Southeast Asian History

A Captivating Guide to the History of Southeast Asia, Thailand, Vietnam, Bali, and the Philippines

© Copyright 2021

All Rights Reserved. No part of this book may be reproduced in any form without permission in writing from the author. Reviewers may quote brief passages in reviews.

Disclaimer: No part of this publication may be reproduced or transmitted in any form or by any means, mechanical or electronic, including photocopying or recording, or by any information storage and retrieval system, or transmitted by email without permission in writing from the publisher.

While all attempts have been made to verify the information provided in this publication, neither the author nor the publisher assumes any responsibility for errors, omissions or contrary interpretations of the subject matter herein.

This book is for entertainment purposes only. The views expressed are those of the author alone, and should not be taken as expert instruction or commands. The reader is responsible for his or her own actions.

Adherence to all applicable laws and regulations, including international, federal, state and local laws governing professional licensing, business practices, advertising and all other aspects of doing business in the US, Canada, UK or any other jurisdiction is the sole responsibility of the purchaser or reader.

Neither the author nor the publisher assumes any responsibility or liability whatsoever on the behalf of the purchaser or reader of these materials. Any perceived slight of any individual or organization is purely unintentional.

Free Bonus from Captivating History (Available for a Limited time)

Hi History Lovers!

Now you have a chance to join our exclusive history list so you can get your first history ebook for free as well as discounts and a potential to get more history books for free! Simply visit the link below to join.

Captivatinghistory.com/ebook

Also, make sure to follow us on Facebook, Twitter and Youtube by searching for Captivating History.

Table of Contents

PART 1: HISTORY OF SOUTHEAST ASIA 1
    INTRODUCTION 2
    CHAPTER 1 - THE FIRST FRUITS OF BURMA 4
    CHAPTER 2 - CAMBODIA COMES ONTO THE SCENE 10
    CHAPTER 3 - THE RISE OF THE KINGDOM OF VIETNAM 20
    CHAPTER 4 - THAILAND AND ITS EARLY KINGDOMS 27
    CHAPTER 5: THE POLITICAL INTRIGUE OF ANCIENT INDONESIA 33
    CHAPTER 6 - BURMA AND THE BRITISH 41
    CHAPTER 7 - VIETNAM, LAOS, AND CAMBODIA OPENED TO THE WORLD 50
    CHAPTER 8 - ISLANDS OF DISCOVERY—THE PHILIPPINES 55
    CHAPTER 9 - THE COMING OF THE COLONISTS AND CAPITALISTS 60
    CHAPTER 10 - SOUTHEAST ASIA CONSUMED BY THE CO-PROSPERITY SPHERE 70
    CHAPTER 11 - SOUTHEAST ASIA AND THE SWEET TASTE OF FREEDOM 84
    CONCLUSION: WHERE LEGEND MEETS REALITY 98
PART 2: HISTORY OF THAILAND 100
    INTRODUCTION 101
    CHAPTER 1 - PREHISTORY / EARLY HISTORY 104

- CHAPTER 2 - SUKHOTHAI PERIOD (1238-1438) 110
- CHAPTER 3 - AYUTTHAYA PERIOD (1350-1767) 118
- CHAPTER 4 - THE THON BURI PERIOD (1767-1782) 124
- CHAPTER 5 - THE BEGINNING OF THE CHAKRI DYNASTY (1782-1868) 129
- CHAPTER 6 - THE MODERNIZATION OF THAILAND AND THE REIGN OF THE GREAT RAMA V (1868-1910) 139
- CHAPTER 7 - THE FINAL ABSOLUTE MONARCHS OF THAILAND (1910-1932) 143
- CHAPTER 8 - THE CONSTITUTIONAL MONARCHY AND MILITARY DICTATORSHIPS (1932-1945) 158
- CHAPTER 9 - POWER STRUGGLES IN THAILAND POST WORLD WAR II (1945-1973) 170
- CHAPTER 10 - THE STRUGGLE FOR DEMOCRACY IN MODERN THAILAND (1973-2020) 186
- CONCLUSION 206

PART 3: HISTORY OF VIETNAM 208
- INTRODUCTION 209
- CHAPTER 1 - THE BASICS 215
- CHAPTER 2 - ANCIENT VIETNAM 221
- CHAPTER 3 - FOUR AND A HALF CENTURIES OF INDEPENDENCE 237
- CHAPTER 4 - THE LY DYNASTY 247
- CHAPTER 5 - THE TRAN DYNASTY 254
- CHAPTER 6 - THE LATER LE DYNASTY 269
- CHAPTER 7 - THE EUROPEANS ARRIVE 280
- CHAPTER 8 - NEW POWERS AND NEW DIVISIONS 285
- CHAPTER 9 - THE FRENCH 292
- CHAPTER 10 - FRENCH RULE 302
- CHAPTER 11 - VIETNAM IN TURMOIL 306
- CHAPTER 12 - HO CHI MINH AND THE FRENCH INDOCHINA WAR 313
- CHAPTER 13 - THE VIETNAM WAR 330

CONCLUSION 338

PART 4: HISTORY OF BALI 340

INTRODUCTION 341

CHAPTER 1 - BALI WITHIN INDONESIA 343

CHAPTER 2 - BALI BEFORE THE COMMON ERA 354

CHAPTER 3 - THE HISTORIC PERIOD 364

CHAPTER 4 - THE MAJAPAHIT EMPIRE 375

CHAPTER 5 - GELGEL AND THE MUSLIM ERA 383

CHAPTER 6 - EARLY EUROPEAN EXPLORATION 397

CHAPTER 7 - BALI AND COLONIAL INFLUENCES 407

CHAPTER 8 - INDEPENDENCE AND DEMOCRACY 419

CHAPTER 9 - EXISTING HERITAGE 433

CONCLUSION 446

PART 5: HISTORY OF THE PHILIPPINES 449

INTRODUCTION 450

CHAPTER 1 - THE PHILIPPINES WITHIN SOUTHEAST ASIA 452

CHAPTER 2 - PREHISTORIC PHILIPPINES (BCE) 466

CHAPTER 3 - PRE-COLONIAL PHILIPPINES (1-1565 CE) 479

CHAPTER 4 - PRE-COLONIAL INDEPENDENT PRINCIPALITIES AND SULTANATES (900-1565 CE) 491

CHAPTER 5 - THE SPANISH COLONIAL ERA (1521-1898 CE) 515

CHAPTER 6 - THE PHILIPPINE REVOLUTION AND THE AMERICAN PERIOD (1872-1935 CE) 537

CHAPTER 7 - THE SECOND WORLD WAR TO THE MODERN ERA (1935-21ST CENTURY CE) 547

CONCLUSION 560

HERE'S ANOTHER BOOK BY CAPTIVATING HISTORY THAT YOU MIGHT LIKE 563

FREE BONUS FROM CAPTIVATING HISTORY (AVAILABLE FOR A LIMITED TIME) 564

REFERENCE 565

Part 1: History of Southeast Asia

A Captivating Guide to the History of a Vast Region Containing Countries Such as Cambodia, Laos, Thailand, Singapore, Indonesia, Burma, and More

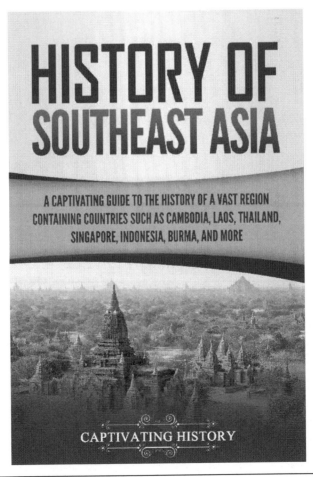

Introduction

It can be said that there was a human presence in Southeast Asia at least as far back as 40,000 years ago. For it was around this time, during the last Ice Age, that archaeologists have traced prehistoric human settlements in places such as Borneo, Flores, and Java. It is believed that during the last Ice Age, when sea levels were much lower, these islands were actually a part of the mainland. This meant that early human travelers from Asia could have easily walked across land bridges to settle the regions. However, the climate change caused by the melting of glaciers some 10,000 years ago rendered these early human inhabitants islanders rather than simply the dwellers of a continental coastline. There is no written record of these early Southeast Asians, but the trappings of civilization that they left behind are still being dug up by teams of archaeologists to this very day.

In fact, in 2004, a major discovery was made when an early human ancestor, said to have been 18,000 years old, was unearthed. These skeletal remains were similar to modern humans except for the fact that their maximum height appeared to be just three and a half feet. This led some to dub these ancient Southeast Asians as hobbits—as in J. R. R. Tolkien's fantastical tale of the same name. Researchers are still not sure whether these mysterious islanders were simply a shorter version of early *Homo sapiens* (modern humans) or were perhaps closer related to an earlier human predecessor such as *Homo erectus*—an upright walking primate with some human attributes.

After the last Ice Age came to a close, the residents of Southeast Asia quickly learned to adapt to their environment. The powerful rivers that cut their course through the lands of Southeast Asia provided for a rise in rich agriculture. It has been suggested that it was in the fertile valleys of Vietnam, Thailand, and Burma that some of the first agricultural settlements arose, with some dating back to around 8000 BCE. In places such as Thailand, Vietnam, Java, Bali, and the Philippines, the people learned methods so they could take advantage of the wet environment, allowing them to produce well-irrigated rice farms. The self-sustaining nature of these farms would fuel the great Southeast Asian civilizations yet to come. The wet environment also encouraged the use of boats for transportation from one place to another. As scattered as the regions of Southeast Asia are, this transport ensured a continuing cross-cultural dialogue between the various peoples of this area.

Southeast Asians had to learn to adapt to their environment, and their ingenuity is seen in the very nature of their settlements. Since the region is prone to flooding, a different style of housing had to be developed. This included a raised platform, meaning it was above ground. By having this, the water could flow under the structure and not flood into the home. These structures, known as stilt houses, still dominate the Southeast Asian landscape today.

Chapter 1 – The First Fruits of Burma

"You most likely know it as Myanmar, but it will always be Burma to me."
-John O' Hurley

Although today we know it by another name, the nation now known as Myanmar has long been called Burma. The country is situated on the mainland, southwest of China, and its first known residents are said to have lived in the region sometime around 11,000 BCE. Archaeological evidence of these early Burmese settlers has been found scattered along the Irrawaddy River, which flows through lower and upper Burma.

Around 1500 BCE, these settlers were using bronze tools and engaging in widespread agriculture. Burma entered into the Iron Age around 500 BCE, and by the 2nd century BCE, natives who spoke a Tibeto-Burman dialect stepped into the realm of recorded history. The Tibeto-Burmans lived in a network of settlements that date back to 200 BCE, and it was from these that the first city-states would form.

Due to Burma's prime location between India and China, these city-states would become heavily involved with trade between two of the major powers of Asia. This trade of goods also brought a trade of culture and ideas, with one of the most transformative being the religion of Buddhism. The Buddhist faith began in India, but it never really caught on with the people of its native soil. Today, India is predominantly Hindu with sizable percentages of both Muslims and Christians, but very few are Buddhists.

Just as Christianity began in Israel and was exported to surrounding lands, so, too, was Buddhism launched from its point of origin to take root in other nations. Buddhism, at least as it pertains to Burma, dates back to at least the 3rd century BCE. These ties of culture and religion maintained a loose confederation among the old city-states of Burma, but Burma would not become a true nation until the rise of the Pagan dynasty in 849 CE.

The Pagan dynasty, also sometimes called the "Bagan" dynasty, is not to be confused with the religious practice of paganism. The Pagan dynasty is derived from a Burmese city named Pagan, in which the Pagan dynasty was centered. The Pagan Kingdom was primarily in control of northern Burma.

Meanwhile, in the south, another kingdom, known as the Mon Kingdom, began to expand. The two kingdoms existed in a state of rivalry until the Pagan Kingdom managed to defeat the Mon Kingdom in 1057 CE, overrunning the former Mon capital of Thaton in the process. This was a devastating loss for the Mon Kingdom, and it's said that the Pagan Kingdom took some 30,000 prisoners in the aftermath.

Among these captives were quite a few Theravada Buddhists. Over time, these Buddhists began to successfully convert their captors to their faith. Although Buddhism, in general, had been known to the Pagans before, it was the Mon captives who proved to be the most successful missionaries. The Mon alphabet also replaced the Pagan traditional Sanskrit script, and terminology derived from the Mon people is still prevalent in Burma to this very day.

After the Pagan Kingdom's defeat of the Mon Kingdom, the realm's reach was consolidated under the powerful King Anawrahta. The details on Anawrahta's rule are scarce, but his legacy was undoubtedly great all the same. In fact, it was great enough to survive his death in 1077, the year his much less competent son, Sawlu, took over.

It's said that Sawlu proved to be so inept that a major rebellion of the Mons erupted in the southern portion of the kingdom in 1084. Sawlu died in the conflict, but his half-brother, Kyanzittha, was able to quickly right the ship, and with the reliable apparatus of the state and military in his hands, he quickly put down the unrest and returned the realm to stability. After getting the kingdom back in order, Kyanzittha proved himself to be a great reformer. Under his leadership, the Pagan Kingdom took measures to standardize laws and customs in the region. This was done with the intention of preventing future rebellions, such as the one that had rocked the kingdom at the beginning of Kyanzittha's reign.

Kyanzittha also made efforts to reach out to the nearby powerhouse of China. By the 12th century, the Pagan Kingdom was powerful enough that it had been duly acknowledged by China's Song dynasty and India's Chola dynasty. However, the Pagans would meet their end when they were invaded by the Mongol hordes led by Kublai Khan.

The ever-encroaching Mongols finally defeated China's Song dynasty in 1279. They then swept down from their holdings in China and began to conduct raids in Southeast Asia, leading to the sacking of the capital city of Pagan in 1287. The leadership of the Pagan Kingdom managed to escape the Mongol grasp, and after they fled, they set up shop farther afield. The Mongols eventually left, but what remained of the Pagan Kingdom was fractured and divided into several self-governing parts.

At the dawn of the 1300s, the main polities of Burma consisted of the regional powers of Lower Burma, Upper Burma, Arakan, and the so-called Shan States. The term "Shan" is actually a name designated for the people of Burma who traditionally speak Tai. And as one might imagine, the Shan States are geographically close to modern-day Thailand, as well as bordering China and Laos. These regional conglomerates were then further divided into various principalities and districts.

As one might imagine, these fractured states were often in discord with each other, and this period would come to have an endless series of conflicts and political intrigue. It wasn't until 1364 that a major player once again came to the Burmese stage in the form of the Kingdom of Ava. Centered around the city of Ava near the Irrawaddy and Myitnge Rivers in Upper Burma, the Kingdom of Ava sought to consolidate not just political power in the region but also cultural power.

The Kingdom of Ava supported the Burmese traditions and became associated as the true inheritor kingdom of the Pagan dynasty. One of the more able rulers of the Kingdom of Ava was a man named Mingyi Swasawke, who ruled from 1367 to 1400. During King Swasawke's reign, a more centralized governing structure was created in Upper Burma.

Unfortunately, the Kingdom of Ava would be the subject of multiple conflicts over the next two centuries and would ultimately be threatened by the neighboring Toungoo Kingdom, which was located in Lower Burma. The so-called Toungoo dynasty dates back to King Mingyi Nyo, who established his court in 1510. King Mingyi Nyo's son, Tabinshwehti, would successfully reunite the remnants of the old Pagan Kingdom.

King Tabinshwehti was a competent and able ruler, and he passed on a vibrant and dynamic kingdom to the man who would succeed him: his trusted general, Bayinnaung Kyawhtin Nawrahta. Bayinnaung would deal the deathblow to the Kingdom of Ava by conquering Ava itself in 1555. The Toungoo dynasty would ultimately control much of the former Pagan Kingdom, but after Bayinnaung passed away in 1581, the principalities he had governed became difficult for his subsequent successors to hang onto.

Things came to a head in 1599 when Arakan, with the help of some soldiers of fortune from Portugal, stormed the major trade city of Pegu (modern-day Bago) and eventually instigated the entire collapse of the Toungoo Kingdom. However, the Arakan were betrayed by their Portuguese allies, and they were shocked to see them break rank and create their own small puppet kingdom in Lower Burma.

Portuguese mercenary Filipe de Brito must have had some delusions of grandeur when he tried to set up his own principality based out of the port city and trading hub of Thanlyin in the year 1603. The Toungoo dynasty was not going to take this lying down, however, and just a few years later, the Toungoo king had rallied his forces under the leadership of Nyaungyan Min, who consolidated Upper Burma by 1606.

However, it was actually the one who succeeded him—Anaukpetlun—who managed to drive the Portuguese from Thanlyin, doing so in the year 1613. The restored Toungoo dynasty would then continue to reign over Burma until 1752 when they were toppled by the Hanthawaddy troops of the Mon people. The city of Ava was burned to the ground, the king was deposed, and the rest of the royal family were put in chains.

After their stunning victory, the Mon people rolled right in and established the so-called Restored Hanthawaddy Kingdom. This incarnation of Burmese political power would be brief, as it was superseded by the Konbaung dynasty, which, by 1759, had managed to piece together all of the former polities of Burma. The Konbaung dynasty faced pressure from Chinese forces in the east, and from 1765 to 1769, it would be subjected to four different assaults on Burmese territory, which were all waged by the Qing dynasty.

Penned in by the Chinese in the northeast, the Burmese forces began to expand their territory to the west instead. While this allowed for expansion without provoking the Chinese, it led to the Konbuang's Burmese border to come in close proximity of what was then British-controlled territory in India. The subsequent wars with Britain would eventually lead to a long and costly colonization process.

Chapter 2 – Cambodia Comes onto the Scene

"Let me reassure that the Kingdom of Cambodia, a country with independence, neutrality, peace, freedom, democracy and human rights as you all have seen, shall be existing with no end."

-*Hun Sen*

It's thanks to ancient Chinese records that we have historical documentation of the very first major governing body to come to prominence in Cambodia. This governing civilization was the Kingdom of Funan, which took root in the 1st century CE. The name "Funan" is of Chinese origin, and it is unlikely that the actual inhabitants of the region called their government by this name. It has been theorized that the Chinese called the kingdom Funan as a geographical designation since it seems to be the Chinese version of the Khmer (a language of Cambodia) word *vnam*, which means mountain. Whatever the case may be, and for the lack of a better term, this 1st-century Cambodian kingdom will be forever known as the Kingdom of Funan.

The Kingdom of Funan was situated around the Mekong River in a region made up of a good chunk of what's called Indochina—the peninsula that juts off the mainland of Southeast Asia. It lies east of India and south of China, and for centuries, it has been influenced by these two giants of Asia.

Initially, the people of Funan were made up of loosely connected communities, each with its own leader. Eventually, these communities fused together under one centralized administration to form a much more powerful kingdom. Important trade routes were established between China and India by the 2nd century, making Cambodia a vital crossroads between the two regions. It was through increased traffic with India that Indian religion, culture, and writing styles began to take root in Cambodia.

Sanskrit writing, in particular, became the glue that held Cambodian intellectual thought together. Sanskrit was the foundation of written languages in Southeast Asia, much like how the Latin alphabet became the main basis of writing across Europe. The subsequent language that developed would become known as "Khmer," but the early lettering of this language was achieved through a variation of Sanskrit.

The Kingdom of Funan was at its most powerful in the 3rd century when it was governed by King Fan Shih-man, a ruler whose realm stretched toward Burma in the west, Malaysia in the south, Vietnam in the east, and Laos in the north. Under the leadership of King Fan Shih-man, the Cambodians were able to beef up their naval power and institute a streamlined bureaucratic government over their growing kingdom. This system forged a loose confederation of local regions under a centralized authority, which managed to keep the regions together without being too burdensome to the specific traditions and local governance of the various regional rulers.

Through its adoption of Sanskrit and Indian religious and legal practices, it is said that the powerful Kingdom of Funan helped to rapidly spread these same ideas all across Southeast Asia. The Kingdom of Funan continued to grow over the next few centuries, but it would eventually be overrun by a new southeastern powerhouse called the Chenla Kingdom. Chenla was initially a vassal state of Funan, but over the years, this former vassal grew powerful enough to challenge Funan itself.

Not a whole lot is known about this period of Cambodian history, and most of the written records we do have relies heavily on Chinese historians from the time. At any rate, the Chenla Kingdom began to decline by the late 7th century, and by 706 CE, Chenla had been divided into two major polities—one in the north known as Upper Chenla and one in the south called Lower Chenla.

Sometime around the 8th century, Lower Chenla was absorbed into nearby Java's powerful Shailendra dynasty as a subservient satellite. However, none of the local Cambodian powerbrokers were prepared for the rise of the next big boys on the block—the Khmer Empire. The Khmer Empire came into being when a man named Jayavarman II rose to prominence and began to lead military strikes against the subservient vassal states of Southeast Asia. He was quite successful in his campaigns, and soon, he was in control of a large swath of territory.

As his fame and power increased, Jayavarman II took on the name "Chakravartin," which translates as "Universal Ruler." King Jayavarman II created a dynasty of what were known as "devarajas," or "god-kings." As the name implies, it was believed that these rulers had been anointed by the powers of heaven to rule over their subjects. Although King Jayavarman II ruled through a policy of "might makes right," it seems that he was a fairly stabilizing ruler. He also managed to bring several principalities under his dominion just as much through political wheeling and dealing as he did through the use of the sword.

Jayavarman II moved the seat of governance to the inland regions of Cambodia's Tonle Sap Lake, founding a capital that would become known as Angkor. Jayavarman II passed away nearly fifty years after the founding of his empire, and after he died, the torch was passed to his son, Jayavarman III. Not much is known about the reign of Jayavarman III, but since there were no major upheavals during this period, it seems that he must have ruled his kingdom well enough. Upon his passing, the throne was then taken by his cousin, Indravarman I.

Indravarman ruled for a little over a decade before he died, passing the reins over to his son, Yasovarman I. Yasovarman invested heavily in the city of Yasodharapura, which would eventually be named Angkor. Some of the longest-lasting fixtures of this king's legacy were the large water reservoirs he implemented in order to take advantage of the region's natural water supply. There are a few inscriptions referencing this king, but they are fairly mythic in scope.

One inscription, for example, states that Yasovarman was "a giant capable of wrestling with elephants and slaying tigers with his bare hands." All of that elephant wrestling must have taken its toll, however, as the great king eventually passed away in 910 after ruling for around twenty-one years. After his demise, his eldest son, Harshavarman, took over. He ruled for some twenty-two years, and he seemed to have reigned over a prosperous kingdom. In fact, an inscription dated to the end of his reign in 922 documents the heavy tax revenue brought in from rice. Known as the Tuol Pei inscription, this artifact is interesting because it makes special mention of how certain religious groups had been deemed tax-exempt. Like in any governing body, taxes were important, but certain religious institutions apparently benefited from this tax-exempt status. At any rate, when Harshavarman died, he passed the baton to his little brother, Isanavarman II.

Isanavarman II's administration was a brief one; it is believed it lasted for around five years. In 928, he was toppled by Jayavarman IV. This king would rule for around thirteen years. Jayavarman IV engaged in many construction projects during his reign, and he wasn't above using slave labor to accomplish his ends. This is evidenced in an official inscription from Jayavarman IV's reign, which records the king ordering some 117 slaves for construction work on a couple of his temples.

Jayavarman IV was followed by Harshavarman II, who only ruled for just two years before Rajendravarman II arrived on the scene in 944. Rajendravarman was yet another temple builder, and under his steady hand, several more religious facilities were constructed, among them the famed Pre Rup temple, which still stands to this day. The Pre Rup temple was built in dedication to the Hindu deity Shiva, and it consists of three levels. It was largely lost to history until French archaeologists stumbled upon the structure in the 1930s. It had been literally buried by the sands of time, but after a careful excavation, much of it was found to still be intact. The structure is said to be representative of Mount Meru—a symbolic feature in the Hindu religion and a theme that can be found throughout Cambodia's ancient Hindu temples.

Out of all of the potentates to grace Angkor, by far one of the most important was Suryavarman II, who reigned from 1113 to 1150. Under Suryavarman II, the kingdom would extend from Cambodia into Vietnam and southern Laos. Eventually, even Thailand would become a vassal state to this powerful ruler. But his most lasting legacy, by far, was the construction of the grand temple complex in the capital city of Angkor known as Angkor Wat. Angkor Wat, which spans across some

400 acres, is the most expansive religious-themed monument on the planet. And the people who built it realized just how big their religious monument was, as indicated by the fact that they named it "Angkor Wat," which actually translates into English as "Temple City."

The fact is, under the rule of Suryavarman II, there was no such thing as separation of church and state. Thus, this "Temple City" was the heart of all political happenings in the empire. Although Angkor Wat was later converted into a religious site for Buddhism, it was originally created in reverence of Hinduism. Indeed, it was supposed to represent Mount Meru, the Hindu center of the universe. And even after Suryavarman II passed, the temple complex was still used for Hindu practice, as was indicated by an inscription made in the temple in his honor. The sacred inscription contained the term *Paramavishnuloka*, which means "He who has entered the heavenly world of Vishnu."

Early Cambodians were indeed dedicated to the religion of Hinduism. This is a religion that Westerners often misinterpret to be polytheistic when, in reality, it is monotheistic. Yes, Hinduism on the surface appears to have hundreds of deities in a pantheon just as robust as ancient Greece, but what many fail to realize is that the gods of Hinduism are believed to be merely multiple manifestations of the one true god called Brahma. In fact, Hindus could be just as easily classified as believers of pantheism since they believe that all of us—me, you, Shiva, Vishnu, a cat, a dog, or even a rock—are all merely manifestations of the same super consciousness/god. While in our separate forms, we may feel that we are separate and distinct entities, in reality, we are just pieces of the same whole. We are made up of the same original energy/god essence that permeates all of creation. Or, as the sacred Vedas of Hinduism proclaim, "Everything is Brahmin." Angkor Wat was built to serve as a testament to this belief system.

In Angkor Wat's memorial to the dead king Suryavarman II, there is an elaborate depiction of how the god-king allegedly merged with Vishnu upon his passing. Hindus believe that when we die, all of our fractured and split consciousnesses, after so many periods of reincarnations/rebirths, will ultimately merge back together. This will ultimately lead to the eventual return to the source of it all—Brahma. If a Hindu were to have a near-death experience and see a bright light at the end of a tunnel, beckoning them to become part of it, they would no doubt assume this to be their consciousness merging back with Brahma, the origin of where it came from in the first place.

Along with being a religious site, Angkor Wat was also a kind of scientific outpost, especially in regards to astronomy. These discoveries have only recently come to light, but it turns out that Angkor Wat was built with an amazing sense of precision, as it seems the massive complex was made into a platform for observing the heavens. Many Hindu mystics and ancient astronomers alike must have spent many hours in quiet contemplation as they scanned the heavens.

The original construction of the complex is shrouded in mystery. Back in the 13th century, a visiting Chinese diplomat was regaled with the tale that the complex was not built by human hands but rather a divine entity who erected the complex in a "single night." However, even those skeptical of Angkor Wat's supposed divine origins have to admit that it was an incredible feat of engineering.

A Portuguese friar named António da Madalena paid a visit to the complex in 1586, and he was awed by what he bore witness to. António described Angkor Wat as being an "extraordinary construction." He even insisted that the sight of it was so incredible that he was unable to "describe it with a pen." However, he tried his best, reporting back to his handlers in Portugal that Angkor Wat "is like no other building in the world. It has towers and decoration and all the refinements which the human genius can conceive of." He then went on to state, "There are many smaller towers of similar style, in the same stone, which are gilded. The temple is surrounded by a moat, and access is by a single bridge, protected by two stone tigers so grand and fearsome as to strike terror into the visitor."

Just two decades after the death of King Suryavarman II, the capital city of Angkor was invaded by the Cham people of southern Vietnam. Angkor Wat itself was ultimately sacked by these invaders in 1177. Despite the "grand and fearsome" visages of the stone sentinels that António later reported on, these intruders apparently wasted no time in seizing control of the temple complex.

The Khmer and Cham peoples have had a long history of warfare with each other. In the year 1177, Cham forces, who were said to have been guided by a Chinese diplomat who had previously visited the city, set sail on the mighty Mekong, making their way to the great Tonle Sap, where they then proceeded to storm Angkor itself. As dramatic as this offensive was, it proved to be a very short-lived victory. After the forces of the Khmer Empire rallied, the invaders were sent running back to the Kingdom of Champa from whence they had come.

This blatant assault proved to be a great political coup for the rulers of the Khmer Empire in the meantime, as it gave them more than enough reason to launch a bloody crusade against the Chams. This resulted in Champa itself becoming a subservient satellite of the Khmer Empire. But even so, the fact that the capital of this great realm had been struck led many of the Khmer elite to question how such a thing could have occurred in the first place. It was in the midst of all of this questioning that a new king—Jayavarman VII—came to power and decided to change the state religion from Hinduism to Buddhism.

Jayavarman VII was said to have been a rather compassionate ruler as it pertained to his subjects. In fact, he was famous for establishing so-called "hospital temples" in which the average citizen could have ailments cared for. Seeming to bear testament to this altruism and concern for the general welfare of the public is a 12th-century inscription about the king at one of these hospitals, which reads, "He suffered the illnesses of his subjects more than his own; because it is the pain of the public that is the pain of kings rather than their own pain."

In light of the Cham invasion, which was followed by fierce warfare with the Cham and then the adoption of Buddhism, the Khmer Empire was going through some rather significant changes. In reality, Hinduism and Buddhism had coexisted to some extent for hundreds of years. But it was Jayavarman VII who became the first king of the Khmer Empire who established Buddhism as the official, preferred religion of the state. This religious shift was similar in scope to when Emperor Constantine of the Roman Empire tolerated and then made Christianity the official religion of the realm in the 4th century.

Thus, in a similar fashion, in the 12th century, Jayavarman VII set the stage for this great transition from the old religion of Hinduism to the newly accepted religion of Buddhism. Although there is no way to know for certain, it is believed that the Cham invasion and the subsequent desecration of the Hindu temple city may have had something to do with it. It could be that this shocking incident led to a loss of belief in the Khmer kings being a manifestation of the invincible Hindu deity. Instead, many began to turn to what seemed to be the more pragmatic Buddhism, which made sense of the recent pain and suffering of the kingdom. After all, the main thrust of Buddhism is its quest to relieve suffering.

This more compassionate bent led King Jayavarman VII to not only secure the borders of the empire but to also greatly improve living conditions within those borders. It was under Jayavarman VII, after all, that some of the greatest infrastructure projects of the Khmer Empire were made. This included new roadways, dams, reservoirs, and, of course, the countless temple hospitals dedicated to the healing and general well-being of the populace. These hospitals were way ahead of their time, and they offered spiritual prayers as well as medicinal herbs for the sick and infirm. At any rate, this great stage of civilization in Cambodia would come to a close in the first half of the 1400s. By then, the Khmer Empire was suffering a great decline while other forces in the region were ready to expand.

Chapter 3 – The Rise of the Kingdom of Vietnam

"Throughout the 20th century, the Republican Party benefited from a non-interventionist foreign policy. Think of how Eisenhower came in to stop the Korean War. Think of how Nixon was elected to stop the mess in Vietnam."

-*Ron Paul*

It is hard to argue against the notion that when people hear of the nation of Vietnam today, they first think of the quagmire that was the Vietnam War, a conflict that pitted communist Vietnamese forces against US troops. But Vietnam, of course, has a rich history that took root long before Marxism was ever in vogue. In fact, the Vietnamese civilization is said to have first flowered in approximately 2500 BCE.

These early Vietnamese settlements, like many of their neighbors, relied heavily on the farming of rice fields. As the settlements became more prosperous and the population increased, local landlords rose up to consolidate their power. This led to a kind of feudal confederacy that remained in place until the much more cohesive civilization of China decided to invade during the 2nd century BCE.

Although southern Vietnam remained largely out of China's reach, the Chinese would be the masters of northern Vietnam for over 1,000 years. However, China's grip on North Vietnam was a tenuous one, and periodic rebellions staged by homegrown Vietnamese insurgencies during this span of time were quite commonplace. The Vietnamese became experts at guerilla warfare in their struggle against the Chinese—a skill that would be realized once again in their 20th-century struggle for self-determination.

However, as it pertains to the Vietnamese struggle against China, things came to a head in 939 CE when Vietnamese forces managed to overthrow Chinese rule once and for all. It was one of the victorious Vietnamese generals—Ngo Quyen—who would become the first Vietnamese ruler of the independent Kingdom of Vietnam, which consisted of modern-day North and Central Vietnam.

King Ngo Quyen reigned for just five years before perishing, and his death sent the Kingdom of Vietnam into a terrible internal war of succession known as the "upheaval of the Twelve Warlords." It was called as such because, in the vacuum of clear leadership, a war was waged by twelve powerful warlords who controlled twelve different regions of Vietnam. The powerful Vietnamese General Dinh Bo Linh eventually wrested control over the twelve warlords in 968 CE, bringing all of Vietnam under his authority in the process.

It must be noted, however, that even with an attempt at centralized control, North Vietnam was always markedly different from South Vietnam. Ever since the start of the Chinese occupation, North Vietnam had become culturally and administratively more Chinese in character than South Vietnam. South Vietnam had become the wild, untamed land of the Cham people, while the North Vietnamese had much more in common with the Han Chinese.

At any rate, when Dinh Bo Linh seized control, it marked the beginning of the Vietnamese Dinh dynasty. The dynasty established by General Dinh would hit a bump in the road in 979 when the emperor, Dinh Bo Linh, who, upon his coronation, was given the name Dinh Tien Hoang, and the crown prince, Dinh Lien, were both assassinated. This left Emperor Hoang's six-year-old son Dinh Toan (who would be given the title of Dinh Phe De) as the heir. Since a six-year-old is obviously not going to be able to rule by themselves, this meant that court officials had to rule through the child.

It was during this period of instability that China's Song dynasty decided to launch a renewed attempt to take Vietnam back as a subservient state. Chinese forces swooped down on North Vietnam in 979. At the onset of this crisis, the great Vietnamese general Le Hoan took over the leadership of the nation. Le Hoan proved himself to be an ingenious leader, and although the odds were stacked against his kingdom, he found ways to offset the more powerful Chinese forces through the use of his brilliant tactics.

Since the smaller Vietnamese military would never be able to face the larger Chinese army, Le Hoan developed a scheme in which he lured the Chinese troops to cross into the narrow confines of Chi Lang Pass. This proved fatal for the Chinese army since it enabled the Vietnamese to systematically pick off the Chinese soldiers while they were hemmed in by the rock walls of the mountain pass. This terrible defeat sent the Chinese packing and reasserted the strength of northern Vietnam.

The northern Vietnamese, in the meantime, began to steadily expand their territory into southern Vietnam, encroaching upon the territory of the Kingdom of Champa. Le Hoan, who had taken the title of "Emperor Le Dai Hanh," died in 1005 CE, and he was succeeded by his son, Le Trung Tong, who ruled for an impressive three days before dying. His brother, Le Long Dinh, also known as Le Ngoa Trieu, proved to be a cruel dictator, but his terrible reign didn't last long, although it was longer than his brother's—he passed away just a few years later in 1009.

After this tyrant's death, the Vietnamese court made what was probably a wise decision by bypassing any hereditary claims to the throne and handing power over to a humble but capable military general by the name of Ly Cong Uan, who would begin the powerful Ly dynasty. One of the first major moves of Ly Cong Uan, whose regnal name was Ly Thai To, was to establish a new capital for his kingdom in what we now call Hanoi.

The Ly dynasty is known for its complex bureaucracy, which was very similar to China's, in which government officials could be trained and officiated through the undertaking of government-sponsored exams. The Kingdom of Vietnam also developed a modern system of taxation, which was used to keep the government apparatus functioning. As for the religion of the kingdom, both Buddhism and a variation of Taoism reigned supreme.

But despite all of this headway, China's Song dynasty was not quite ready to let the Kingdom of Vietnam go. In 1075, it launched yet another assault upon North Vietnam. The Vietnamese were ready, and knowing that an invasion was about to be launched, they actually struck out at the Chinese first, launching devastating attacks against Chinese military mobilizations in the regions of Guangxi and Guangdong.

The Song dynasty itself would then be subjected to invasion by the mighty Jurchen Jin, who defeated the Song military in northern China in 1126. The Jurchen Jin originally hailed from Manchuria, which was northeast of China proper. They would go on to found an empire that would include northern China, Mongolia, and much of Korea.

This major event led the government of the Song dynasty to relocate to southern China, where a new government was established in Hangzhou. The Song dynasty would never again attempt a major military strike against North Vietnam, and it would be completely extinguished by an invading Mongol horde led by the successor of Genghis Khan: the famous Kublai Khan. The Mongol campaign began in 1260, and it ended in 1276 with the capture of Hangzhou, followed by the city of Canton, where the last holdouts of the Song government of southern China were holed up.

With the Mongols in control of China, it wasn't long before they turned their attention to China's southeastern borders and began plotting to take over Vietnam as well. Soon, the Mongols led their forces, along with Chinese troops and naval power, to engage in an assault on northern Vietnam. The Vietnamese, who were by now well versed in defensive warfare, were able to repel the invaders, and the Mongol forces failed in their endeavors. Faced with numerically superior forces, the Vietnamese repeated the same tactics that they had used against the Song dynasty in which they kept the enemy at bay without getting lured into open engagements, as they knew their smaller forces would have been crushed.

North Vietnam also temporarily aligned with the Champa Kingdom of South Vietnam, presenting a united front to the aggressors. The Mongols, meanwhile, who had become stretched entirely too thin, soon had to retreat back to higher ground. Once the Mongol threat had been removed, North Vietnam and South Vietnam began to do battle with each other, as the Kingdom of Vietnam once again began to expand into Champa territory in the south.

These efforts resulted in the Champa Kingdom being reduced to a vassal state of the Kingdom of Vietnam in 1312. But after just a decade, the Champa Kingdom was able to break free, resulting in a war that would last three decades. Very little was gained out of this conflict, and the Kingdom of Vietnam was so weakened that it invited a fresh invasion from China in 1407.

China, by this time, had shaken off its Mongol overlords. Thus, it was the Ming dynasty that sought to make the Kingdom of Vietnam a client state once again. The Vietnamese had known independence for far too long to take this attempted subjugation lying down. By the 1420s, the Vietnamese were launching massive rebellions against Chinese authority. The Ming forces were ultimately defeated in 1426, thereby ending the last attempt by China to directly exert control over Vietnam.

The brief Ming occupation was in many ways more beneficial to North Vietnam than it was detrimental. After all, it was the Ming who introduced siege weapons, such as canons and gunpowder, and other technological innovations, such as the printing press and paper, to the North Vietnamese.

In 1471, a resurgent North Vietnam was able to march on Champa and seized most of the former Champa territory, incorporating it into the greater Vietnam. The destruction of the Champa Kingdom kicked off a diaspora of the Cham people, who moved to other neighboring regions of Southeast Asia. By 1479, the Kingdom of Vietnam had also expanded into Laos, leading to what has been called the Vietnamese-Laotian War. The war ended in 1484 in what was essentially a draw between the two regional powers, as neither side gained much of anything for their efforts.

Over the next few decades, the Kingdom of Vietnam began to deteriorate steadily due to a wide range of factors. These factors included political turmoil, economic distress, and climate change having an adverse effect on agricultural output. With all of these problems, Vietnamese expansion seemed to be at an end. It was right around this time when Vietnam began to shrink back that the outside world came knocking.

Chapter 4 – Thailand and Its Early Kingdoms

"When I was first lady, I worked to call attention to the plight of refugees fleeing Cambodia for Thailand. I visited Thailand and witnessed firsthand the trauma of parents and children separated by circumstances beyond their control."

-Former First Lady Rosalynn Carter

The history of Thailand is one that frequently merges and blends with its neighbors of southern China, Burma, Malaysia, Cambodia, and Vietnam, which all played a major role in the shaping of Thailand. The name "Thailand" itself is derived from the "Tai people." The Tais in ancient times referred to their kingdom as simply "Meuang Thai," which, roughly translated, means "Land of the Tais."

It is believed that the Tai ethnic and linguistic group originated in southern China. Around the year 700 CE, a significant portion of Tais came to live in what now constitutes the modern-day city of Dien Bien Phu in northern Vietnam. These Tais would then gradually move southwest, following the local waterways that would lead them deeper into the territory of what is now Thailand. But just because the Tais made the region their home, that does not mean they were the first to lay claim to the land.

According to a piece of traditional Tai folklore called the Simhanavati legend, the region was first inhabited by the Wa people before the mighty King Simhanavati of the Tais led a brutal assault against them and forced them to flee. This led to the founding of the Tai settlement of Chiang Saen in 800 CE. Soon after this, the Tais of the region developed relationships with their "Indianized" neighbors and began to practice Buddhism. They also developed a form of Sanskrit writing.

All was relatively peaceful for the next few decades, but by 900 CE, war had erupted between the Tais of Chiang Saen and the neighboring Mons of Burma. The war ended up being fairly devastating for the Tais, as their capital was overrun and sacked by the Mons. It wasn't until 937 that the Tais were able to rally their forces and drive the Mons out of the region. However, the Tais would receive another blow in 1000 CE when a major earthquake tore right through Chiang Saen.

This earthquake was devastating, as it leveled the city and left many dead. The situation was so dire that the inhabitants enacted what today we might call a state of emergency, as they instituted a special council just to maintain order. Fortunes would improve enough by 1100, and the Tais would begin to expand their kingdom to the south. As the Tais expanded to the south, they came into contact with Cambodia's Khmer people and began to be heavily influenced by the Khmer culture.

By the early 1200s, Thailand would reach what would be considered its "golden age." By the time the Khmer Empire began to wane, the first major Thai kingdom would emerge. It was in approximately 1240 CE that Pho Khun Bang Klang was made the first ruler of what would become known as the Sukhothai Kingdom. The kingdom was called as such because it was based around the Thai settlement of Sukhothai in central Thailand. This particular Thai kingdom was known to be one filled with rich resources, as it was said to have had an abundance of fresh fish and rice paddies.

During this period, the Thais had peaceful relations with their neighbors, both abroad and at home. In fact, to ensure this sense of peace and tranquility, it is said that if there was any problem, all a resident had to do was ring a bell that was installed right outside of the king's palace, and he would arrive on the scene to settle the dispute. If such accounts are accurate, it must have been surely used as a subject's final recourse over a major disturbance. One has to imagine the king would probably get frustrated fairly quickly if his people were bugging him over every single petty squabble that might erupt.

At any rate, the king was seen by the Thais as a kind of fatherly figure who had their best interests at heart. One of the most memorable kings to rule during this period was the Thai potentate Ram Khamhaeng, who served as the head of the kingdom from 1279 to 1298. Archaeological evidence of his reign has been uncovered in the form of the so-called "Ram Khamhaeng Stele," which is a kind of "inscribed tablet" that commemorates the king's rule. In keeping with the paternalistic nature of the kingship, the stele describes Ram Khamhaeng as a fatherly king who cared deeply for his people. There is no doubt that Ram Khamhaeng certainly was a great and powerful king with a lasting influence. In fact, it is said that he may have been the one who actually established the Thai alphabet. After all, it was on his stele that this script was first seen to be in use.

Another important Thai leader was Maha Thammaracha I, who came to power around the year 1347. Maha Thammaracha established Theravada Buddhism as the main religion of the realm. Theravada Buddhism is essentially orthodox Buddhism, meaning that it was the first main school of Buddhist thought to emerge. Buddhism began in India, but it subsequently spread throughout Asia. As the teachings of the Buddha spread, different branches emerged. By the time it fully reached as far as Japan, for example, the Japanese had developed a variation called Zen Buddhism. Those believing in Theravada Buddhism are originalists, so they reject these later variations. Although the religion originated in India, which was is also the land of Hinduism, Buddhism rejects much of Hindu belief. Buddhism would never quite catch on in its place of birth, but it would spread to India's neighbors in East and Southeast Asia.

Buddhism itself is a unique religion in the sense that it is a religious practice that is not centered around a deity. Buddhists do not believe in a god—they simply acknowledge that a cosmic force exists and that it runs through nature. As such, Buddhism does not focus on pleasing a god as much as it focuses on finding a way to live a virtuous and enlightened life through philosophical concepts, such as the "Middle Way," "The Four Noble Truths," and "The Noble Eightfold Path." By reaching enlightenment, a Buddhist believes that one can break the cycle of rebirth and suffering and reach a state of Nirvana. The Buddha himself is said to have been someone who "awakened" to this ultimate truth. After doing so, he sought to bestow this understanding upon the rest of humanity through his teachings. The Buddha basically taught that we are all trapped in our own false narratives of suffering but can learn to free ourselves from them. Theravada Buddhists furthermore believe that every so often, an enlightened one like the Buddha emerges in order to help the rest of us wake up from the vicious cycle that we are trapped in.

At any rate, it was around the time of Maha Thammaracha that the Thai Ayutthaya Kingdom arose. This dynastic kingdom would last the longest, staying in existence all the way until 1767. During this period, the kingdom of Thailand became an economic powerhouse, taking advantage of its position between several powerful states to become a major trading partner in the region. But as the power of the kingdom grew, the rights of its citizens lessened. Whereas in the past, any subject could ring a bell and state their grievance to the king as equals, during the Ayutthaya Kingdom, there was a clear class distinction. The kings were all powerful, and they were perceived as having essentially a mandate from heaven to do whatever they wished, which, by the way, is definitely not something encouraged by Buddhist belief. Nevertheless, by the 15th century, the Ayutthaya Kingdom was powerful enough to even take on the Khmer Empire, and it is said to have bested their Khmer neighbors in battle on three separate occasions.

During the 1500s, another Thai kingdom called Lanna existed in the north. These two kingdoms would intermittently wage war with each other until the Lanna Kingdom fell to the neighboring Burma kingdom in 1558. The Ayutthaya Kingdom, in the meantime, came into contact with visitors from outside of Southeast Asia entirely when the Portuguese arrived in the region in 1511. Soon after contacts with the Portuguese were made, the French began to take an interest in the region as well. For a while, the feeling seemed to be mutual. King Narai of Ayutthaya, in particular, who reigned from 1656 to 1688, developed close ties with King Louis XIV of France. As the relationship grew, the Ayutthayan king allowed French missionaries to his realm and even installed French soldiers for the kingdom's national defense.

However, this foreign influence led to much dissent and unrest in the king's court. This unrest would continue to grow until it erupted in what would become known as the Siamese revolution of 1688. For it was this year that a popular revolt broke out against the king, which led to his overthrow. The revolt was led by a Thai general named Phetracha, who deposed the king, seized the throne for himself, and drove out the French. The most dramatic moment of this revolution was during the so-called Siege of Bangkok. Bangkok had become a prosperous port city by this time, and the French had some 200 of their troops holed up in a fortress. Some 40,000 Thai troops were said to have waged an assault on this fort, but the French were able to hold them off long enough to negotiate a deal that would allow them to evacuate the city. This move would effectively isolate Thailand from the Western world until Western interests would once again intrude upon the land of the Thais in the 1800s.

Chapter 5: The Political Intrigue of Ancient Indonesia

"Think Indonesia and tourism, and the first thing that comes to mind is probably Bali. Think golf holiday, and most people would dream of Scotland or Ireland. But Indonesia harbors one of the best-kept secrets in the world of travel: it is a golfer's paradise."

-Raymond Bonner

Indonesia is a thriving nation in Southeast Asia filled with a rich and vibrant history. Like many regions of Southeast Asia, Indonesia owes much of its ancient heritage to the subcontinent of India. The name itself, in fact, comes from the Greek appellation of *Indos Nesos*, which literally means "Indonesia." Indian religion and culture were prevalent in Indonesia as early as 200 BCE.

It is around this time that the Indian epic *Ramayana* was written. And within this ancient Sanskrit text, there is mention of a great kingdom called "Yawadvipa" located on the Indonesian island of Java. Not a whole lot can be drawn from this narrative, but it definitely indicates that Java was a known quantity at the very least. Today, Java is the most populated island on the planet, and it holds the bustling Indonesian metropolis of Jakarta.

However, back in 200 BCE, it's not entirely clear what the ancient Indonesian kingdom of Java might have been like, but it was at least noteworthy enough for Indian scribes to mention it in one of their epic narratives. Ancient Indonesia also had close political and mercantile ties with both India and China. Since the islands were positioned between these two Asian powerhouses, Indonesia would have been a valuable weigh station. Some trade, such as Indonesia's extensive export of cloves, traveled far and wide, with this precious Indonesian spice having appeared as far afield as ancient Rome.

Roman historian Pliny the Elder made mention of Indonesian crafts making their way to ports in East Africa, where they undoubtedly then made their way north to Egypt and then across the Mediterranean to Rome itself. The Indonesians had such a presence in the region that it is believed they may have even had a settlement on the island of Madagascar. The Indonesians were indeed a great seafaring people during this time, and there are independent sources that back this up.

For instance, according to the modern-day author and Southeast Asia researcher Colin Brown, there are Chinese records from sometime around 300 CE that speak of the Indonesians having large trading vessels that were as long as 50 meters (164 feet), which would have been loaded with all kinds of precious goods and commodities. It was only once the Roman Empire went into decline in the 4th century that Indonesians began to turn back to primarily trade in East and Southeast Asia.

After this pivotal shift, Indonesia began to transform from a trading outpost and weigh station into a dynamic political entity in its own right. The first known kingdom was centered around the island of Java, and it was called Tarumanegara. This kingdom was ruled by a king named Purnawarman, whose reign has been verified through inscribed stones dating back to 450 CE. Not a lot is known about the kings that immediately came after Purnawarman, but by 535 CE, another powerful ruler by the name of Suryawarman (not to be confused with Suryavarman I—the Cambodian king) seems to have emerged. Suryawarman set up a new capital and established the kingdom of Sunda Sambawa.

Here, the records get a bit murky, and the next we know of Indonesian governance is the kingdom of Ho-Ling, which comes down to us from Chinese sources dating back to 640. As you might have guessed, "Ho-Ling" is actually a Chinese name, and it is most likely not what the actual residents called their kingdom. Some believe that the name is actually a Chinese attempt to pronounce the Indonesian word "Kalingga." At any rate, the Chinese called the place Ho-ling, and that is the name that stuck for this epoch of Indonesian history. According to the Chinese, the ruler of Ho-Ling entered into contact with the Chinese for the purpose of trade, which means Ho-Ling superseded Tarumanegara as the main ambassador kingdom of Indonesia.

As well as being steeped in the mercantile business of trade goods, Ho-Ling was also quite blessed when it came to developing productive farms. During this period, rice production was quite abundant, and the people not only grew enough to keep the locals well nourished but also to have plenty of leftover products to sell to other nations.

Contact between China and Indonesia during this time was quite strong. By the 670s, the Chinese were even sending Buddhist missionaries to the region. This was the case in December of 671 when a

Chinese monk by the name of Yijing left Yanjing (modern-day Beijing) and made his way to the Indonesian island of Sumatra at a town that Yijing called Sanfoqi. The locale was actually the city of Srivijaya. This bustling port city would soon become the capital of a powerful mercantile state based out of the Indonesian island of Sumatra. Upon coming ashore, Yijing made his way to the local raja's headquarters. It was then arranged for him to meet the king, who is said to have taken kindly to the Chinese monk and helped facilitate his Buddhist activities while in the region.

Yijing, as much as he was ready to spread the gospel of Buddhism, was pleasantly surprised that the religion had already taken root on the island. Yijing would later record in his journal, "In the fortified city of Fo-Qi [Srivijaya], Buddhist priests number more than one thousand, whose minds are bent on learning and good practices. They investigate and study all the subjects that exist just as in [India]; the rules and ceremonies are not at all different. If a Chinese priest wishes to go to the West in order to listen and read, he had better stay here one or two years and practice the proper rules and then proceed to central India." Buddhism, of course, originated in India, and when Yijing speaks of going to "the West," he means going west from China to Indonesia and then ultimately on to India itself, which Yijing did himself in December of 672.

Once again, Indonesia was being considered as a weigh station, but this time for religion. The kingdom of Ho-Ling was predominantly Buddhist, but as was and still is the case with most religious factions in Indonesia, this predominant strain was built upon an ancient ancestral religion that heavily influenced the region's variations of religious practices.

Srivijaya, in the meantime, became the seat of a powerful confederation of port cities that were all heavily involved in the trade economy. By the early 700s, this confederacy was essentially a mini-empire with Srivijaya as its seat of power. During this time, Chinese records officially acknowledge the region as a vassal state, recording regular tribute passing from the Srivijayan leader to the emperor of China. But by the middle of the 8th century, the Srivijayan kingdom began to be overshadowed by another Indonesian kingdom, whose name has come down to us as Mataram.

The polity of Mataram would construct some of the first monasteries on the islands of Indonesia, with some of the greatest being situated just north of the Indonesian metropolis of Yogyakarta. In fact, it was near Yogyakarta that the grandest Buddhist temple of them all—Borobudur—was built. This colossal structure is said to have cost quite a bit of money to pay the many hands who helped to construct it. And since this religious edifice had no real monetary return—just spiritual ones—it's generally taken as a sign that Mataram must have been fairly well off to fund such a project in the first place.

Mataram picked up right where Ho-Ling had left off by controlling the mercantile trade of the region with big players such as China. Mataram was also quite successful in growing an abundant amount of rice, thereby ensuring enduring prosperity for the kingdom. The Srivijayan kingdom began to lose favor with China, and once the Chinese began to send their own merchants abroad, they didn't have as much use for the Srivijayans as trading partners. To make matters worse, in 1025, a group of South Indian pirates called the Cholas invaded and sacked the capital. After this assault, Srivijaya never quite recovered its former prestige as a trading hub in Indonesia. At any rate, just as Srivijaya was in decline, Mataram began to take off, and it would reach new heights of success under the leadership of a man named Airlangga.

From his capital of Surabaya, Airlangga held a monopoly over the trade of fine spices and rice production. In 1045, before he abdicated his throne, Airlangga divided his kingdom up between his two sons, with west Mataram being turned into a state called Kediri and east Mataram being rendered into a place called Janggala. Kediri had the better ports and thus proved to be the more capable province.

By the 1100s, subsequent rulers of Kediri had been able to successfully take over and reincorporate Janggala, creating a single powerful kingdom. In addition, they also made the regions of Kalimantan and Bali fall under their sway. However, after about a 100-year run, this expanded Kediri Kingdom would be overrun in 1222 when Ken Angrok of nearby Tumapel, in East Java, seized the territory for himself. Ken Angrok forged yet another capital, Singhasari, which was situated near the Kali Welang River Basin in the vicinity of the modern-day Indonesian city of Malang.

The last leader of this subsequent Javanese empire was a man named Kertanegara, who ruled from 1268 to 1292. During his reign, the Mongol warlord Kublai Khan began pressuring Indonesia to pay tribute to the Mongol Empire. Kertanegara refused to fork out the tribute and dismissed the khagan's representatives outright. This, of course, did not sit at all well with Kublai Khan, and in 1292, he made his displeasure known by way of a massive military invasion in which nearly a thousand ships and around 20,000 troops were sent to lay siege to Java.

However, if Kublai Khan wanted to exact vengeance on the insolent Kertanegara, he was too late. By the time this massive army arrived, Kertanegara was already dead. He had fallen victim to local political intrigue and was assassinated by a local prince by the name of Jayakatwang, who then declared himself king. By the time the Mongols arrived, they were briefed by the happenings and were persuaded to side with Kertanegara's son-in-law, Raden Vijaya, who was struggling to take the throne for himself.

Raden proved to be quite a crafty politician, and he soon would get the best of the Mongol horde. Initially, he won a diplomatic coup with the would-be invaders, as he actually managed to get them to agree to do battle with his enemy, Jayakatwang, the one responsible for Kertanegara's assassination. But as soon as the Mongols did his bidding and took out Jayakatwang, Raden turned his own forces on the Mongols. Not only that, but he also managed to develop a successful grassroots guerrilla warfare campaign in which all of his subjects were galvanized to annihilate the Mongols.

The bewildered Mongols, as fierce as they might have been, were just not prepared for this unexpected onslaught. With enemies assailing them on all sides in an unfamiliar and inhospitable land, they were ultimately forced to retreat. After successfully driving the Mongols off, Raden further consolidated his power and created a palace south of Surabaya where he ruled and reigned supreme of a reconstituted Javanese empire that would become known as the Majapahit kingdom.

Raden Wijaya passed away in 1309, and he would be replaced by his own son, Jayanagara. However, Jayanagara would not fill his father's footsteps very well, and after amassing a scandalous reputation, he perished without an heir in 1328. This ushered in a period of dynastic instability with factions vying for power until the year 1350. In that year, a capable prince by the name of Hayam Wuruk, who just so happened to be the great-grandson of the murdered Kertanegara, made his way to the throne.

Under his steady hand, Majapahit would expand its reach to include Bali, Kalimantan, and Sumatra. During this time, both China and Europe were eager buyers of the spices that Indonesia had to offer, and the spice trade made the Majapahit kingdom quite rich. The Chinese and Europeans were using many of the Indonesian spices for both food seasoning and medicinal purposes.

As was usually the case during this period, it was China who began to pressure the Indonesians for extra perks and privileges when it came to trade. And after the Chinese managed to shake off the Mongols and establish the Ming dynasty in 1368, it wasn't long before China began to demand tribute in the form of favorable trade deals. By the early 1400s, China was sending regular expeditions to exact tribute from the Indonesians. In 1407, a Chinese delegation led by a famous member of the Ming court—Zheng He—found its way to the shores of Java. Zheng He found Majapahit to be a bustling land with a multitude of nationalities engaged in vibrant trade networks. However, it was a tad too rough for Zheng He's tastes, and his chroniclers would later report, among other things, that just about everyone had a knife and that they were all more than willing to use it.

This part of Southeast Asia would more or less lumber on in this same state of both cosmopolitan luxury and violent banditry for the next 100 or so years until new arrivals from farther afield would change the entire landscape of Indonesia for good.

Chapter 6 – Burma and the British

"This is Burma, and it will be quite unlike any land you know about."

-Rudyard Kipling

By the early 1800s, Burma and Britain seemed all but destined for a cataclysmic collision. At this point, Burma was in the middle of its last independent dynasty, that of the so-called Konbaung kings. It was the mighty King Bodawpaya who began to aggressively stab westward, as he took control of the fabled city of Arakan in 1785, which was then followed by the seizure of Manipur in 1814 and the acquisition of Assam in 1817. These territorial acquisitions brought the Burmese right to the border of what was then called British India.

Of course, this led to inevitable conflict and border skirmishes. In 1819, King Bodawpaya passed away and was succeeded by his grandson, Bagyidaw. King Bagyidaw proved to be even bolder than his grandfather and began to consider seizing the British-controlled territory of Bengal for himself. The British were well aware of the threat they faced, and wishing to weaken their competitors, they sought to sow seeds of chaos.

The British fanned the flames of dissent among residents of nearby Manipur and Assam during the early 1820s, hoping the territories would break away from the Konbaung dynasty and provide a more adequate buffer zone. However, the rebellions failed, so cross-border conflicts continued until the so-called First Anglo-Burmese War broke out in 1824.

In the first stage of the conflict, the British managed to catch the Burmese by surprise by striking directly against Lower Burma from a fleet of craft launched from the nearby Andaman Islands. The Burmese had been expecting a land invasion from the borderlands they shared with the British, but the Brits went right around the Burmese defenses and invaded by water. On May 10th, 1824, the British landed, and they managed to seize the strategic port city of Rangoon without much of a fight. This gave the British a toehold right inside Burmese territory, and now it was up to the Burmese to expel the British from their land.

From their perch in Rangoon, the British planned to travel up the Irrawaddy River to the capital of Burma itself. But soon after their arrival in Rangoon, they realized their invasion plans would be difficult as the wet and rainy monsoon season had begun, which made traveling upriver exceedingly difficult. Therefore, the British advance, which initially had much momentum on its side, stalled at Rangoon. The Brits ended up having to hole up for several months as they waited for the long, wet season to end. And throughout the monsoon season, their force, which initially numbered 11,000 strong, had been whittled down to less than a thousand combat-ready soldiers. This was largely due to the plagues of illness that had rocked the British, as they were not well adjusted to the tropical diseases of the region.

In the meantime, the Burmese forces, led by a general named Bandula, began to make their way to Rangoon with tens of thousands of troops and their best artillery in the hopes of driving the British out of Burma for good. Although the moribund and sickly British were stuck in Rangoon, they proved to be an intractable lot when defending the little piece of territory that they had captured. This can be seen in December of 1824 when the Burmese forces launched their assault on British-held Rangoon, as the Burmese were easily pushed back. Interestingly enough, this was the very same year that the British entered into the so-called Anglo-Dutch Treaty, which cut off part of the Malay Archipelago and affirmed British control over Singapore. During this period, Britain was most certainly on the rise when it came to the dominance of Southeast Asia.

At any rate, the British were able to easily cut through their assailants and cause great disorder. Faced with withering, relentless fire from the Brits, General Bandula was forced to call off the attack in fear that his whole army would fall apart. This victory seemed to rally the spirits of the British, and that spring, they finally left the protective confines of Rangoon and ventured toward the city of Prome.

In the skirmishes with the Burmese that followed, General Bandula lost his life, and his army retreated. This allowed the British to advance on Prome without much of a fight. These developments caused much distress to the Burmese king, as he quickly realized that things were not going at all well for the Burmese forces. Desperate to buy some time, the Burmese government reached out to the British and requested an armistice in the fall of 1825. However, these plans were scrapped when the British uncovered a Burmese scheme to take back Prome, and they left the bargaining table. The war would then rage on for much of the rest of 1825.

This same year, in neighboring Thailand, which was then known as Siam, the Siamese government was convinced to enter into a treaty with the British. This treaty saw Siam officially granting its recognition of British-controlled territory in Malaysia. In previous years, Siam had made some significant inroads into Malaysia, conquering the Kedah Sultanate in 1821. This put Siam in close proximity to British interests in the region. After seeing how easily the British were beating the Burmese, the Kingdom of Siam was convinced that it would be in its own best interest to enter into diplomatic relations with the British rather than risk armed conflict. This move would ultimately prove to be beneficial to Thailand since it would remain the only Southeast Asian nation to remain independent and never be colonized by a European power.

However, Burma would not be so lucky. The war continued to go badly for the Burmese, and in time, both parties (the Burmese and the British) once again began negotiations. This time around, the British offered some pretty harsh terms for the Burmese to accept. They demanded that they be handed the territories of Arakan, Assam, Manipur, and Tenasserim, as well as be paid a hefty amount of rupees for their trouble.

As can be expected, the Burmese were enraged at these demands and immediately refused further negotiations. But once the British captured the city of Yandabo, which was not far from the Burmese capital itself, the Burmese began singing a different tune. Knowing that they didn't have much room to bargain, they finally agreed to the terms given to them by the British in a desperate bid to stave off complete collapse. This fear is what led the Burmese to sign the so-called Treaty of Yandabo on February 24th, 1826.

Forcing the Burmese to give up strategic territories such as Arakan, Asam, and Manipur gave the British the breathing room they desired, but now, Burma was just a shadow of what it had been. The kingdom was also heavily burdened by having to pay the British Crown reparations for the cost of the war. This was a humiliation for Burma and, in particular, for the Burmese king, Bagyidaw. It has been said that after this terrible defeat, King Bagyidaw spiraled into a full-blown depression that would haunt him for the rest of his life. In fact, things would get so bad at times that the queen and her family would often have to step in as stewards of the Burmese government while King Bagyidaw spent time recovering from his mental afflictions.

This stewardship was not looked upon favorably by Tharrawaddy Min, the king's younger brother. Tharrawaddy was disgusted by his brother's inability to rule, and he also didn't appreciate his brother's wife and family members stepping in for him. Deciding to put matters into his own hands, Tharrawaddy launched a coup in 1837, and he managed to knock his brother out of power and take his place as king of Burma.

Tharrawaddy Min was determined to reverse his sibling's losses, so he began to engage in wanton saber-rattling against the British. He also began cutting ties with British diplomats, and in the fall of 1841, he sent his forces to Rangoon in what was tantamount to a military parade in order to drive home his ambition to push the British out by force if need be. But despite all of this bravado, Tharrawaddy proved himself to be every bit as unstable as his older brother had been, and after several bouts of mental instability, his own sons had him locked away in 1845.

King Tharrawaddy Min passed away in 1846, paving the way for his son, Pagan Min, to take his place. However, relations between the British and the Burmese would break down once again. In 1851, the governor of Pegu Province took two British sea captains into custody for trumped-up charges of homicide, causing relations to hit an all-time low. The British predictably demanded the repatriation of its citizens, and when the

Burmese government refused, the British sent its forces into Pegu in 1852, kickstarting what would become the Second Anglo-Burmese War.

The British ended up annexing Pegu that December. In the meantime, the Burmese court had begun to fear a complete collapse of the government, and in order to stave off utter annihilation, Burmese officials launched a coup against Pagan Min. After Pagan Min was removed from power, his half-brother, Prince Mindon, who had encouraged the rebellion, was placed on the throne. Mindon was said to have been a devout Buddhist who abhorred warfare. As such, he readily came to the table to discuss terms of peace with the British.

King Mindon Min's delegation met with the British in March of 1853 and pleaded with them to relinquish the territory of Pegu, but the British, knowing how weak a hand the Burmese had, refused to give up their gains. As peaceful as Mindon Min may have been, he could not agree to these terms, so he cut off communication with the British in May of 1853. But despite this breakdown, an uneasy standoff would lead to a return of fairly cordial relations over the next few years. Unofficial channels through irregular diplomacy were opened, which began to promote a much friendlier dialogue between the two nations.

In the meantime, two distinctly different Burmas were shaping up. There was British Burma, which cobbled together the British holdings of Pegu, Arakan, and Tenasserim, and then there was the traditional Burma, which consisted of the remnants of the old Burmese kingdom overseen by the king, Mindon Min. Consolidating what little territory he had left, Mindon Min instituted a new capital in 1860, making Mandalay the new seat of power.

During this period, King Mindon attempted to reform his government, hoping to make his kingdom robust and dynamic enough to keep the British from absorbing even more territories. However, despite all of his efforts, by 1875, the British had gained even more of his ancestral land. The trouble began when the people of the Karenni States, called Karens, rebelled against the Burmese king and attempted to break away. The Burmese king obviously wasn't just going to allow this insurrection of Karens to take place under his watch, so he tried to rein in the rebellion. King Mindon sent in his forces to take control of the rebellious region, but this put Burmese troops right on the borderlands of British Burma. The Brits made their displeasure known and sent their own forces into the region to aid the Karens.

Initially, the British worked out a deal that would have the Burmese government recognize Karen autonomy, thereby creating another strategic buffer between the British and the Burmese. However, King Mindon died just a few years later, breathing his last in 1878. Thibaw Min, Mindon's son, rose to power. Initially, Thibaw Min seemed like someone who could be controlled by his ministers and who would therefore give more leeway for compromise when it came to the governance of the region. But after his wife, Supayalat, suspected that several ministers were plotting against her husband, she convinced the king to have several of them, as well as many members of his own family, executed. This act shocked the British, and when the court was questioned about it, Thibaw Min's officials simply stated that the king was within his rights to rule his own sovereign realm as he saw fit. Burmese and British relations continued to deteriorate.

While Thibaw Min was giving the British the cold shoulder, he was opening up a new dialogue with the French, who were also making rapid inroads in Southeast Asia. This greatly distressed the British, as they were seeking to keep the French from colliding with their own interests in the region. By this point, the British were seeking a pretext to take action against the Burmese kingdom, and by 1885, they seemed to have found it.

Around this time, a local squabble erupted involving the so-called Bombay Burmah Trading Corporation. This was a British company that had been involved in the extraction of trees from the teak forests of Upper Burma for many years, doing so under a direct agreement with the Burmese kingdom. King Thibaw Min had claimed that the company had illegally taken more trees than was stated in their official contract, and therefore, it had short-changed the Burmese government.

The case went to court in Burma, and the British contractors ended up being fined a lot of money. Predictably, British representatives were upset over this move, and they claimed that the charges were false and that the king's corrupt government was simply trying to extract extra money from the British. The British then ordered the Burmese to appoint a British mediator in order to come to a fair agreement.

However, the Burmese refused to oblige the British, leading the Brits to rather belligerently issue their infamous ultimatum on October 22nd, 1885. This ultimatum demanded that a British representative be installed in Mandalay, and it also insisted that any fines or other legal punishments that had been leveled against the contractors be put on hold until the representative arrived. This wasn't the end of the demands, for the ultimatum contained a clause that didn't seem to have much to do with this local dispute at all. According to the ultimatum, Burma would have to consult with Britain should they wish to conduct business with any foreign country. This was obviously an attempt to curtail Burma's growing relations with the French, and it was a complete affront to Burma's own free will, independence, and sovereignty. The king, of course, knew that if he agreed to this ultimatum, he would become merely a puppet in the hands of the British.

So, predictably enough, he refused to give it another thought. This refusal was all the British needed for their pretext to launch what would become the Third Anglo-Burmese War. It's almost a stretch to call this campaign a war. British troops were sent to Upper Burma on November 14th, and by November 28th, Mandalay was in their hands with very little resistance, and King Thibaw was deposed. This almost unclimactic series of events finally led to the downfall of Burma.

Chapter 7 – Vietnam, Laos, and Cambodia Opened to the World

"Fear keeps us focused on the past or worried about the future. If we can acknowledge our fear, we can realize that right now we are okay. Right now, today, we are still alive, and our bodies are working marvelously. Our eyes can still see the beautiful sky. Our ears can still hear the voices of our loved ones."

-*Thich Nhat Hanh*

Vietnam, Laos, and Cambodia had spent thousands of years as separate entities until the French came along and decided to cobble them all together in what would become French Indochina in the mid-1800s. As was often the case with the great European powers of the 19th century, it took the flimsiest of pretexts to launch an ambitious spate of colonization to the far-flung corners of the globe. And this is precisely what happened in the lead-up to the French creation of Indochina.

France had been looking for a reason to carve some territory out of Southeast Asia for some time, and when French Christian missionaries were heard to have been mistreated in Vietnam—or as it was called then, *Dai Nam*—it was all the reasoning that Napoleon III needed to send in French troops to pacify the Vietnamese. It could be argued that Napoleon III was engaging in a bit of "wag the dog" here since embarking on a foreign distraction in Southeast Asia proved to be a great distraction to the political turmoil that was taking place in France.

Napoleon III, who was the nephew of none other than Napoleon Bonaparte himself, had circumvented the French constitution and seized power for himself. He had been democratically elected to serve a term from 1848 to 1852 prior to engaging in a coup d'etat, which had him propped up as dictator. Surely not all of the French were happy with these developments, so when Napoleon III had a chance to turn attention abroad, he leaped at the chance.

Although the French punitive expedition was initially meant to teach the Vietnamese a lesson, it became an all-out colonization effort. The French assault began in the southern reaches of Vietnam, where French forces then marched north and took the city of Da Nang in the fall of 1858. This siege included the use of some 14 gunships and nearly 4,000 troops. The Vietnamese fiercely resisted any attempts by the French to move farther north, and after a few months of being repulsed from northward progress, the French decided to head south to attack the southern city of Saigon (modern-day Ho Chi Minh City) instead.

Saigon did not have the defensive networks that the cities of Central and North Vietnam had, so it was relatively easy for the French to take the city. It fell to French forces on February 17th, 1859. But once the French took over Saigon, they met with heavy resistance in the surrounding countryside, making it difficult to move far beyond the city of

Saigon itself. The French actually decided to enter into peace talks with the Vietnamese in November of 1859, demanding a treaty in which the Vietnamese would pledge to ensure the safety of the Christian clergy in the future.

However, the Vietnamese leadership refused to enter into any agreements, so the battle raged on. The French, in the meantime, were able to bolster their strength with more reinforcements, and in 1861, they were able to march on several strategic settlements along the Mekong Delta in southern Vietnam. These territorial gains led to the signing of the Treaty of Saigon on June 5th, 1862. This treaty guaranteed the religious freedom of Christians in the region, and it also opened up the Mekong Delta to French traders.

According to this agreement, the government of Vietnam had to hand over Bien Hoa, Gia Dinh, and Dinh Tuong, as well as the isles of Poulo Condor. The Vietnamese were also stiffed with the bill for the war and were told to fork over a considerable sum of money. By 1864, the territories of Bien Hoa, Gia Dinh, and Dinh Tuong had been made into a colony, which the French called Cochinchina. The French were then able to expand even farther in 1867 when, after another military defeat, the Vietnamese were forced to cede the regions of Ha Tien, Chau Doc, and Vinh Long.

The next step on the path to French Indochina was neighboring Cambodia, which became a French protectorate later that year. The French, in the meantime, had their eyes on using the Mekong as a means of transport to China. But when the Mekong proved too treacherous, they decided to create a path to China by train, constructing a railroad track originating out of Tonkin (a region in northern Vietnam). The region was not exactly friendly to French interests, and after a French official named Francis Garnier was attacked and beheaded by locals in

1873, the French used the incident as justification to enforce their will. After a steady pressure campaign, both Tonkin and the region of Annam were ultimately made into French protectorates.

China couldn't help but notice these troubling developments in its own backyard, and soon, it would be pulled into a conflict with the French. After the French stormed into Hanoi in the spring of 1882, the Chinese sent in an army of their own to confront the French. Initially, the Chinese tried to negotiate with the French, but the French forces by this point were ready to take Vietnamese territory by force.

Unable to reason with the invaders, China began to take up arms against them, and the so-called Sino-French War erupted in 1884 as a result. As the war heated up, the French sent their gunboats as far afield as Taiwan, where they laid waste to Chinese defensive positions. But as successful as the French were on the water, the Chinese made some headway on land when their infantry managed to push the French troops out of Lang Son. The French were not willing to expend their resources in a long, drawn-out war with China, and they were finally convinced to come to the table.

The subsequent peace talks resulted in the Treaty of Tientsin, with both parties placing their signatures on it in June of 1885. As a result of this treaty, the French would be in control of Vietnam. By 1887, the French holdings in Vietnam and Cambodia merged together to form Indochina. The next development was an outbreak of war between France and the Kingdom of Siam (modern-day Thailand) in 1893 when the governor of Indochina sent a French diplomat by the name of Auguste Pavie over to Bangkok to negotiate the placing of Laos under a French protectorate. The Kingdom of Siam refused to consider any such thing, which led the French to engage in "gunboat diplomacy" to produce an outcome that would be favorable to them. With the heavy artillery of the French Navy encircling Bangkok, King Chulalongkorn (also known as King Rama V) of Siam pleaded with the British for help, but the Brits proved to not be of much use. After washing their hands of the whole matter, they basically told King Chulalongkorn to cut a deal with the French. This forced bargain led to the French acquisition of Laos.

King Chulalongkorn is still remembered as a great king among the Thai people, noted for his massive additions to Thailand's infrastructure. This includes modernization efforts to bring electricity and other amenities to the nation. But when it came to French pressuring for Laos, it seemed that the king of Siam was forced to play a losing hand. He knew that his nation would not be able to stand up to the French military on its own, so Chulalongkorn began to seek ways to strengthen the standing of Thailand as an independent nation on the diplomatic front. It was with this purpose in mind that the ambitious Siamese monarch left his homeland for a tour of Europe in 1897. This marked the first official delegation from Thailand, and King Chulalongkorn used all of his diplomatic prowess with the heads of Europe to make sure that his kingdom—or at least what was left of it—would remain free.

In the early 1900s, the borders of French Indochina would go through some slight adjustments, but for the most part, it remained in place. However, this French establishment of a status quo belied the inner turmoil brewing within the borders of French Indochina, as several underground resistance movements were well underway. But it wouldn't be until the strain of World War Two that the French grip on the region would finally be loosened enough for these movements to truly take root.

Chapter 8– Islands of Discovery – The Philippines

"The Philippines is a terrible name, coming from Spain. Philip II was the father of the inquisition, who I believe died of syphilis. It is my great regret that we didn't change the name of our country."

-Imelda Marcos

The Philippines is a dynamic archipelago of around 7,641 islands located in Southeast Asia. These islands make up some 115,831 square miles, with the islands of Mindanao and Luzon making up the vast bulk of the region. Luzon boasts the capital city of Manila, which was the seat of the ancient Kingdom of Tondo, which ruled from 900 CE until the Spanish came along and took over the islands in the 1500s. Prior to the arrival of the Spaniards, the people of the Philippines were heavily influenced by India. After all, it was the Indian subcontinent that helped shape the culture, religion, and even writing of the islands (the Philippines used a form of writing derived from Sanskrit). All of this, of course, was prior to the arrival of Europeans in the region.

Ferdinand Magellan, a Portuguese explorer, who worked for the Spanish Crown, first stumbled upon the Philippines in 1521. In what was indeed a daring voyage for the day, Magellan had sailed from Europe to the southern tip of South America, rounded the tip, and then continued on in a northwesterly direction across the Pacific Ocean until they ended up off the shores of the Philippines.

There, they made contact with the leader of the islands, Rajah Humabon. The encounter seems to have been a good one, and the rajah even proved to be friendly to Christianity when pressed on the issue. This was important for Ferdinand and his company since they were all fervent Catholics who desired to spread the gospel just as much as they desired to find new lands. After leaving the good graces of the rajah, Magellan and his comrades then made their way to the nearby island of Mactan, but the reception would not be so welcoming there.

In fact, as soon as Magellan's ship landed and he and his crew stepped foot on dry land, they were ambushed by the locals. The attackers seemed to know that Magellan was the leader, and for whatever reason, they directed the bulk of their assault on him. Suddenly, Magellan was having spears thrown at him and scimitar-like blades lunging at his person. Magellan ended up suffering from multiple wounds, and he died right there on the beach. The rest of his shipmates had to quickly dash back to the ship and flee for their lives.

Although the mission would end tragically for Magellan, the rest of the crew would make history nevertheless. After this stop, they would continue west until they were able to circle the tip of South Africa and sail back to Europe, thereby completing the first ever successful global circumnavigation. The Spanish would return to the Philippines decades later in 1565, but this time, it was not as explorers but as conquerors. Led by Miguel López de Legazpi, a group of some 400 Spanish troops took Luzon by force and made Manila the colonial capital of Spain's newest extraterritorial possession.

Manila would become an important center for international trade, as it was now the stopping point for Spanish galleons fresh from Spanish-controlled territories in the Americas. These galleons were typically loaded with silver just mined from Mexico, and with this silver, the Spanish purchased precious goods from China. They essentially worked as an intermediary with Europe, dealing in porcelain, fine spices, and the like.

The Spanish seizure of Manila also had an impact on the Muslim sultanate of Brunei since Manila was considered to be a vassal to the sultan at the time. Brunei had been converted to Islam in the 1400s, some hundred years prior to the arrival of the Catholic Spaniards. After the Spanish converted the Philippines to Christianity in the late 1500s and exerted political control over the region, it wasn't long before an open conflict erupted with the Brunei sultanate. Initially, the Spanish governor of Manila seemed to send the sultan an olive branch, requesting they have friendly relations, but when the governor sought permission to evangelize Brunei with Christian missionaries, the sultan wanted nothing to do with it.

At this time, Spain was an uncompromising religious regime, and ever since the days of the Reconquista when Spanish Christians took back their Iberian Peninsula homeland that had been invaded by the Muslims, the Spanish had been on a never-ending crusade against Islam. When the Spanish Crown decided to declare war on the sultan of Brunei in 1578, this was, in many ways, just the latest battle in this ongoing ideological war.

In Spain's base in Mexico, which was yet another territory that the Spaniards had recently conquered and converted to Christianity, the Spanish had built up a multinational force of Europeans and indigenous Mexicans of various Native American backgrounds, such as Aztecs, Maya, and Incans. This taskforce set sail from western Mexico, traveling across the Pacific Ocean and arriving in the Philippines, where it was reinforced by over a thousand Filipinos.

This fighting force smashed its way into the capital of Brunei—Kota Batu—on April 16th, 1578. The sultan was actually forced to retreat to the higher ground of Jerudong. The Spanish forces were getting ready to chase after him, but they had to call off any further engagements after their camps were rocked by a terrible epidemic of dysentery and cholera.

Weakened from illness, the Spanish retreated back to the Philippines. Relations between Spain and Brunei would eventually normalize, and in 1599, full relations were restored with the understanding that neither side would interfere with the religious affairs of the other. Spanish rule would continue uninterrupted until 1762, which was when the Philippines were briefly taken over by the British.

Spain had been dragged into the so-called Seven Years' War on the side of the French, who were fighting the British. Britain was merciless in its assault on Spanish colonies, assaulting Cuba while simultaneously launching an amphibious invasion of Manila in the Philippines. The British had sent a naval expedition from their colonies in the subcontinent of India, which reached Manila Bay on September 26th, 1762.

This led to the Battle of Manila Bay, in which the Spanish defenders were fairly easily put down by the British invaders. The British agreed to an official withdrawal in 1764, but they would not disperse all of their troops until 1773. Spain remained in control of the Philippines until the territory was lost to the Americans in the Spanish-American War in 1898.

Chapter 9 – The Coming of the Colonists and Capitalists

"I hate imperialism. I detest colonialism. And I fear the consequences of their last bitter struggle for life. We are determined that our nation, and the world as a whole, shall not be the plaything of one small corner of the world."

- Sukarno

The colonization of Southeast Asia followed a fairly standard formula in which European powers would ask a Southeast Asian nation for certain concessions and then use any refusal as a pretext to take them over outright. This occurred in Vietnam when it was demanded upon the Vietnamese government to ensure the protection of Christian missionaries as well as to open up the doors for more widespread trade. When the king of Vietnam refused to appease the French in these demands, Napoleon III decided to launch an invasion in 1858, which would lead to several decades of French consolidation of territory in Southeast Asia.

The same pattern repeated itself in many other locales in the region during this period. Most of the kingdoms of Southeast Asia found themselves at a serious disadvantage when faced with the encroaching Europeans who were just coming off of the Industrial Revolution, which allowed them to make major strides in the advancement of their armed forces. The disparity between the heavily armed Europeans and the lightly armed Southeast Asians is precisely what led to these instances of so-called gunboat diplomacy. In these instances, steel-hulled freighters suddenly showed up at Southeast Asian ports with artillery fully capable of blasting settlements to smithereens if certain demands were not met.

Indonesia was yet another region of Southeast Asia that faced several waves of colonization, but the first real colonizers of this piece of Southeast Asian real estate actually weren't the Europeans but rather a steady stream of Islamic power brokers who began arriving on the scene sometime in the late 1200s. By the time the Portuguese set their sights on the island of Sumatra in the late 1400s, it was firmly under Muslim control.

The exact process of this Islamization is not exactly clear. This transformation was documented in some local legends, but most modern readers—quite frankly—might have a hard time believing them. An Arab scholar named Ibn Battuta visited the region in 1345, for example, and relayed a rather startling story. In regard to how Islam took hold, he related an account of an Indonesian king called Merah Silau who experienced a miraculous conversion.

According to Ibn Battuta, Merah had a vision of Muhammad, in which the prophet spit in his (Merah's) mouth. Shortly thereafter, Merah was supposedly confounded to find himself speaking strange speech. The legend then goes on to claim that soon after, a merchant craft from the Islamic world popped up, and the visitors were able to inform the befuddled king that the odd words coming out of his mouth were the Islamic confession of faith. This tale would have us believe that an Indonesian king miraculously became a Muslim overnight and that his kingdom followed in his footsteps.

If true, this certainly would be quite unique in the history of Islamic conversions since most other instances of nation states turning to Islam occurred after they were conquered by Muslim armies. The Middle East, all of North Africa, and, for a time, even Spain had become Muslim after military conquests. Upon their military defeat, the citizens were typically given the choice of either becoming Muslims or paying the jizya—a tax non-Muslims had to pay in order to keep their religious freedom intact.

As it pertains to Indonesia, however, there is some evidence that perhaps the assimilation of Islam among the locals was a more gradual process involving the influence of powerful Muslim merchants visiting the region over time. But whatever the case may be, by the time the Portuguese arrived on the scene in May of 1498, Islam was firmly entrenched in the region.

The Portuguese were not exactly the most ardent of missionaries, and most of the time, the trade of expensive spices took precedence over the winning of souls. When the Portuguese erected their first small outposts in and around Indonesia, their main concern was loading up their ships with as many valuable commodities as they could so they could then barter them to merchants in the port cities of Europe. The interesting thing about the Portuguese who took daring trips in the early days of European colonization is that many of them gave up any notion of returning home and instead hung their hat in their outposts in Southeast Asia for good.

In fact, more often than not, Portuguese sailors integrated themselves into the local community as much as they could. They married Southeast Asian women and raised whole families. As daring as many of their exploits were in sailing through uncharted waters, much of the time, they were more likely to be assimilated into Southeast Asia rather than actually colonize the region.

However, all of that would change when Dutch explorers arrived around the year 1596. The Dutch had suffered greatly during their voyage, with many of their number perishing from diseases such as dysentery during the trip. Some of the more abrasive Dutchmen had nearly mutinied and sparked fighting amongst the crew. As such, by the time this discontented lot landed in Indonesia, they were a sorry sight to see, as they were sickly, battered, and bruised (literally) from their own incessant infighting.

Nevertheless, they were received well enough by the locals, and they were given every common courtesy that was given to all foreign traders who arrived in the region. They were also given some assistance by the Portuguese who lived on the islands, as they arranged for the Dutch to be introduced to the local potentate. The Dutch explorers were invited to the king's palace, where they signed a basic treaty that recognized their rights to conduct trade in the region.

However, upon going to the local markets, the Dutch were not happy with what they deemed to be price gouging by local sellers. With such high prices on local spices, they realized that they would not be able to make a decent profit for their efforts. The leader of the Dutch explorers, Cornelis de Houtman, apparently was so incensed that he went to the palace and angrily complained. In the process, he managed to infuriate the king's court and was subsequently ordered off of the island.

The crafty Cornelis agreed to leave, but before he did so, he told his men to cause a ruckus. It's said that these devious Dutchmen started a melee, which left several civilians dead, before hopping on their craft and then turning their artillery on the palace itself. They shelled the king's own court, causing extensive damage before sailing off across the waters. As far as international relations go, this first exposure of the Indonesians to the Dutch was just about as bad as it could have been. There would be time to make amends, and by the early 1600s, more Dutch ships would reach Southeast Asia and develop much more cordial relations.

Initially, the Dutch outposts that were established didn't have much to do with colonialism as they did sheer, unbridled capitalism. The Dutch knew that if they could get their hands on a ready supply of spices, they would dominate European markets, as just a small amount of precious spice could bring in tremendous profits. In order to make the most of their financial gains, the financial backers of the Dutch expedition created an official commercial enterprise, which they called the Dutch East India Company. This organization would create the first permanent Dutch outpost in Indonesia, in Banten in western Java. Shortly after the installment of the Dutch in Java, the British, who were maritime rivals, tried to dislodge them.

The British would come to haunt Dutch outposts all over the world. After all, it was the British who famously evicted the Dutch from their settlements in Northeastern America, which they called New Amsterdam. After kicking the Dutch out, the victorious British renamed it New York. The British had tried a similar maneuver in the early 1600s when they tried to push the Dutch out of Java. The Dutch, realizing that they were outgunned, sent for reinforcements while a small faction remained besieged in their island fortress. The British soon tired of the expedition and called off the assault. Shortly thereafter, Dutch reinforcements arrived, and the capital of Jakarta was seized and made into the headquarters of the Dutch East Indies.

The Dutch consolidated their power in the region, and by the year 1682, they were influential enough to demand that the local Indonesian leaders of Banten no longer do business with the British. Although this was decades in the making, the Dutch were finally able to deliver their vengeance upon their archrivals by rendering them *persona non grata* as it pertained to Indonesia.

But as influential as the Dutch were at this point, they were still not colonists in the traditional sense. They merely held onto a powerful outpost in Java. However, throughout the 1700s, the Dutch would slowly gain more and more territory in the region. It was as if the Dutch East India Company transformed from a commercial enterprise into something more akin to a colonial territory. In the process, the Dutch monopoly of maritime trade began to decline.

Part of the reason for this decline was simply due to a decrease in the demand for the spices that the East Indies had to offer. The European thirst for items such as cloves and nutmeg had decreased. In addition to this disinterest, British and French colonies were now growing many of these spices on their own, thereby creating a glut in the market, lowering the price of what was previously a precious commodity. The Dutch just weren't making money off spices like they used to. By 1799, due to massive mounting debt, the Dutch East India Company was disbanded, and what could be called a Dutch colony formed in its place. During this time, the Dutch began to turn their attention inward, particularly on the islands of Sumatra and Java, where they began to coerce the locals into growing profitable sugar and rice crops, which could still bring them some profits on the international market. The Dutch administrators profited from this practice, but the locals they induced to labor for them earned very little for their work.

However, it would be wrong to say that the Dutch did nothing to help their colonial subjects, for the people of Indonesia certainly benefited from the Dutch colonial order, as it protected them from the banditry that had been rife in the region in the past. The locals were also given access to quality healthcare, and as a result, they saw an increase in their overall lifespan. The fact that Indonesians were living longer and healthier lives is easily demonstrated by the population growth on the islands while under Dutch rule.

It is said, for example, that in 1800, there were only ten million people who lived on Java. By 1900, that population had tripled to thirty million, which bears testament to the increase in the quality of life that occurred under the Dutch colonial administration. At the dawn of the 20th century, the Dutch decided to be even more humane to their subjects by instituting public welfare initiatives that expanded access to schools and healthcare clinics. This was done in a legislative move they dubbed as their Ethical Policy. Ironically enough, it was the improved education system in Indonesia that taught many for the first time the ideals of democracy, which led to a rethinking of the colonial system that they were under.

The French, in the meantime, had forged their own mighty colony in Southeast Asia, which they referred to as Indochina, of which Vietnam, Cambodia, and Laos were a part. These countries had very little in common with each other besides the fact that they were forced into a union as part of a French colony. Nevertheless, the French were able to profit considerably from their colonial holdings through the development of raw materials, such as rubber and other valuable trade goods. But even so, the administration of their faraway Southeast Asian colony was often a strain on mainland France. The French had to send an endless stream of

French bureaucrats just to run the place. The colonial structure also wasn't very good for the locals since it deprived them of the chance to have local representatives stand for them in government, as French colonial officials were sure to take all of these roles for themselves. This meant that local workers had no way to address grievances, for example, when faced with inhumane conditions when working on rubber tree plantations. Although the French introduced capitalism to their colonial society of Southeast Asia, the local populace was more likely to be victimized by this cutthroat form of capitalism than to have any tangible benefit from it.

Things weren't much better in British-controlled Burma either. The British took over Burma in three successive waves, which culminated in the seizure of all Burmese territory at the end of the Third Anglo-Burmese War. The British then incorporated these new territorial gains with their holdings in neighboring India. The British were brutal at times when rebellions broke out, especially in Lower Burma, where whole villages were sometimes burned down by British troops.

In an effort to divide and conquer the Burmese, the British often helped foster resentment between various ethnic groups. The British showed favoritism to the Karens of eastern Burma, for example, and gave special perks to Indian immigrants. The Burmese were especially resentful of Indians who came and bought lands that had previously belonged to the Burmese. By the turn of the century, the situation was getting especially tense in British Burma, and several anti-Indian rights movements began to break out as the unrest among the Burmese continued to grow.

In the Philippines, a new colonial aspirant had emerged in the form of the United States. The US had wrested the Philippines from its old colonial overseers, the Spanish, after the Spanish-American War of 1898.

However, once the US gained the Philippines, they didn't quite know what to do with it. Initially, they had feigned sympathy to Filipino rebels, who had been previously struggling to free themselves from Spain. But just about as soon as the US drove the Spanish out, any pretense of liberation had been dropped. Instead, the US annexed the Philippines as its own territory. The Filipinos, who desired freedom, were not going to take this lying down, and they quickly staged an insurgency against the US occupation. A major battle broke out between the Americans and the insurgents on February 4th, 1899.

This knock-down, drag-out fight would become known as the Battle of Manila, and it was the opening action of the Philippine-American War. This battle erupted after a skirmish broke out on the perimeter of Manila, which the US Army was occupying at the time. And what was a minor incident soon spiraled into an all-out war. Some Filipino insurgents tried to take the initiative by taking control of US artillery, but their advantage wouldn't last for long.

The next day, the US troops rallied and began to seize the surrounding territory around Manila, driving out the rebels. The US control of Manila was secured, but guerilla warfare carried on over the next few years. It was not until the summer of 1902 that American forces could claim to have complete authority over the Philippines, and even then, some sporadic attacks were staged off and on against the occupiers.

Part of the reason why the Filipino insurrection against the United States died down was due to a lack of public support among the majority of Filipinos. The long animosity that had galvanized the Filipinos to revolt against the Spanish was just not there when it came to the Americans. For one, the US ran its colony differently from the European model. The US installed a democratically elected legislature and allowed Filipinos to fill every position with the caveat that the US had to approve all major decisions.

In truth, among the general population of the Philippines, the Americans were considered to be the lesser evil when compared with the Spanish taskmasters who preceded them. Just the fact that the US enabled the separation of church and state was a great improvement on the lives of most Filipinos, who previously had to deal with a domineering Catholic Church that dictated just about every aspect of their lives. The Spanish had given local priests considerable powers that they then imposed upon the laity.

Although the US did nothing to interfere with Catholic worship, leaving Catholic churches to stand where they were, US officials made sure that church and state were separated. Such things were brand new concepts to the Filipinos, and they indeed benefited from them. And as the Filipino people began to experience at least a slight increase in their own personal freedoms, they realized that their yoke was much lighter under the American administration.

But no matter how it was administered, the United States, which was itself a former colony of the British, always seemed rather ill-fit to have an overseas colony. The Philippines was far from the US (although not quite as far as they were from Spain), and most Americans knew next to nothing about Filipino culture.

Then again, the Philippines provided a strategic foothold for US interests in the Pacific when the rising power of Japan made its presence known. Pretty soon, it would be the sudden surge of Japanese imperial might that would come to shake all of these Southeast Asian colonies to their very core.

Chapter 10 – Southeast Asia Consumed by the Co-Prosperity Sphere

"To advocate a New Order was to seek freedom and respect for peoples without prejudice, and to seek a stable basis for the existence of all peoples, equally, and free of threats."

- Tojo Hideki

Japan shocked the world on September 27th, 1940, when it was announced that they had signed on to the so-called Tripartite Pact with Nazi Germany and Fascist Italy. Japan had been a rising power ever since the so-called Meiji restoration began in the 19th century, which helped Japan revitalize its armed forces and industrial base. Rather than falling prey to colonization like so many of its Asian peers, Japan had become a colonial power in its own right.

In 1894, Japan went to war with China and wrested control of Taiwan from the Chinese. In 1904, Japan fought Russia to a standstill, and in 1905, it made Korea a protectorate. This laid the groundwork for Japan to annex the entire Korean Peninsula into its burgeoning empire in 1910. Imperial Japan seemed to have plenty of potential, but other world powers weren't quite sure what the Japanese would do with it.

The fact that Japan would side with the Nazis and Italian Fascists was quite alarming, to say the least, but even a couple of months prior to this bold move, Japanese Foreign Minister Matsuoka Yosuke had made an announcement that should have put the world on notice. He declared Japanese designs for a Greater East Asia Co-Prosperity Sphere.

Even though most wouldn't have had much of a clue as to what such a thing might mean, it would have tremendous implications on Southeast Asia in the years to come. Even Japan's signing of the Tripartite Pact should be seen in this light since as part of the terms of Japan joining forces with the Germans and Italians was for the latter two parties to recognize that East and Southeast Asia would be Japan's sphere of influence.

After the Germans steamrolled through western Europe and defeated France in June of 1940, the Japanese began to consider the ramifications of what might happen to French-controlled territory in Southeast Asia. France's early knockout blow left the fate of the French colonies up in the air. Japan knew that if it did not step in, Germany could seize the colonies for itself. As it were, in the immediate aftermath of France's devastating defeat, a French puppet state was established in southern France around the city of Vichy.

Vichy France, as it was known, would be rendered Nazi allies. And although Vichy France was allowed to keep their extraterritorial possessions, Japan soon made it clear that it expected to be given special perks and privileges since Vichy France's colonies were in their projected sphere of influence. Japan had already sparked another war with China (the first took place in the late 19th century) in 1931 with the seizure of Chinese Manchuria. Then, in 1937, Japan struck China again, this time seizing several major cities along China's eastern coast, including Beijing, Shanghai, and Nanjing.

The seizure of Nanjing (also called Nanking), which has sometimes been referred to as the Rape of Nanjing, was particularly brutal. As the appellation suggests, the taking of the city was followed by wanton rape and pillaging committed by Japanese soldiers. Much of the world turned a blind eye to these atrocities. It wasn't until Japan joined the Axis and began to seize former European possessions in Southeast Asia that the rest of the world really took notice.

It actually took some soul searching among Japanese war planners to decide on acquiring Southeast Asian territory while the war in China continued to rage. Emperor Hirohito of Japan was not pleased with the fact that the war with China had not yet been won while the Japanese military was preparing to open up a new front in Southeast Asia. Hirohito even stated to one of his staff his belief that the Japanese armed forces were merely trying to deflect from their failure to quickly defeat the Chinese by distracting everyone with a new engagement in Southeast Asia. By doing this, the Japanese could then blame the lack of progress against China on the European colonies, which had deprived Japan of the plentiful resources in their own backyard that would have helped them more easily subdue the Chinese.

At any rate, despite his skepticism, the Japanese emperor allowed the war plans to continue as his generals intended. Japan's military leadership was absolutely convinced that the war in China could not continue unless Japan made use of the abundant resources in Southeast Asia to help fuel the fight.

Thus, Prime Minister Konoe Fumimaro of Japan okayed the implementation of the Co-Prosperity Sphere. Initially, it did not necessarily mean outright war but rather a gradual integration of Southeast Asian nations into the sphere. Most important for Japan was for world powers, such as the United States and the Soviet Union, to recognize Japan's dominance in the region. And of these two, it was perhaps the Soviets that Japan was the most worried about.

Japan and Soviet Russia were in close proximity to each other, so it was quite easy for the two to get into territorial disputes. In fact, prior to the Russian Revolution of 1917, when Russia was still run by the tsar, Japan had successfully waged war against the Russians. The newest incarnation of Russian power, the Soviet Union, was not willing to take any chances with Japan in the future, which resulted in a large military buildup between Soviet and Japanese territory. This was a source of considerable tension.

In 1939, a border skirmish erupted in Japanese-controlled Manchuria between Japanese and Russian troops. Despite their previous victories against the Russians, in this unofficial battle, the Japanese did not fare so well. Before the situation escalated into an actual war, both parties were able to come to a diplomatic solution, reaching a new border agreement in the summer of 1940, just prior to Japan joining the Axis. At this point, the last thing Japan wanted was a conflict with Soviet Russia.

This provided Japan with yet another reason to expand into Southeast Asia rather than risk Russian aggression in their northwestern backyard. The Japanese wanted to keep the Russians off their back for the time being. And even when the Germans decided to double-cross Soviet Premier Joseph Stalin and invade Russia, the Japanese, themselves feeling double-crossed, wanted nothing to do with it.

The first implementation of Japan's so-called Co-Prosperity Sphere came after the Nazis defeated France. With the fall of France, the Nazi puppet state of Vichy France was created, and Japan felt that the former French colonial territory in Southeast Asia was ripe for the picking. Since Vichy France was ostensibly an ally of Nazi Germany, Japan couldn't immediately strongarm the colonies away from France outright. Instead, the Japanese sought to pressure and bully the French into meeting as many of their demands as they could. The first of these demands was a request that France allow the Japanese to station troops in North Vietnam in order to aid Japan's continued struggle against the Chinese. The Japanese insisted that having a foothold in North Vietnam would be essential in their effort to get the upper hand against Chinese forces. The beleaguered French, predictably enough, didn't disagree, and they gave their approval for the Japanese to begin placing troop deployments in North Vietnam. This was initially meant to be just a small troop detachment, but it wasn't long before there were several thousand Japanese soldiers stationed in North Vietnam.

The next demand that the Japanese squeezed out of the French was full control of the port city of Haiphong, citing it as being vital to their war efforts. Soon, Japan was sending troops at will, establishing airbases, and generally making use of whatever resources they could. By the fall of 1940, it was quite clear who was actually in control of French Indochina. Initially, many of the local Vietnamese freedom fighters in the region must have looked upon the Japanese as liberators, but any hopes that the Japanese had their best interests at heart were rather quickly dashed.

Demonstrating their contempt and lack of any real sympathy for the Vietnamese, the Japanese administrators kept much of the French colonial bureaucracy in place. Nothing really changed for the average Vietnamese resident except for the fact that the Japanese had the final say in what the French colonial authorities could do, and at the end of the day, it was the Japanese who were exacting a profit from their labors. Despite any pretense of being liberators, the fact remained that it was much easier for the Japanese to rule through the French than without them.

Another test to Japanese dominion and the status of French Indochina emerged in June of 1940 when Thailand seized upon French weakness and began saber-rattling against the colonists. Even before France was dragged into World War Two, a steady movement had been growing in Thailand to reclaim the lands that France had taken. These sentiments gained real momentum in 1938 when Thai dictator Field Marshal Plaek Pibulsongkram (better known as Phibun) came to power.

Marshal Phibun, riding on a populist wave, began to speak openly of returning Thailand to its former glory. It was with these intentions in mind that, on June 24th, 1939, Phibun changed the name of his nation from the hated "Siam," which outsiders had essentially given the region, in favor of "Thailand." This name signified that their nation was a home for all Thais, including those currently living under French colonial rule. For an opportunist like Phibun, it must have seemed like the divine hand of fate when German tanks defeated France in 1940. It must have appeared to Phibun that this was just the right time to take on his defeated French nemesis and demand the repatriation of land that France had carved off from Thailand in the past.

Phibun galvanized the Thai armed forces to his cause and launched a war against the French in the region in October of 1940. The French were heavily outnumbered by the Thai troops, and initially, the war went in their favor. By January 6th, 1941, the Thai troops seemed to be close to a major victory in Laos. However, the situation would change rather dramatically only a week later when the beleaguered French cobbled together what remained of their naval craft and launched a sneak attack on January 17th.

The French would turn the tide at the so-called Battle of Ko Chang. This naval battle pitted a French flotilla against a group of Thai craft, and the Thai ships were decimated. This was a devastating blow to the Thai war effort. Although the Japanese were initially content to let the two parties fight it out, after this French victory, they decided to step in and serve as a mediator between the two. Under Japanese "diplomacy," the French were forced to cede the disputed territories to Thailand, and the fighting between the two parties ceased.

The Japanese used their role not as much for peace but rather as a means to further take advantage of the situation. It was from this point forward that Japan would begin to move its own troops into Thailand. As a result, the Thai state would essentially become an occupied puppet of the Japanese. In fact, the Japanese launched an invasion of Thailand on the very same day that they bombed Hawaii's Pearl Harbor.

Phibun's troops vainly tried to hold the Japanese off, but after one day of fighting, Phibun surrendered to Japanese aggression. Phibun would then decide to collaborate with the Japanese, which led to Phibun openly declaring war on the Allied powers on January 25th, 1942. Thailand, of course, was never considered much of a serious threat in the grand scheme of things, but certain Allied powers, such as the British, in particular, would not forget Phibun's perceived treachery.

Meanwhile, homegrown Vietnamese resistance against the Japanese would begin to take shape under the leadership of the communist idealogue Ho Chi Minh. Since Japan was ramping up its efforts against China and squeezing all manner of resources out of French Indochina, the US Department of State began to take a keen interest in the region. In a bid to slow down the Japanese war machine, the US slapped the

Japanese with sanctions, stopping the flow of oil and gas from America to Japan. The British and the Dutch also cut off Japan shortly thereafter.

Japan was dependent on these resources, and without them, it would have to look for more supplies elsewhere. In particular, Japan began to eye British and Dutch holdings in Southeast Asia. However, Japanese war planners were fully aware that any attack on British territory would most likely drag them into a war with the United States. Britain was already fighting off the Germans, and if Japan joined the fray, the United States would surely follow.

At this point, the Japanese figured that war with the US was all but inevitable, so they made the fateful decision to strike out at the Americans first. This preemptive strike came on December 7th, 1941, when the Japanese launched a raid on Pearl Harbor. Similar to the blitzkrieg lightning war that Germany had conducted to quickly overwhelm western Europe, the Japanese hoped to completely cripple the US fleet that was stationed in Pearl Harbor, Hawaii.

Some of the best US battleships, such as the USS *Arizona*, USS *West Virginia*, USS *Oklahoma*, USS *California*, USS *Utah*, USS *Nevada*, and USS *Pennsylvania*, among countless others, were literally blown out of the water. Most were caught completely by surprise, which means they did not even have the chance to take evasive action before their ships were demolished and their crews sent to a watery grave. In all, some 3,500 Americans were killed. With the Americans still digging out the wreckage at Pearl Harbor, the Japanese then unleashed an assault upon British, Dutch, and American holdings in Southeast Asia.

The Japanese seized the Philippines on December 8th, fighting with such ferocity that the unprepared American fleet was forced to evacuate to Java by December 12th, 1941. The Japanese troops that participated in the invasion had been stationed in nearby Formosa, and as soon as they were given the signal, they leaped into action. Incredibly enough, even though the Japanese delivered a blistering defeat to American forces that day, the Americans actually held the numerical advantage. There were indeed more defenders than assailants during the assault on the Philippines, but it is said that many of the colonial troops were inexperienced or irregular units who just did not have the wherewithal to stand up against battle-hardened Japanese troops. In the end, 23,000 American soldiers died or were made prisoners of war, as well as some 100,000 Filipino troops who were also either killed or made prisoners of war.

The Japanese then launched attacks on British-held Malaya, forcing British defenders to retreat to Singapore. After a protracted siege, the Japanese were able to lay claim to Singapore itself on February 15th, 1942. The Japanese war machine then rolled through British Burma, the Dutch East Indies, and other locales, one after the other.

The American defenders who were left behind in the Philippines were forced to surrender to the Japanese on April 9th, 1942. These prisoners of war would come to face some of the worst conditions imaginable. They were routinely beaten, abused, and humiliated, and they were also made to march for long hours with hardly any food or water. One of the most famous of these marches, the so-called Bataan Death March, which had some 80,000 prisoners of war march about 60 miles to their new site of detainment, resulted in several thousand deaths.

With the Japanese controlling both the Dutch East Indies (Indonesia) and the Philippines, the waters around Australia were practically encircled by hostile Japanese troops. Many Australians were concerned that they might be next, but the Japanese would not get that far. That is not to say there were no casualties. The bombing of Darwin was the largest attack mounted by a foreign power on Australia to this day. Japan destroyed several ships while suffering little in return. The attack on Sydney Harbour saw the deaths of twenty-one Allied soldiers. However, in the grand scheme of World War Two, Australia's casualties were more minor. The gains made in late 1941 and in the first half of 1942 would mark the highpoint of Japan's aggression, as its power would only dwindle from this point forward.

After Japan's disastrous defeat at the hands of the United States at the Battle of Midway Island in June of 1942, the Americans began to slowly but surely push the Japanese back. Midway was an all-around disaster for the Japanese, which saw four of their aircraft carriers destroyed. This fact alone put a significant dent in Japan's ability to wage war. After all, it was their aircraft carriers that had enabled the Japanese bombers and fighters to get within range of Pearl Harbor in December of 1941. Without suitable aircraft carriers, a wrench was thrown into Japan's ability to launch long-range attacks across the Pacific.

The Battle of Midway was followed by another important US victory in the Solomon Islands when the US took on the Japanese at Guadalcanal. The Solomon Islands, which had previously been a British possession before the Japanese took them over, was important to the Japanese because they were a key component of their overstretched supply lines. The Japanese also wished to use the Solomon Islands as a launchpad for further attacks across the Pacific.

However, these plans were foiled when the US launched an invasion of the islands, one that was determined to drive the Japanese out. American Marines fought bloody battles with the Japanese for every inch of land they could get a hold of. And while the Marines duked it out with the Japanese on land, US naval forces took on the Japanese navy in the surrounding waters.

The siege would last until February of 1943 when the last Japanese defenders were finally forced to abandon the islands. Interestingly, as Japanese leaders began to sense that the war was not turning in their favor, more consideration was given to additional autonomy to the Southeast Asian nations that were under their dominion. On January 28th, 1943, the recently elected prime minister, Tojo Hideki (commonly referred to as Hideki Tojo in the Western style, where one's surname appears after their given name), began to openly speak of granting some semblance of independence to both Burma and the Philippines.

It seems that, once again, the Japanese hoped that by presenting themselves as liberators, they could gain the active support of Southeast Asians. These words were followed up with action when Burma and the Philippines were both granted a form of independence on August 1st and October 14th, respectively.

Despite the lip service, Tojo Hideki himself never really believed that the nations of Southeast Asia merited independence. In fact, just a few days prior to Burmese independence, Prime Minister Tojo stated to his colleagues, "Burma is more a newborn than a child," insinuating in his own patronizing way that Japan would have to be the guiding hand of the infantile Burmese. Tojo then further assured his colleagues of Burma's ultimate submission to Japan when he stated, "as long as we have our military power, we know we have Burma by the throat."

The most elaborate bit of pseudo-nation building that the Japanese engaged in was when, on October 21st, 1943, they installed an Indian nationalist named Subhas Chandra Bose in Singapore in what was termed the Provisional Government of Free India. Since Singapore is fairly far removed from India, this was obviously a government in exile, which the Japanese hoped would inspire more independence-minded Indians to support their efforts. It was hoped that Indian nationalists on the subcontinent would look upon the Indian-run government in Singapore with pride and inspire them to turn against their British colonial taskmasters in India proper. The Japanese especially hoped that the sight of an armed and independent Indian army in Southeast Asia would inspire all Indians in the region to join their cause. And before the war was out, the Japanese would indeed have Subhas Chandra Bose's forces march on mainland India in a desperate attempt to dislodge the British hold on the region.

But no matter how much Japan claimed that these various regimes were independent, they were really only independent so long as they followed the wishes of Japan. Nevertheless, on November 5th, 1943, the Japanese high command convened the so-called Greater East Asia Conference, which would attempt to present all of Japan's puppet rulers as equals. This was where the future plans for the Co-Prosperity Sphere were hammered out. Here, Japan's efforts were presented as a collective struggle that involved all of Southeast Asia against Western imperialism.

By 1944, however, it was clear to all that the war was beginning to go very badly for the Japanese, and as the Japanese dug in for a tough fight, promises for true autonomy rang hollow. Japan was now on the defensive against the Allies, and it had lost much of any real support from Southeast Asian nations, such as the Philippines and Burma, the latter of which had Allies landing on its soil in March of 1944.

The Japanese, while being bounced out of Burma, actually caught the Allies off guard by driving westward and invading British India. A force of some 85,000 Japanese soldiers, coupled with additional support from Subhas Chandra Bose's Indian National Army, attempted to assault British positions while simultaneously stirring up popular resentment among the locals. It was hoped that a homegrown resistance to British rule would emerge and that, in the chaos, the British would be defeated.

It was also an objective of the Japanese to tie down the British in India so that they would not be able to fight in Burma.

The joint Japanese/Indian forces seized the border town of Imphal on March 29th, 1944, taking the British by complete surprise. The Japanese were then able to shut down the Imphal-Kohima road without much resistance. Emboldened, they then took over the nearby town of Kohima on April 6th. However, the British were not going to take this lying down, and finally, a British/Indian force was assembled to take on the Japanese. This group cut through the blockage of the Imphal-Kohima road, and once a relief force arrived on the scene, the true battle began. The invaders held on for a while, but they ended up retreating completely that July. Driven back to Burma, the Japanese realized they only had a mere toehold left, which was centered around the Irrawaddy River. The Japanese would be kicked out of Burma for good by 1945.

In the meantime, in nearby Vietnam, the Vietnamese resistance to the Japanese was only increasing. The communist-backed rebel forces, known as the Viet Minh, were particularly effective when it came to launching guerilla-styled attacks on the occupying Japanese troops. Nevertheless, by March of 1945, the Japanese had tightened their grip by stripping all French colonies of power so that the Japanese could rule directly over the Vietnamese people. It would be short-lived since the Japanese were inching closer and closer to their ultimate defeat in the Second World War. And as Japan teetered on the very brink of collapse, the Viet Minh actually managed to wrest their own piece of territory from the Japanese in northeastern Vietnam.

This piece of high ground would remain important to the Viet Minh as the group continued its struggle to create an autonomous communist enclave in the decades to come. As Japan neared its inevitable defeat, the Viet Minh grew bolder, and by August, the rebels had actually managed to take both Hanoi and Saigon. Then, on September 2nd, 1945, the Vietnamese rebel leader Ho Chi Minh boldly announced that his Viet Minh had established the first Democratic Republic of Vietnam.

Interestingly enough, this was declared on the very same day that Japan officially surrendered to the Allied forces. However, the Allies didn't take this homegrown declaration of independence very seriously. And, in reality, Ho Chi Minh only controlled a portion of the north, while the French, aided by the British, were attempting to restore the colonial rule in the south. This wasn't an easy task, though, since the communist Viet Minh were roaming the countryside, spreading disorder as much as they could. Things were so bad, in fact, that the British and French actually recruited the recently defeated Japanese to help them fight off the Viet Minh! The Japanese themselves were being consistently assaulted by Vietnamese guerilla fighters, which left them unable to even evacuate themselves from the region until the violence subsided.

As such, the Brits had the French declare martial law until a joint force of French, British, and Japanese troops attempted to put down the ferocious Viet Minh fighters. This feat was finally achieved on September 23rd, 1945. With some semblance of peace restored, the former French colonial infrastructure was put back into place.

Much the same could be said for many other parts of Southeast Asia that the Japanese had withdrawn from. But despite the false promises of the Co-Prosperity Sphere, the nations of Southeast Asia were not going to be satisfied until their true freedom was legitimately realized.

Chapter 11 – Southeast Asia and the Sweet Taste of Freedom

"I did not join the resistance movement to kill people, to kill the nation. Look at me now. Am I a savage person? My conscience is clear."

-Pol Pot

Since much of Southeast Asia had become colonized, the march to freedom was not going to be an easy one. It took local struggles against colonial overlords, two world wars, and further such struggles to achieve something akin to independence, which would then be followed by an attempt to forge statehood from scratch. In much of Southeast Asia, these were the things required in order for any true freedom to take place.

Of all the former colonies to achieve statehood, it was perhaps the Philippines whose road was the easiest. Despite the horrors inflicted upon them by the Japanese, the Japanese occupiers had put a bureaucracy in place of local Philippine leadership, which would serve as the framework for an independent nation state. The Philippines also benefited from the fact that the United States, unlike the British and French, was not absolutely hellbent on keeping the Philippines as a territory. In fact, even before the Japanese occupation, the US had entered into an agreement with the Philippines that aimed to pave the way for a gradual independence by 1946. The plan called for the Philippines to remain under a commonwealth status until full independence could be achieved. The US had even overseen the election of the first president, Manuel Quezon, in 1935. Once the Japanese were kicked out, plans for independence were once again put into place, and the first legitimate independent Philippine state came into being on July 4th, 1946. Although Manuel Quezon had perished from tuberculosis in 1944 while in exile in the United States, a new Filipino president was readily elected in his place.

The British in Burma, on the other hand, had a much more difficult time letting go of their overseas possession. There was a lot of baggage and unfinished business let over after the war, and initially, the British wanted to try those Burmese who had collaborated with the Japanese. Among them was the popular Burmese leader Aung San.

The Burmese revolutionary Aung San had first come to prominence as a student rabble rouser who organized protests against British rule in the 1930s. Aung San eventually went from being a student organizer to leading a revolutionary group, which called itself Thakin. As British authorities began to crack down on the movement, Aung San relocated to Japan in 1940. This, of course, was right on the eve of the eventual Japanese invasion of Burma, an invasion that Aung San had a front seat to, arriving back in Burma in prominence in Burma while riding on the coattails of the Japanese.

Having said that, there was certainly more than enough skeletons in Aung San's closet to merit a closer look by the British, but since Aung San was so popular with the Burmese people, it was quickly realized that such a thing would only make an already chaotic situation even worse. Aung Sang headed the most powerful political party at the time, which was clamoring for independence. This party was the so-called Anti-Fascist People's Freedom League.

With this powerful political backing, Aung San demanded nothing short of complete and full independence from Britain. The British, however, began to stall for time and instead presented a much more gradual process that included a lengthy transition before finally granting Burma its autonomy. This did not at all sit well with the Burmese, and in the fall of 1946, they let the British know by staging massive protests that included a national strike of Burmese police and other low-level bureaucrats. Britain could not ignore this unrest, and by early 1947, British officials were pressured to come to the table.

In January of that year, Aung San himself made his way to London to discuss terms of a final separation of Burma from Britain. It was agreed that a general election would be held that April. Aung San was officially elected by a majority of the Burmese people, although many Karens (an ethnic group in Burma) decided to sit the election out due to lingering feelings of disenfranchisement and frustration with the process. Some believed that by boycotting the proceedings they could convince the incoming administration to approve Karen independence from Burma. At any rate, Aung San would not have long to enjoy his victory, as he was assassinated on July 19th, 1947. The British weren't the ones behind this hit as one might initially expect; it was actually a rival Burmese political party that carried out the hit.

Nevertheless, even though the newly elected prime minister was dead, a new constitution for a free and independent Burma was forged on September 24th, 1947. Aung San's successor, U Nu (also known as Thakin Nu), presided over the British signing of the treaty, which formally acknowledged the new Republic of the Union of Burma on October 17th, 1947. This treaty was officially ratified by the British Parliament on January 4th, 1948, declaring to the world that Burma was indeed a free and independent nation.

But although it was declared free from Britain, Burma would face several decades of tumult and inner turmoil. There would be waves of protest against corruption and multiple outright coups. In the quest to reform the Burmese government, it would be none other than the daughter of the assassinated Aung San, Aung San Suu Kyi, who would rise to prominence as a champion of human rights in Burma. For her efforts, Aung San Suu Kyi was persecuted by the Burmese government and placed under house arrest in 1991. She was finally released in 1995.

Aung San Suu Kyi continued to fight for the rights of the average Burmese citizen, and as a result, she once again ended up in prison in 2000. She was released in 2002, but she was very nearly assassinated in 2003. Nevertheless, in 2010, riding on a tide of popular sentiment, she was elected as state counsellor, which is essentially the Burmese equivalent of a prime minister. Aung San Suu Kyi is well known for her activism, and she is a Nobel Peace Prize winner for her efforts.

However, in recent years, her legacy has been marred by the alleged genocide of Burma's Rohingya ethnic group. It has been claimed that the Burmese military has carried out a systematic genocide of the primarily Muslim Rohingyas and that Aung San Suu Kyi has tried to cover it up. Aung San Suu Kyi actually made an appearance before the International Court of Justice (ICJ) over this issue in 2019, and she not only refused to acknowledge that any genocide ever occurred, but she also defended the actions of the Burmese military. Many around the world who knew her as a human rights activist were quite shocked at this turn of events.

Whatever the case may be, her strong defense of the military certainly didn't do her any favors, and on February 1st, 2021, she was ousted from power in a military coup. Amid claims of widespread irregularities, the results of the previous November election had been thrown out, and Aung San Suu Kyi was forcibly removed from power and placed under arrest. As of publication, both the fate of Aung San Suu Kyi and Burma (Myanmar) remain uncertain.

But as chaotic as the independence of Burma was, it wasn't anywhere near as rough as the Indonesian struggle to free itself from Dutch domination. The Indonesians had declared their independence right at the end of World War Two when the Indonesian revolutionary Mohammad Hatta declared the country's independence on August 17th, 1945. The Dutch, who wished to reestablish themselves as colonial overlords, did not take kindly to this, and it would mark the beginning of a bitter four-year struggle over the fate of Indonesia.

For the average Indonesian, this would become a struggle against each other just as much as it was against the Dutch. The thing that made the Indonesian National Revolution particularly ugly was the fact that hardline revolutionaries came to see prominent Indonesians who had prospered under Dutch rule as enemies to their cause. As a result, it has been claimed that more Indonesians perished from fighting each other during the course of their revolutionary struggle than died at the hands of the Dutch. At any rate, it was only after a major upheaval that the Dutch finally recognized Indonesia as an independent state in December of 1949.

However, even the struggle of the Indonesians pales in comparison to the long, drawn-out saga of the Vietnamese. At the end of World War Two, the Vietnamese guerilla fighters, the Viet Minh, declared independence, much like the Indonesian revolutionaries had. But this declaration was not at all welcomed by the French. With the help of the British, the French reestablished themselves in southern Vietnam while the communist-aligned Viet Minh still had control of the north.

In the spring of 1946, the French came to acknowledge the Democratic Republic of Vietnam (DRV) in the north but insisted that a referendum be held to determine the fate of South Vietnam. Initially, Ho Chi Minh agreed, but the talks broke down, and all-out fighting between the French-controlled south and the communist north erupted anew. The French, in the meantime, tried to put a Vietnamese façade on their presence in South Vietnam by installing Bao Dai, a descendant of the Vietnamese imperial line, as the head of state. In reality, Bao Dai was just a puppet for the French.

In early 1950, the Soviet Union and communist China (Chinese communists took over China in 1949) officially acknowledged the DRV. Since the Cold War between the United States and the Soviet Union was already in full swing, the US was none too pleased with these developments. The United States desired to contain communism, and as the war in Korea was about to prove, the nation was willing to spend much blood and money in order to do so.

Although US troops were not yet in Vietnam by the early 1950s, the US was sending millions of dollars in aid to help prop up the French-backed South Vietnamese. Meanwhile, the North Vietnamese were ramping up their efforts against the South Vietnamese. The North Vietnamese aggression ultimately culminated in the so-called Battle of Dien Bien Phu in the spring of 1954. In a serious of ferocious assaults, the Viet Minh brought the French close to total defeat.

At this point, the French turned to the Americans for help. US President Dwight D. Eisenhower initially intimated that perhaps the United States could conduct some limited bombing campaigns against the North Vietnamese. However, when the notion was brought before the US Congress, it was thoroughly rejected. Eisenhower was not willing to push the issue after that, and the French realized that US military support would not be available any time soon.

As a result of US unwillingness to engage in war, the French were forced to negotiate with the North Vietnamese. This led to a deal in which Vietnam would be officially partitioned into two countries—a communist regime in the north and a French-backed regime in the south. From here on out, the French would no longer have a military presence in South Vietnam, but the United States began to become more and more involved with military aid to the South Vietnamese in a desperate bid to fortify South Vietnam against the communists.

The South Vietnamese Prime Minister Ngo Dinh Diem also received full political support of US officials, even though Diem was increasingly unpopular with the South Vietnamese themselves. Diem was a strident anti-communist, and he systematically cracked down on subversive groups in South Vietnam. However, the more Diem cracked down on them, the more they continued to pop up. Soon, South Vietnam had to deal with the so-called Viet Cong, a communist group backed by the North Vietnamese. In fact, the North Vietnamese had created a vast supply line that ran through neighboring Laos and Cambodia to aid South Vietnamese guerilla fighters. This supply line, which was called the Ho Chi Minh Trail, would become a major thorn in Diem's side. The conflict entered a new phase in November of 1963 when Diem was assassinated. He was then succeeded by a South Vietnamese general named Duong Van Minh, and from here on out, the situation in Vietnam would only get worse.

In 1964, the USS *Maddox* was torpedoed by the North Vietnamese in the Gulf of Tonkin. This led to the so-called Gulf of Tonkin Resolution, which gave US President Lyndon B. Johnson the go-ahead to take military action against the North Vietnamese. This came in the form of a massive bombing campaign conducted against the North in February of 1965 called Operation Rolling Thunder. President Johnson then upped the ante even more by deploying over 180,000 US troops to the region less than a month later.

By 1966, the number of American troops in Vietnam would swell to over 400,000. But no matter how many troops or bombs the Americans threw at the communist Vietnamese, they absolutely refused to give up. Not only that, they only seemed to grow more relentless. After a shocking assault on a US Marine garrison in the South Vietnamese city of Khe Sanh in 1968, the US realized it was stuck in an intractable quagmire. The American defenders of Khe Sanh were able to repel the Viet Minh attackers, but they lost 250 American soldiers in this one battle alone. And even after achieving this hard-won victory, it was clear that it didn't amount to much since the Viet Minh could regroup and attack them all over again.

The real shock would come in the 1968 Tet Offensive when the Viet Minh launched a coordinated massive assault on South Vietnam, attacking over 100 different targets all at once. During the onslaught, even the US Embassy was penetrated, although the invaders were repulsed; however, it came with a great cost of life. By now, the war was incredibly unpopular among the American public, with frequent protests against it staged in cities throughout the United States. Faced with such an unpopular war, President Johnson chose not to run for reelection.

Richard Nixon ultimately became the next US president, and he pledged to bring US troops home.

Nixon's strategy to do this was to launch a massive effort to train and mobilize South Vietnamese troops so that they could take up the bulk of the fighting and allow the US soldiers to withdraw slowly. However, along with withdrawing troops, Nixon also broadened the scope of the fighting by directing units to take on the North Vietnamese supply lines that ran through nearby Laos and Cambodia. Nixon began a bombing campaign within the borders of these two nations, which was widely considered illegal at the time. None of these efforts seemed to have much of an impact on the ability of the North Vietnamese to wage war, though, as was proven in the massive Easter Offensive launched by the Viet Minh in 1972.

Even though Nixon was unable to find a military solution to Vietnam, he didn't cease to look for political solutions. He thought he found one when he opened the door to diplomatic relations with China. The fact that Nixon normalized relations with China was a big deal since no previous US president had even bothered to recognize the legitimacy of the Chinese government after China's communist revolution of 1949. However, Nixon and Chairman Mao Zedong found some common ground, and Nixon was able to use China to gain leverage with Vietnam. By using China to pressure the North Vietnamese, the Viet Minh were persuaded to come to the table to negotiate a potential peace deal.

Unfortunately, all of this was derailed in 1973 when Nixon faced his own political pressure from home in the form of the so-called Watergate scandal. Nixon had been implicated in a bungled break-in of the Democratic National Committee's headquarters during the previous year's election. Nixon was ultimately forced to resign, and in the midst of this turmoil, negotiations with the North Vietnamese fell through. In the end, the remaining US troops were forced to withdraw in 1975, and North Vietnam would take over South Vietnam, uniting the country under one government.

Ironically enough, after all of the bloodshed over whether or not Vietnam should become a communist state, Vietnam would drop much of its hardline Marxist policies in subsequent years and embrace many capitalist ideals simply because they made the nation more prosperous in the long run. After a terrible recession in the late 1970s, Vietnam opened up to private enterprises by the 1980s. Farmers, for example, were permitted to sell surplus produce in order to make a profit. Such measures improved the economy, and Vietnam has continued to embrace many aspects of free-market capitalism to this day. In fact, Vietnam is now a trading partner with the United States and even its old nemesis, France. Was all of that fighting in Southeast Asia for nothing? Perhaps looking back, one could say so, but, of course, as they say, hindsight is always 20/20.

But as rough of a transition Vietnam had, in many ways, neighboring Cambodia had an even worse time emerging from colonialism. The French agreed to grant the Cambodians more say in their government after the war, with reforms being enacted in January of 1946. The French also agreed to get rid of some of the old colonial formalities, such as stuffy titles for colonial officials, and they pledged to establish a locally elected legislature under a constitutional monarchy, which would be headed by the Cambodian royal family. At the time, the royal family was headed by King Norodom Sihanouk.

Even though some local affairs were given over to the Cambodians, matters of major importance, such as international relations, military defense, and even internal policing, would all still be left up to the French. All the same, it was the most freedom the French had ever given the

Cambodians, and many were eager to see it through.

Cambodia's first set of elections were carried out that spring. The two main parties were the Liberals and the Democrats. From an American perspective, the names of these two parties might be confusing on the surface, but their names don't correlate to American politics. The so-called Liberals are actually the conservative wing of Cambodia, whereas the Democrats are the liberal wing.

Now that this little explanation is out of the way, here's how the first election and the next few elections shaped up. In the first few Cambodian elections, the Democrats won the majority of seats. In fact, in 1946, the Democrats won fifty seats, while the Liberals only won fourteen seats. This was a source of great frustration for both the king and the French-backed Cambodian elites who backed the conservative Liberals in their bid for office.

Things turned violent in January of 1950 when a political activist tossed a live grenade into the Democrats' headquarters in the city of Phnom Penh. This assault killed a major leader of the party, a man named Ieu Koeus. This attack stoked the anger of many in the public, and when the economy began to tank later that year, massive discontent began to erupt in the streets. It was in this volatile atmosphere that another election was held in the fall of 1951.

During this election, the Democrats won a supermajority of fifty-four seats, while the Liberals gained a measly eighteen. The French and the Cambodian elites who had dished out a lot of money to help the Liberals were not happy. In fact, they had reached a breaking point, and a coup was staged in June of 1952 to remove the democratically elected prime minister, Huy Kanthoul.

The French officially left Cambodia in 1953, and King Sihanouk ruled more or less by direct decree over the next several years. There would still be the charade of elections, but now, only the candidates backed by the king would prosper. Although he was essentially a dictator, King Sihanouk had some admirable qualities as a leader. He had a good ear to the ground and understood what both commoners and elitists alike expected of him. He also knew what the wider world expected of him. He knew, for example, that anything to do with communists would make him a pariah to the West. As such, King Sihanouk made sure to distance himself from the communist guerillas fighting in North Vietnam as much as he possibly could while not provoking the communists in the process. And in many ways, the fact that he kept Cambodia out of the Vietnam War for so long was to his credit. He masterfully threaded the needle when it came to staying on the good side of both the Americans and the North Vietnamese. He knew, for example, that the North Vietnamese would not tolerate Cambodia allowing the US to station troops on its soil, so when the US floated the notion, he stood firm behind his convictions.

However, both North Vietnam and the United States would later find ways to circumvent the sovereignty of Cambodia. Vietnamese communists often made use of the Cambodian borderlands, and the US eventually conducted bombing runs across Cambodia's border. Nevertheless, Sihanouk largely stood by his principles of neutrality.

By 1970, however, the winds were once again changing, and in March of that year, Sihanouk, who was no longer the king but rather the head of state, was removed from power. There had been several rounds of riotous protests in the preceding months over North Vietnamese communists who were active in Cambodia. Sihanouk was overseas at the time, visiting several nations, including China, the Soviet Union, and some European countries. While Sihanouk's back was turned, his own prime minister, Lon Nol, plotted against him, declared martial law, and forced Sihanouk out. The new government, borrowing from the greatness of Cambodia's previous Khmer Empire, would be called the Khmer Republic. And it was in this tumultuous backdrop that a young Cambodian communist by the name of Saloth Sar, better known by the name Pol Pot, came to prominence. The communists that Pol Pot led would also become known by their own infamous moniker of the Khmer Rouge. The term "Khmer" is in reference to the Cambodian language and ethnic identity, whereas "Rouge" is the French word for red. Communists have been widely referred to as "reds," so essentially, the name was an epithet to refer to communist Cambodians. It was meant as an insult, but the Khmer Rouge would come to embrace the title.

Soon after the Khmer Republic was declared, Cambodia descended into a civil war, with the communist forces of the Khmer Rouge backed by North Vietnam as they fought against the Cambodian government. This was a real slugfest, and even when President Richard Nixon renewed US bombing campaigns of communist targets in Cambodia, the Khmer Republic was still unable to gain the upper hand. Pol Pot's Khmer Rouge was ultimately successful, and Pol Pot and his so-called Democratic Kampuchea would come to power in 1975—the same year that US troops were practically being chased out of neighboring Vietnam.

Pol Pot, in the meantime, would set up a brutal regime that would leave between 1.5 to 2 million Cambodian citizens dead by the time that its brutality had run its course. The Khmer Rouge was so brutal that they even angered their former communist backers, the Vietnamese. After several border skirmishes, Vietnam invaded Cambodia outright in 1978. Conditions in Cambodia had grown even worse, and with the threat of a Vietnamese invasion, the oppression of Cambodians reached horrific new lows.

Ethnic minorities, such as the Cham and especially those who happened to be of Vietnamese background, were routinely slaughtered. It got so bad that, at one point, it has been said that even conversing in another tongue could get one killed. The Khmer Rouge finally came to an end when the Vietnamese forces forcibly dismantled the regime on January 10th, 1979.

Now under the full weight of outside oppression, Cambodia would not regain its independence until 1989, which was when the last Vietnamese troops finally withdrew. Pol Pot died in 1998 while under house arrest. He was seventy years old, and he apparently died of natural causes, although some believe he committed suicide. To this day, there is tremendous outrage among those who feel that Pol Pot never really answered for his many crimes.

Cambodia would begin to really get its act together by the early 2000s. In 2003, the country was deemed to be prosperous enough to be admitted to the Association of Southeast Asian Nations (ASEAN). Cambodia's ultimate liberation was certainly a long time coming, but just as all of the other Southeast Asian nations that had been freed from the grip of colonialism, the taste of freedom was still just as sweet as ever. However, as in some other Southeast Asian countries, Cambodia faces a crisis when it comes to the government, as the country has been run by one party since 2018, despite labeling itself as a multi-party democracy. Thailand is another country that has faced difficulties in regards to the government, for it has bounced back and forth through military regimes and constitutional monarchies. Since 1932, Thailand has undergone seventeen different constitutions. It is hard to know what the future will hold for countries like Cambodia and Thailand, but considering everything they have gone through and how far they have come, there is hope they will establish governments that promote equality and a strong economy.

Conclusion: Where Legend Meets Reality

Southeast Asia is a land of many legends. All one has to do is think of the spectacular grandeur of Angkor Wat, and this much is made clear. The nations of Southeast Asia have histories that reach back thousands of years, and many countless civilizations have risen and fell during the many varied epochs of Southeast Asian dynasties. These regimes navigated through all manner of political intrigue and engaged in battle after battle with opposing forces.

For example, the Kingdom of Vietnam was shaped by the dueling pressures of China to its north and the Champa regime to its south. It was in the midst of this pressure cooker that the Vietnamese learned to be absolute experts at guerilla warfare. Indonesia, on the other hand, with its prime location between the shipping routes of both China and India, became the ultimate weigh station for trade goods, as well as for religion and culture. Throughout history, the majority of the Indonesian population has been Hindu, Buddhist, and Muslim. It is due to this plurality of beliefs that Indonesia today prides itself as a religiously tolerant society. Indonesia, of course, also benefits from its history in the spice trade, and today, it leads the world in many forms of commerce. In fact, Indonesia boasts one of the biggest and most robust economies in all of Southeast Asia.

However, all of these civilizations are dynamic locales that certainly live up to the hype. Tourism is a big business in Southeast Asia because there is simply always something new to explore. Walking through old Hindu temples or retracing the steps of past adventurers such as Marco Polo, Ibn Battuta, or Ferdinand Magellan, you can sense some of the wonder that the Dutch East India Company must have known. After all, Southeast Asia is no ordinary place. It's not just a collection of peninsulas, tropical coasts, and islands. It's also the land of Brahma, Buddha, Islam, and Catholicism. Southeast Asia is a realm of pure wonder—that neverland where the once imagined is suddenly possible.

Southeast Asia was the fabled spice lands that brought sailors far and wide, and it was the rubber-rich trees that drew in both the French and the likes of Imperial Japan. Southeast Asia is indeed plentiful in resources. But the land of Southeast Asia is not only where the rubber meets the road—Southeast Asia is also where the legend meets reality.

Part 2: History of Thailand

A Captivating Guide to the Thai People and Their History

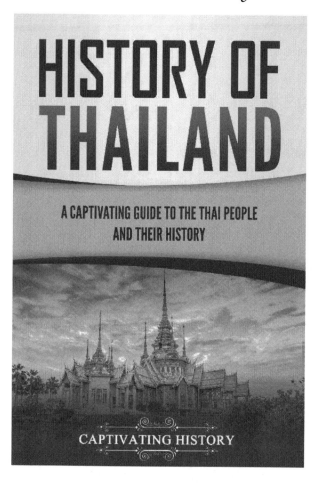

Introduction

Although Thailand's first people are said to have hailed from China and Vietnam, much of their culture was technically adapted from India, Cambodia, and China, and they have had great amounts of Western influence. Despite this, Thailand has certainly forged its own rich and unique history, culture, and national identity. The name Thailand in and of itself has a unique origin story and holds quite a lot of meaning. Though the word Thai is adapted from the Tai ethnic group, who originally arrived in Thailand thousands of years ago, they adopted the name "Thai" in 1238 following the population's liberation from oppressive Khmer rule. Thai translates to "free," which means the country's name holds multiple meanings, both the "land of the Thai," as in the people who occupy it, and the "land of the free." Ironically enough, the country was known as Siam for most of history, and the name would only officially change to Thailand when the country was under an authoritarian military dictatorship.

Thailand's history dates back hundreds of thousands of years ago, many millennia before the arrival of the Tais. Although not much is known about the country before the Sukhothai period, which began in 1238, archaeological sites have revealed that Thailand's territory may have been home to one of the world's oldest agrarian societies and potentially the earliest cultivation of rice.

Migrant travelers from the Tai ethnic group began arriving in the territory that now makes up Thailand around a thousand years ago, and until 1238, they remained under the Mon-Khmer Empire's rule. It was in 1238, upon the liberation from their foreign rulers, that the Tais assumed the name "Thais," which would mark the beginning of the formation of Thailand's unique cultural history. Following its liberation from foreign rule, the country would enter into its Sukhothai period, a time that is often referred to as Thailand's golden era, seeing as it marked the creation and introduction of much of Thailand's current culture, including its language and religion.

By the middle of the 14th century, the Sukhothai Kingdom was absorbed by Ayutthaya, a nearby kingdom, and in time, the population would grow, developing their culture and allowing the kingdom to flourish. Although the Sukhothai period is known as Thailand's golden era, the country would become a powerful force during its 400-year Ayutthaya period. The Kingdom of Ayutthaya would finally be overthrown by Burma (modern-day Myanmar), which would continue to threaten Thailand over the next century.

Those who survived the Burmese sacking of Ayutthaya emigrated to Thonburi, rebuilding their kingdom around this city, which became its capital. In 1782, the first member of the Chakri dynasty ascended the throne, and they have reigned as the kings of Thailand in an uninterrupted chain ever since. King Rama I, the first monarch of the

Chakri dynasty, would swiftly move the country's capital city from Thonburi to Bangkok, where it remains to this day.

Thailand, or Siam as it was known then, would be led by the kings of the Chakri dynasty in an absolute monarchy until a civilian-led coup d'état in 1932. Following the long-awaited revolution, the country was run briefly by a democratic government. This democratic government would last barely two years before transitioning to a military government and eventually a fully fascist, authoritarian military dictatorship. Between the Thai revolution of 1932 and today, the government has repeatedly shifted between democracy and authoritarian military governments due to endless coups, rebellions, protests, and revolutions.

Chapter 1 – Prehistory / Early History

From Before Common Era - The Beginning of the 13th Century

Thailand before the Common Era

Although *Homo erectus* fossils have been found scattered throughout Thailand, recent archaeological discoveries have determined Thailand's first permanent inhabitants settled there around 40,000 years ago. Debatably the most significant and informative archaeological site in Thailand, Ban Chiang, was discovered in 1966 completely by accident when the son of a US ambassador, Stephen Young, tripped and fell, prompting him to notice a buried clay pot in the ground. Ban Chiang, located in the northeast Udon Thani Province of Thailand, contains artifacts that date back to 1495 BCE.

Stephen Young may have stumbled onto ceramic pots, but as further excavations were made, penetrating deeper and deeper within the stratigraphic layers at Ban Chiang, more buried artifacts were revealed that shaped what historians know of Thailand's early history. The discoveries at Ban Chiang revealed early inhabitants might have begun cultivating rice just after 1500 BCE. Other archaeological sites in Thailand, such as Non Nok Tha, where rice chaff was found in pottery, proves the country may have had wet rice agriculture back in 3000 BCE. This is significant since it would make Thailand not only the home to Southeast Asia's oldest known agrarian society but also one of the world's oldest farming communities.

In addition to agricultural discoveries, Ban Chiang contained some of the world's earliest known bronze and copper production tools, which revealed that Thailand might have had one of the most advanced metallurgy industries at the time. These metal-focused excavations, conducted mostly by Chester (Chet) Gorman and Pisit Charoenwongsa, found traces of metalwork, including bronze and iron, dating back to 2500 BCE and possibly as early as 3000 BCE. If these discoveries prove to be accurate, Thailand would have predated metallurgy in Southeast Asia by around 1,000 years and potentially had some of the world's first bronze forgers.

Amongst the ceramics and metal forging tools found at the Ban Chiang archaeological site were ancient bodies, which were often buried within or with these crafted objects, indicating that Thailand's first settlers had burials. The buried bodies that were discovered not only raised questions regarding the early settlers' ritualistic burial traditions but also allowed scientists to run tests that would then lead to further important historical discoveries.

Some studies performed on stable isotopes in the teeth of the people buried at Ban Chiang and other archaeological sites around Thailand have led historians to conclude prehistoric Thailand may have had a matrilocal system (in which a married couple lives with or near the wife's parents). This conclusion stems from test results that found women grew up on local food while men seemed to have been foragers, travelers, or immigrants of some sort, as they had access to a wider selection of foods. The isotopes also revealed the presence of carbon, strontium, and oxygen, which confirms the growth of farming and agriculture. Together, this data implies that men would immigrate and marry into the agrarian societies, suggesting that women may have had relative power and high social status at the time.

After the Common Era - The Tais

While people existed in Thailand far before the Common Era, these people were not, in fact, "Tai" people. Although there is much debate on Thailand's original immigration patterns, the ancestors of the Thais, also referred to as the Tais, are believed to have come from southern China and/or northern Vietnam. Even before immigrating to the land now known as Thailand, as well as other Southeastern Asian countries, the earliest Tai populations, from around the 1st century CE, spoke Tai-Kadai, which is believed to have been Southeast Asia's largest ethnolinguistic group. For most of history, it was maintained that the Tais originated and lived in the valleys along the Yangtze River in China and that difficulties forced them to spread throughout Southeast Asia, eventually reaching Thailand. Now, many scholars and historians believe the Tais came from Dien Bien Phu, a city in northern Vietnam now known for the battles of the First Indochina War. The Tais, regardless of whether they originated from northern Vietnam or southern China, spread southward into Thailand and Laos, as well as to the north and west into China, Myanmar, Vietnam, and India. This would explain why there are large populations with Tai ancestors today, not just in Thailand but also in Laos, Myanmar, China, and Vietnam.

The Tai people are believed to have begun immigrating to Thailand around 1,000 years ago, where they mostly settled in the valleys along the country's rivers. Both before settling in what is now Thailand (dating back to the 1st millennium CE) and after, the Tais had a political organization, known as the müang, which consisted of many small groups of villages ruled by a common hereditary chief or lord, known as a chao. Historians believe that the strengths provided by this political system are what enabled the Tais to immigrate and expand through Southeast Asia as they did.

The Tais established their müangs in the valleys along Thailand's rivers, and their small settlements were agricultural-based communities. They very quickly began farming rice, fishing, foraging, and domesticating animals, such as pigs and fowl for eating and water buffalos for plowing. Over time, the Tais continued to expand their communities throughout Thailand, spreading from the northern valleys into central Thailand, which featured different landscapes than those they were used to, such as plains and plateaus. As the Tais immigrated southward from Vietnam and/or China, slowly populating Thailand, they came into contact with foreign empires and trading centers. The most notable of these foreign empires were the Mon-Khmer kingdoms, which had a major influence on the Tai people and, therefore, on the current Thai culture.

Mon-Khmer Civilizations

During the Tais' emigration to what is today Thailand, they came into contact with people of the Mon-Khmer ethnolinguistic groups. The Mon, similarly to the Tais (at least for much of history), were believed to have originated from China. The Mon spread southward throughout the north, west, and center of Thailand and southwest through Burma, or what is known as modern-day Myanmar. Since the Mon dominated most of what is now eastern Myanmar and west-central Thailand, they quickly established kingdoms centered around their religion of Theravada Buddhism. The first and most influential of these Mon kingdoms is known as Dvaravati, which was established surrounding the Chao Phraya River around the 6th century. Although the Mon inhabited Thailand as early as the 6th century, most modern-day Mon in Thailand were displaced from Burma between the 17th and 19th centuries.

The Khmer Empire was a well-developed polity, which was mostly established in modern-day Cambodia and which is often thought of as Southeast Asia's equivalent to the Roman Empire. Much like the Mon, the Khmer people mostly followed Theravada Buddhism, but they were once primarily based on Hinduism, and many still practiced it. The Khmer Empire's strength, power, and devotion to Hinduism can be attested by the enormous, extravagant temples built at the time. The most important and impressive of these was Angkor Wat, which was constructed in the 9th century in Cambodia. It is not only now a **UNESCO World Heritage Site** but also the world's largest religious monument by land area. Between the 9th and 13th centuries, the Khmer continued to expand westward from Angkor throughout Thailand, inhabiting mostly eastern Thailand along the Cambodian border. Despite the strength of the Khmer Empire, the majority of the current Khmer people in Thailand actually immigrated many years later after being displaced by wars, much like the Mon.

Throughout the 4th to 9th centuries, the Mon and Khmer populations continued to spread throughout Thailand, eventually coming into contact with the Tai immigrants between the 9th and 12th centuries. As the Tai soon became politically dominant (throughout the 13th century,) the Mon-

Khmer populations displaced and assimilated into the Tai culture. Although the Mon-Khmer lost their power in Thailand, their influence is still evident and strong, both in Thailand's past and its modern-day national identity culture. The Tai combined their socio-political system, culture, and language with the Mons' religion and the statecraft and ceremonies of the Khmer to form the distinct Thai culture we know today.

Chapter 2 – Sukhothai Period (1238–1438)

Sukhothai before Thai Rule

Before the city of Sukhothai became the first capital of Thailand (which was then known as Siam) and the birthplace of much of Thai culture, it was, in fact, a Khmer city. Through the study of the still-standing ruins of Sukhothai, historians have theorized that the Khmers constructed Sukhothai at some point between the 12th century and early 13th century. This conclusion was drawn due to the similarities in design and structure with Angkor Wat and other Hindu temples built by the Khmer Empire at the time. The ancient city stood, and still remains, albeit in ruins, in the northeastern Sukhothai Province of Thailand. The impressive feats of design displayed in the city of Sukhothai not only share similarities but also rival those of Angkor Wat. Much like Angkor Wat, the city of Sukhothai is now revered for its sophisticated dams, canals, reservoirs, and other feats of hydraulic engineering. This advanced and sophisticated system, which permitted the city's future inhabitants to produce plentiful harvests and prevent droughts and flooding, certainly aided in the Sukhothai Kingdom's prosperity over the next 200 years.

Although the ruins of Sukhothai still displays evidence of the early Khmer Hindu-influenced construction, it now stands as a monumental Buddhist city, with influences from not only the Khmer but also the Mon and Tai as well. This is due to the immigrating patterns of the Tai people, who arrived in Sukhothai soon after the construction. They intermarried with the locals and formed müangs while remaining under Khmer rule. While the Tais did incorporate parts of the Khmer and Hindu culture into their own (which explains the Khmer influence on modern Thailand's culture), the Khmer Empire was overbearing and overruling. The Tais challenged Khmer authority and succeeded in gaining independence and conquering Sukhothai thanks to a combination of massive immigration, which reinforced the Tai population, and the already declining power of the Khmer Empire (this was due to a separate war throughout the late 12th and early 13th century).

Establishment of the Sukhothai Kingdom

The city was established by a Tai chieftain named Sri Indraditya in 1238. It was named Sukhothai, which quite literally translates to the "dawn of happiness." Following the victory over the Khmers, the Tais became known as the Thais, and the Sukhothai Kingdom was founded, with Sri Indraditya (taking the regnal name of Si Inthrathit) as its king. The word "Thai" was chosen to set the inhabitants of the Sukhothai Kingdom apart from the other Tai-speaking peoples scattered throughout Siam (Thailand), which was still under foreign rule.

King Si Inthrathit ruled the Sukhothai Kingdom, uniting the Thai müangs and leaders. Although Sukhothai remained a small power during his reign, King Si Inthrathit is revered and regarded as a sort of "founding father" of Thailand. King Si Inthrathit ruled Sukhothai until his death in 1270, when his first son, Ban Mueang, took over at a young age. Although much of the history preceding and during the 13th century is shrouded in mystery, historians do know for certain that Ban Mueang's rule was short-lived and that his brother, King Si Inthrathit's second son, Prince Rama, took over the Sukhothai Kingdom in 1278.

King Ram Khamhaeng

It is when the third ruler of the Sukhothai Kingdom, Rama, took power that the kingdom truly grew and prospered. When Ram was only nineteen and still a prince, he aided his father in fighting off a raid from Khun Sam Chon, the ruler of Mae Sot, whom Rama fought in an elephant duel. Although many of Sukhothai's warriors fled, young Rama not only accepted the challenge but also beat Khun Sam Chon. Due to his bravery in battle, he earned the name Ram Khamhaeng, which translates to Rama the Bold (or Rama the Great.) Under King Ram Khamhaeng (also spelled as Ramkhamhaeng), the Thais grew to be the largest population in Siam.

Until its third ruler, Sukhothai had remained quite small, though it grew slowly and amounted some fortune. When King Ram Khamhaeng took the throne of Sukhothai in 1278, he continued to live up to his title of "Rama the Bold" and quickly expanded the Sukhothai Kingdom's influence to the rest of Thailand and Southeast Asia. Ram Khamhaeng extended the boundaries of the kingdom throughout Thailand from the northern city of Sukhothai to the southern Nakhon Si Thammarat. Ram Khamhaeng also expanded the territory and rule of the Sukhothai Kingdom into what is considered to be the modern-day Malay Peninsula, Laos, Myanmar, and Cambodia. He put Sukhothai on the map by establishing diplomatic relations and sending envoys to China, which was, at the time, ruled by the Yuan dynasty. These actions helped prompt trade between the two kingdoms, which encouraged and enriched the Sukhothai Kingdom's economy and influence.

Ram Khamhaeng did more than just expand the kingdom's territory. Under his rule, the city of Sukhothai flourished thanks to both its king and the city's convenient geographical location. Sukhothai finds itself in the north of Thailand, along the Yom River, between modern-day Myanmar and Cambodia. This meant that, at the time, the city of Sukhothai was about halfway between the Burmese Kingdom of Pagan and the Khmer Empire. Due to its convenient midway location, Sukhothai and its neighboring cities, also under the rule of Sukhothai, became profitable centers of production and commerce. The city of Si Satchanalai, which is only a mere 20 kilometers (12.5 miles) or so away from Sukhothai, became the kingdom's main ceramic production and exportation location. The neighboring countries' and kingdoms' demands, combined with Ram Khamhaeng's interest in art, led to the creation of unique pottery in Sukhothai and Si Satchanalai. The artisans of Sukhothai and Si Satchanalai developed a ceramic adorned with a green glaze, which attracted the attention of surrounding countries and spread throughout all of modern-day Southeast Asia. That being said, Sukhothai was not only a major trade city due to its admired ceramics and convenient location, as much of the city's prosperous commerce was due to its tax policies. Unlike many of the surrounding trade cities, the city of Sukhothai allowed people to trade with freedom, as no taxes were added on products.

Although the city of Sukhothai was built as a Khmer city, Buddhism was adopted as the kingdom's official religion during King Ram Khamhaeng's reign. By the end of the 13th century, the inhabitants of Sukhothai were not only devout Buddhists, but the city also became one of the world's largest Buddhist centers. Ram Khamhaeng's successors furthered his work in establishing Buddhism in the region by recruiting monks from other Buddhist nations and building Theravada Buddhist temples, many of which still stand to this day. The Sukhothai residents showed their devotion to Buddhism through art and architecture, developing a unique artistic and design style that spread and influenced future Buddhist images, statues, and temples.

One of King Ram Khamhaeng's greatest and most influential achievements during his lifetime was the creation of the Thai language. Ram Khamhaeng invented the language's writing system in 1283, which has remained mostly unchanged. This means that ancient writings from the 13th century can still be read by almost any Thai person today. One of the most important pieces of ancient writing, which comprises most of what we know about the 13th century today, is the inscription stone that was written by King Ram Khamhaeng himself in 1292. The King Ram Khamhaeng Inscription is an engraved four-sided pillar that tells of Ram Khamhaeng's life starting back at his birth, detailing his mother and father's names—Nang Suang and Sri Indraditya—and that he had four siblings. It is through the inscription stone that we know about the young death of Ban Mueang, Ram Khamhaeng's elder brother. He wrote of how the Sukhothai Kingdom spread throughout Southeast Asia, reaching Phrae and Nan in Thailand and Vientiane, Laos, to the north. He talked about the kingdom spreading to Nakhon Si Thammarat, the Mons' Hongsawadi, and the banks of the Mekong River in the south, east, and west, respectively. The inscription records the invention of the language, and it is the earliest example of Thai script, although Ram Khamhaeng used more words from the Khmer vocabulary than what is commonly used in Thai today. The inscription is split into three parts. The first mostly details Ram Khamhaeng's personal history, the second speaks of the city and kingdom of Sukhothai, and the last, which seems to have been written by a different person, glorifies the king after his death. Within the second portion, there are details of the Sukhothai Kingdom's views and values on religion, economy, politics, and law, much of which is not that far off from beliefs held around the world today.

Even though the Sukhothai Kingdom only existed between 1238 and 1438, a mere 200 years, it is quite literally the birthplace and backbone of modern Thailand's rich culture. The Sukhothai Kingdom's contemporary influence and impact are mostly thanks to King Ram Khamhaeng, who invented the Thai language and officially adopted Buddhism, which allowed the religion to spread throughout the country. In addition to creating the country's language and adopting its religion, he also helped the kingdom flourish, leading to many important traditions and artistic and cultural advancements.

King Ram Khamhaeng died in 1298, and although the kingdom existed for around 140 more years, it steadily lost power after Ram Khamhaeng's death. After the passing of Ram Khamhaeng, the Sukhothai Kingdom was subsequently ruled by his son, Loe Thai. The throne was then usurped by Loe Thai's cousin, Ngua Nam Thum. He was followed by Li Thai (who is known as King Maha Thammaracha I). He was Loe Thai's son, making him the cousin of Ngua Nam Thum. The immediate rulers who followed King Ram Khamhaeng are mostly recognized for continuing to spread Theravada Buddhism throughout Thailand. Perhaps the most notable achievement of these kings is a text entitled *Sermon on the Three Worlds* (later known as *Three Worlds of King Ruang*), which was written by Li Thai, who, at the time, was the heir apparent to the Sukhothai Kingdom. The piece, which was written in 1345, is not only considered to be the first Thai literary work but also had such a major influence on Buddhism that some historians consider it to be the most important Thai text ever written.

Though the Sukhothai Kingdom's influence slowly declined following King Ram Khamhaeng's death, the straw that broke the camel's back was Phaya ("Lord") Maha Thammaracha I's passing in 1370. In addition to his death, which led to many satellite states withdrawing from the kingdom, the decline in Sukhothai Kingdom's power has been attributed to the establishment and strengthening of the Ayutthaya Kingdom, which was located not too far away in the south. Furthermore, it is believed that there were conflicts within the noble families and a decrease in the land's fertility, which would have also greatly influenced the decline of the Sukhothai Kingdom. In spite of the Sukhothai Kingdom's prosperity and affluence, they were challenged by King Borommarachathirat I of Ayutthaya. The once flourishing Kingdom of Sukhothai was forced to submit in 1378, and it was gradually annexed over the years into the Ayutthaya Kingdom. The Sukhothai Kingdom had two more kings following the annexation into the Ayutthaya Kingdom. In 1438, the once-great Kingdom of Sukhothai was finally completely absorbed by the Ayutthaya Kingdom.

Lan Na Kingdom

Although the Sukhothai Kingdom is regarded as the first, strongest, and largest Tai Kingdom in what is now modern-day Thailand, they were not the only Tai kingdom that reigned during this time. Another influential Tai kingdom was also formed during the 13th century, and it was called the Lan Na Kingdom. The Lan Na, which is another one of the first large Tai kingdoms to exist, and its capital city of Chiang Mai were founded in 1292 and 1296, respectively, by Mangrai. Similar to how Sukhothai was originally a Khmer city that was conquered by the Tai, Chiang Mai was originally a Mon city, known as Haripunjaya, which the Tai eventually conquered with Mangrai as their leader. Lan Na's power and influence grew with Mangrai and its subsequent rulers. It remained independent until the 16th century, just around 100 years after the fall of the Sukhothai Kingdom, when it was conquered by Burma (Myanmar). Although the Lan Na and Sukhothai Kingdoms had some contact during their reigns, specifically during an alliance made in 1287, the two kingdoms did not have much interaction at all. This is mostly due to the different cultures and languages that had developed in the two separate Tai kingdoms. While Theravada Buddhism was established as the Lan Na Kingdom's primary religion during Mangrai's rule, it wasn't until Tilokaracha, who took power in 1441, that Lan Na became a hub for the spread of Buddhism. Lan Na became known for its Theravada Buddhist literature and teachings, which spread Buddhism to the Tai people throughout Southeast Asia (including Myanmar and China).

Chapter 3 – Ayutthaya Period (1350–1767)

The Formation of the City of Ayutthaya

The city of Ayutthaya, located almost 350 kilometers (almost 220 miles) south of Sukhothai, was founded in 1350 by its first leader, a Tai named Ramathibodi I. While much of Ramathibodi I's life is unknown, it is believed that he was born in 1314 and was married to the daughter of the ruler of U Thong (which is now known as Suphan Buri). Ramathibodi I became the ruler of U Thong, explaining why he is now often referred to as simply U Thong. When Ramathibodi I took over U Thong in 1347, he moved the city eighty kilometers (about fifty miles) east to an island in the Chao Phraya River. The new city became known as Ayutthaya, which became the first capital city of Siam and remained the capital for over 400 years. The Ayutthaya Kingdom was actually the reason behind the country's original name, Siam, since the neighboring kingdoms and countries referred to the city and the Ayutthaya Kingdom population by this name.

Similar to the Sukhothai Kingdom, the Ayutthaya Kingdom benefited from their timing, as they immigrated to the city of Ayutthaya during the decline of the Khmer Empire. While the Tai, led by Ramathibodi I, gained power, they kept civil relations with the Sukhothai Kingdom and focused their military energies against the Khmer Empire. Besides founding Ayutthaya, Ramathibodi I's greatest legacy was laying many of the foundations of the legal system that was used in Siam until the 1800s. Ramathibodi I spent many years preparing his son, Ramesuan, to take his throne, and he did so upon his passing in 1369. But soon after, power was taken by Borommaraja I (also spelled as Borommarachathirat). King Borommaraja I reigned Ayutthaya for eighteen years, in which time he challenged and seized the Sukhothai Kingdom, forcing them to partially annex with the Kingdom of Ayutthaya.

Borommaraja I's son, Thong Lan, inherited the throne in 1388, but his reign lasted for only seven days, during which time Ramesuan, Ramathibodi I's son, regained power. When King Ramesuan seized the throne from Borommaraja I's son, many were displeased, as Ramesuan was extremely unpopular. Power was instead given to his uncle, Prince Phangoa, known as Borommaracha I, who became the fifth king of Ayutthaya.

Ayutthaya cycled through many more kings, most notably Borommarachathirat II, who ruled during both the downfall of the Khmer Empire and the official absorption of the Sukhothai Kingdom. By the time Ayutthaya conquered the Khmer Empire, they had already expanded throughout parts of Southeast Asia, with their kingdom absorbing much of the former Khmer population. This led the Siamese Ayutthaya kings to adopt many of the Khmer's Hindu practices, most notably the concept of the *devarāja*, or divine king, which would give the king an almost god-like level of power. Under the belief of *devarāja*, the king could only be addressed in a special language and only be seen by the royal family. He also would have the power to sentence anyone in his kingdom to death.

Ayutthaya after the Absorption of Sukhothai

Borommatrailokanat, the eighth king of Ayutthaya, who is better known today as Trailok, ruled the kingdom between 1444 and 1488 when many of the first Hindu-influenced customs came into practice. Trailok focused on centralizing Siam's political power by creating separate governmental departments that would be administered by workers rather than the royal family. These workers would be chosen by the king, who would select those who would help strengthen his administrative power. During Trailok's rule, a hierarchical system was introduced, similar to that of the caste system in India, which assigned *sakdi na* (unit or numerical rank) to the people in different social classes. Ranks within society were assigned based on the amount of land one possessed. The people of Ayutthaya were divided into royalty, nobility, and commoners. They would be further divided, more specifically within the commoners' category, into slaves and freemen. Although the hierarchy placed a clear separation between the classes, there was potential for social mobility through marriage or relations with someone of a higher class. The majority of the population of Ayutthaya, which found itself in the commoners' category, worked in the fields. Although they were not technically enslaved, the freemen still owed a "debt" to representatives of the king and were required to work for them six months of the year.

Despite Hinduism's strong influence on the Ayutthaya Kingdom, most of the population of Ayutthaya was devoutly Buddhist. The religion provided young male freemen with schooling, offering the opportunity for social mobility to those who wished to remain to learn within the Buddhist social order, known as the sangha.

Due to Ayutthaya's easily accessible location within the Chao Phraya River, which connected it to the Gulf of Thailand, the city became a major trade center. Its convenient location proved to be incredibly important during the century when European traders, beginning with the Portuguese in 1511, began traveling to Siam. The Portuguese were subsequently followed by the Dutch, English, Spanish, and French throughout the 17th century. They believed Ayutthaya to be the greatest and most prosperous of the Southeast Asian cities, if not of the world. Modern-day Thailand was put on the international map by King Narai of Ayutthaya, who invited travelers from all over to visit the city. European, Chinese, Indian, and Persian traders settled within Ayutthaya, establishing trading sites and employing missionaries. Furthermore, Ayutthaya sent out their own missionaries to spread Buddhism throughout Sri Lanka, China, and some of Europe. However, in 1688, the Siamese expelled the Europeans due to the pushy, overzealous French Christian missionaries.

The Burmese Conflicts

Despite all of these Western visitors, the Europeans did not pose any real threat to the Ayutthaya Kingdom other than perhaps the overzealous missionaries. Neither did the Asian countries of China, India, and Persia. The prosperous Ayutthaya Kingdom was, in fact, threatened by the Burmese state of Toungoo, which was rapidly rising and expanding in modern-day Myanmar. In the late 16th century, Bayinnaung, the king of Toungoo, helped the dynasty rise to become the most powerful Southeast Asian state. During his reign, he expanded the empire to Laos and finally to Siam, where Ayutthaya fell to the Burmese king in 1569. During the fifteen years following Burma's conquest of Ayutthaya, many Siamese inhabitants were deported as slaves, and those who remained saw their once-prosperous city pillaged.

At only sixteen years old, a Siamese boy named Naresuan was appointed as a vassal by the Burmese, replacing his father, Maha Thammaracha. In 1584, Naresuan recovered Siam's independence after leading a military operation in which he defeated Burmese armies and renounced his allegiance to Toungoo. Ayutthaya prospered once again under the reign of King Naresuan, who took the throne after his father passed in 1590. King Naresuan established the foundation for a strong Siam military force, which managed to not only seize the Cambodian capital, Lovek, but also resist the persisting Burmese conflicts. Almost all Burmese pressure on Siam ceased in 1593 after Naresuan defeated Burma's future prince. The Siam country and the Ayutthaya Kingdom continued to flourish and grow with subsequent kings.

The Ayutthaya Kingdom remained strong, resisting foreign threats while opening itself up internationally for almost two more centuries after Naresuan regained the country's independence in 1584. However, between the years of 1765 and 1767, the Ayutthaya Kingdom entered into a war with the Burmese Empire, known as the Burmese-Siamese War or "war of the second fall of Ayutthaya." As the latter title would indicate, in this battle, the 400-year-old Ayutthaya Kingdom finally fell, being conquered by the Burmese in 1767. Although the Siamese army was strong, the Burmese, led by King Hsinbyushin, invaded with a much larger army, which finally led to the final sacking of Ayutthaya. The battles devastated the city, leaving the once great Ayutthaya Kingdom in ruins. Almost all of the Ayutthaya art and records were burned, and most of the impressive feats of their early ancient architecture were completely destroyed. The majority of the Siamese warriors and people from the Ayutthaya Kingdom were wiped out, and those who survived, such as the royal family, were deported as captives to Burma. Though it was long ago, the impacts of the Burmese-Siamese War still plague relations between modern-day Myanmar and Thailand.

Chapter 4 – The Thon Buri Period (1767-1782)

The Aftermath of the Burmese Conflicts

After the fall of the Ayutthaya Kingdom in 1767, the once-prosperous city of Ayutthaya laid in ruins, and most of the Burmese soldiers who had aided in the pillaging and seizure of the city returned to what is considered to be modern-day Myanmar. Although a majority of the Ayutthaya civilians were killed in the battles or brought as captives to Burma, some Siamese managed to flee before the kingdom was brought to its knees. The remaining Ayutthaya people gathered into clans in the nearby provinces, but as they were now in need of a leader, those in charge of the clans, mostly the remaining governors and other men of importance, proceeded to fight to earn the title of king.

A former governor known as Taksin ended up emerging as the obvious leader and became the king of the remaining Ayutthaya people in

1767. Taksin was born in 1734 in the city of Ayutthaya to a Siamese (Thai) mother and a Chinese father. It is believed that Taksin was enrolled in government service and worked his way up to the rank of governor before the fall of the Ayutthaya Kingdom. During the Burmese battles, Taksin was called to help lead and defend the city and its kingdom from the Burmese threat. Although he and his troops fought alongside the Siamese soldiers in defense of Ayutthaya, it is believed that either late in the year 1766 or in early 1767, prior to the Burmese seizing the city, Governor Taksin and his troops left the capital and found safety in the surrounding provinces.

Settling in Thonburi

Once he was crowned, King Taksin began leading his followers downriver toward the east coast, traveling until they settled in Thonburi, around ninety kilometers (fifty-six miles) south of Ayutthaya. Throughout the whole journey, from their initial departure from Ayutthaya to their final destination of Thonburi, King Taksin and his troops ran into and defeated Burmese troops, earning King Taksin a reputation as a formidable military leader. As this reputation spread throughout the nearby provinces, many men joined King Taksin's troops, which helped to fortify his power and eventually the city of Thonburi.

King Taksin strategically chose to settle in Thonburi, which is just across the Chao Phraya River from modern-day Bangkok, since it would be difficult for the remaining Burmese troops to access while still having an accessible trade location. Upon the arrival of King Taksin and his troops, Thonburi was named the capital of Siam, and men from the surrounding provinces continued to join King Taksin's troops, which eventually turned into a powerful army. Not soon after arriving in Thonburi, King Taksin focused on collecting weapons, strengthening his army, and organizing a resistance to the Burmese invaders still remaining in the country. Once King Taksin had done this, he and his troops returned to Ayutthaya and managed to seize the city back from the Burmese in only two days. After the arduous Burmese rule in Siam, King Taksin drove the remaining Burmese out of the country, liberating Siam once again.

Although the country now known as Thailand was liberated, it was far from united. During the Burmese rule, the people of Siam had split into many factions, all of which were struggling and disorganized. King Taksin conquered the factions, and by 1770, he had unified the country.

Although most of Taksin's accomplishments are military-related, the king did help to restart and rehabilitate the Thai economy. Thanks to King Narai's foreign relations prior to the fall of the city of Ayutthaya, the country already had developed trade relations with China. King Taksin capitalized on these existing relationships and invited craftsmen and merchants from China to settle in Thonburi. Not long after uniting the country of Siam, King Taksin restored the economy, thanks to the Chinese merchants and taxes he put in place. During his time as king, he also strengthened the trade relationships with European countries, such as Great Britain and the Netherlands. The king worked to develop Thonburi and had roads, canals, and temples built, renovated, and restored. During his reign, King Taksin also revived the arts in Thailand, focusing mainly on literature, since almost all of the previous Siamese works had been destroyed in the Burmese siege.

Although the Thonburi Kingdom only existed while King Taksin was on the throne, a mere fifteen years, this era remains one of Thailand's most expansive early periods. In 1769, not long after arriving and settling in Thonburi, King Taksin led his troops to conquer Korat, which is now Thailand's largest province, and Cambodia. In 1772, he returned to Cambodia and attacked once again to assert his power, replacing their king with a Cambodian prince of his choosing. In 1774, King Taksin annexed the city and the Lan Na Kingdom, which had been around since the Sukhothai period but had been seized by the Burmese, and the city was absorbed into the Thonburi Kingdom. By 1776, King Taksin had absorbed almost all of the tribes in Thailand and had truly united the country that had been mostly made of smaller separate factions. By the end of King Taksin's reign, Siam and the Thonburi Kingdom had expanded to include much of modern-day Thailand, the Malay Peninsula, Laos, and Cambodia.

The End of King Taksin's Reign

However, despite all of King Taksin's accomplishments and achievements during his fifteen-year reign as the king of Siam and Thonburi, in 1782, he was forced to step down and was executed. It is said that at the beginning of the 1780s, King Taksin began to lose his mind, and many documents speak of his, what we would now refer to, mental instability. Apparently, King Taksin started to believe he was advancing toward Buddhahood and tried to force the belief of his divinity onto his followers. These actions led to rebellions and dissatisfaction amongst the united Siam people, so much so that King Taksin came close to undoing all that he had achieved during his reign. The country of Thailand and the Kingdom of Siam would have likely crumbled had it not been for a revolution that broke out in Bangkok, with his ministers eventually deciding to have him executed. King Taksin was replaced in 1782 by Chao Phraya Chakri, who was a governor and chief campaigning in Cambodia at the time. Chao Phraya Chakri would later be known as "Great Lord" Rama I and the founder of the Chakri dynasty.

Although Taksin's reign was short-lived, and he was, in the end, dethroned and executed, he is regarded as a hero in Thai history. During his fifteen-year reign, he rid the country of the Burmese threat, which had destroyed the Ayutthaya Kingdom and caused so much suffering to the people of Siam. He also united the country of Siam and expanded its borders to include much of today's modern Thailand. These, along with many of his other accomplishments, are why he is referred to today as "King Taksin the Great." On December 28th, the date he was crowned as the king of Siam in 1767, is celebrated in Thailand as King Taksin Day. There is a shrine erected at Wat Lum Mahachai Chumphon, where the king is said to have stopped on his way to free Ayutthaya from Burmese control. Today, many, including both Thai locals and Chinese visitors, go there to pray on King Taksin Day.

Chapter 5 – The Beginning of the Chakri Dynasty (1782–1868)

Reign of Rama I (r. 1782-1809)

Following the arrival of King Taksin and his people in Thonburi, Chao Phraya Chakri joined and moved his way up in King Taksin's troops until achieving the high leadership position of military commander of the northern provinces. During the Thonburi period, he led Thai troops in Laos, Cambodia, and the Malay states and was regarded as one of Taksin's most exemplary generals. He was actually on a campaign in Cambodia when the rebellions against Taksin were beginning to take place, and he was called back to take his place at the beginning of 1782. He was crowned as the new king on April 6th of that year and became known as Rama I, Phra Phutthayotfa Chulalok ("the Buddha on top of the sky and the crown of the worlds"). He would be the first of his family to rule, and his descendants would continue to reign the country now known as Thailand, with Rama X of the Chakri dynasty recognized as the king of Thailand today.

One of Rama I's first moves as king was to move the capital of the country from Thonburi to Bangkok, which, of course, is still the capital of Thailand today. Bangkok was mostly undeveloped at the time and was, in comparison with Thonburi or Ayutthaya, still a small village. King Rama I had new infrastructures built, with palaces and Buddhist temples constructed in a very similar elaborate style as the Ayutthaya designs. Through establishing these somewhat grandiose temples, Rama I was able to restrengthen the Buddhist religion throughout the country. During his reign, he requested to have many of the essential Buddhist texts translated to Thai, which helped to establish the sangha, which refers to the monastic order in Buddhism.

Rama I also focused on restoring Thailand's cultural arts and heritage, much of which had been lost during the Burmese pillaging of Ayutthaya. This was made easier due to the fact that Rama I's predecessor, King Taksin, had already attempted to revive some of the artistic cultural customs. Rama I had many works of literature brought from other countries, namely India and China, in addition to others, and he strongly encouraged the citizens of Bangkok to reinterest themselves in the arts, which certainly helped lay the foundation for much of Thailand's cultural arts and heritage throughout history and today.

Although King Taksin had driven out the Burmese troops from Siam during the Thonburi period, the Burmese kingdom would continue to threaten the country following Rama I's move to Bangkok. They would be a threat until 1820, when the British army would force Burmese troops to return to their home country and defend their kingdom. The first Burmese attack during Rama I's reign occurred in 1785. It was a massive invasion, and Rama I's troops were barely able to fight it off. Although it was difficult, the Siamese troops managed to repel the Burmese attacks in 1785, as well as those attacks in 1786, 1787, 1797, and 1801, although these later ones were on a much smaller scale. King Rama I would continue to strengthen his troops and expand the kingdom throughout Southeast Asia. By the beginning of the 1800s, under the reign of Rama I as well as Rama II, the Chakri dynasty had extended its power to much of Laos, Cambodia, and Vietnam.

Toward the end of Rama I's twenty-seven-year reign, he published Thailand's first written form of law and issued comprehensive court law codes and court rituals. This codification of law, which was completed in 1805, was adapted from laws that date as far back as King Ram Khamhaeng from the Sukhothai Kingdom. That being said, many of the laws crystalized by Rama I were ones set in place throughout the Ayutthaya period, and they were derived from both Hindu and Buddhist practices. This set of revised written laws were known as the *Three Seals Law*, and it would remain almost completely unaltered until the reign of Rama V in 1882. Rama I reigned as the first king of the Chakri dynasty until his death in 1809. He would be succeeded by his son, who would be known as Rama II.

Reign of Rama II (r. 1809-1824)

Rama II, also known as Phraphutthaloetla Naphalai, was the second ruler of the Chakri dynasty. His reign was fairly short, lasting only 15 years, and during that time, he aided in the reconstruction of Thailand's cultural arts, heritage, and traditions. Rama was enamored with the arts, specifically poetry, and it was under his reign that the great Thai poet Sunthon Phu wrote some of his most influential works, which are regarded as some of Thailand's best works of poetry ever written. Rama II was also himself a gifted artist. During his lifetime, he wrote many famous poems, such as a well-known dramatic rendition of Inao and Sang

Thong, which is a popular dance drama.

Although King Taksin had maintained relations with China, most of Thailand's foreign relations had been closed off since the rule of King Narai during the Ayutthaya period. Under Rama II's rule, Siam reconnected with the West, namely Portugal in 1818 and Great Britain in 1822.

During King Rama II's rule, Thailand would see its first outbreak of cholera, a disease that would continue to plague the country for years to come. The first case in Thailand dates back to 1820. To attempt to fight the plague, King Rama II ordered the population to stay home from work and to focus on observing their Buddhist practices. This stay-at-home decree helped in ridding the country of cholera for the time being. Despite the fact that King Rama's royally ordered quarantine eventually worked, it is estimated that likely around 30,000 people died from the outbreak.

Rama II would rule Thailand from his father's death in 1809 until his own death in 1824, and he would be succeeded by his son, who would come to be known as Rama III. In comparison to his father's rule, Rama II's time as king was mostly peaceful, which allowed him to focus much of his energy on reviving the arts and culture in Siam, laying the further foundation for Thailand's rich arts and culture today.

Reign of Rama III (r. 1824-1851)

Rama III's succession to the throne is considered to be somewhat of a strange and rare occurrence. His father, Rama II, as with most Thai royalty during this era, had many concubines—in other words, a lover with a lower status than a wife—in addition to his wife, who was the queen of Siam until her husband's death. Rama III, also known as Nangklao, was born on March 31st, 1788, in Bangkok to one of Rama II's concubines. Although Rama II had a legitimate son, Prince Mongkut, Nangklao

(Rama III) was chosen to rule upon his father's death instead.

This strange choice by the accession council was due to the fact that from a young age, Nangklao (Rama III) was put in charge of overseeing the country's foreign trade and relations, which made him more experienced than his brother. This experience would explain why much of what is written and remembered about Rama III's reign is related to foreign relations.

Throughout the beginning of the Chakri dynasty, Britain had been increasingly threatening the Burmese kingdom, which was to the benefit of Siam, as it had been battling with the Burmese for many centuries by this point. It was not until Britain increased their military in what is now modern-day Myanmar that the Burmese stopped being a threat to the Chakri dynasty. War was finally declared between Britain and the Burmese kingdom in 1824, and its proximity to Siam left Rama III fearful that the powerful British army might eventually attack his kingdom as well. This thinking led Rama III to agree to sign the 1826 Burney Treaty, which mostly covered trade and economic agreements. The British had failed to get King Rama II to sign this agreement in 1822, as he was certainly less open to the West than his successor. The Burney Treaty would finally permit English tradesmen to operate in Bangkok; however, the treaty had quite limited clauses and high taxes, which would lead to a stricter treaty being put in place later in 1855, after Rama III's death.

Although diplomatic relations had been established between Thailand and the United States, likely by Rama III when he was overlooking the country's foreign relations, no official agreements were signed between the two countries until 1833. That year, the United States and Thailand signed the Treaty of Amity and Commerce, with the very first article claiming the two countries shall have perpetual peace. The other nine articles in the treaty essentially laid out commerce and trade regulations, such as citizens of the United States having free liberty to enter Siam through its ports to sell and purchase in the country's many markets. This agreement is actually the United States of America's very first treaty of any kind made with any Asian country. The treaties between the Kingdom of Siam and the United States, as well as between Great Britain, which were mainly put in place to allow foreign merchants to buy and sell in Siam, would greatly impact Thailand's infrastructures throughout the rest of history.

Rama III's reign would also lead to further strengthening of the Siamese army. Throughout the 1830 and 1840s, under Rama III's lead, the Kingdom of Siam continued to establish and assert their military dominance throughout Southeast Asia, specifically in Cambodia and Laos, where they fought to defend the two aforementioned countries from the Vietnamese. This period also marked a change between Siam and Kedah, now Malaysia, which Siam had been occupying since the start of the 19th century. In 1837, following Rama III's mother's death, many of the officials stationed in Kedah returned to Siam. This space allowed Kedah to finally accomplish what they had been trying to do for over a decade already, which was to launch a rebellion in 1838 against the Siamese. Following the rebellion, in 1839, the Kingdom of Siam realized any further direct involvement in Kedah would lead to more resistance, so Kedah became mostly autonomous, with the two kingdoms entering into a peaceful coexistence.

Much like during his father's and grandfather's reigns, art was of great importance during Rama III's reign. What is unique to Rama III is the amount of outside influence that impacted Thai art. In addition to the numerous Western influences that are obvious within Thai art from this time, the Chinese, who had been inhabiting the Kingdom of Siam throughout the entire Chakri dynasty, also had a great amount of influence. Much of this Chinese influence can be seen in the temple paintings from this time.

Rama III is widely remembered for his accomplishments in foreign relations, which helped put Thailand on the global map and extending its trade all the way to North America. He ruled from his father's death in 1824 until his own death in 1851. Although King Rama III never took a wife, he had fifty-one children. However, seeing as none of them were born in wedlock, in addition to the fact that he never named a successor, the throne finally went to Prince Mongkut, the son of King Rama II and his wife, Queen Sri Suriyendra.

Reign of Rama IV (r. 1851-1868)

Mongkut, also known as Rama IV or by his reigning title, Phra Chom Klao Chao Yu Hua, was born in 1804 and was the first son of King Rama II and his wife, Queen Sri Suriyendra. Although he was the first in line to take the throne after his father's death in 1824, seeing as Mongkut was only twenty in 1824, the throne was instead given to his half-brother, who became known as Rama III. Instead of becoming a military general or working in the royal government, Mongkut became a Buddhist monk, and an accomplished one at that. At the monastery, Mongkut made connections with Christians from both the United States and France, which would lead to enhancing both the West's understanding of Buddhism and the Thais' understanding of Western languages and advancements in the sciences.

During Mongkut's twenty-seven years in a Bangkok monastery, he helped to develop Thai Buddhism into what it is today. While at the monastery, Mongkut was concerned that many of the techniques and practices taught to him were superstitious and strayed away from Buddha's original teachings. Mongkut sought to purify Buddhism once again, and he found more of what he was looking for while traveling to the countryside and encountering Siam's remaining Mon, who practiced stricter Buddhist disciplines than the Siamese people. Inspired by the many practices he picked up from the Mon, Mongkut would go on to found the Thammayut order, which is now one of Thailand's two main Theravada Buddhism denominations.

After spending twenty-seven years in the monastery, Mongkut, also known as Rama IV, took his rightful place as the king of Siam after his half-brother's death in 1851. During Rama IV's reign, he continued to strengthen Buddhism throughout the country. However, he is likely best remembered for his foreign relations. Following Rama III's somewhat restrictive treaties with Britain, in 1855, the queen of England sent Sir John Bowring to demand that the treaties be reestablished and less restrictive. Considering Britain had waged wars on other countries for restrictive treaties, Siam signed the Bowring Treaty in April 1855, which gave the British diplomatic immunity in Siam and removed the tariffs and duties placed on foreigners. Similar revised agreements were also signed between Siam and other European countries, as well as the United States, between 1855 and 1870.

Though King Rama IV's signing of the Bowring Treaty and other subsequent agreements protected Siam's sovereignty, it greatly damaged the kingdom's economy and independence. This forced the king to find other sources of revenue, which led to crops being planted to sell in global markets, canal systems being built to help with exporting goods, and an increase in taxes. In the end, the treaties Rama IV signed did more good than harm since they helped create rapid growth in Siam's economy, put Siam firmly on the global map, and prevent wars that other neighboring rulers had fought due to not adjusting their original restrictive treaties made with the Western countries.

Although the Bowring Treaty was mostly centered around foreign trade, it certainly led to an overall increase of foreign influences on Siam. Prior to the treaties, Siam was ruled by a very strict sovereignty, and though Siam was still ruled by a monarchy following the Bowring Treaty, that strict, uncompromising authoritarian sovereignty would no longer be possible if Siam was to accommodate for the new Western influences. Under King Rama IV, Siam's view of the monarchy became less traditionally strict and more modern, which would strip the royal order of some of their powers but overall prevent any rebellions or wars within the country or with any foreign nations.

Another example of the change brought by the increase in foreign influence was the introduction of Western ideas in Siam's education. European countries once again began sending missionaries to attempt to convert the Thais into Christians, and although they were unsuccessful, they did end up building medical facilities and other Western-styled infrastructures. It was actually American Protestant missionaries that brought over the first printing press and ended up creating Thailand's first newspaper.

Rama IV ensured his children had access to Western advisors, teachers, and tutors who would help enhance their understanding of the changing world. Mongkut brought in French missionaries to teach his kids Latin, math, and astronomy, as well as an American missionary to teach them English. One of these tutors was Anna Harriette Leonowens, a teacher from Britain. Her life would be made into a novel called *Anna and the King of Siam*, which would later be made into the well-known musical *The King and I*. These works were widely popular in the Western world, and despite being riddled with inaccuracies, they would shape much of the West's understanding of Thailand, much to the Kingdom of Siam's dismay. Both of these works are considered to be highly controversial in Thailand, so much so that the book was banned in the country. Even today, theatrical versions of the book are often banned in Thailand due to historical inaccuracies. Anna Harriette Leonowens claims that she greatly influenced Mongkut's son, who would go on to become Rama V; however, it is debated exactly how much impact she had on the future king.

Rama IV ruled the Kingdom of Siam until his death in 1868, and he was succeeded by his son. Rama IV's time as king would mark many changes in Thailand's culture, namely the modernization of the sovereignty and the ceding of many of the royal order's powers. He is remembered for his creation of the currently widely popular Buddhist Thammayut order, but he is perhaps most remembered for introducing many Western ideas, concepts, and infrastructures into the country, which laid the foundation for Thailand's unique culture.

Chapter 6 – The Modernization of Thailand and the Reign of the Great Rama V (1868–1910)

Although King Mongkut was succeeded by his son Chulalongkorn, who would come to be known as Rama V, Chulalongkorn was barely sixteen at the time of his father's death in 1868 and not prepared to run the Kingdom of Siam. Chulalongkorn spent the subsequent five years following King Rama IV's death traveling to neighboring European-colonized countries and observing political and judicial proceedings in preparations to fully take the throne. During this time, a notable minister named Somdet Chao Phraya Si Suriyawong, also known by his personal name Chuang Bunnag, whose family had held important posts since the 17th century, was appointed as the regent. Chuang Bunnag was one of the highest-ranking officials under King Mongkut and had been a key player in the Kingdom of Siam's treaties with the Western countries. Since Chuang Bunnag was such a powerful official under the previous king's reign, he was extremely adept at running the kingdom, and in 1873, when Chulalongkorn was prepared to take the lead, Chuang Bunnag remained as an official and advisor until his death in 1883.

An accurate way of describing Chulalongkorn's ruling style would be "like father like son." In comparison to the kings of the Ayutthaya Kingdom or even the early Chakri dynasty, who didn't allow people of the lower class to see them or look at their face and ruled with god-like power, Rama V (Chulalongkorn) acted more similarly to a modern politician. Rama V went out in public dressed casually (or at least casually in comparison to what kings would normally be seen wearing), and he would allow his face to be printed and reproduced on products such as coins and stamps, which no previous king had allowed before. Although Rama IV had taken great strides to modernize the Kingdom of Siam, it is Rama V who is remembered for defying the outdated traditions and modernizing the country.

Similar to his father, Chulalongkorn focused much of his time on foreign relations. Although previous kings of Siam had made connections and agreements with foreign countries through missionaries and merchants sent to Thailand, King Rama V would travel to countries throughout Europe and Southeast Asia. These trips and the trips taken before his reign while he was preparing to take the throne would inspire King Rama V. These inspirations are demonstrated in ornate European-style structures built during his reign, which would have been similar to what he had seen on his trips, as well as in his choice to defy the traditional practices in Thailand and conduct many modernizing political reforms.

Almost immediately after Chulalongkorn fully took over power at the age of twenty, he began to put in place a series of significant reforms in the country's law, finance, and political structures, much of which were drawn from Western models he had observed while preparing to lead. Unlike the previous kings of Siam, who had relied almost exclusively on the advice of their Siamese officials, King Rama V had many foreign advisors, the majority of which were from Britain. Rama V felt that it was important that all future royalty attend Western-style schools to prepare for their futures in leading positions and that all promising future government and military officials should study in Europe.

Between 1868 and 1910, the country experienced rapid modernization. King Rama V very quickly laid out a new political order and a more comprehensive legal system and legal code, putting a stop to arbitrary laws. He pushed for primary education and enforced military conscription, which together created the foundation of what it meant to be a citizen in the Kingdom of Siam. This, along with the abolition of slavery and state labor, were all accomplished within the first few years of his reign. In 1892, all of these actions led to the separation of the government into twelve ministries, three of which were defense, education, and justice, which is not too dissimilar to the political structures we see today. It was under Rama V that the Kingdom of Siam introduced a police force, a government-run currency-based tax collection, and a modern school system. Although Thailand had been a unified country before King Rama V, the Kingdom of Siam developed a centralized administration that would connect all of its provinces. Finally, as another sign of modernization, Siam began constructing railways, which were finished in 1897 (and extended during the subsequent years), connecting Bangkok and Ayutthaya and, in 1903, to connect to the British Malaysian railroads.

While all of these reforms were happening internally, many of which were due to Western influence, the Kingdom of Siam was gradually losing territory to these same Western countries. Similar to agreements made by King Mongkut with the Western countries, King Rama V skillfully signed agreements that, despite reducing the Kingdom of Siam's independence and landmass, helped the country avoid Western colonization. In 1893, the Kingdom of Siam ceded all Lao territories that they had been occupying east of the Mekong River to France. Similar agreements were made in 1907 when Thailand ceded their landmass in Cambodia to France and in 1909 when they ceded many Malayan states to Britain.

All things considered, despite the land they were ceding to Western countries, Thailand kept its independence and was being globally established as a powerful force. To celebrate Thailand's freedom in contrast to its colonized neighbors, in 1902, the country unofficially became known as *Prathet Thai* or *Ratcha Anachak Thai*, which translates, respectively, to the "country of the free" and the "kingdom of the free." The country's name was not officially changed to Thailand until 1939.

Seeing as Chulalongkorn (Rama V) began his rule so young, succeeding his father in 1868 at the age of sixteen, and ruling until he died in 1910, he had one of the longest reigns in the country's history. Although his extended reign explains how he was able to achieve so much during his time as king, overall, the rapid modern reforms that Rama V introduced into Thailand were completely unprecedented. King Rama V is remembered as one of Thailand's greatest, most successful, and most notable kings.

Chapter 7 – The Final Absolute Monarchs of Thailand (1910–1932)

The Reign of King Rama VI (r. 1910-1925)

King Rama V's successor was his son Vajiravudh, who later became known as Rama VI. Vajiravudh went to Oxford University, making him the first king of Siam to ever have a foreign education. Prior to ruling Siam, he also served in the British army, but he only did so briefly, as he returned home in 1903 after being named his father's successor to prepare himself for the throne, which he would take after his father's death in 1910.

King Rama VI's time spent in Europe greatly impacted many of his social reforms. During his reign, he recodified Siamese law and introduced many Western-inspired laws, banning polygamy and ordering all citizens to adopt surnames. Although some of his Westernized changes were beneficial to the country, such as the creation of the Thai

Red Cross, other changes were of less significance, such as the introduction of the Gregorian calendar. However, many civilians felt King Rama VI pushed the Westernization of Thailand too far. One example of this would be when he strongly suggested that the Siamese stop wearing traditional Thai garb and adopt a more European-style of clothing.

Considering King Rama VI was not only the first ruler of Thailand to have a foreign education (he was also the first one to attend university), it comes as no surprise that during his reign, he greatly aided in advancing the education system. In 1917, almost two decades after returning home from Oxford University, he founded and opened the first university in Thailand, which he named Chulalongkorn University after his father. Although the building was constructed under his father's reign for instructing government workers, under King Rama VI, it became a proper university. Chulalongkorn University, which is still located in Bangkok, is considered to be one of the top fifty universities in all of Asia and the number one institute of higher education in Thailand today. To also aid in advancing the country's education, Vajiravudh (King Rama VI) would continue to push his father's enforcement of primary school for children, and in 1921, he would officially make primary school education compulsory and free for everyone in Thailand.

Ever since King Narai's rule during the Ayutthaya period, Thailand had a large population of Chinese people, not all of which understood Thai or connected with the Siamese culture. King Rama VI not only passed laws forcing compulsory primary school but also an act that everyone in the country had to learn the Thai language. In his quest for nationalism, he sought that all students would learn the language until they were fluent and also be educated on Siamese culture and national duties.

Under King Rama VI, the Kingdom of Siam had access to arts and scientific and technological advancements of other countries around the world, which would help Thailand rapidly modernize at the same pace as the other connected countries. When the country was faced with smallpox, they had access to the British-invented smallpox vaccine, and King Rama VI was able to implement a universal dose of the vaccine to every citizen in Thailand. King Rama VI also established Thailand's very own Red Cross. Although the humanitarian organization was technically around during his father's reign, it was under Vajiravudh that it became recognized by the International Red Cross Committee. King Rama VI also attempted to crack down on Thailand's drug problems, specifically opium, which affected and other neighboring and international countries, which were also seeking solutions to the problem around this same time.

That being said, King Rama VI's globally-accessed advancements weren't only scientific and humanitarian. King Rama VI was also known as a patron of the arts and spent much of his spare time translating international works into Thai. He translated hundreds of famous plays and books, including many of Shakespeare's, introducing Thailand to many Western works of art that weren't previously accessible. On top of translations, King Rama VI wrote dozens of original plays and dramas, almost all of which under pseudonyms and many of which are still beloved in the country today. King Rama VI wrote many of his works, although not all, surrounding the topic of nationalism, a concept that deeply fascinated him. After spending so much time in the West, King Rama VI often compared and contrasted the facets of Thai and Western nationalism, many concepts he would then introduce into his politics.

King Rama VI ruled between 1910 and 1925, which means he oversaw the country during World War I. The Kingdom of Siam fought on the side of the Allies and sent troops to fight alongside them in Europe. In the end, this action certainly aided the Kingdom of Siam in its foreign relations with European countries, namely Britain and France. Fighting alongside the Allies also meant that when the war ended, the Kingdom of Siam was able to bring home the spoils of winning a war, which included an arsenal of German ships. Under King Rama VI, in 1919, Siam attended the peace conference in Versailles and was one of the founding countries of the League of Nations. Following the war, due to both the Kingdom of Siam's strengthened European relations and Europe's loss in power, King Rama VI was able to persuade the Western countries to cede their extraterritorial rights in the country. This would mean that all Western travelers would have to follow local laws and would no longer be granted immunities when they were in the Kingdom of Siam.

King Rama VI never truly struck the right balance between Western ideologies and conserving Thai culture. Although he strongly promoted Thai nationalism, his Western ideas of nationalism with utility in mind led to a great reluctance amongst the civilians. An example of this was when King Rama VI tried to create the Wild Tiger Corps, a military force that was separate from the country's army and under King Rama VI's direct command. This royal paramilitary force resembled the royally-run armies in Britain at the time. This, coupled with the other English and European traditions that King Rama VI was trying to push on the country's people, led to a disgruntled population. Many were offended by his choices and saw them as undermining Thai culture and Siamese heritage rather than modernizing the country as he was intending. Public opinion of King Rama VI was not helped by the fact that (toward the end of his reign especially) he was overspending and leading the country into economic issues. This resentment was shared amongst the corps, and in 1912, some navy and army officials began to plot a rebellion of sorts to restrict the king's power. Although the plan was aborted, the population of Siam remained wary and resentful of the king, as well as the next king. King Rama VI died in 1925, and the throne was succeeded by his brother, Prajadhipok (King Rama VII), who inherited a disgruntled population no longer satisfied with the country's absolute monarchy.

The Reign of King Rama VII (r. 1925-1935)

Generally, a reigning king will choose an heir to the throne many years before the end of his reign, with some successors being chosen from birth and others being decided upon when they become of age and showed potential. Either way, a successor is typically given enough years to prepare for leadership through observing and working their way up in other government. This was not the case for Vajiravudh's brother Prajadhipok, who never expected to be king. Similar to his brother, Prajadhipok had a foreign education, but unlike his brother, Prajadhipok had been attending school to prepare for a career in the military. Prajadhipok, who was also known as Phrapokklao and who would later be known as King Rama VII, attended Eton College, which is an all-boys boarding school for those aged thirteen to eighteen. Founded by Henry VI, Eton College is globally considered one of the most prestigious schools for this specific age range. Following his time at Eton College, Prajadhipok attended the Woolwich Royal Military Academy to further his military training, meaning that a large portion of his teenage and young adult life was spent outside of Thailand, with access to more Western influences and ideologies than his brother. At the beginning of 1925, not even a year before the throne would be passed to him, he became the most likely successor to the throne, even though, unlike the previous kings, he did not have years of preparation or governmental experience. Prajadhipok was only officially and formally announced as the successor to the throne on November 24th, 1925, only two days before his brother would pass.

When King Prajadhipok (Rama VII) began his reign, he inherited a discontent population and some significant financial issues. Due to his brother's extravagant spending, King Rama VII was forced to lay off a good amount of government officials within the first year of his reign. Although the layoffs helped stave off the Kingdom of Siam's fiscal issues for a few years, at the start of the 1930s, Thailand and the rest of the world would be hit with the Great Depression. The Great Depression would force King Rama VII to lay off even more government officials, cutting workers from every ministry and department. At the same time, the resentment many of the middle-class civilians had held during King Rama VI's reign had only grown stronger. With the combination of the dissatisfied working middle-class civilians and now the disgruntled laid-off government officials and the government officials' families, discontentment with the absolute monarchy became the popular opinion. Backed by the majority of the population, newspapers and other media began shining a light and giving voices to the dissatisfied people.

Of course, with all of the press coverage, King Rama VII was aware of the population's growing resentment of the royal family and of the absolute monarchical government. The king was rightfully convinced that he would need to begin moving toward political reforms that would introduce democratic practices, ones that would lessen the royal family's power and give more power to the people. Considering King Rama VII, like his brother, had spent many years in the West, he was open to moving toward a more democratic political system. However, despite his own convictions, the senior and more experienced royal court members did not agree with him. Although these senior government officials certainly restrained him, King Rama VII did not push hard for change, and though he believed that the government needed reforms, he remained outwardly ignorant toward his people's demands. It would be this inactivity in the face of the population's complete dissatisfaction with absolute sovereignty that led to the Thai (or Siamese) revolution of 1932.

The Thai Revolution of 1932

Although a good majority of the Thai population was dissatisfied with the absolute monarchy by the beginning of the 1930s, the Thai revolution of 1932 was actually started by a group of young Thai students who had studied abroad. In fact, they actually began plotting the revolution while living and studying in Europe. The revolutionary movement, known as Khana Ratsadon, or the People's Party, was led by Pridi Phanomyong and Plaek Khittasangkha, better known as Phibun to Western audiences.

Pridi Phanomyong was born in Ayutthaya, Siam, in 1900, making him only thirty-two years old at the time of the Thai revolution of 1932. Born to a Thai mother and a Chinese father, Pridi excelled in school from a young age. His father was a rice merchant, but rather than following in his father's footsteps, Pridi put his time and effort into making his way through school. His dedication to a solid education paid off, as he graduated from secondary school at only fourteen years old, four years ahead of the typical graduation age, and completed law school at the Thai Royal College of Law by the time he was nineteen. He was a shining pupil, and although he was many years younger than his peers, he was awarded a scholarship to the University of Caen in France to study law. He subsequently attended the University of Paris to earn his doctorate. By the time Pridi Phanomyong was twenty-seven, he had graduated with a masters in law and economics and a doctorate in law. The air of revolution was not only present in his home of Siam but also in France as well. Pridi Phanomyong's time in Paris allowed him to observe and take part in the radical revolutionary movements that would help shape France's democratic politics. While in France, Pridi would not only be inspired by the revolutionary socialistic and democratic movements and politics in the country, but he would also meet Major Plaek Khittasangkha, and together they would form the Khana Ratsadon (the People's Party).

Plaek Khittasangkha was born in 1897 in a province north of Bangkok. Plaek Khittasangkha was raised to join the military and would attend the Chulachomklao Royal Military Academy, a military school located in one of Thailand's central provinces. In 1914, at only seventeen years old, Plaek Khittasangkha graduated from the academy and was sent to the artillery, commissioned as a second lieutenant. He spent around a decade in the Siamese artillery corps, where he displayed outstanding natural military instincts, prowess, and intelligence. Plaek Khittasangkha's excellent military performance was rewarded in 1924 when he was sent to advance his military training in France. Plaek would continue to study artillery tactics in France between 1924 and 1927, and in 1928, after returning to Bangkok, he was promoted to major, receiving the title *Luang*. As a result of this, he began going by the name Luang Phibunsongkhram (better known as Phibun to Western audiences). Similar to his future revolutionary counterpart Pridi Phanomyong, it was in France that Phibun began to realize the need for political reforms in the Kingdom of Siam and the power of a people-run revolution. During his time studying in France, Phibun would come into contact with Pridi Phanomyong and many other Thai students who were studying abroad and who were discontent with the Kingdom of Siam's politics.

While there are many factors that led to the Thai revolution of 1932, or as it was called then the Siamese Revolution of 1932, many historians and participants agree that the revolution unfolded as it did due to King Rama V's policies to send students to receive foreign educations. As we saw with King Rama VI and King Rama VII, who both had foreign educations in England, they both became infatuated with Western ideologies. However, unlike King Rama VI and King Rama VII, who were, of course, from the royal family and quite wealthy, the non-royal students being sent to Europe and elsewhere were not as privileged, and they shared similar views on the monarchy as the rest of the country's working-class civilians.

Throughout King Rama VII's reign, the number of scholarships given out by the government to talented non-royal family men significantly increased. Ironically enough, by sending students to study abroad, Thailand's absolute monarchist government was essentially giving out the education that led to its undoing. What awaited the students who studied in foreign countries were lessons of Western democratic politics and freedoms. As Thai students continued to attend foreign schools and connect with one another while abroad, they discussed politics and came to realize that the absolute monarchy in their home country was not only unsatisfying but was also growing to become intolerable.

The number of students from the Kingdom of Siam attending schools in Western countries continued to increase throughout the 1920s, and by the 1930s, it is assumed that there were at least a couple hundred Thai students spread throughout England, France, the United States, the Philippines, and other European countries. Although the students were mostly sent to these countries to get a better understanding of Western practices that could help modernize the Kingdom of Siam, many, though not all, of the students would bring home revolutionary democratic political ideas. Rather than bringing home techniques to help advance the absolute monarchy's political system, many of the students came to the conclusion that the monarchy would have to be entirely replaced by democracy, as they believed this would be the only way to truly modernize the country.

While attending school in France to earn his masters and doctorate in law, Pridi Phanomyong became the secretive face of the revolutionary and somewhat anarchist Thai student movement. Since there were so many Thai students in France, there was already an association of Thai students in France, of which he quickly became the first elected secretary. As he became better acquainted with the students, he was elected as president of the association. While he was president, Pridi Phanomyong would somewhat openly discuss his democratic politics, which connected him to other Thai students with similar viewpoints. After a few years, Pridi had carefully gathered a few close friends and partners that he trusted, and he would often host and attend secretive meetings with them, where they would discuss revolutionary plans for their return to their home country. Through Prayoon Pamornmontri, who was one of the first people Pridi shared his revolutionary plans with and who was also the main recruiter for the revolutionary group, Pridi was connected with Plaek Khittasangkha (Phibun).

Although a revolution was still mostly wishful thinking, Pridi Phanomyong, Prayoon Pamornmontri, and Plaek Khittasangkha yearned for a way to take down the absolute monarchy, creating the People's Party in 1927. Over the subsequent years, Prayoon would continue to recruit fellow Thai students with similar democratic ideologies, and they would go on to play important roles in the Thai revolution of 1932, including Tua Laphanukrom, Nab Phaholyothin, Lieutenant Luang Sinthu Songgramchai, Phraya Phahon Phayuhasena, Phraya Song Suradej, Phra Prasas Pitthayayudh, and Phraya Ritthi Akaney. Many of these new additions to the revolutionary movement had relatively high-ranking positions in the Siamese military, which would help to provide the movement with necessary military troops, equipment, and planning to eventually overthrow the nation's absolute monarchy.

Although the leaders of the Khana Ratsadon (the People's Party) were plotting revolution for the Kingdom of Siam while in France, their dissatisfaction was similarly shared amongst the people who still remained in the country. While talented students and promising military leaders were sent to study abroad, the younger generation of officials within Thailand who had studied at the newly opened Chulalongkorn University was also gaining expertise and discussing the inefficiency of the nation's political system. This should come as no surprise, considering the dissatisfaction in the Kingdom of Siam within the middle and working classes had been growing ever since King Rama VI's reign. This would mean that the monarchy's power was gradually diminishing, and as a monarchy loses favor with its people, they lose leverage and power since they need to avoid creating more discontentment, as that would lead to revolutions and rebellions.

The royal government's public opinion was not helped by the serious fiscal issues the kingdom was facing at the beginning of the 20th century due to King Rama VI's extravagance and the ramifications of the global Great Depression. These financial difficulties would lead to many cuts within the ministries, which would upset not only the laid-off officials and their families but also the general population. Following the layoffs, Rama VII was forced to make extensive changes in the running of the government to account for the loss of so many high-ranked officials. These changes were not positively received, as the population felt important governmental ministries were not being adequately run.

Another factor that added to the population's distaste for the nation's monarchist government was the shady way decisions were made. Although the government wasn't doing anything necessarily worse than in a democratic political system, the royal family would deliberately keep many actions and decisions secret from the population, who wouldn't find out about even the most extreme changes until they were already put into action. Since the government kept all decisions hidden from the population, newspapers and reporters often printed misinformation based on rumors, although many papers would choose not to print gossip-based news at all since any misrepresentations of the rulers' decisions could end their careers.

Overall, the population was dissatisfied with the absolute monarchist government that had been ruling the Kingdom of Siam since its creation as a nation. However, though the entire population was in favor of political reforms and was leaning more and more toward democratic ideals, it would be the younger Thai students who led the revolution. Toward the end of the 1920s, the members of the newly founded People's Party, who had done all of their plotting abroad, began returning home. Once Pridi Phanomyong, Plaek Khittasangkha, and their revolutionary peers had returned to the Kingdom of Siam, they began building up their forces and somewhat secretly promoting their cause. They gathered fellow democratic Thai students and scholars, both those who had remained in Thailand and those who, like them, had studied abroad. Along with students, they also assembled government and military officials, some of whom had been laid off throughout King Rama VII's reign and some of whom were still in office.

Although the members of the People's Party (known in the Kingdom of Siam as the "Promoters") had spent many years secretly plotting a revolution, it was not until they returned home to Thailand that they began putting their plan into action. Phibun (Plaek Khittasangkha) and fellow revolutionary military officials planned the coup, attempting to avoid violence at all costs. At the same time, Pridi Phanomyong and other People's Party members created a detailed political plan that they hoped to institute if the coup went as planned. The political plan consisted of reforms to the people's liberties, equalities, and educational opportunities, as well as the nation's security, finances, and independence.

On June 24th, 1932, with the Khana Ratsadon, or People's Party, leading as the heart of the movement, a fairly small group of students, military officials, non-royal employed and unemployed government officials, and civilians took to the streets to stage a coup d'état. Catching the monarchical government completely off guard, the Bangkok district, which contained the government buildings, ministries, and palaces, were flooded with people, tanks, and armored cars. The revolutionary group captured, arrested, and imprisoned surprised government officials, many of whom were still in their pajamas. While they were arresting these officials, other members of the People's Party handed out flyers to confused citizens with the revolutionary group's manifesto. The manifesto described how poorly the civilians had been treated by the monarchy, with the flyers saying the government treated people as slaves and as animals. It compared the life of civilians, who had to work their lives away to have enough money to live, with the privilege of the royal family and government officials, who could sleep and eat without worry. The manifesto also detailed how Thailand had one of the worst, if not the worst, government besides the Russians and the Germans and how any other country would have already overthrown their government had it been comparable to that of the Kingdom of Siam.

While the People's Party were staging their rebellion in Bangkok, King Rama VII was golfing at a coastal resort a few hours by train from the city. Ironically, the palace he was staying at, which is a summer residence in Hua Hin for the royal family that had been built for King Rama VII only six years before, is named Klai Kangwon, which directly translates to "far from worry." After contacting both his advisors from within the Kingdom of Siam and his foreign advisors from neighboring and Western countries, King Rama VII realized the monarchy did not stand a chance, as they were unprepared and in the minority. To prevent bloodshed, King Rama VII was essentially forced to capitulate and accept the People's Party's constitution and demands. The People's Party had succeeded in ending the absolute monarchy that had existed in Siam since its creation, and according to the requests of the revolutionary group, the royal family was forced to cede their power to the people of Thailand. Although it took many years of plotting, the People's Party managed to carry out a successful, bloodless coup d'état in only a few hours, leading to the institution of a constitutional regime.

Subsequent Events and Effects of the Thai Revolution of 1932

With the growing dissatisfaction in Thailand during the reigns of the last two absolute monarchist kings, a rebellion was bound to happen at some point, as we can see in the aborted rebellion against King Rama VI in 1912 that had been planned by members of the military. That being said, although the majority of people shared their disgust with the royal government, most people did not agree with the People's Party's revolution.

Although the revolution is often looked at in a positive way, especially at the time by non-Thai scholars who didn't yet know how history would play out, the People's Party's coup was not well taken by much of the country. Many civilians, especially those outside of Bangkok who felt a similar discontent with the government, had nothing to do with the revolution at all and felt the rebellion was just a movement that represented the wants of a small group of students, military and government officials, and Bangkok civilians. To them, this revolution was not what the Kingdom of Siam's population as a whole wanted. Considering the fact that the revolution lacked the country's support, the initial success of the People's Party's movement was short-lived.

On June 26ᵗʰ, 1932, less than two days after the Thai revolution of 1932, the People's Party apologized to the ling and the royal family for the radical and offensive manifesto and requested their help. Despite the Khana Ratsadon's (People's Party) promises of democratic change, King Rama VII and his royal family continued to share power with the newly appointed government in a constitutional monarchist system. This constitutional system, with both the new governing powers and the king running the nation together, continued for the next fifteen years, with the royal family's power gradually diminishing throughout that period.

Chapter 8 – The Constitutional Monarchy and Military Dictatorships (1932–1945)

The People's Party's First Decisions and the Constitutional Monarchy

Similar to the revolution itself, which was incredibly well planned and unbelievably successful, with essentially no issues at all despite all that could have gone wrong, the People's Party had been meticulously planning out many aspects of their future government practices. However, unlike the revolution, their well-thought-out new political system did not go as planned.

In 1932, following the coup, Pridi Phanomyong helped to craft the constitution that would detail the king and his role in the government and how the power would be gradually transferred to a new democratic governing order. The transference of power was supposed to occur in three stages. First, the People's Party would appoint seventy government representatives, made up of both members of the People's Party and, in a democratic fashion, new non-royal officials who played no part in the revolution at all. This way, the People's Party would be staying true to their democratic goals without flooding the government with completely new, untrained people. The government would still be made up of many of the king's government officials, who had the experience necessary to train the new representatives to ensure the transition of power went smoothly.

In the second stage, the People's Party would continue to gradually rule out the king's men from governmental positions unless they were chosen by the people to remain. Finally, during the third period, the power would be completely transferred, and the political system would be completely democratic. The plan was that once the government had reached the third stage of the transition plan, all government officials would be democratically elected by the population and not appointed directly by any higher force, so neither the king nor the People's Party would have the power to decide officials; it would instead be up to the regular civilians.

Their goal was for the nation to reach the final government form once at least 50 percent of the population had a primary education, which was a readily growing number due to the efforts of King Rama V and the laws made by King Rama VI. That being said, if half the population had still not completed their primary education within ten years of the creation of the constitution, which was finalized on December 10th, 1932, the final stage would begin regardless.

During these ten years, the People's Party promised to help improve the nation's economy and help send more Thais to receive a post-secondary education. The push for education would come as no surprise since the People's Party was made up almost entirely of university-educated scholars, intellectuals, and military officials. The party set up the University of Moral and Political Science, which would attempt to make higher education more common and widespread throughout the nation. Considering the People's Party inherited a post-Great Depression Thailand, they had no choice but to reform the government's economic policies to help remedy the country's fiscal issues. Some economic changes that the People's Party promised following the revolution and delivered on were putting an end to the overcharging of interest and the confiscation of agriculturalists' properties.

The members of the People's Party were well aware that their new power would require them to tackle some of the financial issues the kingdom had been facing over the past few decades. At the beginning of 1933, not even a year after the Thai revolution of 1932, Pridi wrote an economic plan that he announced to the government, which, at this point, was still dominated by the king's chosen officials. His plan was aggressive, radical, and significantly more democratic and socialist than the old, more conservative government officials were willing to accept. It was even too extreme for the new officials to put into place. The almost communist-leaning economic plan, which detailed Pridi's goals of nationalizing all industrial and commercial assets and enterprises and making all workers into state employees, upset just about everyone.

Pridi Phanomyong's economic plan was so controversial that it was not only rejected immediately with no deliberation, but it also earned him the reputation of a somewhat deranged communist, a reputation that would follow him for the rest of his life. The radical economic plan upset so many people that Pridi was temporarily exiled, and to avoid further complications, the king temporarily suspended the newly formed National Assembly. Although King Rama VII suspended the National

Assembly in order to prevent any more governmental controversies that may turn off more royalists, the People's Party realized that this meant their own power would be temporarily limited. The radical plan also led to the removal of the first prime minister of Thailand, Phraya Manopakorn Nititada, who was elected by the People's Party directly after the revolution, meaning he didn't hold his office for even a full year.

With the People's Party being so new, they feared that even a temporary suspension of the National Assembly might allow the king and his royal order to regain their power over the government. To prevent any attempts to steal back control of the nation, the People's Party's military leaders forced King Rama VII to revive the National Assembly. Less than a year after the first coup, a new coup to reconstitute the National Assembly took place. It was led by Luang Phibunsongkhram (Phibun). While in the process of reviving the National Assembly, Phibun installed a longtime member of the People's Party, Phraya Phahon Phayuhasena, as the second prime minister of Siam.

Between the People's Party's democratic ideologies, Pridi Phanomyong's socialist economic plan, and the military leaders forcing the reconstitution of the National Assembly, the royalists, especially the older and more conservative ones, were not pleased with the new government. The royalists demonstrated their discontent in a countercoup rebellion that took place over the course of a few tense days in October of 1933. Although King Rama VII had no involvement in the rebellion, it was led by his cousin, Prince Boworadet. In this battle, Lieutenant Colonel Phibun's military intelligence and prowess would once again shine, as he led his troops and suppressed the countercoup within only three days of intense fighting. Though King Rama VII had absolutely no involvement or connection to the royalist rebellion in 1933, it was at this point that he felt his position was no longer personally maintainable. A few months after the attempted countercoup, King Rama VII left the country and moved to England, and just over a year after that, he abdicated his role as king. Although Siam was no longer a nation led by a monarch, Prince Ananda Mahidol, who would become King Rama VIII, was named as the successor to the throne, but seeing as the prince was only nine at the time and studying abroad in Switzerland, a regency council would act in his place until he returned.

Phibunsongkhram (Phibun) was already considered to be an impressive military leader following the Thai revolution of 1932, but it took resisting the royalist rebellion of 1933 for him to come into public prominence. Although neither the previous royalist government nor the People's Party, or even the population for that matter, was fully aware of it at the time, Siam was slowly being controlled by its military. Led by Lieutenant Colonel Phibun, as well as other well-trained military officers, the military would continue to strengthen and gain power. Between the years of 1933 and 1938, the military grew and gained experience, even though it was only fighting internally within its own nation. In fact, the new and improved military run by the People's Party would not actually have the chance to face an external force or threat of any kind until 1941.

Only a few years after the Thai revolution of 1932, some obvious cracks were forming in the People's Party. The government was essentially split into three different groups, with the first being the royalists made up of the king's remaining family and conservative elitist royally-appointed officials. The second group was represented by the non-military members of the People's Party and the elected civilian government officials. The final group within the government was the military, led by extreme members of the People's Party and other well-disciplined military generals. The three rivaling factions would continue to battle for the upper hand in the subsequent years following the original revolution of 1932. Ultimately, through a series of military rebellions and coups that plagued the nation in the 1930s, the military wing would unsurprisingly triumph over the other two governmental factions. This would eventually lead to the military dictatorship that would control the country of Thailand for years to come.

Pridi Phanomyong returned to his home country in 1934, after just over a year of exile abroad. Upon returning to Siam, he founded the nation's second university, the aforementioned University of Moral and Political Science, also known as Thammasat University. By opening the university, Pridi was able to deliver on one of his core beliefs and promises at the beginning of his campaign, which was that higher education should be accessible to all who wanted it, not only those of the royal family. The same year he returned, he was elected as the minister of the interior, which would give him responsibility for appointing the governors of the provinces of Thailand, internal security, local administration, citizenship, and other facets of internal affairs. Not long after becoming the minister of the interior, he was appointed as the minister of foreign affairs. During his time holding this position, Pridi attempted to renegotiate all of the unfair treaties between Thailand and foreign, mostly European, countries. He would help to put an end to the remaining foreign countries' extraterritorial rights in Siam and limit the import taxes that Western countries had put in place to take advantage of Siam.

The Beginning of the Military Dictatorship in Thailand

Although Pridi Phanomyong represented the civilian wing of the government, it was essentially upon his return that the government's military faction began gaining power. In 1934, following Phibun's impressive triumphs over the royalists in their attempted countercoup, he became the country's minister of defense. Subsequent to his rise in rank, he would dedicate himself to strengthening the nation's army. Much like King Rama VI or King Rama VII, who also studied abroad, Phibun was inspired by Western governments and ideologies. Unlike the previous kings who seemed to take most of their inspiration from their time studying in Britain, Phibun was enamored and impressed with the Italian military fascist movement led by Benito Mussolini, which was occurring while Phibun had been in Europe. He realized the potential and power of nationalism and saw the effects of government-issued propaganda. On top of working to strengthen the nation's troops, he attempted to popularize military and nationalistic values based on those he had come to appreciate in Italy. He would push Italian propaganda films and started presenting himself as a hero to the Thai people. Though Pridi Phanomyong marked the beginning of many new privileges for the citizens of Siam, at the same time, the government was shifting toward a fascist regime that not only slowed the promised democratic changes down but also took away some of the civilians' rights and equalities.

Phibun was certainly aided throughout his time as minister of defense due to the fact that his backer, Phraya Phahon Phayuhasena, had been the prime minister of Siam. However, after being appointed as the second prime minister in 1933 following the Thai revolution of 1932, Phraya Phahon was involved in a scandal concerning shady real estate deals. After five years as the prime minister of Siam, Phraya Phahon was forced to retire, and the country held its first-ever election in 1937.

The 1937 election in Thailand would elect around half of the seats in the National Assembly. Pridi Phanomyong would be elected as the minister of finance, but more importantly, Phibun would be chosen as the new prime minister of Siam, becoming the country's first elected prime minister. He would assume the position in December of 1938 and began imposing his ultranationalistic beliefs on the population almost immediately. Although he was democratically elected, upon assuming the position of prime minister, the government, under his guidance, began tilting toward complete military fascism. Phibun essentially became the unofficial dictator of Siam. To assert his power, Prime Minister Phibunsongkhram arrested his opposition, especially the remaining royalists and members of the royal family who had long challenged his opinions. By doing so, Phibun was quite quickly dominating the civilians in office and, in many ways, moving away from the People's Party's initial plans of democracy and returning to a government that shared many similarities with absolute kingship.

Since Prime Minister Phibunsongkhram quite openly opposed the Chinese, who had inhabited Siam for centuries at this point, similar to beliefs held by many fascist dictators when it comes to people of other nationalities, the non-Thai civilians clashed with his ultranationalistic views. Phibun very quickly rolled out many policies that were intended to curb the Chinese civilians' success in the country. He tried his best to restrict Chinese education and limited the usage of Mandarin in Chinese schools. Phibun pushed to reduce Chinese immigration to Siam, and in 1939, he officially changed the name of the country from Siam to Thailand. This change was to rid the country of its name that had been assigned by foreigners and to push his anti-Chinese rhetoric that Thailand was the land for the Thai. Ironically enough, "Thai," a name given to the civilians of the Kingdom of Siam in 1238 upon their liberation of the controlling Khmer Empire, translates to "free." Although the Thai and the country of Thailand had been freed from oppressive forces many times throughout history, the name was changed in a period where civilians had their freedoms revoked.

While the democratic Pridi Phanomyong was acting as the country's minister of finance, working on revamping the taxation system to remove unfair taxes not based upon earnings, Phibun was using taxes to reduce Chinese economic power. The Chinese, who had arrived in Thailand centuries before for economic opportunities, had quite successful and prosperous businesses, which Phibun denounced, claiming they were trying to take opportunities away from the native Thais. He offered Thai-owned businesses subsidies and pushed civilians to support them rather than Chinese ones. All of these actions would lead officials with opposing views, especially those of Chinese heritage, to compare the Phibunsongkhram movement against the Chinese to what was occurring to the Jewish population in Germany around the same time (this was just prior to World War II).

While promoting anti-Chinese beliefs, Phibun felt it was necessary that the Thais developed their own culture that was distinct from the Chinese. Although the Thais had established a uniquely rich culture of their own, Phibun felt it had too many close ties with Chinese culture, which had helped to shape it. In 1939, Phibun issued a new national anthem, which, similar to any national anthem, pushes patriotism and ultranationalism. The anthem's lyrics detail the Thai civilians' responsibility and willingness to fight for their nation. Although the song quite fairly speaks of Thai independence, an understanding of the anti-Chinese events surrounding the inception of the song gives another meaning to lyrics such as "every inch of Thailand belongs to the Thais."

Similar to the kings who had preceded him, who had similarly studied in Europe before their reign, Phibun pushed his nationalistic beliefs by introducing new Western practices, which he believed would be necessary to modernize the country. Prime Minister Phibunsongkhram imposed decrees that encouraged the civilians to wear more Western-style fashions, an act that King Rama VI had tried to pass a few decades before and was faced with great adversity for doing so. Phibun succeeded where King Rama VI had failed, though, and prohibited betel chewing and made opium illegal. All those addicted to the substance were prosecuted and jailed. In 1940, he changed the traditional celebration of New Year's from April to the Western month of celebration in January, although the decree didn't take. Today, Thais celebrate both dates and have kept the April New Year's as their traditional celebration.

Thailand during World War II (1939-1945)

While pushing for fascist, Western-style, ultra-Thai nationalism, and anti-Chinese policies internally, World War II was beginning externally. Prime Minister Phibunsongkhram took advantage of France's misfortune in 1940 at the start of World War II and provoked a war with French Indochina to attempt to regain the land that had previously belonged to Thailand. The war waged between 1940 and 1941, but seeing as France was preoccupied in their home country, they were unable to resist Phibun's irredentist claims. Thailand regained their lost territory in Cambodia and Laos with the help of Japanese forces, which helped to form an alliance between the two countries.

As Phibun slowly shifted from being the prime minister to the country's military dictator, his appreciation for Japanese military practices grew. Throughout his reign, he was quite openly pro-Japanese, and an alliance had been forged between the two countries when Japan supported Phibun's claim to lost lands in Cambodia and Laos. At the start of World War II, Japan's own nationalistic views led it to join Germany, and along with Italy, the three countries formed the Axis Powers. Following Japan's attack on Pearl Harbor in the United States, which succeeded since no one saw it coming, Japan plotted a similar surprise attack in 1941 on British Singapore. To be able to reach Singapore unannounced, Japan planned to travel through Thailand, as an attack wouldn't be expected to come from that direction. In 1941, with the intention of surprising Singapore, Japanese troops entered Thailand, and since the two countries had previously forged an alliance, Japan requested the Thai government for the right of passage. The Thai government, not wanting to facilitate an attack on their Western allies, attempted to resist the Japanese troops. However, after only a brief period of battling, Phibun's pro-Japanese views and his realizations that resistance would probably only lead to the partial destruction of Thailand led him to sign a treaty of alliance with Japan, which would allow their new ally to peacefully cross through Thailand.

Just before and during World War II, the once-democratic People's Party had transitioned into a fully fascist military dictatorship led by elected Prime Minister Phibunsongkhram. This, of course, upset almost all of the original civilian members of the People's Party, including Pridi Phanomyong, Phibun's counterpart in the Thai revolution of 1932. Throughout the Phibun dictatorship, many of the civilians holding governmental positions were released of their duties and replaced with those who backed Phibun's fascist views. In 1941, following Phibun's signing of the treaty with Japan, which only strengthened the dictatorship's fascist rule, Pridi Phanomyong resigned as the minister of finance; however, whether it was by choice or force is still unknown. Pridi was assigned the role of regent in place of King Ananda Mahidol (King Rama VIII), who was not only quite young still but also stuck in Europe during World War II.

Following Thailand's treaty with Japan, Phibun and his government declared war on the Western countries that opposed Japan, specifically the United States and Great Britain, at the beginning of 1942. Thailand's signing of the treaty with Japan, Phibun's pro-fascist government, and the country's declaration of war on the United States and Britain would unravel many of the alliances that had been made between Thailand and the Western countries over the previous years and alienate Thailand from the West for years to come.

Considering the fact that the treaty signed between Japan and Thailand was formed not due to the alliance the two countries had built over the years but rather created to end a battle caused by a Japanese invasion, it is not surprising that the Japanese took advantage of their new privileges. Following the treaty, Thailand's government was increasingly undermined by the Japanese occupation, which caused both the Thai economy and population to suffer. The public began to lose trust in Phibun's government, which led to the creation of numerous resistance groups. Pridi Phanomyong, who was by this point anti-Japanese and completely against Phibun's government, led the Free Thai (*Seri Thai*) movement, a resistance group created to rid the country of the Japanese occupation. The Free Thai organization connected with resistance groups based in the West, mainly in the United States, which helped to revitalize Thailand's foreign relations in the future. Pridi Phanomyong, operating within the Thai resistance groups under the codename Ruth, organized rebellions against the Japanese and the Thai government. By 1944, when it became increasingly obvious that the Axis was not going to win, Phibun's government collapsed, and he was forced to resign in July of 1944. A civilian government, led unofficially by Pridi and headed officially by Khuang Aphaiwong, replaced Phibun's government. World War II officially ended on September 2nd, 1945.

Chapter 9 – Power Struggles in Thailand Post World War II (1945–1973)

Democratic Rule Post Phibunsongkhram's First Military Dictatorship

In 1944, Phibunsongkhram (Phibun) was forced to resign as the prime minister of Thailand, and he was replaced on July 31st by Khuang Aphaiwong. Khuang Aphaiwong was the son of a Thai governor, and like many children of government officials, he had gone on to study in the West. Khuang Aphaiwong pursued post-secondary education in engineering in France, and it was there that he made connections to Phibunsongkhram and Pridi Phanomyong. He was even one of the founding members of the People's Party. Although Khuang Aphaiwong would only hold the position of prime minister for a few months following the fall of Phibun's military rule, he would subsequently hold the position again two more times for similarly short periods over the next few years.

Khuang Aphaiwong's first period in office as acting prime minister of Thailand was unusual since he found himself wedged between the democratic civilians of the People's Party, now the Free Thai, and the military leaders that he had openly helped during the war (although he did not really have much choice in the matter if he wanted to keep his job). Though Khuang Aphaiwong was technically the prime minister, many of the decisions made by the government toward the end of and subsequent to World War II were actually made by Pridi Phanomyong, who was working behind the scenes.

In 1945, the last year of World War II, Thailand helped the Allies in every way possible. Pridi Phanomyong retracted Thailand's previous declaration of war against the United States and Britain and allowed the Allies free access in Bangkok. Very quickly after replacing Phibun, Pridi Phanomyong and Khuang Aphaiwong terminated the treaty the previous military dictator had signed with Japan, officially ending their alliance. These swift changes would help remedy Thailand's international reputation and prevent potential military threats from the west from occurring. This likely would have taken place had the government waited any longer. Under its new democratic rule, Thailand returned the territories in Laos and Cambodia that had been taken from France during World War II. Due to all of the reparations made toward the end of World War II, Thailand's global reputation was rectified, and the country was admitted to the United Nations in 1946. Directly following the end of the war, King Ananda Mahidol (King Rama VIII) was able to return from Europe, and Pridi Phanomyong was reassigned as a senior statesman, seeing as he was no longer needed as regent.

Despite the collapse of the military dictatorship bringing about a period of democracy, the government was far from secure. Just as they had at the beginning of the 1930s when the People's Party first took control of the government, many cracks appeared in the newly reigning democratic party. Although Khuang Aphaiwong and Pridi Phanomyong had helped to advance Thailand subsequent to the collapse of Phibun's reign, they were not united and began to fall out around the time World War II ended. Due to these instabilities, Khuang Aphaiwong was replaced by Thawi Bunyaket after only a year in office. Thawi would be replaced not even two months later by Seni Pramoj. Seni had been the original choice, but he wasn't available when Khuang stepped down. This would help to stabilize the party for a short period, but the party would never be truly united during their reign, which would eventually lead to their downfall.

In September of 1945, Seni Pramoj assumed the position of prime minister of Thailand. This would be Seni Pramoj's first stint as prime minister, a position he would hold four separate times over the course of the next few decades, for a combined total of only just about a year. Seni Pramoj was one of many living great-grandsons of King Rama II, and as with almost all of the younger generations of royal family members, he received a foreign education in the West. Seni attended Trent College, which is an English boarding school, and like King Rama VI, he went on to study at the prestigious Oxford University. At Oxford, Seni studied law, and after passing his bar exams, he returned to Bangkok to work as a junior judge. Although Seni was of royal blood, he was never truly opposed to the People's Party's coup in 1932, likely due to his education abroad. That being said, he was not necessarily fond of the members of the People's Party or how they ran the country. There are many rumors surrounding Seni Pramoj's opinions since his views on issues seemed to have greatly changed many times during World War II. At first, Seni publicly and firmly supported Phibun's government, but he seemed to completely reverse his opinions once the government signed the treaty with Japan. Despite his frequently varying opinions, Seni Pramoj became a symbol of the Thai resistance, which would aid him in being chosen as the prime minister at the end of World War II.

When Seni Pramoj was prime minister, he was, to his dismay, controlled by Pridi Phanomyong, just as Khuang Aphaiwong had been. Although the democratic government under Seni flourished, this period led to larger cracks in the People's Party and amongst the democrats in the country. Toward the end of Seni Pramoj's short term as prime minister, the country was suffering due to post-war alliances and reparations made with Western countries. To rid the air of war that remained between Thailand and Britain post World War II, Seni and his government signed a peace treaty in January of 1946, which Britain would only sign if Thailand agreed to post-war reparations, including cripplingly large amounts of rice. These post-war alliances led to serious financial difficulties, which led to the population's discontentment with Seni Pramoj's government. As the population's dissatisfaction grew, Seni left his post as prime minister, which was somewhat unjust since many of the upsetting decisions were actually made by Pridi Phanomyong. This would only aid to further the cracks in the democratic movements in Thailand and forge a rivalry of sorts between Seni Pramoj and Pridi Phanomyong. Seni was replaced by Khuang Aphaiwong, who took the position once again under his unofficially founded Democrat Party, which would be officially founded in April of 1946. This time around, Khuang assumed the position for less than three months.

Khuang Aphaiwong was prime minister for a little over fifty days, but seeing as his party was not properly established, he resigned on March

24th, 1946, following a vote of no-confidence. Khuang Aphaiwong would go on to formally establish the Democrat Party on April 6th, 1946, which would act as a rivaling democratic party to the People's Party and make it clear that the country's democratic forces had separated. Thailand's Democrat Party would illustrate the cracks that had formed in the People's Party, as Khuang Aphaiwong would be joined by Seni Pramoj since they both shared a distaste for Pridi Phanomyong, who had controlled them from behind the scenes during their respective periods as prime minister. The party would attract other democratic-leaning royalists, including Seni Pramoj's brother, Kukrit Pramoj, and members of the Thai resistance who had lost trust in the People's Party and specifically in Pridi Phanomyong.

Although every leader since 1932 had technically been democratically elected, it wasn't until 1946 that the country held its first popular election. This would mean that when Pridi Phanomyong was elected as prime minister in March of 1946, he was the first-ever prime minister elected fully by the people. Similar to when Pridi Phanomyong's People's Party took power in 1932, in 1946, Pridi came prepared to make some significant changes to the country without any delay. He very quickly passed a new constitution that would help to protect civilians' labor rights, return democratic power to the population, and hopefully reduce the military's power in Thailand's government once and for all. Pridi Phanomyong, who had been essentially running the government from behind the scenes since 1944, had finally earned his position as prime minister and intended to make the radical reforms he felt were necessary to restore Thailand, which had been rocked by both World War II and Phibun's abusive military dictatorship, which stripped the citizens of many of their liberties.

Though Pridi Phanomyong made initial progress at the start of his reign, making it seem like Thailand would finally be able to recover from the damages they had experienced over the past few decades, the peace was short-lived. On June 9th, 1946, twenty-year-old King Ananda Mahidol (King Rama VIII), who had only returned to his home country six months prior, was found dead. The young king was found in his bed in the royal palace, with the cause of death a gunshot wound. King Ananda Mahidol's death left just about everyone in confusion. No one was sure if it was an accident, a murder, or even suicide. Even the king's brother Bhumibol, who would become King Rama IX, claimed that it was certainly not a suicide or an accident, but he was still unsure as to what had happened. Seeing as Pridi Phanomyong's officials were never able to solve the investigation, the death was ruled as an accident, although almost no one in Thailand felt the case was closed.

The military leaders from Phibun's rule and the Democrat Party did not agree on much, but in some way, they unknowingly banded together in their mutual suspicion, or at least mutual blame, of Pridi Phanomyong, implicating him as the mastermind behind the death of the young King Ananda Mahidol. Throughout 1946, both the Democrat Party and the fallen military government spread their beliefs of the prime minister's involvement in King Ananda Mahidol's sudden death. The Democrat Party, being a more trusted organization at this point, was responsible for much of the propaganda. Trusted members of parliament from the Democrat Party would claim that Pridi Phanomyong had been the architect behind the king's death and that his death was truly an assassination. No matter what one believed, almost no one believed a proper investigation had been completed by the government or police at the time of the king's death. Pridi Phanomyong's case was not helped by the fact that his government had released very little information about the case, keeping most of the facts hidden from the public.

Whether Pridi Phanomyong was truly involved in the death of King Ananda Mahidol does not matter. In the end, the population lost trust in Pridi and his government, and the controversies surrounding his possible assassination attempt would weaken his government to the point of no return. On August 21st, 1946, after less than barely five months as prime minister, Pridi Phanomyong resigned. Pridi would publicly announce that he resigned due to his poor health, although it is more likely that he was forced by his party to do so. After being one of the leading members of the Thai revolution of 1932, Pridi Phanomyong would spend only a few years subsequent to his return from exile and the two years following World War II with any sort of power in the country. Following Pridi Phanomyong's resignation as prime minister, the position would be filled by various democratic leaders, including Khuang Aphaiwong, Seni Pramoj, and Kukrit Pramoj, who would each hold the office for short periods of time without the previous stability or security. Following King Ananda Mahidol's death, the throne would be succeeded by his nineteen-year-old brother Bhumibol Adulyadej, who became known as King Rama IX and would remain abroad until 1951. He would go on to become the longest-reigning monarch of Thailand and is, as of now, the second-longest reigning monarch of all time.

Pridi Phanomyong fled from Thailand once and for all in 1947. He moved to China and stayed there until 1970, when he then left Asia to return to France, the country that had inspired him to lead the revolutionary movement and push for democracy in Thailand in the first place. From both China and France, Pridi Phanomyong would speak out about his criticisms of the subsequent fascist Thailand governments that would rule throughout the rest of Pridi's life. From fleeing Thailand until his death, Pridi was never able to see true democracy in his home country, nor was he ever allowed to return. Seeing as no one, foreigners included, were allowed to discuss or even write about King Ananda Mahidol's tragic death, up to Pridi Phanomyong's death in 1983, he was regarded by most as a villain, as they saw him as being the one responsible for the assassination of King Ananda. It would not be until the end of the 20th century, when people were allowed to speak of the events surrounding King Ananda's death, that Pridi would be cleared of the suspicions clouding his name and recognized as an important revolutionary figure in Thailand's history. Years later, many scholars have made the case that it is actually more likely that Phibunsongkhram (Phibun) and his allies were responsible for the young king's death, especially considering how much the king's death worked in the military wing's favor. However, it is impossible to know what actually happened, as there are numerous theories regarding the young king's death.

Reinstatement of the Military Dictatorship with Phibunsongkhram as the Prime Minister

The fact that the population had turned against the democratic civilian-run government worked out perfectly for Phibun's military faction. Although Thailand's civilians, as well as foreign countries, had not necessarily gotten over Phibun's alliance with the Japanese and aggressive nationalism, they were even more disappointed with Pridi Phanomyong and his supporters. The intelligent yet manipulative Phibun and his military government played on the population's resentment of the democratic government's decisions after World War II. The military faction knew that the public resented the democratic-approved war reparations that had caused so much economic suffering in the years following the war. Although the post-war reparations were only necessary due to Phibun's decision to join the Japanese in fighting the Western Allies in World War II, the population was so dissatisfied with the crippling reparations that they turned their blame to the democratic government instead. Phibun's reputation amongst the civilians and foreign countries was also aided by the fact that he was always very openly anti-communist. His staunch anti-communism was especially sought after in the 20th century, as communism was growing in Thailand's neighboring countries. This meant that he earned the respect and support from other anti-communist leaders and countries, such as the United States.

In November of 1947, the military, led by Phibun and some other military generals who had backed Phibun during his military government, namely Phin Choonhavan, staged a coup, seizing the democratic civilian government. During the coup, Phibun threatened all those who still backed Pridi Phanomyong; it was during this coup that Pridi narrowly escaped Thailand, never to return to his home country.

Although Phibun and his military party had regained popularity in the country, the military faction was well aware that the population was not quite ready for them to take control of the government again. Thawal Thamrongnavaswadhi was the prime minister at the time of the military coup of 1937, and he still quietly supported Pridi Phanomyong. In their efforts to not anger the civilians while still removing or arresting all those who continued to support Pridi Phanomyong, the military faction named the democratic Khuang Abhaiwongse as interim prime minister until a new election could be held.

In January 1948, around two months after the military coup, the government held a general election, and although the military leaders did well, the military faction chose to keep Khuang Abhaiwongse as the prime minister to avoid any countercoups from the democratic civilians. Khuang Abhaiwongse continued being prime minister, although his power was limited by the military faction. Within a few months, the military powers were dissatisfied with Khuang's overly democratic practices, and in April of 1948, Khuang Abhaiwongse would be forced to resign.

Similar to the military reign preceding and during World War II, Phibun played a major role in leading the military movement. However, the coup of 1947 differs with that of the military reign, as this time around, Phibun shared his political power with two generals: General Phao Siyanon and General Sarit Thanarat. Both of these men had helped Phibun overthrow the People's Party's government in 1947. Over the next few years, during which military power continued to grow, General Phao Siyanon and General Sarit Thanarat would gain power over Phibun, and they would eventually depose him altogether a decade after reclaiming power over Thailand.

In 1948, Phibun would reassume the position of prime minister, which he would keep until 1957. Although he was gradually becoming less powerful than his younger counterparts, a rivalry between General Phao Siyanon and General Sarit Thanarat prevented either one from replacing Phibun. Throughout his term as prime minister, Phibun would share much of his power and make many of his decisions with the help of Phao Siyanon and Sarit Thanarat.

Akin to Phibun's reign as prime minister in the 1930s and early 1940s, Phibun's government was not exactly a true military dictatorship. Although it resembles one, with many of its policies being inspired by fascist governments, a true military dictatorship was not put in place until the power was taken away from Phibun in 1957. That being said, Phibun and his associates led Thailand with an iron fist and reintroduced many extreme, ultranationalist, and freedom-revoking practices, ones that Phibun had instituted during his first period as prime minister. To placate the unrest, a new constitution was formed with the help of the Democrat Party, before Khuang Abhaiwongse and his fellow party members were forced to take their leave. However, not long after, Phibun and his associates reinstituted the 1932 constitution, which would once again limit many of the civilians' rights. In 1946, prior to Phibun assuming the position of prime minister, the nation reverted its name back to Siam to retract some of the extreme nationalism that had led to the change in its name. However, in 1949, Phibun and his colleagues restored the country's name to Thailand, the land of the Thais. Once again, one must notice the irony in this timing, as the country's name also translates to "land of the free." Phibunsongkhram continued his anti-Chinese rhetoric, although this time around, this harassment was celebrated, seeing as the Chinese outside of Thailand were becoming increasingly communist during this time. Phibun reintroduced his Western-leaning beliefs and decrees, many of which were seen as negative, but some, such as the improvement of secondary education, resulted in positive changes for the nation.

Overall, the beginning of Phibun's reign was, unsurprisingly, not overwhelmingly well-received. Over the subsequent years after assuming the post, Phibun and his associates would have to deal with rebellions, coups, and unrest from almost every other governmental faction. Phibun survived rebellions by rival military factions in 1948, 1949, and 1951, though in 1951, Phibun was actually abducted. The military government was able to resist the three coups, and in 1951, following the brief abduction of the prime minister, they revoked the newly written constitution and replaced it with the 1932 constitution, the more restrictive one, instead.

Despite all of Phibun's and his associates' reimposed restrictive practices, the government during this period was and still is celebrated for their anti-communist actions. Immediately after reassuming the position of prime minister, Phibun began fighting the communists both internally within Thailand and externally within Thailand's neighboring countries.

The West began realizing the potential of an anti-communist country located so close to the rapidly growing communist countries in Asia. Phibun once again pushed for the suppression of the Chinese inhabitants in Thailand, this time in the name of fighting communism. Thailand aided the English and Malay troops in fighting against communists located in the south of Thailand around the Thailand-Malaysia border.

During the Korean War, which began in 1950, the United States sent money to help support Thailand's military. The government would use this money to send 4,000 Thai troops to help the United Nations fight against the communist Koreans. The United States' financial support would also fortify Thailand's economy, remedying many of the existing financial issues that had been affecting the country since King Rama VI's reign. Thailand would continue to help the United States and the United Nations fight the spread of communism in 1954 during the Cold War when Phibun helped to form SEATO (the Southeast Asia Treaty Organization), which was an anti-communist defense organization. Despite Phibun's results in fighting communism, both the Thai population and his military faction were growing dissatisfied with his use of power.

Considering General Phao Siyanon and General Sarit Thanarat were gradually becoming more powerful than Phibun, it should come as no surprise that he would eventually be replaced by one of them. As Phibun gained the confidence of foreign countries in his fight against communism, he lost the confidence of the population and his government. The middle- and higher-class citizens were becoming increasingly dissatisfied with Phibun's economic results. Although the nation's economic situation would improve due to the money sent by the United States, Phibun's nationalistic economic plan was proving to be unsuccessful. His military colleagues were equally discontent with his reign, and Sarit Thanarat would up being the one to lead the long-awaited coup against Phibun's tiresome reign. The coup, which took place in September of 1957, would successfully overthrow Phibun and force the man who had introduced the military government to Thailand into exile. In time, Sarit Thanarat would become the prime minister, who would introduce a true extreme military dictatorship to the country.

General Sarit Thanarat and his Successors' Military Dictatorships

In September of 1957, Sarit Thanarat was elected as field marshal, and a provisional prime minister named Pote Sarasin was appointed. In December of that year, a parliamentary election was held. On January 1st, 1958, Thanom Kittikachorn was chosen as the new prime minister, but he was overthrown by Sarit Thanarat on October 20th, 1958, due to another military coup, a system of toppling political leaders that had come to plague the country by this point.

Although Sarit Thanarat was even more fascist and extreme than his predecessor Phibun, he was respected by the population. The day after he assumed his position as prime minister, or rather dictator, Sarit Thanarat suspended the constitution, which would be officially replaced on January 28th, 1959. During Sarit Thanarat's term, he sought to clean Thailand up from crime and corruption and improve the country's economic practices and policies.

Sarit Thanarat only held this position of power until his death in 1963, during which time he would greatly reform the nation and help shape it into the country it is today. Almost immediately after overthrowing the previous government, Sarit Thanarat took Thailand's social issues into his own hands. He launched campaigns against corruption in the national police force, worked to lessen organized crime, and put an end to the drug consumption and trade, specifically of opium, in Thailand. In his short reign, he also completely transformed Thailand's education system, which, up to that point, had been seriously lacking in comparison to Western countries, which explains why most Thai intellectuals and royal family members would attend schools in Europe rather than Thailand.

Unlike the other democratic leaders and the military dictator Phibun, Sarit Thanarat sought the approval of the king, which at that time was still King Bhumibol Adulyadej (King Rama IX). By 1960, Sarit helped reestablish the monarchy's influence to a new generation, which had grown up without the monarchy being involved in the government or politics at all.

Sarit Thanarat would completely restructure the nation's economic policies, which were in serious need of an overhaul. Aided by the money Thailand was still receiving from the United States following Phibun's anti-communist practices, Thailand was able to grow its own products and take advantage of its own resources. Sarit Thanarat spent much of his time in office focusing on growing Thailand's domestic product and their foreign investments. Although the money the country was receiving from the United States was intended for the military, with much of it going toward that branch of government, Sarit Thanarat also used the money to construct new highways, establish rural economic development, build more schools, and make electricity more accessible. Similar to his predecessor Phibun, Sarit Thanarat was openly allied with the United States and was staunchly against communism, which was necessary for the country to keep receiving funds from America.

Despite all of the positive changes that Sarit Thanarat made, he oversaw a truly aggressive military dictatorship. Almost immediately after assuming the leadership position, Sarit dissolved the parliament, and after abolishing the constitution, he suspended all the democratic constitutional rights that the population had once again begun to get used to. Sarit Thanarat's authoritarian regime was marked by the limiting of free speech, which included the banning of newspapers and media that did not favor his political party, and the banning of other political parties. Although Sarit Thanarat was popular and achieved much good for the nation during his rule, his reputation became increasingly negative following his death in 1963. Although Sarit Thanarat had greatly opposed Phibun and the police force's corruption, only after his death did the truth come out about the ruler's own corrupt practices, which would haunt his and his successors' reputations.

In 1963, Sarit Thanarat was succeeded by Thanom Kittikachorn, who kept many of his predecessor's practices in place. Thanom Kittikachorn, who was helped by Praphas Charusathian, the Deputy Prime Minister of Thailand, continued to receive funds from the United States Army in exchange for further help against the communist countries. During Thanom Kittikachorn's military dictatorship, the United States military and, by 1969, over 11,000 Thai troops were involved in the war with Vietnam. Similar to their predecessors, Thanom Kittikachorn and Praphas Charusathian would accept American money that helped stimulate the Thai economy. Although this had been occurring for many years, it was only after Sarit Thanarat's death that people were made aware of the corruption surrounding the intake of American money, as these funds only helped to increase the gap between the rich and those beneath the poverty line.

Toward the end of the 1960s, between the dissatisfaction for the government's oppressive authoritarian rule and the obvious corruption occurring with the American money, the people, especially those in the working and middle classes, were displeased with the country's government. It would seem, once again, the rebellions would be in the hands of students. A revolution movement, led by students who had received foreign education and picked up democratic ideals in Europe, began holding public demonstrations to oppose the fascist government. The nation's discontent would continue to escalate between the end of the 1960s and the start of the 1970s until that fateful day of October 14th, 1973.

Chapter 10 – The Struggle for Democracy in Modern Thailand (1973–2020)

The 1973 Thai Popular Uprising

By the beginning of the 1970s, Thailand had endured twenty-five years of interrupted, strict military dictatorship rule under Phibunsongkhram (Phibun), Sarit Thanarat, Thanom Kittikachorn, and Praphas Charusathian. Similar to the years that led up to the Thai revolution of 1932, which overthrew the absolute monarchy, discontentment was growing amongst the population, who were tired of autocratic rule. These frustrations would be demonstrated through various student-led protests throughout the 1960s and the beginning of the 1970s. Thailand's dictator, Thanom Kittikachorn, just as King Rama VII had been before he was ousted, was well aware of the population's growing dissatisfaction. To try and placate the civilians, Thanom introduced some insignificant democratic reforms and promised to bring the country back toward a democratic government once communism, both internally and in neighboring countries, was triumphed. In 1971, Thanom Kittikachorn would remove the minor democratic changes he had made and reimpose the military rule, and in 1972, a new constitution was created that would strip the population of more freedoms than ever before.

In 1972, students from different universities in Thailand formed the National Student Center of Thailand (NSCT), with Thirayuth Boonmee, an engineering student, as the face of the movement. Throughout 1972 and 1973, the NSCT would organize dozens of nonviolent protests, which were intended to call out the Thai government's corruption, the American military occupation, and the mistreatment of civilians. Following a truly successful campaign against corrupt Japanese businesses, the student movement gained over 100,000 members and the confidence necessary to tackle the task of overthrowing their own government. The military rule did not prevent the students from protesting so long as it was nonviolent, and the king of Thailand actually encouraged them.

By the fall of 1973, the movement had gathered nearly half a million supporters. Throughout the months preceding the October revolution, the National Student Center of Thailand secretly created a new constitution and attempted to gather signatures from government officials and public figures who opposed the military rule. However, throughout the end of September and the beginning of October, the police began arresting protestors and became overall more aggressive against the supporters of the movement. All of this tension culminated on October 14th, 1973.

On October 14th, 1973, the student-led protesters flooded the streets and surrounded the royal palace, seeking to speak with the king to request he disband the military rule. Even though the protest began at around sunrise, the October 14th protest gathered more people than ever before, and this larger group meant that the police would not be able to easily disband or arrest all the protestors. To attempt to disperse the large group of protestors, the police released tear gas and became even more aggressive toward the group than they ever had before. This violence was met by rioting from the students, which the police responded to by bringing in armored cars, tanks, helicopters, and military troops. Machine guns were fired from every angle, with the crowd chaotically dispersing, trying to find cover. Many of the surrounding buildings were occupied by government officials, though, and other shelters, such as police booths, had been set on fire by the rioters. Finally, after more than half a day of protesting and rioting, the king stepped in to prevent further bloodshed and declared that Thanom Kittikachorn and Praphas Charusathian had resigned and fled the country. Only after the protest came to an end would the full gravity of the brutal fighting be known. The violence of October 14th, 1973, killed at least seventy-seven people and wounded hundreds. It is estimated at least 800 people were seriously injured.

A Brief Period of Democracy Following the 1973 Thai Popular Uprising

Seeing as King Bhumibol (Rama IX) had gained more influence throughout Sarit Thanarat's and his predecessors' dictatorships, he would be the one to call to an end to the fighting during the brutal 1973 revolution. He also appointed the new prime minister, Dr. Sanya Dharmasakti (or Thammasak), who was a former chief justice, a close advisor to the king, and the former dean of Thammasat University. In a speech made by Dr. Sanya Dharmasakti after being appointed as the interim prime minister of Thailand, he declared that he would draw up a new constitution, form a new government, and move the country toward democracy as quickly as possible. The National Student Center of Thailand (NSCT), who had helped overthrow Sanya Dharmasakti's predecessors, would aid in the creation of the new constitution and would help prevent counterprotests and violence against the nation's new democratic leader. The NSCT's hard work would be appreciated by the government and monarchy until they disbanded exactly a month after the revolutionary protest of October 14th, 1973. Sanya Dharmasakti's new democratic constitution was enacted in 1974, and under his leadership, the country had another brief period free from autocratic government. Although Thanom Kittikachorn was forced to flee Thailand following the events of the 1973 Thai popular uprising, he kept his position as supreme commander of the armed forces, which he operated from abroad, allowing him to retain significant power within the country.

Return to Military Government

Although Thailand was finally free of the military dictatorship that had been in control of the country for over a quarter of the decade, the nation was, once again, far from peaceful. Following the separation of the National Student Center of Thailand (NSCT) in 1973, the left-winged, democratic students split up into smaller student groups that became gradually more radical throughout the years following the Thai popular uprising. Public opinion of their radical leftist beliefs was not aided by the fact that the government could not triumph over the growing communist governments in neighboring countries, specifically in Vietnam, Cambodia, and Laos. Sanya Dharmasakti's government was unstable, and the population was growing fearful of the potential spread of communism throughout Thailand.

While the fascist military government had stripped the population of many of their rights, they at least had the military prowess to fight the growing communist threats from within and outside the country. The working- and middle-class civilians began forming anti-communist groups to protest the leftist government and to rival the democratic-verging-on-communist student groups. The population, even those who were left-leaning, felt that Thailand required a government that would be stronger than the growing communist threats, and they became dissatisfied with the government's unstable democratic rule. The population's discontent grew and culminated in the bloody and violent 6 October 1976 massacre between the two opposing groups. While the population's discontent grew, Thanom Kittikachorn returned to Thailand. Despite his aggressive policies only years before, upon his return, he was appreciated and celebrated by the royal family and much of the country's population. In 1976, with the support of King Rama IX and the unhappy middle- and working-class civilians, the military overthrew the democratic government and reinstated authoritarian rule. Although it would be Thanom Kittikachorn's return to Thailand that would lead to another coup, he did not directly participate in the new military government.

Considering the end of democracy would bring about another fascist military rule, those who did not agree with the change of government were forced underground. Many of the radical left-leaning students and civilians who had opposed the military government and had helped to take down the military rule during Thanom Kittikachorn's dictatorship would go into hiding in the country's jungles. The population's original unrest toward these radical leftist student groups was not unfounded since many of the extreme students would go on to join communist groups, namely the People's Liberation Army of Thailand (PLAT), which would later become known as the Communist Party of Thailand.

The new military government, led by Thanin Kraivichien, was quick to reinstate the extreme authoritarian practices that the country had gotten used to in the decades before. Almost immediately after taking power,

Thanin Kraivichien and his military government abolished Sanya Dharmasakti's democratic constitution and dissolved the parliament. Although the military government had placed Thanin Kraivichien in the role of prime minister to replace the previous democratic government, he very quickly became extreme in a way that even the military government knew would not be accepted, especially so quickly after replacing democracy. With the increased threat from the Communist Party of Thailand and with Thanin Kraivichien's government only focusing on external military affairs, the population was once again growing dissatisfied with the country's leadership. In 1977, the military government led another coup against their own leader, who was replaced with the less extreme General Kriangsak Chomanan.

A Democratic Shift in the Military Government

Although Thanin Kraivichien had been appointed as the prime minister by the authoritarian military government, his staunch right-wing military and political views were too extreme even for the military. He was replaced with Kriangsak Chomanan, who was on the complete opposite end of the spectrum. In the end, he would prove to be too democratic for the military. Kriangsak Chomanan helped establish some democratic practices within the government, including sharing the decision-making process with a parliament, a practice that had been terminated by his predecessor. Under Kriangsak Chomanan, the government enlisted more civilians in official positions, which would, in turn, give some power back to the people of Thailand. He also granted pardons to the radical left-wing revolutionary students, who had been jailed due to their extreme views in the 1976 massacre and when Thanin Kraivichien took over the country. Kriangsak Chomanan would quickly roll out a new, more democratic constitution, and he claimed that he planned to give more power to the parliament in later years. Kriangsak Chomanan's time in office marked a strange time in the country. During his term, the war against communism in the surrounding countries would continue to rage on, leaving many refugees of war trying to enter Thailand's borders. This would force him to adjust the country's strict immigration policies to accept the incoming refugees, who mostly came from Cambodia. Although his time as the leader of Thailand was short-lived, he would achieve many important democratic reforms that would help steer the country toward a less aggressive authoritarian rule in the coming years. By 1979, the military had become increasingly dissatisfied with Kriangsak Chomanan's democratic-leaning practices. Unlike the previous prime ministers, who almost all had resigned due to public resentment following a coup, Kriangsak Chomanan resigned voluntarily. Upon his resignation in 1980, the position of prime minister would be filled by Prem Tinsulanonda.

Prem Tinsulanonda is most notably remembered for eliminating the communist threats within Thailand. Although the Cold War was still raging on during his time as prime minister, the population of Thailand and other foreign countries were beginning to believe that the extreme anti-communist beliefs of Thailand's previous prime ministers were outdated. General Prem Tinsulanonda negotiated with the Communist Party of Thailand and granted amnesty to all Thai insurgents, many of whom had joined the communist movement when they were only young university students. With Prem Tinsulanonda as prime minister, Thailand's economic situation vastly improved. However, despite his improvements to the community, he was still more autocratic and military-driven and less democratic than his predecessor. Throughout his time in office, many rebellions and coups were launched against Prem Tinsulanonda and his military government, and the opposition would even go so far as to attempt to assassinate him. Aware of the public's resent toward him, Prem Tinsulanonda would hold a general election in 1988. He would subsequently be replaced as prime minister by Chatichai Choonhavan, who had won the greatest number of votes that election, making him the first elected government head since the reestablishment of the military government.

The Business Era

Chatichai Choonhavan, the leader of the Chart Thai Party (Thai Nation Party), would be elected prime minister of Thailand, who would help establish an unstable parliamentary rule rather than a military rule in Thailand. Chatichai Choonhavan sought to improve not just Thailand's financial situation but also the economy of Southeast Asia as a whole. Following the communist wars that had plagued the region for years, Chatichai Choonhavan claimed he wanted to transform Indochina from a battlefield into a marketplace. Chatichai filled his government with rich businessmen, and although he helped to improve the nation's and region's economic situation, his practices were extremely corrupt. After it was revealed that political positions were being illegally bought and sold, Chatichai Choonhavan was overthrown in a coup by the National Peacekeeping Council in 1991.

The coup was led by General Sunthorn Kongsompong and Commander in Chief Suchinda Kraprayoon, and although the former would have a larger role in overthrowing Chatichai Choonhavan's government, the latter would end up as the figurehead of the movement. Although Chatichai Choonhavan was not respected once his government's true corrupt practices were revealed, he was at least democratically elected by the people. The overthrowing of his government worried the population, as they did not want to lose their democratic privileges once again. To placate the civilians, the National Peacekeeping Council junta assured the population that proper elections would be held and that the respectable businessman Anand Panyarachun would be appointed as the interim prime minister. Although Anand Panyarachun was appointed by the military-run National Peacekeeping Council, he did not align with them politically and openly disagreed with their practices.

Thailand's Black (or Bloody) May

During the 1992 general election in Thailand, Narong Wongwan from the Justice Unity Party was elected as the new prime minister. However, he never truly assumed the post since he was involved in a scandal not long after being elected. The position of prime minister was instead given to General Suchinda Kraprayoon, who was one of the primary members of the junta that overthrew the Chatichai Choonhavan government. General Suchinda Kraprayoon assumed the position, despite the fact that he had assured the population that he would not become nor run for prime minister following his extreme coup d'état only years before.

The population was not pleased with this change, seeing as they had not chosen General Suchinda Kraprayoon and also due to his promises that he wouldn't assume the leadership position. His ascension in office was met with discontentment from the middle and working classes. Led by Chamlong Srimuang, they formed resistance movements and demonstrated their dissatisfaction with many large-scale protests.

The country was once again divided, this time into those, mainly the military and government, who supported Suchinda Kraprayoon and those led by Chamlong Srimuang, mostly the civilians, who wanted to finally achieve a stable democracy in the country. Unlike the previous revolutions, the democratic movement was not led by students but by a Thai politician and ex-army general. The population's unrest would culminate in May of 1992, which would come to be known as Thailand's Bloody May or Black May. Chamlong Srimuang led over 200,000 protestors to demonstrate in Bangkok, where they were met with resistance and violence from the pro-Suchinda Kraprayoon military. Although the battle only lasted for three days, between May 17th and May 20th, 1992, it is regarded as one of the bleakest periods in Thailand's modern history. Similar to Thailand's popular uprising of 1973, the violence of Bloody May only came to an end when King Bhumibol (Rama IX) intervened. King Bhumibol summoned both the democratic Chamlong Srimuang and the right-wing Suchinda Kraprayoon and delivered a famous discourse to the two men. In the translated words of King Bhumibol: "The nation belongs to everyone, not one or two specific people. Those who confront each other will all be the losers. And the loser of the losers will be the nation...For what purpose are you telling yourself that you're the winner when you're standing upon the ruins and debris?" Only after the king summoned both rivaling leaders could the country account for the damages done during the three days of violence. Bloody May would lead to thousands of arrests, hundreds of wounded civilians, and hundreds of unexplained disappearances. Although there were less than one hundred officially reported deaths, many believe that there were hundreds of more deaths that were hidden from the public eye or never reported upon. Losing almost all public support following the violence in the country's capital, Suchinda Kraprayoon resigned as prime minister, and Anand Panyarachun was reappointed as interim prime minister by the king until Thailand could hold proper elections.

The Most Democratic Government to Date

Democratic Government

The period following Thailand's Black May in 1992 would be the nation's most democratic period to date. The few months Anand Panyarachun spent as prime minister brought many democratic changes for the population, leading up to a democratic election in September of that year. In contrast with many other foreign countries, which only have two or perhaps three major parties, in Thailand's September 1992 election, there were five parties out of the eligible twelve parties that would amass competitive vote counts. With the votes spread between these five parties, no party would gain an absolute majority in this election or the subsequent elections held in 1995 and 1996. That being said, the Democrat Party, which was founded in 1946 by Khuang Aphaiwong, would head the government throughout the next decade due to its successful coalitions.

In 1992, Thailand's Democrat Party was headed by Chuan Leekpai, a former lawyer who had joined the Democrat Party and became a member of parliament in 1969. By 1991, Chuan Leekpai had risen in the party's ranks, and in 1992, when the Democrat Party took hold of the government, Chuan Leekpai became the country's prime minister. The newly elected prime minister would immediately begin making democratic social reforms, including making strides toward women's equality and lowering the voting age to eighteen to allow a wider margin of the population to elect future politicians. He also established an administrative court and enlarged the House of Representatives.

Despite Chuan Leekpai's rapid political and social democratic reforms, he was extremely slow in making any economic reforms. Although he had the support of the democratic left-leaning population, his approach to Thailand's finances left a good portion of the population dissatisfied. Although the divide had been gradually growing for years, it was during Chuan Leekpai's time in office that Thailand's civilians would truly be split between leftist democratic and right-leaning conservative political beliefs. Bangkok and the nation's southern towns and big cities would find themselves dominated by the more democratic population, while those in the northeast and central plains of the country tended to lean more toward conservative pro-military beliefs.

As Thailand's financial situation continued to worsen, public opinion of Chuan Leekpai, especially from the more conservative Thais, worsened as well. Thailand held another general election in 1995, and this time, Chuan Leekpai did not come out on top. That being said, Chuan Leekpai would be reelected in 1997.

Banharn Silpa-archa and Chavalit Yongchaiyudh, respectively, were the country's prime ministers between Chuan Leekpai's bookend periods in office. The former's time as prime minister was short-lived due to corruption scandals, and the latter would inherit one of the nation's worst economic periods to date. During 1997, while Chavalit Yongchaiyudh was serving as prime minister, Thailand's currency, the baht, was severely depreciated in comparison to the United States dollar at the time. The devaluing of the baht would essentially cause the Asian financial crisis, which would completely ruin Thailand and other Southeast Asian countries' economies in the subsequent years. Before the end of 1997, the Thai stock market would completely drop, and the nation would acquire severe debt due to necessary financial help from the International Monetary Fund (IMF), which would only aid to cripple their economy over the following years. Although many people associate the country's economic crisis with Chuan Leekpai's poor economic practices in the years preceding the Asian financial crisis, Chavalit Yongchaiyudh would take the brunt of the blame and would resign in late 1997. The country held an election once again in 1997, and Chuan Leekpai was once more elected as prime minister. During Chuan Leekpai's second term, the government was unstable, just as the two democratic governments run by his predecessors had been. Although Chuan Leekpai's government would enact a new constitution that would allow the population the most democratic freedoms they had ever seen, with the constitution having been completed during Chavalit Yongchaiyudh's time in office, Chuan Leekpai did little to aid the struggling economy. Chuan Leekpai would hold his position as prime minister until the country's election in 2001.

The Thaksin Era

Chuan Leekpai was succeeded by Thaksin Shinawatra, who was the founder of the Thai Rak Thai ("Thais Love Thais") Party. Thaksin Shinawatra had originally trained to be a police officer and even earned a scholarship to study criminal justice in the United States to advance his career. Over the years subsequent to earning his degrees, Thaksin Shinawatra rose in the ranks of the police force and spent much of his spare time focusing on computer technology, which he was extremely gifted in. Unfortunately, he could not find employment in the field, seeing as it was the 1980s. Toward the end of the 1980s, Thaksin Shinawatra would leave the force and begin investing time and money into his technological businesses, joined by his wife, Potjaman. The road was not easy for the pair, but by the end of the decade, Thaksin Shinawatra's dedication paid off, as he would found a mobile phone operator and a telecommunications company, which would, by the 1990s, make him one of the wealthiest people in Thailand.

Thaksin Shinawatra had brushed with politics throughout his career, but it was not until 1994 that he would take a vested interest in becoming a member of the political sphere. In 1998, he founded the Thai Rak Thai (TRT) Party, which would be elected as the governing party in the 2001 election. Thaksin Shinawatra would officially succeed Chuan Leekpai as prime minister in February of that year. In many ways, Thaksin became the politician that much of the population had been waiting for, seeing as he understood the economy, believed in democracy, and aligned politically with the views of the more conservative population in northern and northeastern Thailand. With his impressive business record, he was also supported by Thailand's elite business owners.

When Thaksin and his party assumed office at the beginning of 2001, he almost immediately set out on delivering the promises that he had made during his campaign. The rapid reforms were a welcome change, seeing as how his predecessors were criticized for their ineffective, slow output speed. Thaksin increased his popularity with the rural population, as he commenced rural development and set forth agrarian debt relief. During his time as prime minister, Thaksin Shinawatra set up a more affordable and accessible healthcare system to help the lower-income population in Thailand and invested and reformed the education system. Thaksin was largely respected due to his swift actions throughout his entire time in office. This was not just limited to delivering on his campaign promises but also in his response to the 2004 Indian Ocean tsunami.

Despite all of Thaksin's positive reforms made throughout his time as prime minister, his private business practices made him somewhat of a controversial leader. Before he was elected as prime minister, Thaksin Shinawatra and his Thai Rak Thai Party funded campaigns and advertising with private funds, much of which came from his own financial resources. Seeing as this had not yet been done before, many people saw this practice as buying votes. Throughout his term, he would face many prosecutions on different accounts relating to his secretive financial and business practices. Although he would be reelected in the subsequent election, and although he was extremely popular and highly praised, Thaksin's time in office was marked by the incredible scrutiny relating to his potential fraud, corruption, and cronyism.

An election was held in 2005, and for the first time in Thailand's history, Thaksin Shinawatra and his Thai Rak Thai Party won by an absolute majority, which would give the party a majority of the seats in parliament and give Thaksin ultimately more control than his democratic predecessors had. However, before a year had passed, Thaksin would become increasingly controversial. He would sell his self-founded telecommunications company in early 2006, but he was secretive about the taxes involved in the selling process. On top of that, Thaksin Shinawatra had begun taking advantage of King Bhumibol's old age in an attempt to gain more power before the king's successor took over. To add fuel to the fire, in his later years, Thaksin Shinawatra was addressing foreign insurgencies with military force rather than political solutions. Overall, the population became dissatisfied with their once beloved leader, as it seemed he was attempting to manipulate the royal family, the parliament, and the population.

Toward the end of 2005, the population's resentment was growing, which they demonstrated through rallies staged in the nation's capital. The resistance movement, which was run by the urban middle class, became known officially as the People's Alliance for Democracy (PAD) and unofficially as the Yellow Shirts since, as the name would suggest, they wore yellow shirts at their rallies. Although Thaksin was aware of the growing urban dissatisfaction, he was still confident in the rural population's support, and at the beginning of 2006, he called for an election to prove his popularity. While his party did win by a majority, the election had been boycotted, and the results were ruled invalid. Although Thaksin remained as interim prime minister throughout the year, by the fall, he was overthrown by a military coup led by Sonthi Boonyaratglin, who would assume leadership until being replaced by Surayud Chulanont. Thaksin Shinawatra would be exiled from the country, and his finances would continue to be investigated. In 2008, Thaksin was prosecuted and served time on the grounds of corruption.

Surayud Chulanont would hold the leadership position until the country would hold its first election following the coup of Thaksin Shinawatra in 2008. Samak Sundaravej, who helped to form his pro-Thaksin People Power Party (PPP), was elected as prime minister in the 2008 election. Considering his support of the ousted prime minister, many believed Samak Sundaravej and his government were controlled by Thaksin Shinawatra behind the scenes, although these claims were never proven to be true. However, regardless of Thaksin Shinawatra's involvement in the government or not, the urban middle-class population who had protested Thaksin's leadership were not pleased with their new government.

Protests by Both the Yellow Shirts and Red Shirts

Considering the fact that the newly elected People Power Party was completely pro-Thaksin, political unrest continued to grow. The Yellow Shirts (People's Alliance for Democracy, or PAD), which was an ever-growing democratic, Thaksin resistance group, continued to stage protests following Samak Sundaravej's election as prime minister. They felt that no change had been made from their last protest that had helped to overthrow Thaksin since Samak Sundaravej was essentially no different than his predecessor. They believed that Samak was merely standing in until the government could get Thaksin back in office. In September of 2008, Samak Sundaravej, who was forced to resign due to illegally accepting payments for TV cooking show appearances, was succeeded by Somchai Wongsawat, who was actually Thaksin's brother-in-law.

The election of Thaksin's brother-in-law, Somchai Wongsawat, unsurprisingly caused significant political unrest in the country, especially those in the Yellow Shirts (PAD) movement. To oppose the growing anti-Thaksin Yellow Shirts movement, those who had remained supporters of Thaksin formed a rival movement called the United Front for

Democracy Against Dictatorship (UDD), which, somewhat similar to their opposition, became known as the Red Shirts due to the color of their uniform. Many of the Red Shirts lived in rural northern and northeastern Thailand, although there were some urban supporters of the movement as well.

Over the subsequent years, the two groups clashed many times, with the yellow-shirted PAD members protesting in hopes of electing a new anti-Thaksin government and the red-shirted UDD supporting Thaksin and his successors' governments. In 2008, the anti-Thaksin PAD flooded the Bangkok airports with protestors, which grew to become violent quite quickly. Only a few months later, on December 2nd, 2008, Somchai Wongsawat was forcibly removed from office and replaced by the Democrat Party's leader, Abhisit Vejjajiva. Meanwhile, the red-shirted UDD organized their own protests, which became significantly more frequent and aggressive following the removal of Somchai Wongsawat.

The Red Shirts' protesting would culminate at the beginning of 2010 following Thaksin's guilty charges of corruption during his time as prime minister. The pro-Thaksin movement protested both the government's order to seize Thaksin's fortune and Somchai Wongsawat's replacement, who they demanded should resign. In March of that year, the Red Shirts flooded Bangkok's commercial district, where they protested for two months. Although the first month of protesting was mostly nonviolent, by mid-April, the government became more aggressive toward the Red Shirts' occupation of the city's shopping district. As a result, the second month of protesting became increasingly more violent until May, when the military finally used force to remove the protestors. This would end in a bloody battle on May 19th, with shopping centers being set on fire, hundreds of protestors being arrested and/or injured, and almost 100 people being killed.

These protests would not bring the Red Shirts any real success until July of 2011, when the pro-Thaksin Phak Puea Thai Party (PPT) was elected, with Thaksin's younger sister, Yingluck Shinawatra, as its head. Although Yingluck Shinawatra would become Thailand's first female prime minister, she was a wildly controversial leader. Her election would be met with political unrest from those in the People's Alliance for Democracy (the Yellow Shirts movement), who believed she was only a proxy for her brother. At the beginning of her term, she swiftly aided those who had been affected by the country's heavy monsoon rains, but her positive public opinion was short-lived. First, Yingluck Shinawatra was involved in a scandal surrounding corrupt rice sales, which ended up greatly crippling Thailand's economy, and then her government attempted to introduce an amnesty bill. This bill would have granted amnesty to all the politicians involved in the previous years' political drama, including Thaksin. This was, of course, met with political protests from the Yellow Shirts. Shortly after attempting to pass the amnesty bill, Yingluck Shinawatra would be forced to resign, and her position would be filled once again by an interim prime minister.

The End of Democracy and the Beginning of a New Military Dictatorship

Yingluck Shinawatra's interim successor, Niwattumrong Boonsongpaisan, was in office for around two weeks before the government was overthrown once again by another military coup in 2014, this time led by the highest-ranking member of the Thai military, General Prayuth Chan-ocha (or Prayut Chan-o-cha). In May of 2014, General Prayuth Chan-ocha assumed the position as the nation's prime minister, a position he still holds today at the beginning of 2021. General Prayuth Chan-ocha would immediately invoke military law, and although it was certainly not the first time the population of Thailand had endured an authoritarian military dictatorship, the shift of power was incredibly difficult, as the nation had become quite used to democracy.

Prayuth Chan-ocha's military government sought to establish stability in the country that had faced so many struggles for power in the years since the fall of the monarchy; thus, his government became known as the National Council for Peace and Order (NCPO). In the year following the 2014 coup, Prayuth Chan-ocha stripped the population of many of their democratic rights under martial law. He quickly imposed a curfew, limited public gatherings, banned media that spoke out against his government, and took away the right to protest for both the Red Shirt and Yellow Shirt movements. On April 1st, 2015, just under a year after assuming the leadership of the country, Prayuth Chan-ocha lifted martial law and created a constitution, which underwent many alterations over the next few months until finally being released in August of 2016. On October 13th, 2016, King Bhumibol (King Rama IX), the monarch who had brought the spotlight and influence back to Thailand's royal family, passed away at eighty-eight years old. He was succeeded by his son Vajiralongkorn, who would become known as King Rama X, the country's tenth king in an unbroken familial chain of monarchs known as the Chakri dynasty. King Vajiralongkorn is associated with many controversies; their full extent is unknown, as after ascending the throne, Prayuth Chan-ocha enacted strict lèse-majesté laws, which prevents anyone from speaking ill of the king within or outside of the country. These lèse-majesté laws are just another example of Prayuth Chan-ocha's strict authoritarian rule, which upset both the population of Thailand and the foreign countries with whom Thailand once held strong alliances. In response to foreign pressure, Prayuth Chan-ocha promised the country would hold an election in 2017, and although this would be delayed, Thailand would have its first election since being placed under martial rule in 2019. Prayuth Chan-ocha was reelected as prime minister, and his government still remains in power as of January 2021.

Conclusion

As of January 2021, Thailand is still led by a military government, which may come as a surprise to those who did not have a full grasp of the tumultuous political history of the country. Between the years 1238 and 1932, the country was led by an absolute monarchy. During the Sukhothai, Ayutthaya, and Thonburi periods, the kings would help to forge much of the nation's unique culture through establishing its traditions, religion, and language. In 1782, King Rama I, the first member of the still-ruling Chakri dynasty, would take the throne and move the capital city to Bangkok. Between 1782 and 1932, the country, which was controlled by Rama I and his relatives, would establish its global presence and modernize many of its practices, beliefs, and traditions into what they are today. Though Thailand, then known as Siam, spent its entire history until the 20th century under an absolute monarchist rule, foreign countries were developing their own governments, which were separate from the ruling crown. It would be Western-educated Thai students, who had begun their plotting in Europe, who would overthrow and finally put an end to the absolute monarchy through the Thai revolution of 1932.

Following the Thai revolution of 1932, the government was almost never stable, as it constantly shifted between democratic and authoritarian military governments. The curious thing was that every time the democrats would take office, Thailand would need a stricter government to carry them through economic challenges or military threats, and every time the military government took office, they would help solve those issues but take their autocratic rule too far, stripping the population of their rights, which would end in protests and revolutions. For the past six years, the government has returned to a military dictatorship. However, who knows how long it will last, as the country has never been able to strike a balance between the two radical forms of government.

Part 3: History of Vietnam

A Captivating Guide to Vietnamese History

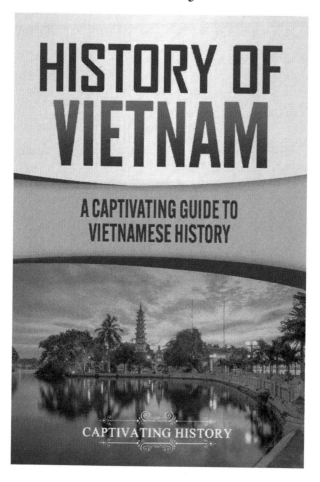

Introduction

Before the Common Era, the area in and around what is now known as Vietnam was populated by a wide variety of people from differing ethnic groups. It was not until about the 11th century that the word "Viet" was used to describe the land occupied by the Viet people, first known as the "Lac" or "Lac Viet."

Within Vietnam today, there are still a number of different ethnic groups. Though the majority of people in Vietnam speak the same form of the Vietic language, about 10 percent of the population (nearly ten million people) speak a Chinese dialect, Khmer, and a number of languages native to the remote highlands of the country. For many in the educated classes, French was a second language for many years, though that has been replaced by greater numbers of people speaking English as a second language.

Though all the people who are citizens of Vietnam are Vietnamese, that does not mean all the people are ethnically the same. The majority ethnic group is the Kinh, which comprises a little less than 90 percent of the people. The Kinh majority inhabit the Red River Delta in the north, the central coastal delta area, the Mekong Delta in the south, and most of the major cities.

There is a total of fifty-four recognized ethnic groups in Vietnam. The largest non-Vietnamese ethnic groups are the Tay, Thai, Muong, Hoa, Khmer, and Nung. Each of these groups numbers about one million people and are located in various places in the country, mostly in the western borderlands with Cambodia and Laos and in the mountain highlands in both northern and southern Vietnam. Other groups number from hundreds of thousands to only several hundred people. To keep things a little simpler, in this book, all of the people of Vietnam will be referred to as "Vietnamese" unless it is imperative to specify an ethnic group to more fully understand the history.

Modern Vietnamese is written with Latin letters ("A, B, C, D," etc.) but with a variety of unique diacritics to adjust the alphabet to spoken Vietnamese. For example, the Vietnamese kingdom of the early 11th century was called "Đại Việt." You can see the diacritical marks on the "D," "a," and the "e." For the ease of writing, this book leaves these diacritical marks out for the most part. (Speaking of reading and writing, Vietnam has one of the highest literacy rates in Asia—some 95 percent of the population can read and write.)

The Vietnamese language and its offshoots are branches of what linguists call the Austroasiatic language family and are descended from the Mon-Khmer language group.

ArnoldPlaton, based on the maps Austroaziatisch.PNG and Se asia lang map.png, edited by Nnemo, Copyrighted free use, via Wikimedia Commons
https://commons.wikimedia.org/wiki/File:Austroasiatic-en.svg

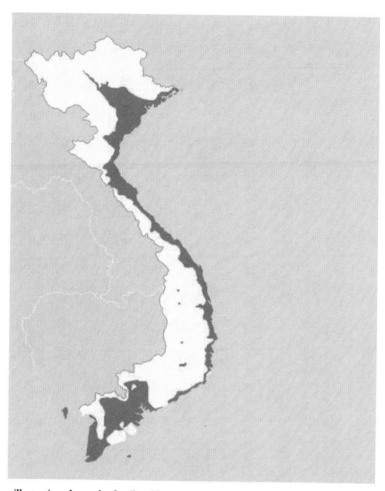

The top illustration shows the family of languages that include Vietnamese. On the bottom, the dark green shows areas where Vietnamese is the dominant language. yellow represents minority language groups.
Kwamikagami at English Wikipedia, CC BY-SA 3.0 <https://creativecommons.org/licenses/by-sa/3.0>, via Wikimedia Commons https://commons.wikimedia.org/wiki/File:Natively_Vietnamese-speaking_areas.png

In ancient times right through to the early modern era, the emperors, kings, and tribal and clan leaders of the various peoples of Vietnam struggled with China, their giant neighbor, for the right to govern themselves, sometimes successfully and sometimes not. These struggles were not always military; at times, they were political, economic, cultural, or some combination of all three.

There were also times during the many centuries of Chinese influence that the people of Vietnam and China enjoyed peaceful and harmonious relations, but this was always with the understanding that China was the "superior partner." The Vietnamese ensured some modicum of self-rule as long as they sent proper tribute to the Chinese in terms of riches, goods, deferential language, and political obedience.

When the Chinese dynasties became weak and more concerned with staying in power or were focused on other issues closer to home (for example, the arrival of the English and other Europeans in the late 17th and early 18th centuries), the Vietnamese made bids for greater autonomy or even complete freedom from Chinese influence. From 1802 to the early 1880s, the Vietnamese Nguyen dynasty ruled, for the most part, free from Chinese influence.

In the 1880s, the French, who had arrived in Vietnam in the 1850s, essentially took over the Vietnamese kingdom but allowed the Nguyen royal family to remain as figureheads. French rule lasted until 1940, when the fall of France to the Nazis resulted in Germany's allies, Japan, asserting itself in Vietnam. One would have thought the Japanese would have only remained in the country until 1945 when Japan was defeated, but many Japanese remained behind to be used by the returning French as an interim police force while they reestablished their own control of the country, something which earned the French few Vietnamese friends.

From 1946 to 1954, the French fought a bloody war against the Vietnamese communists, which resulted in a French defeat and the creation of North Vietnam. Communist attempts to conquer the south through a variety of means in the post-WWII "Cold War" resulted in increased American involvement in Southeast Asia with the aim of keeping South Vietnam free of communism. As you may already know, the Vietnam War (1963-1975) was a shocking defeat for the United

States and resulted in the unification of Vietnam under the Communist Party of Vietnam.

In 1978, the Vietnamese launched an invasion on neighboring Cambodia after a series of cross-border incidents. The Vietnamese victory there put an end to the genocidal regime of Pol Pot, but it also incurred the wrath of China, which was a Cambodian ally and had been estranged from Vietnam for some time. After a month of heavy fighting, both sides declared victory. The Vietnamese remained in Cambodia, and the Chinese seized some land along the northern Vietnamese border and in the South China Sea.

In 1986, the Vietnamese government began a serious effort to modernize the economy of the country and move it from a primarily agricultural state to an industrial one. In doing so, they have gradually eased controls on free enterprise, and today, Vietnam, while still relatively poor in comparison to First World nations such as the United States and Japan, enjoys a much higher standard of living than could have possibly been imagined in 1975 at the end of the Vietnam War. We hope you will enjoy learning more about the history of Vietnam, one of the most fascinating countries in the world.

Chapter 1 – The Basics

In 1965, US President Lyndon B. Johnson greatly increased the number of American troops in Vietnam. At the time, many people were saying that Johnson was "sending American boys to fight and die halfway across the world to a country most Americans had never heard of and couldn't find on a map." And in 1965, this was true. In 1975, most Americans could easily find Vietnam on a map, and many wished they had never even heard of the country.

Today, Vietnam is very seldom a topic in American or Western news media. Still, lately, as of September 2020, Vietnam has been praised for its early and effective response to the Covid-19 pandemic. The nation has had relatively few cases, especially when you consider its vicinity to Wuhan, the province in China where the coronavirus is believed to have originated.

That being the case, many people in the United States and elsewhere once again might have trouble finding Vietnam on a map and likely don't know much about the Southeast Asian nation other than the Vietnam War.

The population of Vietnam in 2018 was approximately 97 million people. The bulk of the population lives near the nation's long coastlines.

The capital of Vietnam is Hanoi, which is located near where the Red River empties into the Pacific Ocean/South China Sea after a journey of about 750 miles from Yunnan province in China, through the mountains and forests of north Vietnam, to the delta region between Hanoi and Vietnam's main port of Hai Phong. The population of Vietnam's capital is 7.7 million people, which includes its immediate surroundings.

Vietnam's "second city," Ho Chi Minh City (better known to many Americans as its older name of Saigon), is located in the far south of the country and is also situated in a river delta area, the Mekong Delta, which was the scene of much fighting in the Vietnam War. Ho Chi Minh City is the most populous city in Vietnam, with 10.4 million people.

Mekong Delta

The Erica Chang, CC BY 3.0 <https://creativecommons.org/licenses/by/3.0>, via Wikimedia Commons https://commons.wikimedia.org/wiki/File:Mekong_Delta,_Vietnam_-_panoramio_(3).jpg

Other large metropolitan areas include Hai Phong (population 2 million), the central city of Danang (1.3 million), and the ancient royal city of Hue, located on the central coast (population 500,000). Other significant population centers dot the coastline, while the interior of the country is still mostly rural but with some larger towns and villages.

An approximate four million Vietnamese (or people who identify as ethnically Vietnamese) live in countries around the world, primarily the United States, Australia, France, and South Korea. A significant number of people from Vietnam who belong to the minority ethnic groups of the country also live in other nations around the world. The vast majority of these people are refugees from South Vietnam and/or their descendants.

Since Vietnam has been governed by the communists since 1975, organized religion has been suppressed and discouraged, though many Vietnamese hold private beliefs, probably more than the government suspects. The CIA World Factbook and other references estimate that some 82 percent of the country are non-believers. However, there is believed to be an estimated 7.8 percent Buddhist, 6.6 percent Catholic, 0.9 percent Protestant, and 0.1 percent Muslim. Two other belief systems unique to Vietnam are the Hoa Hao and Cao Dai, which comprise about 3 percent.

In the United States, the Vietnam War is sometimes referred to as "the first televised war." During the war, the news media had relatively unfettered access to the troops and the battlefield. Often, Americans would be watching live reports from the battlefield while they were eating their dinner (Vietnam is half a day or so from most US time zones).

The overwhelming impression that most people got of the geography of Vietnam was that it was all jungle, and while rainforests do cover much of the country, especially in the south, not all of that is what one might typically identify as "jungle" in the sort of Hollywood sense. Although the southern quarter of the country, especially inland, has much jungle, Vietnam's wooded areas are very similar to the forests of other nations, especially when one considers the northern part of the country.

Much of the country, especially in the north and south, is covered in rice paddies, as rice has been the main agricultural crop of the nation for centuries. Other agricultural products include sugarcane, cassava, sweet potatoes, a variety of nuts, and corn. In the central highlands of the country, coffee and tea are widely grown. Vietnam is the second-largest coffee exporter in the world. To this day, especially in the rice fields, cultivation is highly labor-intensive, and it is done by hand and oxen.

Some fruit is grown, such as bananas, mangoes, and coconuts, and the rubber tree plantations that were widely destroyed during the war are making a comeback.

Agricultural work still employs half of the nation's labor force, though agriculture only contributes to about 14 percent of Vietnam's gross domestic product (this figure also includes lumber and fishing production).

Since the 1990s, Vietnam has made a concerted effort to modernize its economy, and today, it is beginning to take some consumer manufacturing business away from China since Chinese salaries and production costs have increased. Manufactured goods include a variety of wood products, electronics (both industrial and consumer), and construction/packaging materials. Amazingly, one of Vietnam's largest trading partners is the United States, which imports about 20 percent of Vietnam's exported goods.

Vietnam is resource-rich for its size, and it has significant deposits of coal, phosphates, manganese, bauxite, and rare earth elements, which are used in the making of computers and smartphones. It also has some deposits of offshore oil and natural gas, which are major points of contention with China.

Vietnam is 331,210 square kilometers in size (310,070 land/21,140 water), which makes it approximately the same size as Italy, whose shape is somewhat similar. As mentioned earlier, the climate and geography of the south and north are quite different. The country is only 1,100 miles north of the equator, and it's located somewhat between the Indian and Pacific Oceans, which makes it humid in virtually all areas of the country throughout the year.

The north is subtropical, with a climate similar to Louisiana in the United States. As one moves southward, Vietnam becomes a tropical country, with the aforementioned jungles beginning to form at about the "waist" of the nation. Near the southern coasts, the climate is much like Florida most of the year—hot and exceedingly humid, with a mean temperature of 82°F/27.7°C. In the extreme and remote northeast of the country, in the Hoang Lien Mountains, the average temperature is 46°F/8°C, and sub-zero temperatures have been recorded at times.

The Hoang Lien Mountains in summer
Christophe95, CC BY-SA 4.0 <https://creativecommons.org/licenses/by-sa/4.0>, via Wikimedia Commons https://commons.wikimedia.org/wiki/File:Ho%C3%A0ng_Li%C3%AAn_S%C6%A1n_mountains_from_Sa_P a.jpg

Vietnam is susceptible to monsoons, which strike with regularity, though the devastatingly destructive monsoons that frequently come ashore in India and Bangladesh to the east are rare. However, because of its coastal nature and the mountains, which hem much of the country in the east, rainfall in Vietnam is quite high. The "rainy season" runs from August/September to December in much of the north and from September to December in the central coast and the south. Most of the rain falls in an exceedingly wet stretch in October and November. Overall, about 60 to 95 inches of rain falls annually, though, in some places, that is frequently exceeded and comes closer to 200 inches of rain in a year.

Chapter 2 – Ancient Vietnam

It is an old adage that the "victors write history." In the case of ancient Vietnam, this is quite true. With very few exceptions, what we know about Vietnam before 1 CE was not recorded by the Vietnamese themselves. Some parts of their history, such as wars, natural disasters, myths, laws, and dynastic records, were recorded by the Vietnamese, but virtually all of it was destroyed or removed by the Ming dynasty in around 1400 CE. Therefore, much of what we know about Vietnamese history before 1400 does not come from the Vietnamese themselves, and it should be taken with a grain of salt.

The borders of today's Vietnam were not the home of the Vietnamese people of ancient times. Today, most historians and anthropologists believe that the Vietnamese "nation" (meaning those who identified as Vietnamese, though it should be noted that did not become a word until much later) originated in China, south of the Yangtze River, and expanded south into the area of the Red River Delta near today's Hanoi, which was the southernmost border of their territory.

China itself was a land of many clans, tribes, and different ethnic groups (today, there are fifty-five recognized ethnic groups in China). Under the great emperor Shi Huangdi (sometimes spelled as Shih Huang-ti), these groups were brought under the control of one dynasty, the Qin, in 221 BCE. One of these groups was known as the Nan Yue or Nan Yuet, meaning "Southern Yue(t)" people. "Yue" or "Yuet" (one sees both in history texts) is a stone ax that is designed to be carried on the shoulder. The earliest reference to these people comes from circa 1300 to 1046 BCE on bone inscriptions from the late Shang dynasty in China. This was the earliest recorded Chinese dynasty, which ruled from 1600 to 1046 BCE.

The bone inscriptions record questions about the Yue people, such as "Will the Yue be made to come?" and "Will Yue be obtained?" These are messages asking if the Yue people will bow before the Shang or if they will be conquered and added to the Shang Empire.

The pronunciation of the Chinese "Yue(t)" sounds very clipped, and the Vietnamese pronunciation of the word is "Viet." Thus, the Nan Yuet was the "southern Viet" people, but at this time, south meant the Red River Delta, not as in the former South Vietnam.

Late in the 1st millennium BCE, Shi Huangdi and others began to press southward toward the borders of today's Vietnam. The Nan Yuet were apparently not eager to submit to Shi Huangdi, his warlords, or his governors, but they were not in a position to resist such great power, so they fled farther south. As they did, not only did the area of the Red River Delta become populated with Nan Yuet, but large numbers of them pressed farther south as well.

The lands to the south of the Red River Delta were not empty, as they contained a variety of different peoples and tribes, among them Mon-Khmer and Tai speaking peoples. The Khmer are the ancestors of today's Cambodians and have occupied various areas of Southeast Asia for millennia. The Tai mentioned here should not be confused with the Thais of today's Thailand—they are two entirely different groups of people. Also occupying parts of Vietnam were the Cham people, who populated areas in the central part of the country, especially near the coast. While the Khmer and the Tai were from mainland Asia, the Cham are an Austronesian group, meaning they originated from various islands and offshore areas of the region and migrated by sea to today's Vietnam. Over time, many of the people in the area began to refer to themselves as the new immigrants to the area did, as "Viets." However, both the Khmer (especially in the south) and the Cham retained their own identities and kingdoms, and both would fight a series of wars with the Viet people.

It should also be remembered that not all "Yuet" people left China. A sizable portion remained in today's China. Some would become subsumed by intermarriage and integration, while others would retain their "Viet" identity for some time, living in the border areas of China and Vietnam in a time when the borders were fluid and war frequent.

The Vietnamese creation myth explains the spread of the Viet people from China to Vietnam. According to this legend, there was an immortal fairy living in the mountains. She is called Âu Cơ. She fell in love with Lạc Long Quân, "Dragon Lord of the Lac," who rescued her from an attacking monster while she was flying back to the mountains from the sea. She bore one hundred eggs, but unfortunately for the pair, both suffered from extreme homesickness. The fairy needed to return to the mountains and the dragon lord to the sea. They agreed that they would each take fifty children and raise them alone. Âu Cơ returned to the mountains of northern Vietnam, and Lạc Long Quân went back to the southern sea.

In addition to Âu Cơ, Vietnamese spiritual beliefs included many mother spirits. Most of these represented water in some way, as water is not only necessary for life, but it is an important element of the Vietnamese environment. Vietnam can be incredibly rainy, as we have seen. The Red and Mekong Rivers, along with many others, play important economic and social roles, and the sea is never far away, especially for those in the central part of the country.

Ask any Vietnamese, and they will tell you that while the people of both northern and southern Vietnam are one people, the people from the two regions are very different. Northerners are said to be more reserved and quieter, while the southerners are more outgoing and brusquer—just like a fairy and a dragon.

Vietnamese culture differed from Chinese culture in a number of important ways. Firstly, there was their language. Not only was the spoken word different, but so was the written word. Originally, the Viet used Chinese characters, but over time, these morphed into a unique written language called Chu Nom, meaning "the southern letters," which, of course, reflected the location of the Viet people. Today, Vietnamese use the Latin script brought to them by the French, though with a myriad of tonal/diacritical marks.

Another very significant difference was the structure of Chinese society from about 600 BCE onward compared with that of the Viet people. Given its size and history, there were obviously a great number of influences on Chinese culture, such as geography, history, influential rulers, natural and man-made disasters, wars, and much else. Here though, we are speaking about the philosophical underpinnings of Chinese society for much of its history. There are four major influences on Chinese religious philosophy: Confucianism, Taoism, Buddhism, and traditional folk beliefs. (Note: some historians refrain from calling Taoism and Confucianism "religions" and call them solely "philosophies," while others see the same kind of spiritual and moral elements contained in other religions around the world in their guiding principles and history.)

Though Taoism did have some effect and influence on elements of Vietnamese society through the centuries, it was the philosophy of Confucius (or "Kongzi/Kong Fuzi," meaning "Master Kong") that played a much greater role. That role was not always positive, at least not in the eyes of many Vietnamese.

Confucius is thought to have lived sometime in the 6th century BCE. Throughout the centuries, other philosophers added to Confucius's writings to give us Neo-Confucianism, which played a major role in both China and Vietnam in the Middle Ages and beyond.

When the Han dynasty (200 BCE-220 BCE) came to power in China, the philosophy of Confucius became what we today might call the "state religion." Almost every aspect of Chinese society was touched by Confucian thought. Perhaps most famously, Confucius's *Analects* (his writings) became the basis of the Chinese civil service examinations, the first such examinations in history. Upon obtaining a successful score or a passing grade on the exams, one entered the government service on a local, provincial, or perhaps even national level. There were tests for each level, with each becoming progressively more difficult and less accessible to the "lower classes of the upper classes." Essentially, the exams were tests on the writings of Confucius, famous commentaries on them by other great thinkers, and, to an extent, how they applied to everyday life or government affairs. A great number of topics were covered in the civil service exams, as you can see from the two questions below.

Discuss: Pei Du presented the idea that the Prime Minister should be able to discuss plans with sages and advisers in his own house. (Note: during Pei's time, every discussion needed to be done at court before the emperor.)

Can people learn goodness by themselves, or do they need great teachers to guide them? If we want to restrain the spread of evil thoughts around the country and encourage Confucianism, what can we do?

In 111 BCE, the Han dynasty moved south (meaning the southern parts of China not yet under their control and what is today northern and north-central Vietnam). When they did, they brought along concepts of Confucianism with them. Vietnamese rulers and their courts lived, for the most part, according to Confucian tenets until Vietnam achieved its independence from China in 939 CE, then again for a short time in the early 1400s when the Chinese invaded once more.

There were many benefits to the Confucian system, most specifically, the organization of the civil service. Confucianism also teaches benevolence, the love of humanity, moderation in all things, and harmony with nature. To some degree or another, these are human values that are not unique to the Chinese or the Vietnamese, but the Vietnamese had some issues with Confucianism.

Firstly, Confucianism was a Chinese belief system. Within that small sentence, you can see two problems. Vietnam was being dominated by a foreign power to whom they were forced to pay tribute. And secondly, over the centuries, Vietnamese society had developed into an almost matriarchal society. While women were infrequently the rulers of the country, they held great influence at the highest levels of court, and they were the authority in the home and, many times, the village. This holds true to a great degree to this day. Perhaps a better adjective is "matrifocal," as the mother is the focus of society, the glue that holds the family and society together.

Chinese society was quite the opposite. Though the empress and other female members of the royal family could wield great power at times, there was no doubt that Chinese society was a male-dominated one, from the top down.

But how does this relate to Confucianism? One of the pillars of Confucian philosophy is the ideal of filial piety. Volumes have been written in many languages just on the notion of Confucian filial piety itself, but for our purposes here, "filial piety" means loyalty to the family within a strict hierarchy—with the father and other males at the top. In the case of an empire, this begins with the emperor and proceeds down into the provinces, cities, towns, and villages. The empire was envisioned as a great family, with the emperor as the "great father." Within the home, this meant that the father held virtually all the power.

At the top levels of Vietnamese society, Confucian ideas were adopted or imposed. At the lower levels of society, Confucian ideas were taught and spread from city to village with varying levels of success. This spread of ideas that went against Vietnamese beliefs caused confusion and strife within their society.

Another aspect of Confucianism that was resented by the Vietnamese was the emphasis on the subordination of the individual. For many reasons (perhaps partially due to the rugged nature of Vietnam's geography and definitely due to the influence of Buddhism, which we will elaborate upon later), Vietnam had developed into a society where the individual was responsible to himself or herself first; this is in marked contrast to Chinese society to the present day.

When the Han defeated Vietnam, or "Nan Yuet," in 111 BCE, they did not intend to rule the Vietnamese directly, at least at first. They demanded regular tribute and men to fill the ranks of their armies when needed, but other than that, they generally let the Vietnamese be. However, by 40 CE, the Han dynasty had experienced a number of rebellions within China and was no longer in the mood to allow its various foreign regions to govern themselves. Under Emperor Guangwu, they began to impose direct Chinese rule on Vietnam and other regions.

The Han began to enforce Chinese law and administrative structures on the Vietnamese. They also demanded changes to the structure of Vietnamese society and began to try to shift the territory of the Nan Yuet from a somewhat matriarchal one to a strictly paternal one. For example, the traditional Chinese marriage system had the new bride move into her spouse's home, which was ruled by the father. In Vietnamese tradition (until only recently), the prospective son moved in with the bride's family, which was usually headed by the mother.

These changes were not welcomed by many Vietnamese. Two of them were the Trung sisters: Trung Trac and Trung Nhi. (As with much of Asia, in Vietnam, the family name comes first. This is sometimes temporarily changed in the case of international business or permanently when one immigrates to the West, but it is the most obvious example of the importance of family in many Asian cultures.)

The Trung sisters (known in Vietnam as Hai Ba Trung, "Two Ladies [named] Trung") were members of the Vietnamese upper class and lived in rural northern Vietnam, likely on the Red River. They were highly educated and had both been instructed in the martial arts of the time. Their birthdates are unknown, but Trung Trac was the elder, and they were probably born in the first decade of the first millennium.

The Trung sisters were directly affected by the Chinese emperor's order regarding the structure of Vietnamese marriage and family life. The Trung sisters were the designated heirs of their father's property and position/titles (he was a local law officer), something that did not happen under Chinese Confucian rule.

The Trung sisters were also married to the same man, Thi Sach, which was not an unknown situation at the time. Thi Sach was accused by the local Chinese governor of plotting against the Chinese and was beheaded. There were reported Chinese atrocities, including mass murder and rape. However, the Chinese accounts of the Trung rebellion do not mention these at all.

In response, the Trung sisters began a large and open rebellion. They gathered together many of the leading families of northern Vietnam, and within a short time, they had taken over a swath of land that stretched from within today's Chinese territorial border with Vietnam southward to the city of Hue on the central coast. In about a year, they controlled some sixty-five cities and towns. In 40 CE, at Me Linh in the Red River Delta, the Trung sisters declared themselves queens of the area (no one is sure what they called their territory).

Of course, at this time, news traveled slowly, and the Han Chinese imperial capital of Chang'an (today's Xi'an in central China, which is noted for its Terracotta Army) was over 900 miles away. Thus, to get the news, formulate a plan, organize an army, and get their forces to Vietnam took time. The empire of the Trung sisters lasted three years, from 40 to 43 CE.

However, when the Chinese did arrive, it was in overwhelming strength. The first battle, which took place near present-day Hanoi, was a defeat for the Trung sisters, as were the following two battles. Rather than be taken captive, the sisters drowned themselves at the confluence of the Day and Red Rivers in 43 CE. Today, they are Vietnamese national heroes, with pagodas and streets named for them throughout the country.

The failure of the Trung sisters' revolt ushered in 500 years of Chinese rule (43–544 CE).

The relationship between the Vietnamese and Chinese during this time was one of stress and tension. It was not really in a direct way, although local rebellions would appear from time to time; it was more as if there was a tension under the surface. Chinese rule during these years would intermittently be harsh or relatively lenient. In essence, the Chinese generally administered over the province by using Vietnamese officials to attend the day-to-day affairs, such as collecting taxes and tribute. Very generally speaking, the Chinese were satisfied if they received their tribute and taxes and if the Vietnamese (at least at the top) observed the Confucian tenets. A later Vietnamese saying from the late 1600s could apply to this earlier period as well: "Phap vua thua le lang," or "The imperial order falls before the rules and customs of the village."

There were pluses to being a tributary of the Chinese empire. In times of peace and imperial stability, trade flourished, as China had a seemingly never-ending need for goods and resources of all types, especially Vietnamese wood. Pirates operated off the coastlines, some of them Chinese, some Vietnamese, and some from other lands, such as today's Indonesia. To a degree, Chinese power could act against these marauders, and China kept the peace to a large degree between the peoples of Southeast Asia.

Still, foreign rule is foreign rule, and in 544 CE, another sizable revolt erupted in Jiaozhi province, which was what the Chinese called the area around the Red River Delta and the mountains and forests to its west. At this time, the central and southern parts of today's Vietnam were tribal and clan areas, which, for the most part, were not tributaries of the Chinese.

In addition to the simple fact that the Viet people were being ruled by foreigners, many in the area chafed at the changes the Chinese were continually trying to impose or reinforce upon them. Along with Confucianism, the Chinese Taoist philosophy also made inroads into Vietnam.

Originating at about the same time (2500 BCE) as Confucianism, Taoism was originally a philosophy rather than a religion. It extolled a natural order like Confucianism, with which it blended over time. However, unlike Confucian and other thoughts, Taoism included much about the nature of the universe and the "Way" or "Tao" of life within it. Much of Taoism was passive, involving meditation and a reverence for nature to a much greater degree than Confucianism. Over time, Taoism also developed aspects of religion, with monks, temples, rites, etc. In addition, Taoism had elements of ancestor worship within it, which fit very well with traditional Vietnamese beliefs.

As a result, some of what Taoism taught melded well with traditional Vietnamese beliefs, but one aspect, in particular, was problematic. Throughout Vietnamese history, some leaders, whether they be political or cultural, have had a quality that went against a major tenet of Taoism. That is *Te* ("tay").

Te is spiritual power and can refer to a spirit or deity of some kind. *Te* can also refer to power as made manifest in human beings and human relations. Traditionally, great leaders (whether male or female) among the Vietnamese have had a quality called *uy tin* (pronounced "wee tin"). This has many meanings, including a sort of charisma, an ability to lead, a desire to help the people, and a feeling of patriotic empathy. People who have this quality can be easily recognized, and many times in Vietnamese history, they have been chosen to lead, whether by a movement, a village, an association of some type, or a political party. The keyword here is *chosen*.

"Te," on the other hand (at least in everyday terms), can be described as "raw power." Rather than being chosen by the people or a movement, a person (or family, party, etc.) seizes power and then uses power and force to get what they want.

In a nation that valued *uy tin*, a Chinese philosophy that sometimes seemed to value *Te* over anything else was foreign. So, in 544, a rebellion arose in the Red River Delta.

The problems in this area started long before. In the late 300s and early 400s, the ruling Jin dynasty in China split into the Eastern Jin and Western Jin, then fell in 420. The period between 420 and 589 is known in Chinese history as the time of the Northern and Southern dynasties, as warring factions, warlords, and powerful families fought each other for power. As the different groups of China fought each other, Chinese power in Vietnam waned. The Vietnamese knew the time was ripe for an attack.

The eastern part of the Red River Delta was virtually impassible on foot or horseback, and it had not been mapped by the Chinese for decades, if not longer. On Chinese maps, the area was much smaller than it was in reality. The silt and erosion of the Red River had reclaimed much of the land (or rather swamp and jungle-like delta) from the sea. The Chinese didn't even know this land was there, but the Vietnamese did, and rebels gathered there in the thousands.

A later Vietnamese source described the area: "It is covered with thick forest and shrub and there is a hard base in the middle of it, around which there is nothing but mud and swamp. The place is hard to travel for humans and horse and can only be reached by canoes. But if one does not know the route he would be still be lost and fall into the water and be bitten by worms or snakes and die." This sounds like the perfect place from which to launch a guerrilla war, and this was exactly what the Vietnamese had to do, for they were vastly outnumbered by the Chinese.

The leader of this rebellion was Ly Bi, who was actually Chinese. He saw an opportunity to form his own kingdom of Chinese and Vietnamese people in the south. Ly Bi looked back in history for a name for his kingdom and found it in the 200s BCE. The leader of that rebellion, Zhao Tuo (in Vietnamese, "Trieu Da"), had called his kingdom Nan Yue- ("the Kingdom of the Southern Yue"). This implied it was separate from China but that it was also an equal kingdom, at least diplomatically. Because of the internal struggles going on within China, Zhao Tuo's kingdom was recognized by the Chinese in 204 BCE. Over the course of the next 107 years, the new dynasty in Nan Yuet was called the "Zhao" in Chinese and the "Trieu" in Vietnamese. Zhao Tuo, his son, and grandson expanded their empire to the south and west, laying the first foundations for the borders of today's Vietnam, as you can see below.

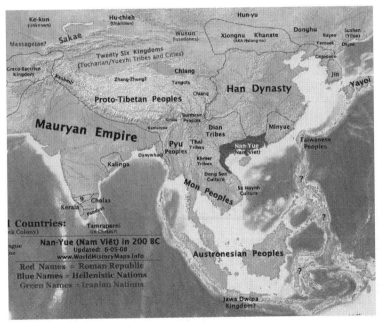

Illustration 7: Here, you can see how much of the Nan Yue Kingdom comprised part of southern China in 200 BCE.
The original uploader was Sea888 at English Wikipedia., CC BY-SA 3.0 <https://creativecommons.org/licenses/by-sa/3.0>, via Wikimedia Commons https://commons.wikimedia.org/wiki/File:Nam-Viet_200bc.jpg

Partly inspired by Zhao Tuo, Ly Bi successfully repelled a Thai invasion from the south in 543, as well as two Chinese attacks, but in 545, the Chinese attacked again and defeated his army of 20,000 men. Ly was forced to flee to the western mountains of northern Vietnam, but he was ambushed by Lao tribesmen in 548 and decapitated. His head was delivered to the Chinese for a reward.

Still, Ly Bi had left a strong army to his heirs, and the Chinese were more concerned with events farther north, so the Ly family and army came back, defeating the Chinese in 550. From 550 to 571, the Ly family ruled the Nan Yue Kingdom, though bickering within the family and the ruling classes weakened them. The Chinese returned in 571, attacking on and off until they overthrew the Ly family and reestablished Chinese control under the new Sui dynasty (589-618). The Chinese gave the region a new name, which would stick in various degrees up until French dominion in the 19th and 20th centuries. They called it the Protectorate of Annam ("the Pacified South"). When the French took over what is known today as Vietnam, they called a large part of it "Annam" and the people in it "Annamese," which loosely translated to "pacified southerners." As one might expect, this was not something the Vietnamese liked.

Ly Bi's kingdom wasn't tailored to Vietnamese society. Ly didn't overthrow the Chinese Confucian system, as he had grown up in it. He just replaced Chinese rule with his. The Trung sisters, who had set up a brief "kingdom" of their own, would've recognized Ly's empire as alien, as it was not really Vietnamese.

One of the things that Ly Bi is noted for was the incorporation of Buddhism in the governance of his realm. Unlike Taoism and Confucianism, Buddhism was not Chinese. It had originated in India and spread to Southeast Asia in the 200s BCE, mostly in the southern and western areas, though some believe it spread from China about 400 years later.

Buddhism, like Christianity and Islam, has many sects. Though there are many schools of Buddhist thought, the main branches are Theravada Buddhism, Mahayana Buddhism, and Vajrayana Buddhism. Most Vietnamese practiced a form of Mahayana Buddhism, as do Buddhists in Vietnam today (though their number is far lower than before 1975). For some time, though, various Buddhist schools of thought were influential in different parts of the country.

Like many other areas of the Buddhist world, the Vietnamese took the teachings that came from India and made it their own. Elements of Taoism and native spirit worship (such as that of Âu Cơ and Lạc Long Quân, as well as elemental river, forest, wind spirits, etc.) were fused with elements of Chinese folk worship and the teaching of the Buddha and the great Buddhist masters.

Ly Bi recognized the influence of Buddhism in the country, which was mainly in the rural areas at the time, and one of the first things he did was erect an eight-foot-tall statue of the Amitabha Buddha, the great savior Buddha. Contemporary sources indicate that by this time, Buddhism had really taken root among the people, and they practiced the chanting of sutras (sayings or rules from Buddhist scripture) and had come to believe that Buddhist monks had magical, superhuman powers.

Eventually, another form of Buddhism, known in Vietnamese as *Thien* and to the Japanese and others as Zen, also arrived in Vietnam. Zen emphasized meditation and contemplation more than the study of texts and the chanting of sutras. Later, in the early 20th century, a new, unique Vietnamese religious sect known as the Hoa Hao rose up. It incorporated aspects of Buddhism and especially emphasized the value of the individual's practice of religious rites and thought rather than the teachings of hermit monks and old writings. Throughout time, the Vietnamese have become determined to do things their way, with varying degrees of success.

During the Chinese Tang dynasty (618-907), the official religion of the Chinese Empire was Taoism, which has some similarities with Buddhism (meditation, the transient nature of existence, etc.). At times, Taoist monks and officials were tolerant of Buddhism in Vietnam, and at other times, they persecuted it, especially in times of rebellion or imperial weakness. They tore down temples and frequently destroyed bells, which held a special place not only within some forms of Buddhist prayer but also in Vietnamese culture. Occasionally, archaeologists will find these bells in digs throughout the country, and they have even been dredged up in rivers.

Chapter 3 – Four and a Half Centuries of Independence

The Battle of Bach Dang River in 938 changed Vietnamese history and is remembered today as one of the greatest Vietnamese victories of all time. The Battle of Bach Dang River secured Vietnamese independence for 400 years, and it was yet another example of the Vietnamese defeating a much larger force with guile and determination.

How and why did the Battle of Bach Dang River come about? Well, in 903, the Tang dynasty in China collapsed, leading to years of division and conflict. In the northern and central regions of China, a new dynasty, known to history as the Later Liang dynasty, rose up in 907. In the south, in and around today's Guangdong region, a monarchy known as the Southern Han arose. In other areas of the country and even within these two larger polities, other families and clans claimed they were destined to rule China or at least a large part of it. These included groups with the dynastic names of Wu, Chu, Wu-Yue, and Min. The latter two ruled in the southeast, and they were the names of former Yue kingdoms conquered by the Chinese in the 1st millennium BCE.

With all of the power struggles in China, it is not surprising that men vied for power in Vietnam. Administratively, the Chinese and Vietnamese governments called the region of today's northern and central Vietnam "The Peaceful Sea Army," with the "peaceful sea" being the South China Sea. In 905, Khuc Thua Du, a man from a prominent family, took over as commissioner of the Peaceful Sea Army. He pledged his support to the Later Liang dynasty, sent tribute, and also managed to keep the Vietnamese out of the Chinese power struggles going on at the time.

In 911, Du's grandson, Khuc Thua My, in the hopes of inheriting his grandfather's position, sent a rich tribute of gold, silver, ornamental vessels, and other gifts to the Later Liang court. They, in turn, granted his wish, making Khuc Thua My the acting governor of Vietnam/Annam and sending him a banner and an ax, which were ceremonial symbols of his office.

Fourteen years later, in 923, the Later Liang fell apart due to internal strife and the efforts of a varied assortment of military men. Khuc Thua My sent an embassy to the Southern Han king in an effort to get in his good graces, but this was not going to work after more than eighteen years of the Khuc family pledging loyalty to the Later Liang. In response to My's embassy and gifts, the Southern Han king, Liu Yan, wrote, "You, sir, have always reckoned to be a mere pretender." Then he sent in a force that ended the Khuc family's rule in Vietnam.

In place of the Khuc family, the Southern Han put one of their vassals, Duong Dinh Nghe, after he began a powerful rebellion that threatened to drag on for years. The Southern Han gave Duong Dinh Nghe the title, but they also sent along Chinese officials to essentially rule behind the scenes.

The Chinese referred to their land as the Middle Kingdom, as they believed the rest of the world surrounded it and that it lay directly under Heaven. They also thought other people were inferior to them. This attitude is reflected in the directions Chinese officials in Vietnam were given by their superiors. A Chinese official once said, "the people of 'Jioazhi' [the ancient Chinese word for Vietnam] are fond of rebellion; you can simply lead them with halter and bridle, and that is all." They were told to rule the "aboriginals" (the Vietnamese) indirectly through tribal chiefs. Again, it is important to note these tribal chiefs were not women, for China, unlike Vietnam, was a male-dominated society from the top down.

Duong Dinh Nghe, in his family's base in Ai (south of the Red River Delta), set himself up as a local warlord and ruled northern Vietnam with an iron fist, which was resented by the people. In 937, Duong Dinh Nghe was assassinated, and the killer, General Kieu Cong Tien, set himself up as the new ruler. Nghe's son-in-law Ngo Quyen led an army against the assassin, who appealed to the Southern Han for help.

The Southern Han sent a large fleet and soldiers numbering at least 20,000 men. This force was commanded by Prince Liu Hongcao, the son of the Southern Han emperor Liu Yan, who followed his son with additional forces. The prince led his fleet up the Bach Dang River, a northern branch of the Red River Delta. There, Ngo Quyen had planned a surprise.

The Vietnamese fleet consisted of hundreds of small boats, which was no match for the larger Chinese vessels in a fair fight on open water. Still, the Bach Dang River was wide enough near the seaport of Hai Mon for the Chinese to bring their numbers to bear down upon the Vietnamese ships. To counter this, Ngo had developed a plan far in advance: he ordered his army to line the river bed with large sharpened stakes, tipped with iron. These were placed in the water at low tide. At high tide, the water covered the stakes and made them invisible. The tides in the Red River Delta are strong and deep; at high tide, the Chinese ships would be able to clear the stakes with room to spare.

The Vietnamese knew their enemy would have to sail up the Bach Dang River to reach the port of Hai Mon to use it for resupply and reinforcement. As the Chinese fleet sailed down the coast, Vietnamese messengers kept Ngo Quyen informed of their progress. When high tide approached, Ngo Quyen ordered his fleet of small boats to harass the Chinese as they turned into the river, luring them farther upstream.

The Chinese, whose decks with lined with archers, believed they could defeat the Vietnamese then and there, and they recklessly followed them upriver, at which point, the strong tide turned into a low tide. Water rushed back out to sea, taking with it the large Chinese ships, whose size made it more difficult to move against the water. As the Chinese fleet was pushed back toward the sea by the tide, the thousands of stakes pushed into the river bottom became exposed. As a result, hundreds of Chinese ships had their hulls breached by them. Those ships that weren't damaged by the stakes crashed into others, making a bad situation even worse.

Armored and untrained Chinese soldiers drowned by the score. Those whose ships sank and settled on the river bottom were immobile, but the hundreds of smaller Vietnamese ships were not. They circled the Chinese fleet like a swarm of angry bees fighting off a bear.

The Chinese lost over half their men and most of their ships. The Chinese prince was killed. The Southern Han emperor, who was following his son's fleet, learned of the defeat and turned back to China. Ngo Quyen named himself king and ruled from the ancient fortress of Co

Loa, which sits about sixteen miles north of the center of Hanoi today.

Vietnam was free from Chinese rule for the time being.

After the Chinese: "Dai Viet"

After the Chinese had gone, Ngo Quyen gave the area of northern Vietnam the name "Dai Viet," or "Great Viet." No longer would the Vietnamese live in the "Pacified South" or be a part of the "Peaceful Sea Army." Instead, it took its place next to China, ostensibly as an equal—at least in the minds of Ngo and the Vietnamese.

The Ngo dynasty, which was established by Ngo Quyen (who took the imperial name of Ngo Vuong, or "Ngo the Uniter") in 939, lasted only twenty-six years, and its founder only lived for five years after the Battle of Bach Dang. Before he died, he made his brother-in-law regent for his young son, Ngo Xuong Ngap. But as has happened so many times in history when an older man is made caretaker of power until a prince comes of age, Ngo's brother-in-law, Duong Tam Kha (a general during the Battle of Bach Dang River), usurped the throne, gave himself an imperial name, and named Ngo Xuong Ngap's younger brother (Ngo Xuong Van) his adoptive son and heir. Ngo Xuong Ngap knew his time was short unless he went into hiding, which is what he and a number of his followers did.

Duong Tam Kha proved to be a very unpopular ruler, and many revolts began against him, both in the countryside and within his own court and family. In 950, his adopted son overthrew him and forced him into exile, never to return. Ngo Xuong Van then went and found his elder brother and brought him back to the court to share the throne. To many Vietnamese, this was the right and honorable thing to do, but Ngo Xuong Ngap was a harsh ruler and soon became a dictator in the provinces he oversaw. Perhaps the most interesting thing about his rule was his death: he had a heart attack while having sex in 954.

In 965, Ngo Xuong Van died, and Ngo Xuong Ngap's son, Ngo Xuong Xi, took the throne, but he wasn't sure long he would stay there. The lords and governors of the twelve provinces that made up Dai Viet were fighting among themselves for power, and it would only be a short amount of time before the strongest of them came looking for his throne and head. This is known as the "Time of Rebellion" in Vietnamese history.

From 966 through 968, Vietnam was torn apart by rebellions and rival claimants to the throne. In each of the twelve provinces of Dai Viet, a warlord set himself up as the absolute ruler with aspirations for more power, but the politics and power plays of the time were so rapid and ever-changing that none of them could climb to the top. This is why this period is also called the "Anarchy of the 12 Warlords."

In 924, a man named Dinh Bo Linh was born to Dinh Cong Tru, one of Ngo Quyen's generals, who died while his son was very young. Dinh's mother took the boy back to her village and raised him there, where he attended school and made a name for himself as one of the smarter boys of the region. When he came of age, he became a soldier under one of the twelve warlords, Tran Minh Cong, who soon elevated the young man to the rank of general.

Soon, Dinh Bo Linh's skill as a soldier led him to defeat the other eleven warlords, and he was addressed as the "King of Ten Thousand Victories." When his benefactor and adoptive father, Tran Minh Cong, died around 967, Dinh Bo Linh took over his territory, which had been the strongest of the twelve.

By 968, the other warlords of Vietnam had either submitted to Dinh Bo Linh or been defeated by him. He then took command of the country and renamed it Dai Co Viet, or "Great Buddhist Viet." Though Dinh still modeled the civil service after the Chinese, Vietnam's own brand of

Buddhism came to the forefront in Vietnamese life. He also married a woman from the Ngo dynasty to help legitimize his rule.

Though Dinh Bo Linh had subdued the other warlords, his country was weak and divided after so many years of civil war. Despite the fact the Chinese troops had been from the kingdom in 938 at the Battle of Bach Dang River, Vietnam still lived in the shadow of its giant neighbor and had to be wary. Still, Dinh Bo Linh named himself the emperor of Dai Co Viet and declared his country to be free from Chinese "guidance."

These relations with China changed in 971 when a new Chinese dynasty, the Song (960-1279), defeated the Southern Han and established rule over most of China. Recognizing that this new Chinese power would have to be placated, Dinh Bo Linh sent an embassy to Emperor Taizu of China. In return, the Chinese recognized Dinh Bo Linh as "Giao Chi Quan Vuong" ("King of Jiaozhi," which was what the Chinese had called Vietnam previously). Still, Dinh Bo Linh was able to secure a non-aggression treaty with the Song emperor in exchange for sizable tribute sent every three years. This would seemingly make Vietnam a vassal state of China, and in China's eyes, it was, but Dinh Bo Linh still called himself emperor, not king, of Vietnam and ran the country without Chinese interference.

Dinh Bo Linh made a number of reforms in the short time he was in power. He strengthened the army and set up a new civil service with a hierarchy of military and civilian officials. He also made treason a crime punishable by being fed to a caged tiger or being boiled alive. Dinh was killed by a palace official in 979. His eldest son was also killed. For a very short time, Dinh's youngest son was emperor, but he was soon overthrown by one of Dinh's generals, who then killed many of Dinh's supporters in the court and began an affair with Dinh's widow. This man was Le Hoan (pronounced "Lay Juan"), and in 980, he became the founder of a new Vietnamese dynasty known as the Early Le dynasty (to differentiate it from the later Le dynasty of 1428 to 1789).

One of the first things that happened upon Le's ascension to the throne was that the Song dynasty made plans to retake Vietnam. They saw the infighting within the Vietnamese upper classes, and around this time, the Cham people of today's central and southern Vietnam began to enter into small-scale conflicts with the Vietnamese along their borders.

Relations with China were complicated after Le Hoan took power. In a series of diplomatic letters and missions, he and the Chinese played diplomatic games, including Le Hoan lying to the Chinese that Dinh Bo Linh's son was still the king. After a year of frustration, the Chinese had had enough, and Le Hoan and his court knew war was coming.

The Chinese planned a two-pronged attack on Le's capital, and to do this, they had to sail up the Bach Dang River. The Song apparently didn't remember or didn't know about the Southern Han's defeat there in 938, but Le Hoan remembered. He planned exactly the same welcome for the Chinese as Ngo Quyen had decades earlier, and the Chinese fell for it again. The ground forces of the Chinese invasion lost their way and became divided in the unusual and rough terrain of far northern Vietnam, where they were defeated by the Vietnamese.

All of the surviving Chinese generals were executed by the Song emperor upon their return to court, and that was the end of Chinese efforts to reclaim Vietnam for some time. Le Hoan was smart enough to know to act from a position of strength, and he sent diplomats to the Song and received Song diplomats himself. Le Hoan accepted ancient Chinese titles, such as the "Governor of Annam" and the "Peaceful Sea Military Governor," in order for the Chinese to save face, but he refused to bow before the Chinese ambassador (who was essentially the representation of the emperor) and marched his army past the ambassador in a clear signal of military strength.

To the south, the king of the Cham people, Parameshvaravaran I, seeing that the Vietnamese were occupied with the Chinese, launched an invasion on Dai Co Viet. His goal was to take the capital of Hoa Lu, which is about fifty miles south of present-day Hanoi. This effort failed when the Cham fleet was destroyed by a storm. Because Le Hoan was busy with the greater threat of the Song Chinese, he sent diplomats to Parameshvaravaran I, hoping to establish peace and good relations, but this was rejected. When the Chinese were defeated, Le Hoan turned upon the Cham and sacked their capital. (The Cham remained a power in the region until it was utterly defeated by the Vietnamese in 1471.)

This leads us to another important aspect of Vietnamese society at the time: a hard-to-define quality known as *phúc d'uc*. Generally speaking, *phúc d'uc* means "virtue" and the opportunity to lead a virtuous life filled with good deeds. Someone who has the quality of *phúc d'uc* is someone to be followed, not out of fear of their power but because they are a good, righteous, and humble person. And since they are a good, righteous, and humble person, they are favored by the gods or spirits. *Phúc d'uc* is, in a way, the Vietnamese version of Mathew 5:16: "Let your light so shine before me in such a way that they may see your good works, and glorify your Father who is in heaven."

An old Vietnamese story has the first leader of the Early Le dynasty possessing *phúc d'uc*. According to this story, before he came to power, Vietnam was fraught with problems. There were bandits on the roads, bad storms, poor crops, and the threat of the Chinese, among others. According to the story, Le Hoan prayed to the gods, saying, "I am a person of little virtue, but I am first among my people. If you will help me, I will rule wisely. If there's any wrong, don't blame the people for these things—I will take the blame on myself." And when he finished, all was well, at least according to Vietnamese lore.

Le Hoan reformed the government and reorganized the country. Officials and village elders were put in charge of smaller communities, but Le Hoan's sons were made provincial governors with the power to tax (unfortunately, they also were allowed private armies). He named many Buddhist monks as advisers and administrators instead of the army of Confucian civil servants that had existed before. Le Hoan built roads and canals, issued bronze coins, and built many new temples and government buildings.

Le Hoan, who had taken the imperial name of Dai Hanh, died in 1005. His successors fought over the throne. His immediate successor, who built on the infrastructure of his father, was assassinated by his brother, Le Long Dinh, who was the third and final Early Le emperor. Le Long Dinh, whose imperial name was Khai Minh, also had an unfortunate ailment that gave him another name: Le Ngoa Trieu, which means "the one who rules while lying on his throne," This was because he had an excruciating case of hemorrhoids.

Le Ngoa Trieu was exceedingly cruel, much in the manner of the Roman emperors Nero and Caligula, as he tortured prisoners and others for his own personal entertainment. He also faced ten rebellions throughout the country in the five years of his rule, no doubt in part as a reaction to his cruelty. He put down the rebellions, but he still died early. This was due to his ill health, which was likely brought on by his unhealthy lifestyle.

In 1009, Le Ngoa Trieu died. It was said that the real power lay behind the scenes with a man named Ly Cong Uan, who busied himself with the administration while the emperor ate himself to death and attended orgies. When Le Ngoa Trieu died, the imperial court decided to place Ly Cong Uan on the throne, ushering in the Ly dynasty (1009-1225).

Chapter 4 – The Ly Dynasty

Ly Cong Uan took the imperial name of Ly Thai To ("Supreme Forefather").

One of the early marks of the Ly dynasty was its responsiveness to the common people and its opening of positions of power in the administration to those who were not of noble or wealthy birth. Ly viewed the people as his children, and just as a father would, he wished to hear his children's wishes and problems. To this end, it is said that he put a large bell in front of the palace, and whoever rang it was entitled to take their problem directly to the emperor. How often this was employed or whether it's just a story about how the Vietnamese viewed Ly Thai To is unknown. What is known is that Ly's spirit is among the most honored in the country even today, with temples and/or special areas within temples dedicated to the "Supreme Forefather."

One of the most notable accomplishments of Ly Thai To was the moving of the imperial capital from the mountain fortress area of Hoa Lu to what was then called Thang Long (meaning "Ascending Dragon")—the location of today's Hanoi.

The moving and building up of Hanoi was significant. Hanoi is located in a relatively flat area of the country, and it is surrounded by rivers and waterways. It is not really a defensible city, at least not geographically. However, economically and politically, the move from Hoa Lu to present-day Hanoi makes a lot of sense. The waterways, fields, and flat landscape created more economic opportunities, and the flat scenery, new roads, and waterways made political communication more effective.

The Ly emperors were noted for their Buddhist beliefs and sponsorship of temples, but they also saw the value of Confucianism and its organizational qualities. Actually, most historians now refer to the Confucianism of this time as Neo-Confucianism, as the Chinese philosophy had been appended with new writings that emphasized the more practical aspects of life. The teachings of Confucius had also been on the wane to a degree in the 900s in China and were only deeply reestablished in the court with the rise of the Song dynasty, hence the term "neo," or "new."

A later Ly emperor, Ly Thanh Tong, built the first university in Vietnam, the Imperial Academy, in 1070. The university functioned as a Confucian education center for men who were not from noble families, and it prepared them for both the Confucian-style civil service exams and a life in government. The Ly emperors were the first to base their rule on written laws rather than the traditional and imperial command.

Previous dynasties were marked by their reliance on the military for power, and the Ly did have sizable armies when it was needed. However, they based their rule on law and economic stability. This is one of the reasons why the Ly are remembered so fondly in Vietnam today.

Though the Ly deemphasized the imperial reliance on a standing army, the 12th and 13th centuries were not peaceful times in Vietnam or really anywhere in the world.

Like other Vietnamese dynasties before it, the Ly dynasty depended greatly on Chinese goodwill and sent periodic tributes to the Chinese emperor. Vietnamese rulers also received titles from the Chinese, which were an honor but were also insulting to a degree. Since the Chinese, for the most part, did not want or were not able to rule Vietnam directly without a massive invasion, they were generally satisfied with receiving tribute from the Vietnamese. They also expected to be addressed diplomatically in a way that indicated their "superior" position. Since the Vietnamese did this, they were left free to govern their kingdom as they liked.

However, between 1075 and 1077, the Vietnamese and Chinese again fought a costly war. In the decade or so before the Ly-Song War was fought, a series of problems on the Vietnamese/Chinese border arose. In one instance, a tribal chief, whose territory lay in China just over the Vietnamese border, rose up to proclaim his own kingdom. As one can imagine, this was a mistake. The Song Chinese sent an army to the area and crushed the rebellion.

The problem for the Vietnamese was two-fold. Much of the Song army remained on the border, and many of those who left the army, along with other Chinese, began to settle on both sides of the border. Another group of Chinese ex-soldiers began to settle in areas in China that the Vietnamese were dependent on (and allowed access to for a price) for imports. The soldiers began to deny them access to the area, angering the Vietnamese ruler.

Additionally, in 1075, Emperor Shenzong of Song was told by his councilors that Dai Viet was being defeated by the Cham people in today's central Vietnam and had only 10,000 men in its army. Hearing this, Shenzong took actions that were sure to anger the Vietnamese. First, he mobilized an army. Second, he ordered that all territory under his command were not to trade with the Vietnamese and blocked Vietnamese goods from entering Tibet, which Shenzong considered to be another part of his empire.

To Emperor Shenzong's surprise, the Ly emperor at the time, Ly Nhan Tong (r. 1072-1128), put two of his most trusted generals in command of the army, which consisted of 100,000 men. Most of these men were volunteers, indicating the popularity of the Ly. Before the Chinese could act, the Vietnamese invaded China and took over two prefectures in today's Guangxi province in October 1075.

The Chinese emperor only heard about the Vietnamese invasion in early 1076, after which he sent reinforcements to the area. These were defeated by the Vietnamese. Adding insult to injury, the Vietnamese decapitated the local governor, then marched to the nearest large city, Yongzhou, and laid siege to it for forty-two days, facing a strong defense. When they entered the city, the Vietnamese went on a killing spree, murdering nearly 60,000 people.

By this time, the Song had amassed a large army, but the Vietnamese retreated before a battle could fully take place. At the same time, the Song emperor called upon his other vassal states, Champa (home of the Cham in central Vietnam) and the Khmer Empire (today's present-day Cambodia and part of Thailand), to attack the Vietnamese.

The Chinese entered Vietnam, captured the leader of the Vietnamese army who had beheaded their governor, and was marching toward the Vietnamese capital of Thang Long by 1077 when they were halted by strong fortifications. Once again, the Vietnamese employed the same wooden spike trap that they had at Bach Dang River, although this time at a different location. They managed to kill over 1,000 Chinese soldiers. This forced the Chinese to take a roundabout route toward the capital, where they engaged and defeated the Vietnamese near Phu Luong.

At this point, the situation was looking grim for the Vietnamese and the Ly dynasty. They were surrounded in a defensive circle around the capital, facing hundreds of thousands of Chinese. One of the commanding generals, Ly Thuong Kiet, stood before his soldiers and read a poem to boost their morale. This episode and poem, "Nam quoc son ha," is as famous to the Vietnamese as "Don't fire until you see the whites of their eyes" of Bunker Hill fame is to Americans or the "Never was so much owed to so few by so many," which was spoken by Winston Churchill to the British in WWII.

"Nam quoc son ha" means "Mountains and Rivers of the Southern Country," and it is also known as "Vietnam's first Declaration of Independence." Like many poems translated into foreign tongues, it loses something in translation, but rest assured, on the right occasion, the recitation of the poem will bring tears to Vietnamese eyes. (Needless to say, the poem has been read at fateful moments in Vietnamese history.)

The mountains and rivers that carved the southern empire where dwelled the Southern Emperor. Its sovereignty is the will of nature and is written in the script of Heaven. What gives these invaders the right to trespass? They shall, in so doing, see themselves defeated and shamed!

Despite the Vietnamese efforts to stay strong, the Song broke through Vietnamese lines and came near the city before the Vietnamese rallied and pushed them back across the river. At the same time, the Vietnamese coastal defense and fleet of small vessels attacked and distracted the Chinese fleet attempting to come to their army's aid.

The Vietnamese made a peace overture to the Song. Vietnamese casualties were mounting, but so were the Song's—they had lost some

400,000 men and were losing more every day to the diseases of the hot climate. An agreement that gave the Song some borderlands was written up and signed in 1077/78. Some years later, the two sides met again and hammered out a more permanent agreement.

The Ly also engaged in wars with other territories and kingdoms in the area. Years before the Ly-Song War, in 1014, the Vietnamese were attacked by a combination of Vietnamese rebels and an army from the Dali Kingdom, which had the unfortunate luck of being sandwiched between China, Vietnam, the Khmer Empire, and powerful Tibetan and Burmese kingdoms. Still, its location and resources made it strong enough to stay relatively independent, though it was still a vassal of China, much like Vietnam.

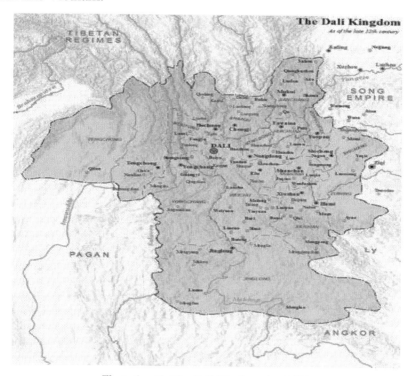

Illustration 11: The Dali Kingdom circa 1014
SY, CC BY-SA 4.0 <https://creativecommons.org/licenses/by-sa/4.0>, via Wikimedia Commons
https://commons.wikimedia.org/wiki/File:Dali_Kingdom.png

In 1014, the Dali leader and Vietnamese rebel Ha Trac Tuan allied and moved into Ly territory in today's Chinese province of Yunnan and the Vietnamese province of Ha Giang. They remained in possession of the region for only a short time before Vietnamese reinforcements arrived and crushed the invasion.

Throughout the reign of the Ly dynasty, peace and conflict occurred on a semi-regular basis between the Ly and the Cham to the south. This would escalate in the centuries to come, as the Vietnamese emperor and people expanded southward to house and feed their growing population.

Chapter 5 – The Tran Dynasty

By the early 1200s, the Ly dynasty was in disarray. Trade with China flourished, and relations were actually better than they had been for some time. The Chinese, while still viewing Vietnam as a "vassal," changed the status of its neighbor to the south from what they called an "internal vassal" (meaning that Vietnam was part of China) to an "external vassal" (meaning that while Vietnam paid tribute, it was its own kingdom with its own king, laws, and customs). Additionally, the Chinese emperor sent impressive gifts to the Ly emperor in 1172, not because he viewed the Vietnamese ruler as an equal but because of the good relations between the two kingdoms. As a side note, the Chinese dynasties never viewed anyone as an equal, which became a real problem when the Europeans arrived.

Within Vietnam at the turn of the 12th and 13th centuries, the ruling classes had become quite wealthy from the peace and trade with China and elsewhere. Some upper-class families, who had sons in the military, the civil service, or served as influential Buddhist monks and who had daughters marrying into other important families, grew not only rich but also influential. This was the case from the provincial level to the Ly emperor's court.

From about 1128, military strongmen were the powers behind the throne. The decline of the Ly dynasty is usually marked with the ascension of Ly Cao Tong (r. 1175-1210) to the throne.

Ly Cao Tong came to the throne at the age of three, with the kingdom being ruled by a regent in his name. Internal power struggles took place during this time, with empresses, concubines, princes, and other influential figures vying for power or even the throne. In 1181, one of these princes led an army against the emperor and looted the capital, though his coup ultimately failed.

The rule of Ly Cao Tong mirrors the stories of a lot of monarchical families throughout history and the world. By the time he came to the throne, the Ly family had been in power for over 200 years. The later Ly kings and Ly Cao Tong, in particular, became more and more interested in living a life of excess than administering to their kingdom properly.

During his reign, Cao Tong was noted for building palaces and pagodas almost everywhere he went, spending money that needed to be spent governing the country and preventing famine, which struck a number of times during his reign. Rulers the world over know that famine is one of the surest guarantees of political trouble and rebellion, and multiple uprisings took place during Ly Cao Tong's reign because of this.

Some of these uprisings were minor and localized, but others were larger and more destructive. The years 1192, 1198, 1203, 1208, and 1210 all saw major rebellions.

While Cao Tong built pagodas and pleasure palaces, a powerful family named Tran gained influence in the court and throughout the Red River

Delta area. Its leader, Tran Ly, was a rich fisherman from the eastern end of the Red River, where it meets the ocean. In addition to fishing, the Tran were also pirates, seizing weaker vessels all along the coast. This piracy brought wealth to the area, and the Tran family spent their money wisely, not only helping improve the area but also buying influence at court.

Along with their judicious use of money, the Tran family also used a time-honored way to gain influence—they married into the royal family. Tran Ly's daughter, Tran Thi Dung, married the Ly crown prince, and in 1210, he became Emperor Ly Hue Tong. Despite Ly Cao Tong's death, the countryside was still wracked by rebellions and disorder. And although the country had a new emperor, it was still run from behind the scenes, this time by the Tran family, specifically the new queen, her brothers, and her cousin, a man by the name of Tran Thu Do, who was also the queen's lover.

In 1224, the last Ly emperor, Hue Tong, abdicated the throne in favor of his seven-year-old daughter, who already had a marriage arranged with Tran Thu Do's eight-year-old nephew. The little girl was "convinced" to abdicate in favor of her "husband," and he became the first emperor of the new Tran dynasty.

Legend has it that Ly Hue Tong had been approached by Tran Thu Do and told, "Old things should disappear." He committed suicide shortly thereafter. The next year, the remaining members of the Ly family gathered together in a Buddhist temple to weigh their options and pray for their ancestors. Tran Thu Do had his men surround the temple and kill the last remaining members of the Ly family.

The first Tran emperor was Tran Thai Tong (r. 1226–1258), the eight-year-old boy mentioned above, although he was essentially a figurehead. His father was the regent, but it was his uncle, Tran Thu Do, who actually ruled the country.

Earlier, we mentioned the Vietnamese notion of *uy tin*, the idea that a person may have charismatic, positive qualities that people choose to honor and follow. The idea of *uy tin* fits in nicely with many Buddhist ideals, such as selflessness and humility. This quality, along with the qualities of *phúc d'uc* ("virtue"), was possessed, or was at least said to be possessed, by people such as Ngo Quyen, the victor of the Battle of Bach Dang River, and Le Hoan, the founder of the Early Le dynasty.

By contrast, the Tran ruled with *Te*, the notion of ruling with power. Since this is a Chinese word, the Vietnamese identified the concept with the ruling Chinese.

Among the first things Tran Thu Do did was to attack Buddhism. Buddhism's influence on the ruling Ly had been in decline since about 1210. This is coincidentally the time the Tran family began to seize power in the court.

The three different Zen Buddhist sects prevalent in Vietnam faded, both with the deaths of some of its older masters and the deaths of its monks at court. The Tran court also began to withdraw its support for many of the Buddhist sects and temples, and Buddhist officials who passed on or were forced out were replaced by Confucian ones.

The ascension of the Tran marked a slow return of the influence of China and Confucianism. Another one of the first things the Tran dynasty did was to reintroduce the civil service examinations on the Chinese classics, which had not been done since before 1100. These exams were not held at regular intervals but rather at the discretion of the ruling family. However, the Tran family held more of these exams as their rule continued. As a practical matter, this meant that the administration of the Vietnamese empire was conducted by men educated and trained in the Chinese tradition, not the Vietnamese.

The Tran also reduced the chances of complicated plots being hatched, which had marked the later years of the Ly dynasty, ones of which the family had been a part. They made rules reducing the ability of in-laws to access power, and they also kept power in the family by encouraging the marriage of cousins to one another, which was not unique by any means, as this occurred in ruling families in Asia and Europe.

The first hundred years of the Tran were marked by prosperity and high agricultural output. This was helped by a period of mild climatic changes with high but not excessive rainfall. Where rain did cause flooding, the Tran built a system of dikes, which helped both agriculture and transport.

Labor was cheap during this period. At a time of rising prosperity and agricultural output, rich families employed thousands of serfs on their estates. These people were not quite slaves, but they were also not free. Serfs were tied to the landowning family and had very few rights. Peasants were allowed to own land, and a large number of peasants became medium-sized landowners, but those without land were subject to be rounded up and impressed into serfdom. This had been the case throughout Vietnamese history, but it increased under the Tran dynasty, as more and more land turned to agriculture, especially in the Red River Valley.

One of the interesting things the Tran rulers did when they first came to power had to do with an old spiritual practice known as geomancy. This may not be something familiar to most Western readers, but you might know a little bit about it if you've heard of the Chinese practice of feng shui. Feng shui is the purposeful location of a building, house, furniture, and windows, among other things, because it is thought to be a "power" spot or fortuitous in some way. Now, feng shui is not really geomancy, but it is related. By definition, geomancy is the "art of placing or arranging buildings or other sites auspiciously," and "divination from configurations seen in a handful of earth thrown on the ground, or by interpreting lines or textures on the ground."

Vietnamese geomancers studied the layout of the ground, as well as the planned location of a building (especially palaces and temples) and perhaps, more importantly, gravesites. Vietnamese folk beliefs include ancestor worship (as does Buddhism and Confucianism). Ancestors were the reason for your existence, and simply put, they "watched" over you. If you took care of them (meaning venerated them in the proper way and secured a gravesite that was fortuitous and powerful), they would take care of you.

There are all sorts of guidelines for the proper burial of a respected family member based on their birth year and the surrounding location. For instance, people born in the years of the Tiger, Dog, or Horse should be buried (with the direction being from head to foot) facing either east or west. South is all right, but north is said to bring bad fortune. On the other hand, those born in the years of the Pig, Cat, or Goat should be buried facing north or south but never west.

Additionally, graves must not be placed in areas with insufficient soil or too much water, as there is the danger of erosion. Trees that are too big are not good either. Aside from the danger of roots digging into a grave after time, big trees are believed to bring stomach and chest ailments to close living relatives. A good source of light is needed, meaning the grave should not be in shadow too often (for example, at the foot of a hill or mountain).

When the Tran family came to power, they went about and claimed as many auspicious sites as they could for their graves and those of their descendants. People who were already buried that the Tran family disliked, such as past emperors, were reburied in less auspicious places.

Until the French colonized Vietnam, there really wasn't a city at the location where Saigon/Ho Chi Minh City stands today. There were two very large settlements: one to the north and one farther south, with much land and water between them. When the French came, they began building in the area between these two ancient settlements, not realizing that there was (at least in Vietnamese minds) a good reason for the empty space. According to traditional geomancy, the two settlements, Gia Dinh to the north and Cholon in the south, were located in auspicious places. When the French began building the rest of what became Saigon/Ho Chi Minh City, they built between the settlements, which was in a "bad" place according to traditional geomancy. (If you are interested in learning more about geomancy, you will find a good source of information about this and the belief that some Vietnamese hold about the effect of this location on the Vietnam War at the end of this book.)

When the Tran family came to power, the first thing they needed to do was to find a way to get along with China, something Vietnamese rulers have been doing since the beginning of time.

For the most part, the Ly dynasty had had fairly good relations with China, and the Chinese wondered if the Tran dynasty would maintain this relationship. The Song court even discussed whether or not it would be best if the Chinese invaded Vietnam, got rid of the Tran family, and placed a puppet emperor on the Vietnamese throne. However, as some documents of the time indicate, diplomats believed that any invasion of Vietnam would be too costly in many ways. Some Chinese troops had been allowed in Vietnam under the Ly dynasty to guard Chinese interests, but some Chinese officials believed even this was too much.

Here are some quotes from the superintendent of maritime trade of the southern Chinese province of Fujian. Occupying "Jioazhi," which the

Chinese still called Vietnam, would be "extremely expensive" and also that "the Government of our present dynasty, out of affection for the army...deemed it advisable that our troops should no longer be kept in this pestilential climate for the purpose of guarding such an unprofitable territory." Those were excerpts from a message written in 1206. They could have easily been written by an American in 1966.

It was likely a good idea for the Song to keep as many of their troops at home in the 1200s, though, in the end, it did them no good. The reason for this is quite simple: the Mongols.

The Mongols were already in control of much of the Asian steppe and the Middle East, and they were pushing into the fringes of Europe by the late 1200s. By the fifth decade of the 13th century, the Mongols, under the most famous of Genghis Khan's grandsons, Kublai, pushed into northern China and sent the leaders of the Song dynasty fleeing southward with their armies, many of them into Vietnam and others into more remote parts of China.

By 1257, the Mongols had reached the southern borders of China. They sent a demand to the Tran dynasty: let us in to destroy the remaining Song armies or suffer the consequences. Emperor Tran Thai Tong refused, and when he did, the Mongols crossed the border.

On January 17th, 1258, the Mongol forces, which numbered around 15,000 men, engaged the Vietnamese army. It is unknown how large their army was, but it did include 200 war elephants. The Vietnamese army was led personally by the emperor on his own elephant. At first, the Mongols were awed by the elephants, but the Mongol general Uriyangkhidai ordered his men to fire all of their arrows at the elephants' exposed feet. The huge beasts panicked, crushing many Vietnamese and causing a confused Vietnamese retreat. Tran Thai Tong escaped by boat to an offshore island near Hanoi (then known as Thang Long). Five days later, the Mongols took the Vietnamese capital.

Some sources say that Uriyangkhidai left Vietnam because of the poor climate, which was taking a toll on his army. Others say he left because he pursued the retreating Song forces back into China on Vietnam's western border.

The Song were defeated in 1276. By that time, the Vietnamese had established a relationship with the Mongols—one very similar to earlier Chinese dynasties. All the Mongols requested was tribute, and in return, the Vietnamese would be left alone.

Immediately to the south of Dai Viet was the kingdom of Champa, which was the next object of Mongol focus. In 1281, a Mongol diplomatic mission visited the Champa king, Indravarman V, and demanded the submission of the Cham to Kublai Khan. The Champa king agreed, but he only did so under duress and because many of his advisers pushed him to make an agreement. Soon, Indravarman organized an army to fight the Mongols, who invaded in the early spring of 1282.

The Mongols invaded Champa with a small force of 5,000 men and 100 ships. The relatively small size of the Mongol force (especially its navy) was due to the losses they had suffered in the second invasion of Japan in 1281 (the first had ended in failure in 1274). King Indravarman, who was an old but wily warrior, and his son led their army into the hills and forests of central Vietnam after ambushing the Mongols and conducted a guerrilla war against them for two years. The Mongols finally left the country in 1284 to get reinforcements.

At the end of 1284 and in early 1285, the Mongols reinforced their southern army and invaded Vietnam with the idea of conquering both it and the Champa kingdom. In January 1285, the Mongols invaded Vietnam and pushed toward its capital yet again, capturing it after a series of costly battles. The Vietnamese retreated southward toward Champa and westward into the mountains, destroying anything that might be of use to the pursuing Mongols.

Over the next few months, the Mongols attempted to catch elements of the Vietnamese forces in a series of pincer movements, including an amphibious landing in the southern part of the kingdom. They were also intent on capturing the Vietnamese emperor, who was now Tran Nhan Tong, but they failed each time, though a large number of lesser Tran princes defected to the Mongols.

A few months later, the Vietnamese launched a surprise attack on the Mongols in Thang Long from the west and south, and they won a series of stunning victories, which was helped by the climate and disease. By the middle of 1285, the Mongols had fled Vietnam, losing tens of thousands of men, who were either killed and captured. Their leading general was even executed by the Vietnamese.

What happened next is really astounding. Kublai Khan, who was bent on invading Japan for the third time, decided to focus all of his energies on Dai Viet, and in 1288, he sent a massive fleet southward to invade it, starting with the Vietnamese capital. To do this, his fleet sailed up, of all things, the Bach Dang River.

Kublai Khan and his generals apparently didn't know their history because, as you have might have already guessed, the Vietnamese lured the Mongol fleet upriver at high tide. As the strong tide receded, the Mongol fleet was pulled back toward the ocean, and in the ever-shallower water, their ships were dragged onto long wooden metal-tipped poles driven into the mud. Those ships that weren't sunk by the poles collided with other Mongol ships. Many sank, and many were grounded. All the while, Vietnamese soldiers fired thousands of arrows and catapults at them from both banks. And this was how the third and final Mongol invasion of Vietnam ended.

After the Mongol invasions, there was a period of peace and prosperity. The first influential members of the Tran dynasty, Tran Ly and Tran Thu Do, were from relatively humble origins (they were fishermen) and did not have a formal education. Later Tran emperors and their courts were known for their accomplishments in the arts, such as poetry, calligraphy, painting, music, and drama. Much of the poetry and drama of the Tran court focused on patriotism and the Tran victory over the Mongols. This was not just entertainment but also propaganda, as it bolstered the Tran dynasty in the eyes of the people and instilled a sense of national pride.

The Tran dynasty also changed how Vietnamese was used. Before the Tran, everything was written in Chinese. Vietnamese was the spoken language of the people and was used in oral history, but Chinese was seen as the more "educated and civilized" language. The Tran dynasty began to use the Vietnamese written language in virtually everything and encouraged its widespread use in the country. This was known as *chu nom* ("Southern characters"), which were Chinese characters modified and fitted to Vietnamese words. This, too, was a way of separating the Vietnamese culture from the Chinese one and placing it on an equal footing. This also encouraged the recording of Vietnamese oral histories and folk tales in the native language. The first Vietnamese medical almanac was written in *chu nom* during this time. The Tran dynasty also fostered performing arts, such as plays and dance. Many of these, like the written stories of the time, were set to nationalistic and patriotic backgrounds.

In the second and third decades of the 1300s, the Tran dynasty was faced with change, and much of that was based on the changing climate. In the first part of the 1300s, Vietnam and much of Asia were subject to much warmer weather and greater rainfall than normal. This caused flooding, which destroyed crops, resulting in hunger and other human tragedies. Rebellions and uprisings against the Tran family, especially in the southern and western parts of the country, which were away from the Tran center of power in the Red River Delta, rose up. However, the Tran dynasty managed to hold onto power.

The first part of the 1300s was marked by heavy rainfall and higher temperatures, but the rest of the century was marked by the beginning of what is known to climate historians as the Little Ice Age, which brought cooler temperatures and drought to many places around the world. Once again, the Tran were faced with problems beyond their control, as drought affected harvests and caused unrest.

It's important to note that the Vietnamese, along with the Chinese, subscribed to the notion of the Mandate of Heaven. This is similar but not the same as the idea of the divine right in the West. Put simply, having the Mandate of Heaven meant that the ruler had the blessing of the gods (or spirits or Buddha or whatever higher power the ruler ascribed to because of fortuitous events. So, when things began to go badly, it was believed that the Mandate of Heaven had been removed and that it should be given to someone else. In the 1200s, it was clear that the Tran dynasty had the Mandate of Heaven: they rose to power, united the country, defeated the Mongols, and enjoyed a blossoming of the arts and a period of prosperity. This began to change with the problems that arose in the 1300s, with the main one being food shortages. But there were other problems as well, such as corruption, whether financial or moral.

The first three emperors after the Mongol invasions—Tran Anh Tong, Tran Minh Tong, and Tran Hien Tong—all enjoyed periods of relative peace and prosperity. Tran Anh Tong, in particular, was seen as a force for good, cracking down on corruption in the court and gambling within the country. These Tran rulers also promoted Buddhism as a way to increase virtue and decrease vice in the country.

The Tran dynasty also introduced an interesting notion into the way Vietnamese emperors were chosen and trained. As they aged, they would choose their heir, and this did not have to be a son. Frequently, it was a son-in-law. Either way, the "emperor-to-be" would be groomed for some time, and when the older emperor and the court deemed it time, the heir would become the emperor. The older man would then go into semi-retirement in a smaller palace in the imperial compound and become the "retired" or "sage" emperor.

The reign of Tran Anh Tong (1293-1314 as emperor, 1314-1320 as retired emperor) was also marked by relatively friendly relations with the Champa kingdom to the south. Remember, there were considerable differences between the Cham and the Vietnamese, as they are two ethnically different people. For instance, the Cham descended from the Austronesian people of the Pacific islands and practiced Hinduism. At times, such as when the Mongols invaded, the Vietnamese and the Cham would fight together. At other times, they would be at each other's throats fighting for land, resources, or both.

But in 1306, relations between the Champa kingdom and Dai Viet were good. The Champa king, Simhavarman III, was eager to gain a stronger relationship with the Vietnamese, for the Cham faced enemies to the west and also the powerful Khmer of today's Cambodia. Simhavarman III offered Tran Anh Tong pieces of territory that bordered on Dai Viet in exchange for taking a Vietnamese princess, Tran Huyen, as a bride. Eager to gain territory and form an alliance that might prove useful again, Tran Anh Tong accepted, and the deal was done.

However, one year later, Simhavarman III died, and as Hindu practice at the time called for, the Champa court prepared to send Simhavarman III to the next world by cremation. He would be accompanied by his wife, the Vietnamese princess Tran Huyen. Tran Anh Tong sent one of his generals to Cham to retrieve Huyen Tran, which he managed to do. (Vietnamese literature has many stories about this general, Tran Khac Chung, running away with Princess Huyen, but most are highly fictional.)

The next year, Simhavarman IV, the new Champa king, informed the Vietnamese that he was not going to abide by the peace treaty signed by his father, and the Vietnamese invaded, capturing the Champa king and appointing a more friendly successor. Relations between the two kingdoms deteriorated from then on.

The Cham and the Vietnamese fought a serious conflict in 1471 in which the Cham were defeated, losing most of their army and land. Most of the surviving Cham fled to Cambodia, where they form a small minority, as they do in today's Vietnam. After the conflict, two puppet Cham kingdoms, which were small in size, remained until 1653 and 1832, respectively.

The Decline of the Tran

In 1357, a new emperor took power: Tran Du Tong. When he was under the tutelage of Senior Emperor Tran Minh Tong, he seemed to be fit for the throne, as he was reserved and hard-working. However, after the death of Tran Minh Tong, Tran Du Tong became extravagant and spent lavishly on his court and the building of palaces. Though theater flourished under the Tran dynasty, which, in retrospect, is a good thing, at the time, the performing arts were considered extravagant and almost sinful. This was not unique to Vietnam. At various times in Japanese history, the theater and its actors were subject to repression, and in many parts of Europe, acting was considered an almost sinful way to make a living, as one was perceived as being a professional "liar."

When Tran Du Tong died at the young age of thirty-three, his place was taken by his appointee, a nephew who was not viewed as being part of the Tran family proper. This nephew, Duong Nhat Le, was also extravagant in his spending and neglected his duties as emperor, which left much time for those around him to plot against his unpopular rule.

Over the course of the next twenty years, the throne changed hands a number of times, including by assassination, and the Vietnamese were defeated quite badly by the Cham, though a victory over them in 1390 sort of stabilized the situation for a time.

In the late 1390s, a court official named Ho Quy Ly rose to power. A series of power moves ensued, including plots by the Tran emperor to sideline Ho Quy Ly, but this came to naught when he passed away in 1394. The next emperor barely held onto power, and in 1398, Ho Quy Ly forced him to abdicate in favor of the emperor's three-year-old son. He was killed a year later on Ho's orders. Nearly 400 other court officials and people viewed as loyal to the Tran were also killed on Ho Quy Ly's orders. Ho Quy Ly then placed himself on the throne, claiming descent from the original royal family of the Yuet people in China.

The new Ho dynasty had a very short life. In 1407, after fighting a series of unpopular wars against the Champa kingdom, Ho Quy Ly had to face a new Chinese dynasty, the Ming, which had replaced the Yuan dynasty of the Mongols. In 1407, the Chinese invaded Vietnam with an overwhelming force, captured Ho Quy Ly, and sent him into exile in China.

The Chinese ruled Vietnam directly for twenty years. In 1428, the third Ming emperor, the Yongle Emperor, decided that Vietnam was too costly and troublesome to rule and pulled his troops out, leaving behind a power vacuum and much destruction, including the destruction of many Vietnamese texts, temples, memorials, and other important cultural artifacts.

Chapter 6 – The Later Le Dynasty

The Le dynasty lasted from 1428 until 1789. For a time, the Le family ruled directly as emperors of Vietnam, but they were supplanted by warring factions, powerful individuals, and the arrival of the Europeans in Asia in the form of the French.

In 1428, the Yongle Emperor removed Chinese troops from Vietnam. As was mentioned at the end of the previous chapter, he had decided that the occupation and administration of Vietnam were too costly in both financial and political terms. He was helped along in that decision by the founder of the Later Le dynasty, Le Ly (r. 1428-1433), who had led a long guerrilla campaign against the Chinese. Today, he is known as "Le Loi," for reasons that will be explained.

Statue of Le Loi in front of the municipal hall of Thanh Hoa province, his home. *Nguyễn Thanh Quang, CC BY-SA 3.0 <http://creativecommons.org/licenses/by-sa/3.0/>, via Wikimedia Commons https://commons.wikimedia.org/wiki/File:Le_Loi_statue.JPG*

As you can likely tell from the picture above, Le Loi is a legendary figure in Vietnam. He is credited with not only throwing the Chinese out of the country but also taking Vietnam on its own path, one that was mostly free from Chinese influence. The origin story of Le Loi is similar to that of the heroes of many countries, so it is difficult to separate truth from fiction. But sometimes in history, that difference doesn't matter all that much.

Le Loi was from a wealthy aristocratic family. It is said that a wise, older man from another important family, Nguyen Ty, was searching for someone of good repute (someone with *phúc d'uc*) to free Vietnam from

Chinese rule. Even in his teens, Le Loi already had a reputation for fairness and intelligence, and Nguyen Ty prevailed upon him to lead the Vietnamese people to freedom. Or at least so goes the story.

Another interesting fact about Le Loi is that his name was really Le Ly. You see, the word "Ly" means "profit" in Vietnamese. In a sometimes-followed ancient Chinese/Vietnamese custom, no one could say the name of the emperor or even write it. Since the word "Ly" was an everyday word, a workaround needed to be found. Thus, his name was changed from "Ly" to "Loi," as was the Vietnamese character. When he took the throne, Le Loi took the name Le Thai To.

One of the most important things Le Loi did was remove almost all traces of Chinese law from Vietnamese life. His court and that of his son wrote a Vietnamese law code based on Vietnamese traditions, customs, and the rules of previously "independent" Vietnamese dynasties, such as the Early Le dynasty. This was known as the Hong Duc code.

Le Loi also issued a proclamation declaring the independence of Vietnam, which is sometimes read on national holidays and is often cited in times of national trouble. Here are the first few lines:

> Our Great Viet is a country where prosperity abounds. Where civilization reigns supreme.
>
> Mountains, rivers, frontiers have all been divided;
>
> For the customs are distinct: North and South.
>
> Trieu, Dinh, Ly and Tran
>
> Built our Nation,
>
> Whilst Han T'ang, Sung and Yuan
>
> Ruled over Theirs.
>
> Over the Centuries,
>
> We have been sometimes strong, and sometimes weak,

But never yet have we been lacking in heroes.

Of that let our history be the proof.

Though the Hong Duc code was based mostly on Vietnamese traditions and ideas, the Le dynasty based the administration of their government on Confucian, or rather Neo-Confucian, structures, with a hierarchy based not only on an aristocratic background but also the civil service exams. Le Loi died in 1433, spending the last two years of his reign fighting against the mountain tribes of western and northern Vietnam, with various degrees of success. He left his son, Le Nguyen Long (better known by his imperial name "Le Thai Tong"), a guide for ruling based on virtue and diligence, warning him against vices, such as women, gambling, and luxurious spending. Le Loi also told his son not to surround himself with sycophants and to listen to others without taking bribes.

The Hong Duc code was, in a way, Le Loi's letter to his son transferred into law. It was a remarkably modern set of laws and statutes. For example, the code allowed women to inherit wealth and property on an equal footing with men, something they had not been able to do under Chinese law. The code also included spousal immunity (the right of a spouse to not have to testify against their husband/wife), punishments for statutory rape, prohibited ex post facto laws, statutes of limitations, and much more. Before his death, Le Loi set about redistributing land to his followers and former officials who had sworn allegiance to him, as well as reforming property and agricultural codes.

Le Thai Tong is considered to be the greatest of the Le emperors. In addition to presiding over many of the changes mentioned above, he also expanded Vietnamese territory. The early Le period included a movement called *Nam tien*- ("the march to the south"), during which both the Vietnamese nation and Vietnamese people expanded southward from their traditional borders, which ended with China in the north, the mountainous Laos area to the west, and the Champa kingdom to the south.

Obviously, the Vietnamese who desired to expand the borders were not going to expand northward. To the west, the land was mountainous; it was easy to defend for the tribes and clans there, and it also did not include much arable land. That left one direction—southward into the Champa kingdom, with its fertile fields, forests, and rich fishing areas.

In late 1470, another conflict began between the Vietnamese and the Cham. Unfortunately for the Cham, their location left them rather isolated from any help against the stronger Vietnamese. The only people who might have helped the Cham were the Chinese, but when the Cham asked for their help, the Chinese emperor simply wrote a stern letter to Le Thanh Tong, which essentially said that China was not going to interfere. The Cham also asked help from the neighboring Khmer people, but they were turned down, as the two kingdoms had recently fought their own wars against each other.

The Vietnamese force that invaded the Champa kingdom was massive. In fact, it was the largest in Asia at the time, excluding China. Nearly 300,000 Vietnamese, who were divided into an amphibious and a land force, invaded the Champa kingdom and defeated the smaller Champa army of 100,000 men. Much of Champa was added to the Vietnamese kingdom, and many Cham were enslaved by the Vietnamese. The war ended with the total defeat of the Cham, but because of the high financial cost of the war, the Cham were left with only a handful of autonomous zones in their former empire, which were required to pay tribute to the Vietnamese. All of the former Cham trade routes were taken over by the Vietnamese, and Vietnam now extended from its border with China all the way to the Mekong Delta.

When Le Thai Tong died in 1442 after almost nine years in power, the Le dynasty began a slow decline.

By the early 16th century, the Le dynasty had seen one weak and ineffective ruler after another. The country was breaking down, and the people fell into civil war in the early 1520s. Within the court, there were various factions and sub-factions vying for power. Two of the most powerful families were the Trinh and the Nguyen. They watched as a military strongman rose to power. His name was Mac Dang Dung.

The leaders of the two powerful families fled south and took the emperor with them so he wouldn't fall under Mac Dang Dung's control (and to stay under theirs). In 1524, Mac Dang Dung captured the leaders of the two families and had them killed. He then proclaimed a new Le emperor, Le Xuan, but he was emperor in name only. Mac Dang Dung was the power behind the throne, and he set up a system much like the Japanese shogunate, but this only lasted a few years until he decided to take the throne himself. He then killed all of the Le royal family members he could get his hands on and proclaimed a new dynasty, that of the Mac, in June 1527.

To the south of Hanoi is Thanh Hoa province (birthplace of Le Loi), and this was where much of the fighting took place. After the killing of much of the Le family, large numbers of the rich and aristocratic families of Vietnam joined with the Trinh and Nguyen families to fight against Mac rule. The fight against the Mac dynasty was ostensibly fought in the name of the Le dynasty, but most knew that if the Trinh and Nguyen factions defeated the Mac, it would only be a matter of time before the two families fought each other.

Over the next sixty years, Dai Viet was at war with itself. Factions rose and fell. Generals and influential family members climbed to the top only to be assassinated. They switched sides, betrayed one another, and involved non-Vietnamese tribes in the fighting. At one point, Mac Dang Dung asked the Chinese Ming dynasty for help, ceding them land in the north for the promise of no further Chinese intervention in Vietnam once the civil war was over. Eventually, the Chinese sent some aid and troops, but Vietnam was a quagmire, and they withdrew to deal with problems elsewhere in their empire. It should be remembered that the Chinese did not withdraw from Vietnam because they could not defeat the Vietnamese militarily—their military was much, much larger than anything the Vietnamese would have been able to muster. They withdrew due to the same reasons as before: cost, political opposition within the Chinese court, and problems elsewhere in their territories. These are the same problems that would occur in the 20th century when the West, in the form of the French and the United States, would become involved in Vietnam.

When the Mac were finally defeated in 1592, Vietnam, over the course of a few years, became divided. The detailed history for the reasons for this would (and has) taken up thousands of pages in much longer and more exhaustive histories on Vietnam. For our purposes here, we are going to keep it simple: the northern part of Dai Viet became the territory of the Trinh family, and the southern part became the territory of the Nguyen.

The maps on the following pages might be helpful in understanding the growth and divisions of Vietnam in the 1500s.

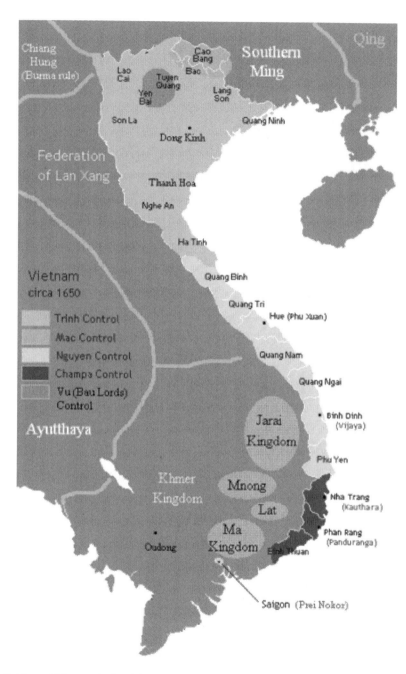

The divisions of Vietnam in the 17th century. As you can see, the Mac retained a small territory on the Chinese border. The Vu were tribal lords in the defensible highlands.
https://commons.wikimedia.org/wiki/File:Vietnam1650.GIF

Over the course of the next 300 years, the Trinh and Nguyen struggled for control of the country. At rare times, they worked together when faced with external threats.

The Trinh

As you might imagine, northern Vietnam, which was under the Trinh, was highly influenced by China. Some of this influence was from China directly in the form of quid pro quo. As you have seen throughout this book, the Chinese have influenced Vietnam since the beginning of recorded history, and under the Trinh, Chinese culture in the form of Confucianism, Taoism, law, and much else was dominant.

The growing influence of China in Trinh Vietnam caused a shift in Vietnamese life. Some of this was obvious, such as law, civil service, and religious and spiritual beliefs. However, much of this shift in northern Vietnamese life was gradual. On a national level, the ruling Trinh brought in more and more Chinese ideas, but in response to this, the power in everyday life in Vietnam devolved to the local/village level. Over time, a tacit agreement was reached—the Trinh would let the villages run their own affairs as long as the villagers would send their sons to defend Trinh interests in times of war. The same type of arrangement also pertained to taxes (in a general way, as Vietnam was still a feudal society, and large landowners had the power to tax). All the Trinh asked was for them to pay what they owed, and in return, the Trinh would leave them alone. However, sometimes the taxes were too onerous, which caused revolts.

The Trinh used a surviving branch of the Le family to keep up appearances and the image of continuity, but the Le emperors under the Trinh were merely figureheads, as the various Trinh warlords held the real power.

Vietnamese intellectuals and religious figures retreated with the ascension of Chinese ideas in the Trinh court and upper classes. The intellectual classes of scholars and monks did not guide policy decisions under the Trinh, as they had with other rulers to varying degrees before. The Trinh ruled by using *Te* (power). To most Vietnamese at the time, all of the Trinh rulers lacked that unique Vietnamese quality of *phúc d'uc*.

One of the most famous Vietnamese poems was written about the Trinh under their rule. The poem, "Sam Trang Trinh," by Nguyen Binh Khiem, laments that Vietnam (at least in the north) was not ruled by virtue and wisdom but rather power, intimidation, money, and death. The writings of Nguyen Binh Khiem are treated by many Vietnamese (especially in the exile community) as a sort of prophecy, foretelling the conditions that need to be met in Vietnam for communism to fall.

The Nguyen

In central and southern Vietnam, the Nguyen ruled, doing so in a much different way than the Trinh. At times, of course, the ruling family resorted to force and the use of raw power to keep their position, but as opposed to the Trinh, the Nguyen embraced Vietnamese ways and kept Chinese influence as small as possible.

In addition to promoting and encouraging Vietnamese Buddhism and folk beliefs, the Nguyen also controlled a much more arable part of the country, as well as fishing lanes that they zealously guarded. Putting it plainly, the Nguyen were better off than the Trinh.

The Nguyen also used their money to try and negate the one advantage the Trinh had: numbers. As you know, the northern part of Vietnam was/is the oldest, as it had been settled thousands of years prior to the partition between the Nguyen and Trinh. Obviously, this gave the Trinh an advantage militarily, and the Nguyen were determined to negate this advantage. They did it in the same way as the American government in the 1800s did when colonizing land in the American West—they gave it away or sold it for cheap.

From 1627 to 1672 and again from 1774 to 1775, the Trinh and Nguyen fought one another for control of Vietnam. In these wars, the Nguyen had a number of advantages. For one, they were on the defense (the Trinh couldn't expand into China to the north, and the land to the west was practically worthless). Second, the battles mainly took place where Vietnam was the narrowest, making the movement and maneuvering of large armies very difficult. Third, the Nguyen had possession of heavily fortified cities in the area, which goes hand-in-hand with the last advantage of the Nguyen—they had contact with Europeans. The Europeans supplied the Nguyen with small but effective quantities of firearms, as well as the training to use them. (Strangely enough, European military aid on land went mainly to the Nguyen. However, the Dutch supplied a small number of ships to the Trinh, while the Chinese supplied ships to the Nguyen. In 1643, the Nguyen, in their Chinese ships, defeated the Trinh in their European vessels.)

Between 1653 and 1656, the Nguyen launched an invasion of the north, which, at first, seemed destined to succeed but ultimately failed due to the leadership of the Trinh general and de facto ruler Trinh Tac. The Nguyen were pushed back into their own territory, and the war continued in a stalemate. The Trinh tried to push south one more time in 1672 but failed, and in 1673, the two sides agreed on a truce. For their part, the Nguyen recognized the Trinh-sponsored Le emperor. On the other side, the Trinh agreed to stop their invasion plans and let the Nguyen govern the south as they wanted.

In the end, neither side would "win." In the 1770s, a rebellion broke out in the south under the Tay Son brothers, who removed the Nguyen government in the south with the help of the Trinh. However, ten years later, they would attack and remove the Trinh in the north.

Chapter 7 – The Europeans Arrive

The first Europeans to arrive in Vietnam in numbers were Portuguese missionaries who had come from their missions in India in the 1500s. These Dominican missionaries found little traction among the Vietnamese and did not stay.

A few decades later, Catholic missionaries began to arrive. These were mainly Jesuit missionaries, many of whom had previously worked in Japan but had been expelled by the first shogun, Tokugawa Ieyasu, in 1614 when he closed the nation to virtually all foreigners. The first Jesuits were a mix of Italian, Spanish, and Portuguese priests and brothers (monks), but it was a Frenchman, a priest by the name of Alexandre de Rhodes, who had the most impact on Vietnam.

De Rhodes was born in 1593 in Avignon, in today's France. At the time, Avignon was under the direct rule of the pope and the Catholic Church. At the age of twenty, de Rhodes went to Rome to begin what he believed was his calling—missionary work. He spent twelve years in Rome with the Society of Jesus, also known as the Jesuit Order, which had been founded by Ignatius of Loyola in 1540.

The Jesuits were considered the most zealous of all Catholic missionaries, and they frequently involved themselves in politics, not only in Europe but also in the countries they "visited" as missionaries. Many critical things have been said of the Jesuits, and many of them are deserved. However, they were also among the most highly educated and innovative men of their time.

Generally speaking, the Jesuits, as opposed to their brethren in other orders (the Franciscans and Dominicans), attempted to teach Christianity in a way that made sense to the local population. They also learned about their culture rather than impose European culture on them. This was one reason for their amazing success in many areas of the world. Unfortunately, it was also one reason for their downfall, as the other orders grew jealous of the inroads the Jesuits made with indigenous populations.

Alexandre de Rhodes was a man who wanted to learn about the people with whom he was sharing the word of God. When he arrived in Nguyen-controlled Vietnam, he studied Vietnamese with a Portuguese Jesuit named Francisco de Pina, who had been there for some time and who had developed a Latin-based script for the Vietnamese language. Pina was a polyglot, and he knew not only Vietnamese but also spoke fluent Japanese as well. He created a Latin book on Japanese grammar that was the building block for other Europeans. Pina was among the handful of Jesuits preaching and studying at the first Catholic church permitted in Vietnam. This was in Danang on the south-central coast of the kingdom.

When de Rhodes arrived in 1624, he organized the teaching of Catholic Christian doctrine in Vietnam, and the faith slowly began to spread in the country. To further the spread of Catholicism, de Rhodes translated and adapted the Catholic catechism into Vietnamese. For example, the work starts with the phrase "The Way of the Virtuous Sky Lord" rather than references to Jesus Christ, of whom the Vietnamese had no knowledge. The catechism was the first book written with Vietnamese Latin characters. De Rhodes also wrote the first Vietnamese-Portuguese-Latin dictionary, which was published in Rome in 1651.

De Rhodes studied and worked at Danang for three years before being sent north to the Hanoi (then Thang Long) region in 1627. For three years, de Rhodes worked in and near the court of the Trinh king, Trinh Trang. He reportedly converted some 6,000 Vietnamese to the Catholic faith and wrote a devotional called Ngam Mua Chay, which concerns itself with Christ's Passion and is still popular today among Vietnamese Catholics.

De Rhodes was expelled from the Trinh territory in 1630, but not because the Trinh were overly worried about the spreading of the faith, though that was a concern. Trinh Trang was more worried that de Rhodes was a spy for the southern Vietnamese rulers, the Nguyen. De Rhodes then moved to the Portuguese concession of Macau, where he lived and worked for the next ten years. He returned to Vietnam in around 1640 and spread the word for six years before the Nguyen king, Nguyen Phuc Lan, determined that Catholicism was a threat to the country and sentenced de Rhodes to death. This sentence was commuted, and de Rhodes was instead expelled from the country, never to return. However, it is estimated that by 1640, 80,000 Vietnamese in the south and an equal number in the north had converted. One of the reasons for that success was de Rhodes's efforts. Besides his evangelizing, de Rhodes wrote to the bishops assigned to Vietnam and Southeast Asia, stressing his success and the hunger of the Vietnamese for Christianity.

He also approached French and Spanish trading companies for funds. He continued to do this when he returned to Rome after his expulsion from Vietnam.

Christianity never amounted to more than a sizable minority in Vietnam, but it was an influential one, especially in the south. Though the faith had success among all strata of Vietnamese society, many converts were from the upper classes, and many were women. Remember, Vietnam, as opposed to China and many (but not all) Asian nations, was a place where women held great power. Vietnamese folk religion had also always emphasized the role of the "Ten Mao," the old sainted mother watching over all things.

By the 1600s, the following of the Virgin Mary had spread throughout Catholicism. This had not always been the case, but by the end of the Middle Ages, Mary was seen as an intercessory figure from human beings to God.

If you remember, the Vietnamese creation myth involved a female spirit/fairy named Âu Cơ. The Vietnamese have adhered to the ideas of yin and yang ("dark and bright") almost since the beginning of time. This idea, which originated in China millennia ago, stresses the balance of the universe, with the "yin" being the passive, female principle and the "yang" being the active, male principle.

In Vietnam in the 17th century, many religious people had begun to believe that yin and yang were out of balance, with the yang principle ascendant, meaning there was too much stress on the ideas of power, will, and force. They also believed that the traditional Vietnamese idea of *phúc d'uc* ("virtue") had faded dangerously into the background. With the arrival of Christianity, and as de Rhodes put it, the "Virtuous Sky Lord," who sacrificed himself for the people, some Vietnamese saw a way to return to better times when the world was more in balance. To them, the

Virgin Mary might be an iteration of the "Ten Mao."

Alexandre de Rhodes was never sent back to Vietnam. Instead, he was sent to Persia to spread the word there, and he died there in 1660.

Chapter 8 – New Powers and New Divisions

The first part of the 18th century was a time of peace in Vietnam. The Trinh in the north and the Nguyen in the south managed to get along well enough from 1700 to 1765, but in that last year, things began to change for the worse in the country.

In the south, the ruling Nguyen lord, Nguyen Phuc Khoat, died. His successor was the twelve-year-old son of one of his concubines. In his place, an unpopular regent ruled the Nguyen lands, which were involved in wars in present-day Cambodia with the Khmer people, as well as with the Siamese (Thais), with whom they vied for control of Cambodia.

These were unpopular and expensive wars, and they weakened Nguyen rule considerably. In 1769, the Siamese ruler launched a powerful offensive to regain Siamese/Thai control of Cambodia. At this point in time, Cambodia included the most southern provinces of today's

Vietnam, south of Ho Chi Minh City. As the Nguyen weakened, the Trinh in the north saw an opportunity to expand their territory and invaded the south (to be more exact, the central part of today's Vietnam).

However, in the mountains of southern Vietnam, a new power was rising. This was the Tay Son. The name comes from the village from where the brothers came. Actually, the Tay Son were three brothers whose last name was Nguyen (no relation to the ruling family, though it does not make things less complicated when it comes to keeping track of the names). Their first names were Nhac, Lu, and Hue, of which Hue became the most powerful and influential.

The time for rebellion was right, as the war was going badly for the Nguyen. Not only that, but the Nguyen court was in the hands of an unpopular regent. Nguyen rule was seen by many Vietnamese of all classes as increasingly corrupt and inefficient. The rule of law was breaking down, and bandit gangs were the de facto rulers of many areas of the country.

Throughout history, tribal and village leaders who raised the flag of revolt have presented themselves as "men of the people," only reluctantly taking up arms against the government when there was no other choice. This was how it went with the Tay Son in 1772. They organized not only their extended family and clan but also poor people from the surrounding areas and tribes in the more remote areas of the south and western highlands.

The stated goal of the Tay Son was to restore the Le emperor, fight corruption, and reduce the power of wealthy landlords by redistributing land and reforming feudal laws. Within a year, the Tay Son, led by Nguyen Hue (who was either the middle brother or the youngest), had beaten the Nguyen armies that had been sent westward to defeat the rebellion.

Modern statue of the Tay Son brothers in Vietnam.

Ba_anh_em_nhà_họ_Nhạc.JPG: The original uploader was Liftold at Vietnamese Wikipedia.derivative work: Phó Nháy, CC BY-SA 3.0 <https://creativecommons.org/licenses/by-sa/3.0>, via Wikimedia Commons https://commons.wikimedia.org/wiki/File:Nhac_Brothers.JPG

By the next year, the Nguyen were in serious trouble. The Tay Son had taken an important southern port and won over the rich traders there. The Nguyen had made peace with the Siamese but at the cost of recently conquered territory, which sent a message of weakness to both their supporters and enemies. Making things even worse, the Trinh invaded the northern part of the Nguyen kingdom and seized their capital, Hue. The Nguyen were forced to move their capital and forces to Saigon and the nearby area, but that only made their problems worse, as they were then forced to give up much of the land in the south that was away from the coast to the Tay Son.

In 1776, the last stronghold of the Nguyen was taken by the Trinh, and almost the entire Nguyen family was killed, with one member escaping and fleeing to Thailand for help. The Tay Son now ruled most of the south. The oldest brother, Nhac, proclaimed himself emperor, contrary to the wishes of the most powerful brother, Hue. The Trinh immediately declared war on the Tay Son.

Although these powers were technically at war with each other, the next decade saw both sides strengthening their positions rather than engage in all-out war. In 1785, the Tay Son, led by Hue, defeated an invading Siamese army, which was headed by the last remaining member of the Nguyen.

By 1786, the Trinh were considerably weaker than they had been. Like the Nguyen, their rule had deteriorated and was seen by many in the country to be corrupt and ineffective. Seeing this, the Tay Son invaded Trinh lands and defeated the Trinh army in one final decisive battle. The Trinh king and his family fled to China, and Hue married the Le princess, Le Ngoc Han, giving himself entry into the royal family. Hue's brother Lu died in 1787, leaving the two other brothers vying for control. In the end, after much political maneuvering and a brief battle, the brothers agreed to partition the country among themselves. However, Nhac would die in 1788, leaving his territories to Hue.

If you recall, earlier in this book, we told you that the French began to refer to much of Vietnam as "Annam." They did this because that's what they had heard it called in China. From a Vietnamese point of view, this was an insult, as "Annam" means the "Pacified South." Tay Son brothers Nhac and Lu had governed the former Nguyen territory in the south, which was, to them, the "pacified south." When the French used the term, it was taken by the Vietnamese as one of foreign conquest.

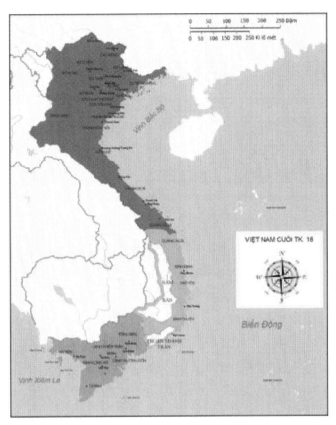

Division of Vietnam, end of 19th century. Blue ruled by Hue, gold by Nhac, and green by Nguyen Anh.
A (talk · contribs), CC BY-SA 4.0 <https://creativecommons.org/licenses/by-sa/4.0>, via Wikimedia Commons https://commons.wikimedia.org/wiki/File:Vietnam_at_the_end_of_18th_century_(Vi).png

As you can see in the map above, the far south of Vietnam was ruled by the last of the Nguyen kings, Nguyen Anh. He had staged a comeback with the help of the Siamese and asserted control over the southern area. Over the course of the next few years, he would enlist the help of the French in his attempt to reclaim not only old Nguyen lands but also the rest of Vietnam. He was helped by the early death of the strongest Tay Son brother, Hue, in 1792. The Tay Son successors were no match for the armies of Nguyen Anh, as they were joined by the French, Siamese, and the Qing dynasty of China. In 1793, Nguyen Anh defeated the remaining Tay Son, who were backed into an ever-shrinking pocket in the center of the country.

In 1802, after having given himself other titles as he won victories, Nguyen Anh proclaimed himself emperor of all Vietnam, which was the first time this had ever happened. Surprisingly, the Chinese recognized him as such. Nguyen Anh gave himself the imperial name of "Gia Long" (pronounced "Zy-ah Lawn"). This name was a combination of the old Vietnamese names for Hanoi and Saigon (Thang Long and Gia Dinh, respectively), symbolizing his rule was from north to south.

When Gia Long came to power, he began, as others had done before him, to swing back to "Chinese" ideas, meaning the ideas of Confucianism. Neo-Confucianism heavily stressed the importance of family and the family hierarchy and, by extension, the emperor and the ruling clan. All instructions came from the emperor, and everyone below him was required to follow them. Gia Long even brought the Chinese law code to Vietnam, verbatim and in Chinese characters. Since Gia Long was the first person to claim lordship over Vietnam as we know it today, his word and his power went far. Even the Chinese Qing dynasty recognized his right to rule and call himself "King of the State of Vietnam," a title that had been achieved with much haggling. It was also the first time that the country was called "Vietnam" rather than "Dai Viet" or another name.

The Neo-Confucian ideas of Gia Long were in opposition to the ideas of the most powerful Tay Son brother, Nguyen Hue, who stressed Vietnamese principles over Chinese principles. Though Hue had died fairly early in his rule, he was still a popular personality in Vietnam and was venerated, especially in the north.

Hue's spirit of "Vietnamese-ness" can be heard in this speech, which is still popular in Vietnam today:

In the sky, constellations have their own place, and on Earth, each nation has its own place. The Chinese do not belong to our race, their intentions must be different than ours. Chinese have always taken advantage of our nation, riches and people. A hero has always risen up to fight them. How can they not know about the prior defeats...I am taking control of the army—you are men of free will and I ask you to follow me.

As you can see, Hue was asking for help, not demanding it.

Gia Long demanded it, and this caused great resentment over time, but he successfully used a number of different strategies to rule. First, he used raw power. Then, he used bribery and favors, dispensing them to officials high and low. Third, he allowed the villages to, for the most part, rule themselves. As long as they paid taxes, provided men for the army, and paid him lip service, he generally let them be.

Gia Long also set up powerful warlords in the different regions of the country, who were relatively free to govern as they saw fit. Gia Long ruled central Vietnam directly but set up powerful governors in the north and south to rule for him. Many historians point to this period as a time when the differences between regions really became pronounced.

Gia Long came to power in 1802 at the age of forty and ruled until 1820. By this time, the French had begun to assert themselves in the country. By emphasizing *Te*, or "power," and Neo-Confucian ideas, Gia Long had inadvertently set up Vietnam to be taken over by a stronger power with more money and exotic ideas, some of which appealed to great numbers of the people.

Chapter 9 – The French

Until the arrival of de Rhodes and his success in interesting French officials in Vietnam, most of the Europeans in the country were Portuguese. Following de Rhodes, the French Society of Foreign Missions, an organization of French Catholic clergy and businessmen/aristocrats that is still active today in spreading the Catholic faith in Asia, began to make inroads in Vietnam.

Soon a rivalry emerged between the French and Portuguese missionaries, and the pope was forced to step in. The Portuguese believed that Vietnam "belonged" to them according to a prior papal order, the Treaty of Tordesillas (1494), which essentially divided the Americas and Asia between the two dominant sea-going Catholic powers of the time, Spain and Portugal. In 1738, Pope Clement XII divided Vietnam into spheres of influence between the French in the south and the Portuguese in the north. Clement's order simply caused more competition between the two nations.

In the 1750s, the French allied themselves with the Tay Son brothers, especially Hue and the nobles surrounding him. By the end of the decade, the French had managed to convince the regime to expel the Portuguese, and with that, the French became the sole European nation allowed to proselytize and do any sort of meaningful business in Vietnam.

From the middle of the 1700s to the end of the century, most Vietnamese were rather ambivalent toward the French. There was not a lot of them, though their numbers were slowly increasing, especially near Saigon, Hanoi, and the imperial city of Hue in the center. The French also brought new technologies, which slowly made their way in relatively controlled numbers to the Vietnamese imperial army, and a new faith that appealed to many Vietnamese.

It was that last aspect that bothered Gia Long when he took the throne in 1802. He kept his eye on the French and attempted to control their access to parts of the country and the numbers of missionaries. However, he did see the advantages of having the French as an ally against Vietnam's many potential enemies: China, Siam/Thailand, the Khmer, and perhaps other Europeans who were eager to exploit his kingdom, such as the British, who were turned away multiple times by Gia Long, likely with the French whispering in his ear.

Gia Long's son, Minh Mang (r. 1820-1841), was openly hostile to the French and virtually all other foreigners, not only Europeans but other Asians as well. He particularly despised Catholicism and wished to reinforce Confucian ideas.

Contemporary sketch of Emperor Minh Mang
John Crawfurd, CC0, via Wikimedia Commons
https://commons.wikimedia.org/wiki/File:King_of_Cochin_China_Minh_Menh_by_John_Crawfurd_book_Published_by_H_Colburn_London_1828.jpg

In the first years of his reign, Minh Mang rejected a number of trade deals and further alliances proposed by the French. Five years after he ascended the throne, he ordered that no more Catholic missionaries would be allowed to enter his kingdom. Shrewdly, he appointed a number of high-ranking French clergy to his court, not so much to take their advice but to keep an eye on them. His policy was much like that of the Japanese shoguns, who had kept the influence of foreigners in Japan very limited since the 1600s. Ming Mang made the following statement to members of his court and a representative from China:

> There has always been a strategy for halting the advances of barbarians. Our own court deals with the Westerners according to the following principles. If they come here, we do not oppose them; if they leave, we do not chase them; we simply treat them as barbarians. If their vessels come to trade, we only permit them to anchor at Tra-son. When exchanges are finished, they must depart. We do not let them remain ashore for long, and we do not allow the local people to trade directly with them. Thus, even if they are cunning and deceitful, there will be no openings of which they can take advantage in order to cause troubles.

When a rebellion against Minh Mang's rule erupted in the south in 1833, the French were quick to support it. The leader of this rebellion, Le Van Khoi, was a Catholic, and he had gained the support of local Vietnamese Catholics and others, including a powerful Catholic regional warlord. Within a very short time, Le Van Khoi's forces had seized the area around Saigon and six other southern provinces. Over the next two years, Minh Mang's forces struggled to regain control of the area.

Once back in control, Minh Mang ordered the arrest of both Vietnamese and foreign Catholics throughout the country. Many of them were executed, sometimes in a brutal fashion. One method of death included the pulling off of flesh by red-hot prongs. One of the French Jesuits who had supported Le Van Khoi suffered this fate. His name was Joseph Marchand, and he is now a saint in the Roman Catholic Church.

Naturally, the death of Marchand and other Catholics angered the French, and they did not lessen the zeal with which Catholic missionaries arrived in Vietnam, albeit done secretly. Minh Mang's successor, Thieu

Tri (r. 1841-47), was even more hostile to the French and Catholicism than Minh Mang. He proscribed the teaching of Christianity, in particular Catholicism, and wherever his officials could find them, Catholic missionaries and Vietnamese were thrown into prison.

By the 1840s, the French were beginning to recover from the era of Napoleon and its aftermath. Having spent much of the 1820s and 1830s somewhat under the eye of the other European powers, the French were beginning to feel a renewed nationalism. By the early mid-1800s, the European countries were done fighting with each other (for a time) and had turned to increased efforts to colonize the rest of the world. Each nation's power and prestige were increasingly tied to the size and wealth of its overseas empire.

Part of this reassertion of French power, and European power in general, were the reactions of European/French governments when their nationals were mistreated by foreign powers. The Europeans often referred to them as "savages," but to be fair, Minh Mang and thousands of others throughout history referred to non-Vietnamese as "barbarians."

In 1847, the French sent two warships to Danang, Vietnam, to add muscle to the negotiations to release two imprisoned French missionaries. The negotiations broke down, and when they did, the French ships opened on the city of Danang, sinking three Vietnamese naval vessels and doing damage to coastal forts and buildings in the city.

In response, Thieu Tri ordered all coastal forts to be strengthened and an increase in the production of cannons. He also ordered the deaths of all foreign missionaries in Vietnam, which essentially meant all Frenchmen, and the "eradication" of Catholicism in the country.

Thieu Tri died soon after issuing this order. His orders were not carried out because most knew that doing so would likely provoke not only a French response but possibly an all-out war with Europe. After all, the English had just defeated the Chinese in the First Opium War, something no one in Asia could have predicted.

Tu Duc became emperor in 1847 and ruled until 1883. His long reign saw various actions against the Vietnamese and French Catholics, but many of his harsh orders were not carried out by his minions. Some were actually Catholic themselves, and others did not wish to provoke an incident with the French in the areas under their control. Still, from time to time, incidents occurred, and with each one, calls went up in Paris and the rest of France for action to be taken in Vietnam.

In 1847, shortly before Tu Duc became emperor, two French warships were sent to Danang to negotiate with Thieu Tri's government for the release of two French missionaries. When they arrived, they were attacked by a sizable Vietnamese fleet. Though outnumbered, the French ships were much more modern and commanded by men experienced by years at sea in combat. The Vietnamese were defeated at great cost, and the missionaries were released.

In 1857, two Spanish missionaries working with the French Society of Foreign Missions were killed at Tu Duc's command. The timing could not have been worse for Tu Duc and his supporters. The French were incensed about the treatment of Catholics in Vietnam and the limitations put on their ability to trade in the country. Not only that, but Europe was in the midst of its second great race for empire-building when Tu Duc acted against the missionaries and Catholics in 1857/58, and France had gotten off to a lousy start.

The first European Age of Imperialism had begun with Christopher Columbus's voyages and ended with the American Revolution and the convulsions of the French Revolution and Napoleon Bonaparte, a time when Europe turned inward out of necessity. Now, however, European relations, while sometimes frosty, were peaceful for the most part. The

European nations realized how destructive a war among themselves could be and that a world of riches was waiting to be claimed, seized, or traded for.

Because of European suspicion of France after Napoleon and the damage done internally in that country, France got a late start in the race for colonies, which started anew in the 1800s—at least compared to its main rival, England. Before England could claim and conquer the entire world, the French wanted a piece of it, and Southeast Asia was the biggest, richest, unconquered land out there. It also lay between Britain's Indian possessions and its possessions in China, where France also had interests. A French possession along the sea routes between these two immense areas might come in handy in time. The French were also lagging behind Holland, Spain, and Portugal, which were all much weaker countries at the time, in the race for a mighty empire. This galled many Frenchmen to no end.

Also driving the French initiative for colonies was Napoleon Bonaparte's nephew, who would become president of France from 1848 to 1852 before, like his famous (and much smarter) uncle, naming himself emperor of the French in 1852. His rule ended in 1870 when he was defeated by the Prussians and removed from the throne in the latter's drive for German unification. In 1858, the French put together a powerful fleet of 14 warships along with 3,000 French marines, 300 Catholic Filipino soldiers, and a number of Spanish ships. Once they were assembled, they were sent to Vietnam to teach Tu Duc a lesson.

The French, under Admiral Charles Rigault de Genouilly, appeared offshore at Danang and proceeded to shell the city and land troops. The Vietnamese surprised the French with the strength of their resistance, and the siege went on for a year and a half before the French took the city. In actuality, more French casualties occurred from disease than combat.

During the siege and occupation, Genouilly implemented plans to strike at other parts of Vietnam.

In February 1859, a reinforced French/Spanish fleet, with French/Spanish/Filipino troops aboard, sailed up the Mekong River to attack Saigon. After a series of intense attacks and Vietnamese counterattacks, the European force besieged the strongest position in the city, the Citadel of Saigon. They captured it and blew it up, knowing they were not strong enough to hold it. Genouilly left a 1,000-man force in Saigon to hold the city while he returned to Danang (which the French called "Tourane") to deal with matters there. He soon realized that his forces were only strong enough to hold either Saigon or Danang, not both, and Danang was evacuated.

Over the course of the next two years, the French and the Vietnamese fought a series of battles and sieges in southern Vietnam. The French outgunned and outclassed the Vietnamese technologically, but the Vietnamese had the numbers and were fighting for their homeland—well, sort of. Many Vietnamese had turned away from Tu Duc and the imperial regime.

This happened for a variety of reasons. The seeming French superiority caused many Vietnamese to believe that the emperor and his family had lost the Mandate of Heaven. A sizable number in the south had become Catholic. Most others, not taking sides, retreated into intellectual or village life, waiting to see which way the wind blew while they rode out the storm.

In 1862, the Vietnamese and French signed the Treaty of Saigon, ending the war. Tu Duc was motivated by the necessity of keeping his throne and dealing with a sizable Catholic rebellion in the south, which he hoped the French would influence to cease. (The French tried, but the rebels refused to lay down their arms. As part of the agreement with Tu

Duc, he was given a free hand to deal with this rebellion—it seems as if French Catholics were more important than Vietnamese ones.) The Vietnamese army was also outgunned, and while the soldiers had put up a valiant fight, they could not hold out against continued French attacks. For the French, the treaty would end the increasing casualties and the great cost of the war.

The Treaty of Saigon forced Tu Duc to cede the area known as "Cochinchina," which included Saigon and the region south of it. The French also received a number of islands off the coast and in the Mekong Delta, which would give them control of the major trade routes there. In addition, Tu Duc gave the French control of his foreign affairs and international trade. Cochinchina became a French colony, and the Vietnamese emperor was essentially a puppet ruler.

In 1867, the French in Cochinchina, led by Admiral Marie Benoit de La Grandiere, grew concerned about the strategic position of Cochinchina vis-a-vis the north of Vietnam and the Khmer territories to the west. He led a French expedition into central coastal Vietnam. The governor there, Phan Thanh Gian, told Vietnamese forces to stand down to avoid useless bloodshed, then killed himself. He is a national hero in Vietnam today. All of southern Vietnam was then under French control.

Around sixteen years later, the French were engaged in a war with China, facing raids on their interests in northern Vietnam by Vietnamese troops, Chinese bandits, and the Chinese army. For much of 1883, the French waged a costly but brief war against the Vietnamese and their Chinese allies in Tonkin (the northernmost area of Vietnam). They besieged the imperial city of Hue and forced the Vietnamese court, which had already been greatly weakened internally and externally, to allow the French to take Tonkin as a "protectorate." All of Vietnam was under French control, as were neighboring Laos and Cambodia.

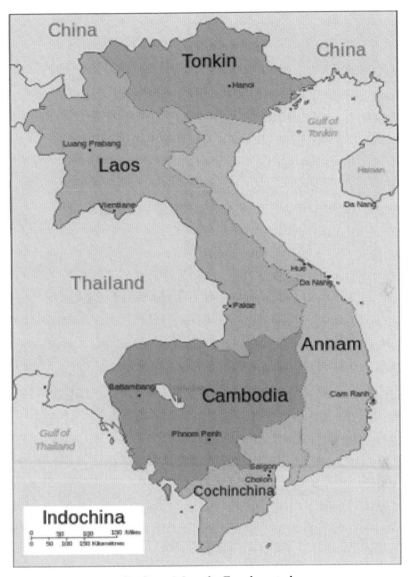

Southeast Asia under French control
Bearsmalaysia, CC BY-SA 3.0 <https://creativecommons.org/licenses/by-sa/3.0>, via Wikimedia Commons https://commons.wikimedia.org/wiki/File:French_Indochina_subdivisions.svg

Chapter 10 – French Rule

From 1883 to 1954, with an interval during WWII, the French ruled Vietnam. The succeeding emperors were mere figureheads who were to be "consulted" out of diplomatic nicety, but French officials governed the country, at least at the very top and at the provincial level. Locally, French officials could not govern without at least a tacit agreement from the Vietnamese bureaucracy, which, to a large degree, came to enjoy French largesse and the privileges that came with governing for a rich European power.

Today, the only real reminders of the French colonial period in Vietnam is the architecture of some of the larger Vietnamese cities, particularly Hanoi and Ho Chi Minh City, which the French were determined to make as "European" as possible. Visitors to the old quarter of Hanoi often reflect on how much the area looks like Paris, which has survived despite the intense bombing of the Vietnam War in the 1960s and 1970s.

After the French left Vietnam in the 1950s, for a time, many of the upper class in Vietnam (particularly in the south) spoke, read, and wrote French, some almost exclusively. In what became North Vietnam, speaking French publicly was not a smart thing to do after the communists took over, though Ho Chi Minh and many of the original elder statesmen of the Communist Party of Vietnam spoke fluent French, having gone to school in Paris.

What else did the French offer? Well, it would come back to haunt them, but at least on the surface, the French offered the Vietnamese the same rights that Frenchmen were given in the famous French revolutionary document, the Declaration of the Rights of Man and of the Citizen. This document, like the American Declaration of Independence and Bill of Rights, enumerated the rights and freedoms that Frenchmen (and those "under their protection") were born with and could enjoy.

Among the rights in the French document were the assertion that all "men are born and remain free and equal in rights," and they were to enjoy the same "unalienable" rights as Americans: property, liberty, resistance to oppression, equality before the law, right to due process, the right to participate in government, and the freedom of religion.

But were these rights observed by the French in Vietnam? The answer is a little complicated. When the Vietnamese ignored the fact that the French were the rulers of their country and lived peacefully, most Vietnamese enjoyed some semblance of these rights. The keyword here is "semblance." As French rule continued, it became clear to many Vietnamese that the French and the Vietnamese upper classes were able to enjoy these "rights" more than those at the bottom or who saw things differently. Still, many of these rights were honored only in the breach.

For many Vietnamese, French rule did provide some protections and improvements. The French built schools throughout the country, mainly in the cities. These were based on the French "lycee" model, giving many Vietnamese their first formal schooling. The French also invested heavily in infrastructure: the building mentioned above, French city-planning, paved roads, better erosion control, a degree of advanced agricultural techniques, and much else.

Perhaps, though, at least for Vietnamese Catholics, the French guaranteed the freedom of religion, and this, for the most part, was honored. Under previous Vietnamese rulers, people of varying religious beliefs had been persecuted. At times when Chinese Neo-Confucian ideals were emphasized, Vietnamese folk religions, as well as Buddhism, were discouraged or repressed. At other times, Catholicism was put down, as we saw in the previous chapter. Under the French regime, religious freedom was guaranteed, as long as religious leaders did not advocate for Vietnamese independence, which most of them refrained from until at least the 1930s.

In the late 1800s and early 1900s, various socialist ideas were becoming popular in Europe and France. With the growth of industry in France (and much of Europe in general) came a shift in the economic landscape. Great wealth was created, as was great poverty. The most militant of these socialist groups evolved into communist parties in the early 1900s.

"Communism," as described by German economic philosophers Karl Marx and Friedrich Engels, was less a revolutionary idea to change the economic landscape of Europe and the world and more of an irresistible economic force. Going hand in hand with that other revolutionary theory of the time, evolution, communist theory declared that economics was an evolutionary timeline. It was a historical inevitability that capitalism would collapse upon itself due to its unequal distribution of wealth and privilege. In the communist stage of economic development, workers would collectively own the means of production and private property. Classes would be abolished, and equal rights would be enjoyed by all in a "workers' state." Communism also propagated the idea that the wealthy capitalist countries of the West (and their native puppets) kept down the population of their colonies and held attitudes of ethnic and racial inequality.

By the early 20th century, increasing numbers of upper- and upper-middle-class Vietnamese sent their sons (and sometimes daughters) to France to receive a European education. At the time, Europeans had a decided edge in many areas, such as engineering, technology, science, medicine, and business.

In some cases, sending the youth of Vietnam to France was a practical move. They could learn to become officials in the French government or enter the European business world and enjoy the benefits and privileges it could provide. In some cases, young Vietnamese were sent to France to learn about French culture, government, and society to better navigate the world of colonial Vietnam. While there, many Vietnamese were exposed to the ideas mentioned above, whether Marxism, other socialist ideas, or the ideas presented in the Declaration of the Rights of Man and of the Citizen.

One of these was a young man from a lower-middle-class background. His name was Nguyen Sinh Cung, but he is better known as Ho Chi Minh.

Chapter 11 – Vietnam in Turmoil

Vietnam in the first part of the 20th century was like a tea kettle on a hot stove when the water first starts to boil. If you watch an old-fashioned tea kettle, you'll hear the water boil inside before you see any indications of steam coming out of the spout. Then, occasionally, you'll see little explosions of steam shoot out of the spout or the lid. If the lid isn't tight enough, you'll see and hear it rattling on top of the stove. Unless you take the kettle off, there is only one inevitable outcome: the water is going to boil, and steam will come billowing out.

The first three decades of the 20th century were a period of great and rapid change in Vietnam. By the end of the 1800s, the French had cemented their rule of the country, and while many Vietnamese worked for the colonial power, the levers of power—meaning the courts, the police (and secret police), and the army—were all in the hands of the French. Sectors of Vietnamese society seemed to avail themselves of one of four main choices. Firstly, they could cooperate with the French and seek out a place for themselves in the ruling political and/or economic hierarchy. Most of those who did were either from the imperial family and its many branches, from the upper economic classes, Catholics, and merchants.

Secondly, they could peacefully, at least at first, attempt to use French ideas against the French, meaning that the Vietnamese, who had their own press, though it was controlled, and their own village and provincial councils, could assert the rights enumerated in the Declaration of the Rights of Man and of the Citizen. After all, if liberty was guaranteed to all men, why then were the Vietnamese under France's thumb? A growing number of Vietnamese, especially in the north, also turned to the other Western idea of socialism, the very idea that French workers were embracing in their own battle for a better life.

Thirdly, and this could work hand in hand with the above, the Vietnamese could simply oppose the French as conquerors, as they had done for centuries with the Chinese. This was simply opposition based on nationalist ideas, which sometimes were combined with others, such as communism.

Fourthly, the Vietnamese could do what they had done for centuries: wait. Many Vietnamese at the turn of the century and in the first decades of the 20th century seemed to believe that, at the time, the Vietnamese ruling classes were not deserving of the Mandate of Heaven. The imperial family had been corrupt, power-hungry, and had oppressed the people. The French were also power-hungry and oppressed those who voiced ideas in opposition to their colonization of the country, but they also offered much that the previous rulers had not, such as access to education (which was much more widespread under the French than it had ever been before), new technology, access to markets and ideas from the rest of the world, better healthcare (at least in the cities), and perhaps a better standard of living. Many Vietnamese seemed to say to themselves, "Until the French showed that the heavens were not on their side any longer, we'll go with them, or at least not oppose them. If and when it seems the wind is blowing in a different direction, we'll go that way."

There were a number of significant movements and important figures in the first three decades of the 1900s. One was Phan Boi Chau. Phan Boi Chau was an intellectual from an upper-class family that had helped rule the country under the restored Le dynasty and fought against early French domination. His journey toward a Vietnamese independence movement began with his moving away from the Chinese Neo-Confucian ideas the imperial family had absorbed and implemented. Then, rather than look for a person of great power, as the Chinese or Japanese might have done, he cast about looking for a man of virtue that might lead Vietnam away from the French.

In 1903, he formed a revolutionary group called the Reformer, modeling it on the ideas of Chinese rebel leader Sun Yat-sen (the founder of Nationalist China, which existed from 1911 to 1949). Phan Boi Chau also wrote two of the most influential Vietnamese books of all time: *Letter from the Ryukyus Written in Tears of Blood* (1904) and *History of the Loss of Vietnam* (1905).

The Ryukyus, which Phan Boi Chau wrote about in his book, are a Japanese island chain. He traveled to Japan in 1904/05 as the representative of various Vietnamese independence movements to look for support. The Japanese had successfully resisted European attempts to infiltrate and dominate the country as they had in Vietnam, China, and other areas of Asia. They had also pitted the Western countries against each other economically to modernize their country and make it a regional power.

Phan Boi Chau, the Vietnamese, and most of the world (particularly the Western-dominated nations of Asia) were stunned when the Japanese defeated Russia in the Russo-Japanese War, which was fought from 1904 to 1905. To Phan Boi Chau, "a new and strange world had opened up," but he needed to open the eyes of his countrymen to see it. He wrote one of the most famous paragraphs of early 20th-century Vietnamese literature in response to Japan's victory and the need of Vietnamese leaders to open the eyes of their people: Even though the Universe was shaken by American winds and European rains, our country was still in a period of dreaming in a deep sleep. Our people were still blind and resigned to their lot. It is only because in former times, we shut our doors and stayed at home, and stayed at home, going round and around in circles of literary knowledge and Chinese studies. To say frankly that our people were deaf and blind is no exaggeration.

Phan Boi Chau traveled through Japan and China in his search for both support and ideas to implement in a new theory of Vietnamese independence/government. Eventually, his writings and activity placed him in the headlights of the French, who pressured the Japanese to expel him from their country. He then traveled to Hong Kong, Thailand, and then China again to help in the revolution that overthrew the Chinese Qing dynasty and put Sun Yat-sen in charge of a new government.

Until 1925, Phan Boi Chau worked and organized various movements, gaining support, especially in the northern provinces near China. There were occasional localized Vietnamese uprisings against French rule that many hoped would grow, but they were put down harshly. In 1925, in Hong Kong, Phan Boi Chau was tracked down by Vietnamese agents of the French secret police and taken back to Vietnam. Rather than martyr him, the French placed him under close house arrest in Hue, where he died in 1934. The interesting thing about

Phan Boi Chau's capture is that some historians say he was betrayed by Ho Chi Minh, who had agreed to meet Phan Boi Chau to talk about common efforts. Other historians, especially Vietnamese Communists, say this never happened and that Phan Boi Chau looked upon Ho as his successor in the Vietnamese independence movement.

Phan Boi Chau
https://commons.wikimedia.org/wiki/File:PhanBoiChau_memory.JPG

We will discuss Ho Chi Minh in a moment, but first, let's talk about two unique belief systems that rose up in the 1920s and 1930s that provided many Vietnamese with a spiritual underpinning to resist French rule and restore Vietnamese national pride.

In the 1920s, a new spiritual movement grew in Vietnam called Cao Dai, which is short for the Vietnamese phrase Đại Đạo Tam Kỳ Phổ Độ ("The Great Faith for the Third Universal Redemption"). Caodaism is a set of beliefs that incorporates elements of Taoism, Buddhism, Confucianism, evangelical Christianity (Protestant missionaries began arriving in Vietnam at the turn of the century), and Roman Catholicism.

Cao Dai originated in the southern part of the country and generally remained localized. Today, there are an estimated one to two million adherents to the faith, mostly in the Mekong Delta, the western highlands, and Ho Chi Minh City. In modern-day Vietnam, religious life is closely monitored by the Communist Party of Vietnam, but in general, as long as religious leaders refrain from politics, they are tolerated.

Cao Dai uses similar rituals as the Roman Catholic Church but does not recognize any one person (living or dead) as a "savior" or the spiritual leader of the religion, although the "church" is headed by a "pope." At the very top of the Cao Dai hierarchy is the "Jade Emperor," who is essentially God but with a definite Vietnamese tinge.

The religion also recognizes Vietnamese folk beliefs in spirits and the power of the balance of yin and yang. Adherents also believe they can communicate with the afterlife through the use of a Ouija-like board. The main goal of Cao Dai is the recognition of a universal brotherhood of man, and this provided the impetus for many Cao Dai believers to resist the French. (Interestingly, the bestselling author, Graham Greene, was an adherent of Cao Dai beliefs.)

In the late 1930s, another Vietnamese spiritual movement began. This was Hoa Hao, an amalgamation of Buddhist and Vietnamese folk beliefs. It was started by a Buddhist monk named Huynh Phu So, and it is similar to Zen Buddhism in its stressing of simplicity. The Hoa Hao movement was highly nationalist and militarist in nature, and its members originally joined with the Viet Minh (Ho Chi Minh's military movement in the 1940s/50s) to fight against French rule. Huynh Phu So was later killed by the Viet Minh, as they believed his movement was both anti-communist and too strong. Today, Hoa Hao, like Cao Dai, still has followers in Vietnam, perhaps around three to four million. Again, these are mostly in the south and west, and again, like all religions, it is closely monitored by the state.

In Cao Dai and Hoa Hao, we see early attempts to assert Vietnamese nationalism and rebellion against the French. The ideas of Phan Boi Chau were an amalgamation of ideas from various Asian independence movements, but Cao Dai and Hoa Hao were uniquely Vietnamese. Strangely enough, the movement that finally ousted the French from Vietnam was provided to the Vietnamese by the Europeans, many of whom were French. This was communism.

Chapter 12 – Ho Chi Minh and the French Indochina War

To this day, the figure of Ho Chi Minh is intertwined with both Vietnam as a country and the Communist Party of Vietnam. "Uncle Ho," as he was called by many, is still a revered figure in Vietnam today, and though he died in 1969, years before the Vietnam War was over, his face is the one most Americans of the Vietnam War era recognize. While he was ostensibly the head of North Vietnam, by the mid-1960s, Ho had very little to do with the intimate planning of the war.

Ho Chi Minh
https://commons.wikimedia.org/wiki/File:Ho_Chi_Minh_1946.jpg

Ho's given name was Nguyen Sinh Cung, and he was born in 1890 in northern Vietnam. His father was a scholar in the imperial government at the local level and stressed education for Ho and his three siblings. By the age of ten, Ho spoke and wrote Chinese and was writing poetry in two languages. He would also learn to speak French fluently and passable English. At the age of ten, his father gave him a new name: Nguyen Tat Thanh, or "Nguyen the Accomplished."

Around the turn of the century, his father refused a better position in the imperial government, but he refused it because it would have meant working with the French. However, this did not prevent Ho from getting a French education in the imperial city of Hue. Also attending the same school were Vo Nguyen Giap, the architect of Vietnam's future victory over France and who played a pivotal role in the war against the US; Pham Van Dong, who became Vietnam's prime minister after Ho's death; and Ngo Dinh Diem, future president of South Vietnam and Ho's enemy.

Much of Ho's early life is difficult to parse out. The mythology around him generated by the Communist Party of Vietnam is full of truths, half-truths, and outright fabrication (think of US President George Washington's cherry tree story or his throwing a silver dollar across the Potomac). In his twenties, Ho traveled to the United States, France, England, and the Soviet Union. Some communist mythology states he led indigenous rebellions in other parts of the developing world.

What we do know is that Ho hoped to study in France. For many Vietnamese, this was a way to get a "leg up" economically, and for some, it was also a way to get to know their enemy. When Ho voyaged to France in the years before WWI, he was not a communist or a revolutionary. Much like his father, he likely had visions of a Vietnam without the French, but this was probably more of a nebulous idea than a concrete notion, though he claimed to have taken part in anti-French protests in Hue in 1908.

Ho made his way to France slowly via cargo ship. He worked for his passage as a cabin boy and cook's helper. He crossed the Pacific to the United States sometime around 1912. When exactly he arrived is not known, but a letter from Ho to the French authorities for Vietnamese affairs is post-marked from New York in December 1912. In New York, he worked as a baker in a hotel. Later in life, Ho claimed to have also worked for a rich family in New York and for General Motors.

Some historians believe that Ho made friends with members of the Korean community in New York, who were working to free their country from foreign domination (Korea was fought over by Russia, China, and Japan in the early 1900s). Many believe this was where Ho's ideas about Vietnamese independence and revolution began. While in New York City, Ho attended meetings of black revolutionaries and read the writings of black nationalist leader Marcus Garvey.

In 1913, Ho shipped off to England, working there for about a year as part of the kitchen staff in a hotel, and then worked on a ferry between England and France. Many believe that by the time he arrived in France, which Ho said was in 1917 but which French records state was 1919, he had given up on the idea of attending the Sorbonne as one of the first "colonials" to do so and began to work as a revolutionary writer and reporter.

While in Paris, Ho had a roommate named Phan Chu Trinh, who was a Vietnamese "constitutionalist," meaning he believed that the Vietnamese should fight the French using their own words and laws against them. Phan Chu Trinh wrote for a Vietnamese expatriate newspaper, and in it was a column called "Nguyen Ai Quoc," or "Nguyen the Patriot." Ho worked for the paper as a photo assistant and occasionally wrote a column in the "Nguyen Ai Quoc" section. Later, when Ho was on the run from various authorities, he would use the name "Nguyen Ai Quoc" as an alias.

Ho was working at the paper when the Bolshevik Revolution broke out in Russia. It was at this time that he read an article by Vladimir Lenin about imperialism that woke him up to the benefits of communism. Later, Ho reported that after reading this article by Lenin, he had a vision—he was to become a great political leader.

In 1920, Ho attended a famous meeting of French socialists. At that meeting, French socialism split into two branches: the more moderate socialists and the radical communists that adhered to the ideas coming out of Moscow. Ho backed the Moscow group, and in 1923, he left Paris for the Soviet capital.

While in Moscow, Ho attended university, which was essentially an indoctrination course on Soviet communism and how to spread it. By 1925, Ho was in China, working for the revolution there and living under the name Nguyen Ai Quoc. It was while he was in China that he was accused of betraying Phan Boi Chau to the authorities. Ho may or may not have turned Phan Boi Chau over. One theory is that he wanted to "make a martyr" out of Phan Boi Chau so the world could focus on the cause of Vietnamese independence. Others believe he had nothing to do with it, as Phan Boi Chau never denounced Ho Chi Minh.

In 1927, the Nationalist leader of China, Chiang Kai-shek, carried out a purge of communists in China. The bulk of the communists, including future leader Mao Zedong, went into hiding, forming an army in the hinterlands. Ho Chi Minh returned to the USSR, then returned to Southeast Asia by a long boat trip that finally landed him in Thailand, where he began work as an agent of the Soviet-directed "Communist International," or "Comintern."

For the next few years, Ho worked as an agent in Asia before getting into trouble with the British authorities in Hong Kong. The British threatened him with deportation to Vietnam, but by this time, the French authorities had become aware of Ho's work in organizing revolutionary cells in Vietnam from abroad. A return to Vietnam would mean a death sentence for Ho, something the British court was not willing to pursue, so Ho was released. He donned a disguise, went to Shanghai, and eventually made his way back to Moscow.

From 1933 to 1938, Ho remained in Moscow, studying and teaching at the Lenin Institute, a school for revolutionaries and "wannabe" revolutionaries from third-world countries. Ho was in Moscow during Joseph Stalin's "Great Terror" of 1937 and the purge trials that followed. Many foreign communists fell victim to Stalin's purges, but Ho reportedly backed Stalin wholeheartedly, and he came through unscathed. This helps prove one thing about Ho Chi Minh—he was a survivor.

From 1938 to 1941, Ho worked with Chinese Communists. He also was given the title "Senior Comintern Agent in charge of Asian affairs," at least covertly in revolutionary circles. From 1936 onward, the Chinese (both Nationalists and Communists) were fighting against the Japanese, who had invaded the eastern coastal areas of China and the major cities there. Ho not only worked to further communism but also to organize cells to fight against the Japanese, an enemy he would soon face at home.

In 1940, the Japanese took over French Indochina, which included Vietnam. This was essentially a bloodless invasion due to the surrender of France to Japan's ally of Nazi Germany in June of that year. The puppet French Vichy government gave orders to their men in Vietnam, most of whom were right-wing and willing to collaborate, to allow the Japanese in. For the most part, the Japanese took over the resources of the country directly or bought them from French landowners without competition.

Japan maintained a relatively small force in the country, allowing the French to maintain order.

In 1941, Ho Chi Minh returned to Vietnam after almost twenty years away and was recognized as the senior communist leader, with the backing of Moscow. Ho was joined by his old friends Vo Nguyen Giap, Pham Van Dong, and others, including a ruthless man named Le Duan, who would later become the premier in North Vietnam, supplanting Ho and directing the Vietnamese effort against the United States.

Ho and other leaders, including non-communist nationalists of varying movements, became more involved in what became known as the Viet Minh (the "League for the Independence of Vietnam"). The Viet Minh had actually formed in the mid-1930s in China, but it was not able to engender much enthusiasm in the fight against the French. However, with the Japanese now involved, the Viet Minh gained new life. A great part of this new energy came from Ho and his inner circle, who had never engaged in open warfare (guerrilla or otherwise) before but had experience at clandestine activities. Ho and his men soon assumed leadership of the movement.

Ho also brought a degree of support from Chinese Communists and the Soviet Union. Most of this support was in the form of advisers and money, as neither the Chinese nor the Soviet Union was able to spare much in the way of weaponry, as they were involved in their own struggles for survival. In addition, moving weapons all the way to Vietnam was difficult because of its location.

The one nation willing and able to aid the Viet Minh against the Japanese and the Vichy French was the United States, which entered the war against Japan in early December 1941 after the Japanese attack on Pearl Harbor.

The Viet Minh's struggle against the Japanese took a couple of different forms. Their main bases were in China, and their main operating area was in the north, which was mostly countryside. In the cities of both the south and the north, the Viet Minh were limited to agitation, sabotage, propaganda, and espionage/reconnaissance, as Japanese and French forces were concentrated in the cities and were too strong to assail.

In the more remote regions of the north, but in some other rural parts of the country, the Viet Minh were more aggressive. They essentially set up a shadow government in many villages, collected taxes, ran a rudimentary judicial system, recruited new personnel (both men and women), and attempted to spread communist ideas where possible. It was easier to spread these ideas in the north, as Catholicism and other religious movements were stronger in the south. The Viet Minh also had varying degrees of success in aiding villagers suffering from hunger and losses due to the occupation.

As the war went on, the Americans were able to bring increasing amounts of weapons and other military supplies to the Viet Minh, who had set up large bases in some of the most inaccessible parts of northwestern Vietnam.

By 1945, the Japanese were clearly losing the war. However, their strength in China, Vietnam, and parts of eastern Burma was still immense. The problem was that Japanese supply lines, at sea, in the air, and on the ground, were practically nonexistent by this point in the war.

In March 1945, the Japanese took direct control of Vietnam from the Vichy French, and their rule became increasingly more desperate and harsher the worse the war went for them. One of the side-effects of the Japanese taking direct control was that the US was deprived of much of its intelligence on Vietnam, for it had cultivated agents within the French government. That same month, an interesting event occurred. An American OSS (Office of Strategic Services) agent with the unusual name of Archimedes Patti went to see Ho Chi Minh to retrieve an American pilot who had been shot down over Vietnam and rescued by the Viet Minh. Patti was directed to get the pilot out of Vietnam and to remain there to both help the Viet Minh against the Japanese by assessing their needs and evaluating the movement.

While there, Ho Chi Minh asked Patti if he could arrange a meeting between Ho and the famous American general Claire Chennault, who was the commander of the US air forces in the China theater and the founder of the famed "Flying Tigers." Patti agreed as long as Ho didn't ask for supplies or active support. Ho acquiesced to this caveat, as he had another mission in mind: he wanted a picture of himself with Chennault.

The meeting took place in southern China, and Ho got his picture with perhaps the most famous American in Asia. When Ho returned to Vietnam, he used this picture to show not only his comrades but also leaders of other movements that he, Ho Chi Minh, had the backing of the United States of America. Since no one else was at the meeting, and he had a photograph with a famous American general, Ho's position became even stronger.

In August 1945, Japan surrendered to the Allies. No one was exactly sure what this meant for Vietnam. However, the Vietnamese under Ho and other independence leaders knew —it meant Vietnam would be run by the Vietnamese. The French had other ideas. The leader of the Free France resistance and the first leader of France after WWII, Charles de Gaulle, had issued a statement prior to the Japanese surrender stating that France was expecting to move back into Vietnam, though his statement did enumerate some "concessions" to the Vietnamese that allowed them a few more rights and privileges than had existed before the war. Still, the

French would oversee the government with a governor-general at its head.

Obviously, Ho Chi Minh and many other Vietnamese were opposed to this, and in August 1945, when the Japanese surrendered, a series of strange events occurred. After surrendering, the Japanese gave the Viet Minh a considerable number of French weapons they had seized when they took over in March, perhaps because the Viet Minh, which was now increasingly dominated by the communists, was the strongest force. The Japanese also turned over many of Hanoi's public buildings to the Viet Minh rather than the remaining French. Additionally, the Japanese threw a sop to the French by turning over a large number of Vietnamese non-communist nationalists, leaving the Viet Minh the most powerful group without a doubt.

On August 24th, the Vietnamese took control of Hanoi. Ho Chi Minh, who had taken the name openly in 1944, read what he called the Vietnamese Declaration of Independence. It began with the famous words, "All men are created equal," and then went on to quote the French Declaration of the Rights of Man and of the Citizen. Ho astutely was playing to not only the Vietnamese but also to any Americans and French who might be sympathetic to his cause. And after WWII, there was a considerable number of them, at least on the political left.

While Ho was announcing his declaration, his compatriot, Vo Nguyen Giap, issued an order abolishing all political parties except the communists. In the north, the communists were the strongest, but in the south, a nationalist movement called the **VNQDD** (for *Viet Nam Quoc Dan Dang*, or the "Vietnamese Nationalist Party") was more powerful. They were allied with the Hoa Hao movement, which had millions of followers, especially in the south. However, when this order came down from Hanoi, the leaders of the **VNQDD**, knowing they would likely have to face the returning French, were unwilling to fight against their own countrymen and stood down.

From late August to mid-September, the Viet Minh attempted to extend their control over not only northern Vietnam but also the south. At this point in time, Ho claimed there were some 500,000 members of the Viet Minh, most of them armed. The real number was likely closer to 100,000, which was still a sizable force.

Ho knew that domination of the country was a race against time. If he (meaning the Viet Minh) could establish some semblance of centralized rule in southern Vietnam, it would be much harder for the French to return, and de Gaulle had left no doubt that they would. French prestige, which had been destroyed during the war, "demanded" it, at least in French eyes. The French armed forces were more numerous in the south, as the former Vichy collaborators turned into loyalists when the war ended.

In the north, Chiang Kai-shek, the leader of Nationalist China, was determined to accept the surrender of the Japanese 38th Army in Vietnam. Chiang was also interested in regaining some Chinese influence in Vietnam and was not interested in the French returning to the north. The sizable Chinese force that received the Japanese surrender refused to make preparations for the French to return, which was basically an unstated way of saying to France, "You might have to fight us now too." With the Chinese army virtually guaranteeing Viet Minh independence in the north, at least for the time being, Ho moved to cement the Viet Minh's grip on northern Vietnam, which he had proclaimed as the Democratic Republic of Vietnam. When he did, Ho realized that he had both a position of power and of weakness. He was strong in the north, but he was weak in the south, where he was about to get even weaker since French troops, along with a sizable number of their British allies, soon moved into Saigon and began to spread out.

In March 1946, Ho and the French came to an agreement. The French would establish what they called the Indochinese Union (meaning Vietnam, Cambodia, and Laos). Within this union, Ho's government would exist as a "free state," which is a somewhat nebulous term. The French also agreed to two other provisions, which they had no intention of honoring from the start. They would limit French forces in the north to 15,000 men, and after a time, a vote would be held on the issue of unifying Vietnam.

The status of southern Vietnam was the problem. For three months, Ho and the French met in Vietnam and in France to negotiate the status of the south. Within a very short time, it was clear that neither side was going to budge from their position. Along the "border" between southern and northern Vietnam, incidents occurred between French and Viet Minh forces, which escalated into a full-scale war in December of 1946.

In response to the communists' virtual takeover of the northern part of the country, the French placed the former emperor, Bao Dai, back on the throne. He had ruled as a figurehead under the French and Japanese previously before abdicating when it seemed as if the communists might take the entire country. Bao Dai was the nominal ruler of what the French called the State of Vietnam, which included both the north and the south.

French rule in the northern part of the country was essentially limited to Hanoi and the villages and towns of the Red River Delta. Outside of some large bases, including one at Dien Bien Phu in the west of northern Vietnam (see map above), the countryside was the domain of the Viet Minh.

From 1946 to 1949, the war between the Viet Minh, whose military wing was commanded by Vo Nguyen Giap, and the French was a low-level guerrilla conflict, with Viet Minh raids on French police stations and other government buildings. This was done not only to secure weapons and any possible intelligence but also to prove to both the French and the Vietnamese people that French colonial power was not invincible.

Atrocities were committed by both sides, and torture was widespread. Interestingly enough, the French made use of a significant number of former German Waffen-SS men, who had fallen into their hands at the end of WWII. These men were given a choice of fighting in the French Foreign Legion or remaining in prison for a considerably longer period of time. Needless to say, many men chose to work for the French. Units from other colonial French possessions, including virulent anti-communists and anti-Vietnamese forces from other French Indochinese territories, added fuel to the fire.

The Viet Minh were not exactly popular either, especially in the south, where the war remained a guerrilla conflict until its end. The Viet Minh used excessive force in their takeover of villages and provinces, and they killed anyone who resisted them or might conceivably do so. In 1948, the Viet Minh went on a killing spree throughout the country, assassinating literally thousands of political opponents, village leaders, and Vietnamese who worked for the French. This year, 1948, remained in the memories of many South Vietnamese throughout the 1950s, 1960s, and early 1970s before their defeat. Many Vietnamese in those decades were sure that a repeat of 1948 would occur should the North Vietnamese win the war—and it did.

Around 1949, other foreign powers became involved in the war. This year is significant because it was the year Mao Zedong and the Chinese Communist Party came to power in China. When they did, one of the first things they began doing was sending arms, supplies, and advisers to their old friend, Ho Chi Minh.

When the Chinese began meddling in Vietnam, along with Soviet advisers and approval, the United States felt forced to aid the French. As both sides brought in more and more weapons, the conflict in Vietnam became a more conventional one.

The French Communist Party was a powerful political force in post-WWII France. Even among the non-communist left, there was little support for the war. Aside from the classic communist arguments about the "rights of the working class and the peasants," many Frenchmen could not see the logic in dominating a people who did not want them in their country. After all, hadn't the French themselves just gone through the same experience from 1940 to 1945?

Of course, there were many moderate and conservative Frenchmen who supported the war. Many of them simply believed it was a matter of regaining France's "honor." Others saw the economic possibilities of Vietnamese resources, as they would help France recover from WWII. Still, others believed that the Vietnamese were not ready for self-government, at least a Western-style democracy, and the French should remain for some unspecified period of time in order to prepare the way for Vietnamese self-government.

Some of the men who were opposed to the French war in Indochina and later American involvement were not leftists per se. Some, like Jean Sainteny, had been French officials in Vietnam at some point in time. Others, including Paul Muse and Jean Lacouture, had worked for the government or the military.

These men and their writings were very influential in creating the anti-war movement in France and later in the United States. In the reference section at the end of this book, you will see a series of lectures by Professor Stephen Young, who worked in Vietnam with the CIA and the American/South Vietnamese government in the late 1960s and early 1970s. Professor Young's thesis is that these men, who had really not traveled in Vietnam outside of Hanoi, Saigon, and Hue and who had had very little interaction with the Vietnamese people themselves, provided false ideas about the Vietnam conflict.

Young's arguments have some merit. According to Professor Young, essentially, Muse, Sainteny, and Lacouture argued that Ho Chi Minh and the Viet Minh were more Vietnamese nationalists than communists. They also argued that the Viet Minh and later the Viet Cong were the embodiment of Vietnamese nationalist feelings and long-held resentments toward the French, Japanese, and other foreigners. What they got wrong, says Professor Young, is that the Viet Minh and Ho were indeed communists of the first order and could be expected to impose a radical foreign idea on the country if they won. Young also argues that the vast majority of the Vietnamese people were anti-communist, but they lacked a coherent ideology or charismatic leadership to put those feelings together in an effective form. This last argument holds water, especially when applied to the south.

Later in the 1960s, as the US became increasingly more involved in Vietnam, these three Frenchmen made tours of the US, speaking at colleges and in front of government committees. Their word was taken as gospel even though they had never really spent time in the Vietnamese countryside or among its people. A main tenet of the mainstream American anti-war movement was that Ho Chi Minh and his followers were nationalists and could be dealt with as such, overlooking Ho's decades of education in and work for the USSR and the Chinese Communists.

In 1954, the First Indochina War came to a head at Dien Bien Phu. The French had constructed a large fortified position from which they could venture out into the western Vietnamese highlands to fight the Viet Minh, who held a strong position there.

Dien Bien Phu was actually a series of separate strongpoints, some with overlapping fields of fire for machine guns and others far afield. The Viet Minh strategy, which had been devised by Vo Nguyen Giap, called for surrounding the French position and cutting off the individual strongpoints one by one, beginning with the weakest and most vulnerable.

The French position was surrounded by hills, some of them very steep and seemingly inaccessible. In combination with the airpower and artillery, the French believed the geography itself would prevent the Vietnamese from using the hills as a fighting position. In addition, the fields around the base were devoid of protective vegetation.

However, despite French beliefs, which were tinged with more than a little racism, the Vietnamese used those hills. And not only did they bring tens of thousands of men into the hills, but they also brought artillery and anti-aircraft guns that had been supplied by the Chinese. This artillery was carried mostly by hand, with teams of men hauling the equipment. The Vietnamese also dug fortified positions into the hills, many of them on the far side, which were out of reach and sight of the French. The artillery would fire over the hills before being pulled back into the mountainside on rails. When the French airpower inevitably arrived, the cannons were out of sight.

Vietnamese artillery not only pounded the French infantry and artillery positions but also repeatedly destroyed the airfields used by the French to bring in supplies. Eventually, the number of planes bringing in supplies, which included tractors to fix the airfields, lessened to the point where the fields could not be effectively repaired, and supplies began to dwindle.

After some time delivering morale-crushing artillery and anti-aircraft fire, the Viet Minh began assaulting French strongpoints. They did not fall easily. The French forces included highly trained and motivated paratroopers, the French Foreign Legion, and many colonial troops, many of whom, like their comrades, had had years of combat experience in WWII. The Viet Minh casualties were far higher than the French. Attackers almost always suffer more than the defenders, but the Vietnamese could afford it, while the French could not. Eventually, French reinforcements ceased coming in, and these reinforcements were limited in number due to transport issues. The French forces began to go hungry and thirsty. Medical equipment began to run low, and every few days, the Viet Minh drew the circle tighter around them.

The French probably held out as long as they did because they knew that being a prisoner of the Viet Minh was likely going to be brutal, although they realized it was just as likely for them to be killed on the spot. However, every man has his breaking point. The French at Dien Bien Phu surrendered on May 7th, 1954, after six weeks of battle. Like the Germans at Stalingrad in 1942/43, the more realistic among the French knew that the war in Vietnam was over.

Two men who ended an empire: Vo Nguyen Giap (l) and Ho Chi Minh (r) in 1945
https://commons.wikimedia.org/wiki/File:Giap-Ho.jpg

While the Battle of Dien Bien Phu was going on, the French government of Pierre Mendes France was negotiating with the Viet Minh. Mendes France was against the war to begin with and saw nothing but the further loss of lives and money at a time when France was still recovering from the Nazi occupation and WWII. He had planned a gradual French withdrawal from Vietnam, with elections and milestones to be met before troops were fully withdrawn, but the French defeat at Dien Bien Phu and the later smaller French defeats nixed all of that.

The Geneva Conference, which ended in July 1954, was a complicated series of talks that created the formal division of Vietnam at the 17th parallel. There was to be a demilitarized buffer zone ("DMZ") between the two states, and though the North Vietnamese strongly opposed the division of the country, a proposal by the Vietnamese that stated future elections would decide the future of the country made the division a done deal.

The Vietnamese emperor, Bao Dai, who was actually living a luxurious life in France, named Ngo Dinh Diem (Ho's former schoolmate and intensely Catholic enemy) as the prime minister of South Vietnam. A year later, with the Americans' approval, Diem removed Bao Dai and named himself the president of the Republic of Vietnam, which was South Vietnam's formal name.

Although the Americans later became heavily involved in Vietnam, they had refused French pleas to send aid and airpower to assist them at Dien Bien Phu. However, WWII had happened only nine years before, and the Korean War had just ended in 1953. No American wanted to get into a war in a country they couldn't even identify on the map.

Chapter 13 - The Vietnam War

American involvement in Vietnam accelerated after the French left. The French withdrawal was rapid, but enough French troops stayed behind in the South to prevent a Viet Minh takeover after the peace talks. Ho Chi Minh's forces needed to consolidate their rule over the new Democratic Republic of Vietnam ("DRV," also known as North Vietnam), and military infrastructure had to be set up in the South, which happened rather rapidly.

When the peace talks in Geneva ended, no one on either side was under any illusion that the terms of the agreement would be followed. The French needed the North Vietnamese to state categorically that they accepted the division of the country and would not interfere in the South, while the North Vietnamese needed the French to say that elections to unite the country would be held in the not too distant future. Both sides, therefore, "saved face" and could point to the other as the reason for a protracted conflict.

However, France was in no position to continue in Vietnam. Its colony in Algeria was experiencing a rebellion that would eventually turn into a savage guerrilla war, and France itself was increasingly divided between left and right. With the tacit understanding that the world's first superpower, the United States, would "oversee" events in Southeast Asia, the French left. Their other colonies, Laos and Cambodia, would experience the same pain as Vietnam over the next twenty years, and Cambodia would experience one of the true horrors of the 20th century, the Khmer Rouge genocide in the mid-1970s.

The Vietnam War does not have an extensive chapter dedicated to it in this book, as the topic has been covered thoroughly in another *Captivating History* book, allowing us to focus on other aspects of Vietnamese history with which people aren't as familiar. If you are interested in learning more about the war, you can find the book here: https://www.amazon.com/Vietnam-War-Captivating-Second-Indochina-ebook/dp/B0782VG27Q There are also some excellent sources at the end of the book to check out.

However, no book on Vietnamese history would be complete without a look at this war. For our part, here is a very brief overview of the conflict.

In the late 1950s, the North Vietnamese organized a force known as the National Liberation Front of Southern Vietnam, better known to history as the Viet Cong (the term is a contraction of the Vietnamese for "Vietnamese Communist"). Throughout the later 1950s, the forces of Ngo Dinh Diem and the Viet Cong fought a savage but relatively low-level war for control of South Vietnam.

Diem was a formidable enemy. He had crushed the criminal gangs that controlled much of Saigon and had subdued some of the more militant members of the Hoa Hao sect who were attempting to set up a government based on their ideals. The only thing preventing Diem from becoming the sole power in South Vietnam was the Viet Cong. In an intense offensive in 1956, Diem's forces pushed the Viet Cong in South Vietnam into remote villages and forests near the Cambodian border. For all intents and purposes, South Vietnam was Diem's, except for the fact he relied on economic and military aid from the United States.

At times, Diem bristled at the "advice" of the US, whose interests were mainly represented in the country by the CIA and a small contingent of military advisers, mostly members of the new elite US Army force, The Green Berets.

In 1959, the North Vietnamese slowly began to regain strength in South Vietnam. They created the 1,000-mile-long "Ho Chi Minh Trail" in the jungles and highlands of western Vietnam, Laos, and Cambodia. They also created an amazing logistical system that functioned in fits and starts until the end of the war despite intense US efforts, which included massive bombing campaigns.

In July 1959, two US military advisers were killed at a Vietnamese military base when it was attacked by the Viet Cong. A few months later, a sizable Viet Cong force attacked and defeated two South Vietnamese companies. Throughout 1960, the Viet Cong launched a series of offensives, most of them in remote parts of the country, and set up what they called "liberated zones," where they established shadow governments that essentially ran village affairs. Much of this was done through terror and threats.

Throughout the early 1960s, the Viet Cong slowly gained strength in the South. They were supported by Chinese Communists, who sought to supplant the Soviet Union, with whom they had had a severe break, as the leading force for "anti-imperialism" in Asia.

It's estimated that about 40,000 to 50,000 North Vietnamese soldiers came to direct Viet Cong efforts in the South. By 1962, the Viet Cong had grown to about 300,000 men and women.

With the growth of the Viet Cong came increased American involvement. By 1962/63, the number of Green Beret and Special Forces units in the country had grown to a couple of thousand. While they were directed to simply advise (at least publicly), American advisers were taking part in the combat against the Viet Cong throughout the South, serving alongside their comrades in the Army of the Republic of Vietnam, better known as "ARVN."

In 1963, about three weeks before the assassination of US President John F. Kennedy, President Diem was killed. Diem had grown increasingly autocratic and was engaged in a suppression campaign against the Buddhist majority in South Vietnam. He had also appointed family members to high government positions, especially his brother, Ngo Dinh Nhu, who became the head of South Vietnamese intelligence and the secret police. In addition to nepotism and a growing trend toward dictatorship, Diem allowed a culture of corruption and bribery to grow in the country. By 1963, this was feeding North Vietnamese propaganda and causing many South Vietnamese to at least begin looking at the Viet Cong as an alternative, if not joining them outright.

It was determined that the leaders of the South Vietnamese army would remove Diem, and they had the okay from the United States, whose advice was being increasingly ignored by Diem. In a series of botched events, including a series of mysterious phone calls involving US State Department officials, Diem and his brother were killed in the back of a van in Saigon and replaced with a military regime. Many point to the assassination of Diem as the event in which the United States had gone past the point of no return in Vietnam, but another event in 1964 made greater US involvement almost inevitable.

This was the famous Gulf of Tonkin incident, in which US Navy vessels, which were on an intelligence mission off the coast of North Vietnam, came under attack at least once by North Vietnamese vessels. A second attack occurred, but it may have been a case of "friendly fire."

When the North Vietnamese fired on the US Navy, a response was guaranteed. Some say that Ho Chi Minh was against instigating greater US involvement in the country. Instead, they point to Le Duan, who had become a leading figure in the Communist Party of Vietnam, saying that he had encouraged it, knowing that without defeating the United States in one way or another, Vietnam might never be united under the communists.

Beginning in 1965, the United States began a massive buildup of troops and firepower in Vietnam and in the surrounding regions. As the American effort increased, anti-war feelings in the US began to grow, albeit slowly. These were fed by a number of notions: the writings of Frenchmen Muse, Sainteny, and Lacouture; the increasing "anti-establishment" feelings of the times, which sprung from the civil rights movement and other cultural shifts; and the idea that Americans should not be fighting and dying for a country they had not heard of.

However, today, people often forget that a sizable majority of Americans supported the war effort, at least until 1968. They felt that the United States could not and should not "lose" another nation to communism, that the South Vietnamese did not want to be communist (which most of them did not), and that American prestige and power in the world, vis-a-vis the Soviet Union and Communist China, was at stake.

From 1965 to 1967, the Viet Cong and the forces of the United States, along with sizable contingents from US allies, such as South Korea, Australia, and New Zealand, fought an increasingly intense war. Over time, the war would expand to include the bombing of North Vietnam, which began in earnest with the Nixon administration as a way to force the North Vietnamese to the peace table; the widespread use of the poisonous defoliant "Agent Orange," with its cancerous results; the broadcast of live combat and casualties into American living rooms on the evening news, which was also a factor contributing to anti-war sentiments; and the reporting of American atrocities in the country, most notably at My Lai.

In 1968, the North Vietnamese and Viet Cong launched a nationwide offensive in the South during the Vietnamese New Year's holiday of Tet. All over South Vietnam, Viet Cong forces launched intense attacks. The overwhelming majority of them were aimed at South Vietnamese forces, not the Americans. However, Viet Cong insurgents managed to assault the US Embassy in Saigon, and the prolonged siege to recapture it was televised back in the US.

Most people think the Tet Offensive was a Viet Cong victory. It was not. Many people believe the South Vietnamese army fought poorly. Sometimes it did, but in 1968, when it was under good leadership, it fought well. The Tet Offensive and the US/South Vietnamese counteroffensive nearly destroyed the Viet Cong, and they retreated back to the border areas to lick their wounds and resume a very low-level war.

However, a combination of factors that came from the Tet Offensive led the American public and government to believe that the US was losing or would lose the war. First, American military officers had been saying that victory was "just around the corner" for some time. The Tet Offensive seemed to prove them wrong and that the Viet Cong were stronger than ever. Second, the optics of the US Embassy siege were demoralizing. Third, footage of a South Vietnamese officer executing a Viet Cong insurgent in the street had Americans doubting the "goodness" of their allies. Fourth, after the Tet Offensive, the most trusted newsman in the country, Walter Cronkite, went to Vietnam and reported on what he thought he saw. His conclusion? The war could not be won. When US President Lyndon Johnson heard this, he is reported to have said, "If I've lost Cronkite, I've lost America." Johnson refused to run for another term as president.

When Richard Nixon was elected president in 1968, he was determined to find a way to extricate the United States from Vietnam, but he knew that American prestige would take a serious hit if he simply ordered American troops to leave. Additionally, his senior foreign policy adviser, Henry Kissinger, was a friend and reader of Jean Sainteny, the Frenchman who believed that Ho was a nationalist who could be bargained with. Ho died in 1969, so the question remained unanswered.

From 1969 to 1973, Nixon and Kissinger pushed the North Vietnamese to negotiate peace, with their prime condition being the existence of South Vietnam. At times, the North Vietnamese would signal their willingness only to refuse or throw up roadblocks. In 1972, when talks reached a standstill and the North Vietnamese refused to return to the table, Nixon ordered the increased bombing of the North with large numbers of B-52 bombers and other US aircraft. Over the course of just three years, more explosives were dropped on North Vietnam than on Germany in WWII.

By 1973, the North Vietnamese returned to the negotiating table. By this time, Nixon was facing an emerging Watergate scandal, a slowing economy, and an American public that was demanding an end to the war. It should also be noted that American troop levels had been dropping since 1969. On the other hand, the Vietnamese were facing the near obliteration of the North and its economy. Whenever they threatened to leave the peace table, Nixon would threaten to bring back the B-52s.

In the end, the North Vietnamese agreed to a separate North and South and the gradual removal of American troops from the country. Both sides knew that it was just a matter of time before the North Vietnamese resumed their war of unification, but Nixon and the Americans held out some hope that the South Vietnamese would be able to hold their own.

Obviously, they could not. In the spring of 1975, North Vietnam launched what it called its Spring Offensive. It was carried out almost exclusively by North Vietnamese troops, tanks, and planes. By April 30th, 1975, South Vietnam ceased to exist.

Conclusion

When the North Vietnamese overran the South, hundreds of thousands of Vietnamese fled the country. Many of these did so by flimsy watercraft—they became known as the "Boat People" as a result. The millions of Vietnamese living in the United States, Canada, Australia, France, and elsewhere are either refugees themselves or descendants of refugees.

In 1978, the Vietnamese invaded Cambodia. At the time, Cambodia was controlled by the extremely radical Khmer Rouge, who, among other things (like the killing of a million of its own people), drove out or killed tens of thousands of ethnic Vietnamese from their country. In response to these atrocities, the Vietnamese invaded Cambodia and toppled the Khmer Rouge regime of Pol Pot.

Unfortunately for the Vietnamese, China was a close ally of Cambodia. Chinese and Vietnamese relations had soured since the end of the war due to deteriorating Chinese influence and boundary disputes. The

Vietnamese invasion of Cambodia gave China the opportunity to settle these disagreements.

Smartly, the Chinese notified both the US and the Soviet Union, with whom the Vietnamese had grown closer to, that they planned on waging a short and very limited war against the Vietnamese. They did so, gaining the disputed territories in the process.

For their part, the Vietnamese could claim they had inflicted more casualties on the Chinese than vice versa, which was true. However, they also claimed they had "discouraged" the Chinese from invading the entire country, which was not true.

Since 1978, Vietnam has been at peace. In the mid-1980s, the government, following the Chinese model, began to gradually open the nation's economy to free-market ideas. The Vietnamese economy has blossomed, with some interruptions. Today, Vietnam is a prime tourist destination for thousands of Americans, and relations between the two countries are friendly, if not "close." After all, both have reason to keep an eye on China.

We hope that you have enjoyed this brief history of Vietnam and the Vietnamese people. It is a history of repeating patterns, tragedy, and, at the same time, a great will to advance and succeed in spite of seemingly overwhelming odds.

Part 4: History of Bali

A Captivating Guide to Balinese History and the Impact This Island Has Had on the History of Indonesia and Southeast Asia.

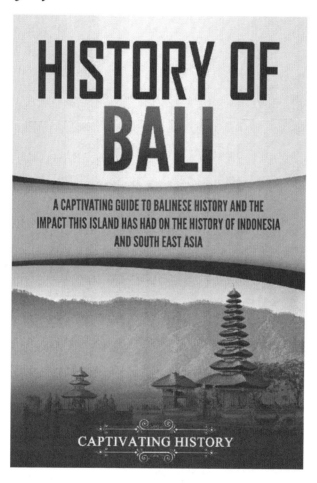

Introduction

The unassuming island of Bali in maritime Southeast Asia is a brilliant jewel in the crown of archipelagic Indonesia, drawing millions of tourists year after year to its magnificent beaches, lush tropical forests, and unique cultural heritage. Known for centuries as "the Island of the Gods," Bali boasts a multitude of temples representing the spirituality of the peoples that have landed on her shores since ancient times. The most intrinsic of these magnificent temples are those dedicated to Balinese Hinduism, an endemic blending of Buddhism, Hinduism, animism, and indigenous beliefs introduced from Java by the Majapahit Empire half a millennia ago.

Bali's mystique and its historical reluctance to submit to foreign powers made her an even brighter jewel, a rare gem that had yet to be snatched by force during the colonial era. After a three-hundred-year-long resistance, the island finally came completely under Dutch suzerainty at the turn of the 20th century, which would be followed shortly afterward by the impact of the world wars and then inevitably the creation of Indonesia as an independent republic.

Whether through breathtaking scenery, the island's World Heritage status for the subak rice irrigation system, a wealth of culture—whether it be music, dancing, or its history of colorful religious pantomimes and parades—or the impact of its ornate ancient temples, Bali still mesmerizes visitors to its shores as it has done since prehistoric times. With a lack of natural resources or the valuable items that maritime traders of old required for gain, it is curious why Bali attracted so much attention and intrigue throughout history. The Balinese talent of morphing to suit the changing times has kept an exceptional and vulnerable culture protected through each successive wave of foreign interference. Bali exists as a living monument to the past, unchanged in many ways and still a refuge for those seeking spiritual and existential solace.

Perhaps the island is simply fortuitously positioned along the arc of the Indonesia island chain, quietly hiding from the real world, but perhaps it was the magical work of an ancient Hindu priest who built strings of sea temples to protect her shores. Whatever has kept Bali resistant to metamorphosis over the ages remains there still, quietly celebrating the beauty and touching story of this extraordinary island.

Chapter 1 – Bali within Indonesia

The history of Bali needs to be understood within the context of its geographical position within Southeast Asia and, more specifically, as a province of the archipelagic nation of the Republic of Indonesia. Indonesia's thirty-four provinces constitute more than seventeen thousand islands that spread in an arc from the Indian to the Pacific Oceans and are bordered by Asia to the north and Oceana (including Australia) to the south. Indonesia is composed entirely of islands and is the largest island country in the world. Indonesia, along with Malaysia, Papua New Guinea, the Philippines, the Solomon Islands, and Timor-Leste, form an oceanic area known as the Coral Triangle. The Coral Triangle is an ecologically significant region of abundant coral and marine life that is recognized as the global center of marine biodiversity conservation. Referred to as the "Amazon of the Seas," the Coral Triangle covers an area of 5.7 million square kilometers of ocean waters that contain almost 80 percent of the world's shallow-water reef-building coral species, almost 40 percent of global reef fishes, most of the world's sea turtles, and other unique marine wonders.

Southeast Asia can be divided into mainland and archipelagic, of which Indonesia is a part of the latter. The mainland of Southeast Asia can be called by the historical name of Indochina, which is essentially a large peninsula consisting of the countries of Cambodia, Laos, Myanmar, Mainland Malaysia, Thailand, and Vietnam. As part of maritime Southeast Asia, the region of islands, including modern-day Indonesia, Malaysia, Singapore, southern Thailand, the Philippines, Brunei, East Timor, and Taiwan, can also be referred to as the Malay Archipelago or by the historical 14th-century name of *Nusantara* ("outer islands"). The word *nusa* is a derivative of this name and means *island*. The Indonesian archipelago has been a valuable area for trade since as early as the 7th century CE when regional empires traded with China and India, being replaced by colonial trading powers from the 1500s onward. European colonial influences were active in Indonesia until as late as the mid-20th century, with the Dutch ultimately being the dominating power in the region for 350 years. The concept of a sovereign Indonesia emerged as late as the early 20th century, with the country gaining independence from all colonial powers in 1945, after the surrender of the Japanese at the end of the Second World War. However, the last remaining colonial influence, the Dutch, would not accept Indonesia's sovereignty until 1949 following an armed conflict.

Indonesia's national motto, *Bhinneka Tunggal Ika* ("Unity in Diversity"), reflects its multitudinous ethnic and linguistic population groupings and the rich cultural diversity for which it is known. While Javanese is the largest linguistic group, the national language is Indonesian—a standardized version of the Austronesian Malay language. Despite Islam being the dominant religion in Indonesia, historical influences of Hinduism, Buddhism, and Christianity have resulted in widespread religious pluralism.

Modern-day Indonesia is constituted of thirty-four provinces divided into seven geographical regions: Sumatra, Java, Kalimantan, Sulawesi, Western New Guinea (Papua), the Maluku Islands, and the Lesser and Greater Sunda Islands. Whereas Sumatra, Java, Kalimantan, Sulawesi, and Western New Guinea are large islands or sections of large islands in their own right, the Sundas and Moluccas are island groupings whose sovereignty is often shared with other Southeast Asian nations. Sumatra is the second largest island (after Kalimantan) of the Indonesian chain, and it extends adjacent to the south of the Malaysian mainland. Java follows the island arc of Sumatra and is not only the most populated island in Indonesia (representing 56 percent of Indonesia's population, over 140 million people) but is also the most populated island in the world. On the northwestern coast of Java, the Indonesian capital of Jakarta is home to almost eleven million people and is the second most populated global urban area after Tokyo. Together with Borneo (most of which consists of Kalimantan) and Sulawesi, these four islands constitute the Greater Sunda Islands. All Indonesian provinces—except Bali, which is predominantly Hindu—are majority Muslim, and it is the most populous Muslim majority country in the world.

The province (*propinsi* or *provinsi*) of Bali is part of the Lesser Sunda Islands. The Lesser Sundas are known in Indonesian as the *Kepulauan Nusa Tenggara* ("Southeastern Archipelago") or the *Kepulauan Sunda Kecil* ("the Lesser Sunda Archipelago"). Together with the four large islands of the Greater Sunda Islands, they make up the Sunda Islands, which are commonly named for and were formed by the volcanic Sunda Arc. The Lesser Sundas extend west-east from the arc of Sumatra and Java, stretching from Bali in the west to the Tanimbar Islands in the east. The Lesser Sundas toward the east also commonly fall under the

Indonesian island grouping of the Maluku (Molucca) Islands as well. The Maluku archipelago lies between the Indonesian islands of Sulawesi to the west and New Guinea to the east (and northeast of Timor). The Maluku Islands, as well as a small island grouping to their south called the Banda Islands, were historically referred to as the "Spice Islands" by colonial-era maritime traders due to their natural abundance of nutmeg, mace, and cloves. The island of Bali is not easily navigable since it is surrounded by coral reefs, which made it extremely difficult to approach in times past. The currents that separate Java from Bali to the west are very strong, and the south is often lashed by heavy seas.

The island country of Indonesia is a geological product of the volcanic activity of the Pacific Ring of Fire and possibly other seismic belts. The Ring of Fire is an inverted horseshoe-shaped zone of intense tectonic forces that encapsulates most of the Pacific Ocean and extends in and around Indonesia and most of the archipelagic section of Southeast Asia. The Ring of Fire is associated with persistent and seismic earthquakes and volcanic activity, which are a result of shifting continental plates that lie deep below the ocean's surface within the earth's lithosphere (or outermost solid layer). Globally, there are seven major tectonic plates, as well as a number of smaller plates, that are in a continual and gradual process of movement or drift. The relative motion of plates at the places where they meet creates friction and results in earthquakes and volcanoes and subsequently the formation of mountains or trenches. The Pacific Ring of Fire is specifically marked at its extremities by the process of subduction, whereby two plates push against each other. Through this convergence, one plate is pushed below another, ultimately forcing it to be recycled into the earth's mantle (a deeper, hotter, and more viscous layer of the planet).

The eastern islands of Indonesia (most of the Lesser Sundas except Bali, Sulawesi, the Maluku Islands, and all other landmasses toward the east) are often associated with the Ring of Fire, but there is scientific disagreement as to whether the western islands can be included with the Ring of Fire. These islands are also associated with the Alpide Belt. The Alpide Belt is a seismic zone that stretches from western Southeast Asia along the mountainous regions of southern Eurasia through the extent of Europe to the Atlantic in the west. In geological terms, western Indonesia includes the Greater Sunda Islands, as well as Bali, Lombok, Sumbawa, and Sangeang, which are politically part of the Lesser Sundas.

Lesser Sunda Islands, Indonesia, showing Bali at the far west, adjacent to Java. Lencer, CC BY-SA 3.0 <https://creativecommons.org/licenses/by-sa/3.0>, via Wikimedia Commons https://commons.wikimedia.org/wiki/File:Lesser_Sunda_Islands_en.png

Regardless of which geological arc Bali is formed, it was the result of tectonic subduction of the Indo-Australian Plate under the Eurasian Plate and the subsequent lifting of the ocean floor above sea level. The deformation of the upper Eurasian Plate has resulted in a string of volcanoes (stratovolcanoes) lying west-east across the northern lands of Bali, although it is not itself a volcanic island. The youngest of Bali's volcanos are the easterly most ones, of which the youngest is Mount Agung, or *Gunung Agung* ("Great Mountain"). It stands at 3,000 meters (close to 10,000 feet) above sea level and remains active.

In general, the soils of Indonesia are subject to deep chemical weathering and rapid erosion because of perpetually high temperatures and heavy precipitation. The tropical rainforest areas experience replenishing cycles of decomposition and nutrient renewal, but these soils are not necessarily ideal for agriculture because once the forests are cleared, the exposed land is subject to significant erosion and mineral leaching. The presence of active volcanoes, such as Agung on Bali, hold the potential for the replenishment of eroded or leached soils since the earth is replaced periodically by volcanic ash, which renews the amount of soil as well as its nutrient value in time. In particular, the rice paddy irrigation systems on Bali transport this nutrient load from higher altitudes to lower altitudes that are being farmed, and so, the nutrient value of volcanic deposits is beneficially used. Balinese farmers have historically regarded volcanoes as homes to fertility goddesses who bring bounty to their fields.

In geophysical terms, Bali is part of the Sunda Shelf, from which the Sunda Islands derive their name. The Sunda Shelf is an extension of the continental shelf (land edge) of Southeast Asia. Interestingly, all the Lesser Sunda Islands east of Bali (from Lombok onward) are not part of the Sunda Shelf, and a steep undersea gradient separates Bali from much of east and southeast Indonesia, which rest upon the adjacent Sahul (Australian) continental shelf. The biogeographical division that separates the landmasses of the Sunda and Sahul Shelves is known as the Wallace Line. This line was identified by the British naturalist and explorer Alfred Russell Wallace in 1859 during his exploration of the East Indies. Wallace (1823-1913 CE) was the co-author of Charles Darwin's *Origin of the Species* and traveled through maritime Southeast Asia in the 19th century, investigating flora and fauna. The line was later given its name by an English biologist and a staunch early supporter of the theory of evolution, Thomas Henry Huxley, who was also born in the 19th century.

The Wallace Line demarcates a distinct difference in fauna and flora between the west and east of this hypothetical boundary according to the continental origins of the landmasses. The western side of the line is distinctly Asian, and the eastern side, also known as Wallacea, is a transitional zone or buffer between Asia and Australia, and it contains a mix of both Asian and Australian species. While this division refers mostly to fauna (animal species), it is also apparently for floral (plant) species as well, although not as specifically. The Wallace Line runs through Indonesia, separating Borneo from Sulawesi, and most notably through the Lombok Strait, separating Bali from Lombok.

The Sunda Shelf that extends from the Southeast Asian continent is a result of erosion of the main continent and volcanic activity that accumulated and was compacted around the continent's edges over the millennia as sea levels rose and fell through the various ice ages. Sundaland is the name given to the exposed areas of land that were visible during the last ice age (24,000 to 17,000 BCE). This extended Asian landmass included the Malay Peninsula, Borneo, Java, Sumatra, Bali, and other surrounding islands. Around approximately 14,000 BCE, rising meltwater from the end of the last ice age filled the low-lying areas between the islands that are present today. The seas between the islands cover ancient peneplains, which are seismically stable plains in the final stages of fluvial erosion.

The Sunda Shelf is typically characterized by low seismic activity and on the whole is considered stable, except for active volcanoes on Sumatra, Java, and Bali, which are technically an adjunction to the Sunda Shelf known as the Sunda Arc—the volcanic arc created by the subduction of the Indo-Australian and Eurasian Plates. The complicated pattern and history of geological formation on and around the Sunda Shelf and the erratic creation and dissolution of land bridges with the Asian continent have given rise to a high level of biodiversity, as well as a significant degree of biological endemism, including local discontinuities, such as across the Wallace Line. On Bali itself, thick deposits of volcanic ash have created good soil fertility and resulted in agricultural prosperity for the islands. The Balinese islands were once connected to Java during low sea levels in the various ice ages, and their fauna and flora are distinctly Asian.

Of Indonesia's approximately 270 million people, 1.5 percent (more than four million people) resided in provincial Bali in 2019. The province of Bali is constituted of four islands: Bali, Nusa Penida, Nusa Lembongan, and Nusa Ceningan, covering a land area of almost six thousand square kilometers (0.3 percent of the land area of Indonesia). The capital of Bali—Denpasar—lies to the south and is home to more than 90 percent of the provincial population in its greater metropolitan area. The three smaller islands are clustered to the southeast. The main island of Bali is what is commonly referred to as Bali in historical and contemporary terms and has been the location for the rise and fall of the events of the provincial archipelagic cluster. Bali is divided into eight administrative regencies (*kabupaten*), as well as the city (*kota*) of Denpasar. The eight regions are Badung, Bangli, Buleleng, Gianyar, Jembrana, Karangasem, Klungkung, and Tabanan. Klungkung includes Bali's three small satellite islands. Each of these regencies has its own local government and legislative body. These *kabupaten* developed during the 17th-century rulership of Bali when its single monarchy began separating into distinctive kingdoms. Although historically there were nine kingdoms, the eight resulting regencies have largely kept the boundaries that can be seen today.

More than 80 percent of Bali practices the Hindu religion today, with 12 percent being Muslim, 5 percent Christian, and 0.5 percent Buddhist.

Ethnically, most of Bali are indigenous Balinese, with the remaining population constituting other Indonesian ethnicities. Since much of Bali is mountainous—essentially, it is a continuation of the central mountain chain of Java—most of the population of Bali is centered toward the south of the island on the lowlands. The combination of the climate, the mountainous north, and volcanic soils have made for an exceptionally rich agricultural heritage, and rice fields cover the southward-descending slopes that lead to the sea. The northward-descending slopes of Bali that face the Java Sea are steeper and used for coffee plantations. Unlike the less populated areas of Indonesia, where indigenous vegetation consists mostly of broadleaf evergreen forests, most of the vegetation on Java and Bali is dominated by cultivated plants. The remaining indigenous areas are characterized by hilly tropical rainforests. The coastal vegetation of Bali consists mostly of mangroves, mangrove palms, and swamp forests in locations where there are no beaches, human habitation, or other development. The mountainous areas of Bali consist of alpine and subalpine vegetation.

Certain fauna and flora are endemic or sacred to the Balinese, such as the rare Balinese climbing bamboo and the sacred frangipani flower. The Balinese tiger, now believed to be extinct, once roamed the western forests. Leopards and macaque monkeys are still found in Bali, and teak and giant banyan trees are amongst Bali's coveted arboreal treasures. Deer and wild pigs roam freely on the island. On Java, the endemic Javanese peacocks and single-horned Javan rhinoceros can be found, although the rhinoceros are critically endangered and mostly contained within wildlife preserves. The endangered and protected orangutan primate is native to Borneo and Sumatra. Overall, Indonesia is home to forty thousand species of flowering plants (including five thousand species of orchids). Like the fauna of Indonesia, many of these species are unique to the region and sometimes endemic to the specific island(s) on which they occur. Indonesia is home to three thousand species of trees, which are often used for indigenous or commercial purposes. These trees include ironwood, sandalwood, woody rattan, and others that produce unique fruits, nuts, and other beneficial products.

The Ubud Monkey Forest, Bali.
Michelle Maria, CC BY 3.0 <https://creativecommons.org/licenses/by/3.0>, via Wikimedia Commons
https://commons.wikimedia.org/wiki/File:Monkey_Forest_Park,_Ubud,_Indonesia_-_panoramio_(7).jpg

Bali is the westernmost island of the Lesser Sunda Islands, lying just 3.2 kilometers (2 miles) east of Java, separated by the Bali Strait. To the east of Bali, Lombok lies twenty kilometers (about twelve miles) away across the Lombok Strait. Bali lies about eight degrees south of the equator and experiences a tropical climate with little distinction between seasons in terms of temperature. It averages around 30 degrees Celsius (86 degrees Fahrenheit) with high humidity year-round. The wet monsoon season from October to April usually brings heavy rains, particularly from December to March. The main island is approximately 150 kilometers wide and 110 kilometers long from north to south and is home to 99 percent of Bali's population. Over the last fifty years, Bali has become an increasingly popular tourist destination and draws people from around the world to its pristine forests and beaches, unique fauna, rich coral reefs as part of the Coral Triangle, cultural heritage, and cosmopolitan nightlife. The island of Bali draws at least 80 percent of its economy from tourism-related businesses and is the main Indonesian tourist destination. The Balinese way of life is deeply spiritual, aesthetic, and cultural, with worship, dance, and other art forms being the most important part of life on the island.

Chapter 2 – Bali before the Common Era

One of the first known specimens of *Homo erectus* (upright humans but before modern man) were found on Java, dating from between one million and 700,000 years ago. Similarly, paleolithic evidence (dating from 1,000,000 to 200,000 BCE) has been found on Bali, indicating that it was also inhabited by very early man during this time. Ancient tools such as hand axes were found in the villages of Sembiran and Trunyan in the north and northeast of the main island, respectively. Further evidence of *Homo erectus* exists in Bali from the Mesolithic period (200,000-30,000 BCE). This later evidence suggests more advanced peoples who used more sophisticated tools such as arrow points and tools made of animal bones. These Mesolithic peoples lived in temporary caves such as those found in the Pecatu hills of the Badung regency. The first sign of modern man (*Homo sapiens*) began in about 45,000 BCE as continental people migrated south from the mainland and began replacing *Homo erectus.*

The presence of Paleolithic and Mesolithic man on Java and Bali suggests that the islands were more accessible during certain periods in history, like the ice ages when sea levels were lower and when land bridges existed between areas that are now islands divided by the sea. By the Neolithic period (starting in about 10,000 BCE), sea levels had risen to produce the arrangement of islands we know as Indonesia in the present era. Humankind also developed the maritime navigation skills and technologies (boats) to move from the mainland to these islands, as well as between the islands. But the early peoples of the Neolithic period most importantly relied on nature for this migration, specifically, ocean currents, tides, and winds, and, most importantly for Southeast Asia, the seasonal monsoons.

The concept of a monsoon is prevalent throughout the tropics and is most commonly associated with wet weather. However, monsoons refer to wind, specifically to a seasonal change in the direction of the prevailing (strongest) winds of a region. A monsoon season can bring dry or wet conditions throughout the tropics, depending on the direction from which the wind is blowing. Monsoons traveling overseas, particularly warm seas, will bring wet weather. Monsoons traveling overland will bring drier weather. Monsoons blow from colder to warmer regions, and these winds determine the climate for most of Southeast Asia. Technically, summer monsoon winds blow from the southwest during June to September, and winter monsoon winds, or trade winds, blow from the northeast from October to March.

However, this general pattern of monsoon winds is attributed to the Northern Hemisphere, and most of Indonesia, specifically Bali, are within the Southern Hemisphere (but only slightly within the Southern Hemisphere). Local weather patterns, including the specific arrangement of larger islands near Bali (such as Sumatra), also affect its experience of monsoon weather and create anomalies in the island from experiencing a typical tropical monsoon weather pattern. Although Bali's true wet season is in its summer (October to March), since it is so close to the equator, it can experience year-round rains brought by alternating monsoon winds. Sir Stamford Raffles, a British statesman and governor of the Dutch East Indies in the early 19th century who wrote *The History of Java* (published in 1817), noted that all of the Southeast Asian countries situated within ten degrees of the equator experienced "one eternal summer" that is not distinguished by hot and cold but by wet (hot and rainy) and dry (hot and humid) weather. The humidity and torrential rain of Bali's wet monsoon season (December to March) are critical for agriculture. The wet monsoon season is essential for much of Southeast Asia since many of these countries do not have extensive natural or manmade irrigation or damming systems, either near their croplands or underground in the form of deep aquifers. The wet monsoons provide necessary water for both livestock and crop farming.

Historically, early exploration is considerably attributed to monsoon wind patterns in Southeast Asia. However, the ancient monsoon winds did not specifically follow modern calendars because of the earth's axial precession. Both early migratory peoples and ancient trade mariners used monsoon wind patterns to discover and explore new lands. Monsoon winds and their associated currents were essential in assisting ancient cultures to navigate their small, indigenous seafaring crafts to foreign lands, such as the Indonesian archipelago, which was only accessible via sea. Recent archaeological evidence along the coasts of Southeast Asia, India, and the Middle East provides persuasive evidence of a network of mariners in ancient times, dating to approximately two millennia before the Common Era, roughly around the time that Bali began to be settled.

The monsoon winds of Southeast Asia altered the surface currents of its seas and oceans to enable smaller craft to navigate along the maritime trade routes. Since ancient sailing and rowing vessels were smaller and either powered by sails or people, they relied mostly on the direction of the prevailing winds to set their direction. Much of Southeast Asia began being populated sometime between 6,500 BCE and 4,500 BCE (the Neolithic period) by the Austronesian peoples. The Austronesians are an ethnically and linguistically related people who originated from mainland Asia. There is one popular historical theory that suggests Austronesians migrated via Taiwan to populate maritime Southeast Asia, but another suggests Austronesian migration patterns originated from Indonesia/Wallacea (of which Bali is a part). Regardless of the various theories of the initial migratory patterns of this ethnic group, the mainland origins of the Austronesians were most likely mainland southern China and mainland northern Southeast Asia. The preexistence of archaic settled tribes throughout mainland southern Asia meant that natural population expansion moved southward and into maritime Southeast Asia, Oceana, and the Indian and Pacific Oceans.

Archaeological evidence, such as linguistics, human and animal DNA, ocean voyaging technology, and pottery, has been used to link approximately 350 million people currently living in Madagascar, Southeast Asia (and, in part, within mainland Asia), Oceana (including areas of mainland Australia), and the Pacific islands with a common genetic source. Known as the Austronesian peoples, it is thought that they moved from southern mainland China and either through Taiwan or Indonesia (or both) in an outward expansion over thousands of years. Although different evidence points to different potentials for the spread of the Austronesian peoples, they share commonalities that indicate the hereditary sharing of knowledge and resources. Some of this indigenous knowledge included ocean voyaging technologies, such as ocean sailing canoes, farming methods like the irrigated rice terraces, domesticated animals like wild pigs and chickens, and cultivated plants like taro, banana, breadfruit, and sugarcane. Since the Austronesians' staple food source was rice, they are most commonly associated with the complex irrigation systems still evident today in much of Southeast Asia. These cascading rice paddies (fields) are known in Bali as the subak system.

The modern-day family of languages spoken in much of the Indonesian archipelago is part of the 1,200 contemporary Austronesian languages. The Austronesian language group covers a vast maritime geographical area and includes about 20 percent of the world's languages. The Austronesian expansion was most likely the result of growing population numbers reliant on new lands for cultivation, which would have been exacerbated by resource-poor small islands and the necessity to continue expanding. It is also likely that many of the new lands discovered by the Austronesian peoples were uninhabited or sparsely inhabited, allowing for the development of new, independent settlements or, in some cases, cross-pollination of ethnicities.

The Austronesian peoples were thought to have begun inhabiting Bali and its surrounding islands in approximately the second millennium BCE. The tools discovered in Bali include rectangular adzes (work axes) and agricultural tools, as well as red-slipped decorated pottery. The early Austronesian settlers cleared rainforests for their villages, and they made plaited crafts as well as boats. They ate pork and chewed betel—a peppery vine with cultural value. Like many early people of Bali, the Austronesians settled mostly in the mountainous regions of the island. They buried some of their dead (possibly of higher social status) in unusual and distinctive oval stone sarcophagi. The sarcophagi were decorated with human head illustrations or zoomorphic figures, and because the sarcophagi were small and pod-like, the bodies sometimes had to be folded into three to fit in the coffins. These coffins were used into the Bronze Age (up to the first millennium BCE).

There is evidence of bronze and iron metallurgy on the Southeast Asian islands occurring in about 500 BCE, which is believed to be more than that simply traded with other regions. Dong Son drums were also traded at this time from Vietnam to the Sunda and surrounding islands. Indian pottery dating from circa 200 BCE to 200 CE has been unearthed in Bali and Java, proving Bali was part of ancient trading routes with greater Asia. It is likely that by 500 CE, Southeast Asia was the site of prolific inter- and intra-regional trade, but it is also likely that one of the main sources of this burgeoning life—Taiwan—became increasingly removed from Nusantara life. Rising sea levels since the end of the last ice age meant that the sea-crossings that may have been manageable in the millennia that initiated Austronesian expansion were growing wider and were possibly climatically more dangerous to navigate.

The Austronesian explorers were thought to have used outrigger canoes and proas to navigate to new lands. Unfortunately, these conclusions are drawn mostly upon the indigenous vessels used by the Austronesian peoples of today, as well as reports by the early European explorers. It is supposed that most of the evidence of early sailing vessels has been destroyed by the climatic conditions of the tropics and the erosive and destructive effects of the ocean. It is also possible that early colonists destroyed indigenous vessels in order to hold the native peoples captive on the islands and, therefore, more under their control.

Outrigger vessels are those where the hull is supported by a lateral stabilizing force such as a second float, and a proa (or a prau) is a type of multi-hulled (usually double) outrigger sailboat. These watercraft inventions, as well as others, were the most important technologies of the

Austronesian peoples and were what enabled them to cover significant distances of the oceans and colonize vast tracts of Southeast Asia and the Pacific.

An example of a "flying" (very fast) proa with a crab-claw sail. These multi-hulled outrigger sailboats of the Austronesian peoples may have been used to explore new lands. Similar craft are used by Austronesian people to this day.
https://commons.wikimedia.org/wiki/File:Proa_(PSF).png

Stone tools dating from approximately 2500 to 2000 BCE have been discovered in Cekik on the western end of Bali (modern-day Gilimanuk). Also at Cekik, as well as inland at Sembiran, indications of a Bronze Age people dating from the 3rd century BCE have been discovered. Evidence from these sites reveals communities of fishermen, hunters, and farmers. It is evident that these early peoples of Bali had knowledge of metallurgy and acquired the skills to cast or smelt copper, bronze, and iron. These Bronze Age peoples are thought to have originated from Indochina, specifically the Dong Son area of Vietnam, and brought metals and metallurgy skills with them. The Dong Son Bronze Age culture was named after a village of northern Vietnam (the Red River Valley) and existed from approximately one millennium before the Common Era to about the 1st century of the Common Era.

The Dong Son were themselves originally believed to have migrated from the southern Chinese mainland to northern Vietnam, bringing their farming (specifically rice cultivation) and metallurgy techniques with them. Although the Dong Son were also skilled in ironwork and carried traditional cultural Chinese artifacts with them, they are best known for their pervasive and high-quality bronze kettle drums. Dong Son religious stone monuments were also a mark of their culture and are similar to those found in Polynesia. Like all Austronesian peoples, the Dong Son were great seafarers who traveled and traded throughout Southeast Asia and whose people naturally chose to settle in certain parts of the various archipelagos. There is evidence that Balinese people acquired the Dong Son metallurgical techniques between the 8th and 3rd centuries BCE. Although the raw materials to make bronze (copper and tin) needed to be imported, it seems that the Balinese had acquired the skills to both mold and decorate tools, weapons, jewelry, and drums.

The development of the Indonesian Pejeng drum was an early 1st and 2nd century CE adaptation of the Dong Son kettle drum. They are one of the region's finest examples of localized metalworking. The Pejeng drums were named after the Bronze Age village of Pejeng in Bali. These drums differed from traditional Dong Son drums in that they were longer and were cast in two pieces using wax molds. These drums were produced extensively on the islands of Java and Bali during the first millennium CE.

The Balinese variation, specifically, is one of the most sophisticated artifacts of Indonesia's prehistory. The finest example of the Pejeng drum is the Moon of Pejeng, the largest example of its kind in the world and currently on display at the temple of Pura Penataran Sasih in Pejeng near

Ubud (southwest Gianyar). The Moon of Pejeng is considered highly sacred by the local people and is thought to have been an important relic of early rice cultivation rituals. The village of Pejeng lies in the Petauan River valley, which, along with its neighbor the Pakerisan River valley, forms the epicenter of the southern Balinese region of earliest rice cultivation. These complex irrigated rice fields are the most important inherited origins of early Balinese peoples.

The six-foot-long (187-centimeter-long) Pejeng Moon drum is thought to have been carved about three hundred years before the Common Era. Balinese legends tell that the drum was originally one of the wheels of a chariot that pulled the real moon through the night sky. One night, the wheel broke from the chariot and fell to the earth in a tree in Pejeng. The wheel shone as brightly as the moon and was extinguished and cooled by a passing thief who climbed the tree and urinated on it! The thief paid for this sacrilege with his life, but the drum was kept as a sacred relic by the villagers.

Top: Neolithic (6,500– 4,500 BCE) stone sarcophagus, Bali Museum.
PHGCOM, CC BY-SA 3.0 <https://creativecommons.org/licenses/by-sa/3.0>, via Wikimedia Commons https://commons.wikimedia.org/wiki/File:Neolithic_stone_sarcophagus_Bali.jpg

Bpttom: A Pejeng kettle drum dating from the 1st-2nd Century CE.
Metropolitan Museum of Art, CC0, via Wikimedia Commons
https://commons.wikimedia.org/wiki/File:MET_2001_433_93_O1_(cropped).jpg

Archaeological discoveries in Bali suggest that human settlement before the Common Era happened in stages but that these migrations were limited and independent of one another. Maritime Southeast Asia is known to be a melting pot of cultures, specifically Indonesia, which boasts a mix of an estimated 250 ethnic groups. Bali is similar in the diversity of its ethnic origins. Contemporary ethnicities in Bali are a unique genetic blend of Chinese, Malay, Polynesian, Melanesian (Pacific peoples), Indian, and Javanese. However, it was the arrival of Hindu merchants from the 1st century CE and onward that made the most significant impact on the population expansion of ancient Bali.

Chapter 3 – The Historic Period

Much of the ancient and historical movements of people through time have arisen from common interests regarding trade. The Austronesian peoples were some of the first to create a maritime trade network across the Indo-Pacific. They traded seacraft, paan (an end product of the betel leaf, like chewing tobacco), and cultivars crucial to farming, such as coconuts, bananas, and sugarcane. Trade networks such as these connected dominant material cultures like India and China. As early Austronesian trade increased, spices became the main imports moving from east to west, surpassing other commodities and products. These early forerunners of the global spice trade eventually developed into the Maritime Silk Road—the multicultural trade network that connected Africa, Europe, China, Southeast Asia, the Indian subcontinent, and the Arabian Peninsula from the 2nd century BCE until the 15th century CE.

India's connection to Southeast Asia was extremely important to the merchants of Arabia and Persia (Iran) in the 7th and 8th centuries. However, by the 11th century CE, the expansive Muslim Seljuk Empire blocked the route of commodities west and instigated the medieval Crusades. The Seljuk Empire was a vast medieval hegemony that stretched from the Levant in the west to the Hindu Kush in the east, and it was bordered by the Persian Gulf in the south and included most of central Asia. Similarly, the Ottoman Empire negatively impacted the spice trade in the mid-1400s, igniting the age of maritime discovery and European colonization as voyages left Europe and rounded the continents in search of commodities. Spices produced in Near and Far Eastern countries, such as cinnamon, clove, turmeric, cassia, cardamom, ginger, and pepper, were in high demand to nations on the ancient spice route. The "Spice Islands" of Indonesia (the Maluku or Molucca Islands and the Banda Islands) were kept secret by the traders, and they developed fantastical tales about the source of the spices to protect these commodities.

The historical period of Bali stretches from the start of the Common Era until the Majapahit Empire in 1343, although it was most active from approximately the seventh millennium of the Common Era. The greatest influences in that time were from influxes of people from India, Java, and China. The Austronesian and Dong Son peoples constituted the original settlers of Bali. The next significant group was approximately four hundred people who moved from eastern Java, more specifically the village of Aga, in about the 8th century CE. They settled in the remote mountainous area around the volcano named Gunung Agung ("Great Mountain"), believing that mountainous areas brought them closer to the gods. These Aga communities prospered and remain a significant Balinese population group today. However, the Bali Agas' strictly preserved cultural code means that, to this day, their communities remain separate and isolated from much of Balinese life, particularly that familiar to modern-day tourists.

Aspects of Aga life, such as clothing and architecture, have been retained through the centuries. For example, the ancient and traditional geringsing fabric unique to the Bali Aga village of Tenganan Pegringsingan is made using an ancient technique of color dyeing or the double ikat method (a form of tie-dyeing). The geringsing fabrics are black, red (rust), and neutral, and they are considered sacred by the Bali Aga, particularly when it comes to healing. "Gering" means illness, and "sing" means no. The geringsing are often ascribed supernatural powers and are patterned with Hindu motifs or other inspirational cultural patterns, such as the frangipani flower (*jepun*). Geringsing are used extensively for cultural and religious ceremonies within Tenganan Pegringsingan village life. References to geringsing exist within ancient Javanese literature and Buddhist poetry. The 1365 poem *Nagarakretagama* (*Nagarakrtagama*, *Desawarnana*, or *Desavarnana*), written by the Buddhist sage Mpu Prapanca, describes curtains of the infamous Javanese Majapahit ruler Hayam Wuruk as being made of geringsing.

Tenganan (Bali Aga) women wearing the geringsing-patterned cloth.
Kresnanta, CC BY-SA 4.0 <https://creativecommons.org/licenses/by-sa/4.0>, via Wikimedia Commons https://commons.wikimedia.org/wiki/File:Rejang_Ala_Tenganan.jpg

The most pervasive and lasting influence of population influx for ancient Bali was by peaceful Indian traders who began arriving on the island in the 1st century CE. The traders are thought to have been from southern India and Sri Lanka, and they moved simultaneously into Indochina and southern China. These Indian mercantile spiritualists would most likely have largely settled in Java—Bali's closest, largest, and most resource-laden island neighbor—before moving across to Bali. From the historical period onward, Java's and Bali's histories have been inextricably linked.

The Indian merchants introduced both Hinduism and Buddhism to Bali. Hinduism was an ancient way of life that had been practiced on the Indian subcontinent since before the second millennium BCE. Buddhism, which was founded in the late 6th century BCE, was becoming entrenched as a world religion at the time, spreading throughout Asia and Southeast Asia along the trade routes. Mahayana Buddhism was brought to Bali, which is one of the two main branches of ancient Buddhism. This branch is the less traditionalist branch of Buddhism (as opposed to Theravada Buddhism) and is the most widely practiced form of the religion today.

The first written records discovered in Bali were Buddhist inscriptions on clay tablets, which were discovered inside stone Buddhist stupas, or ceremonial containers, known as stupikas. These votive writings, which date from the 8th century CE, were found in villages in the regency of Gianyar. Along with the stupikas, which indicate the presence of Buddhism in Bali, the Blanjong Pillar (*Prasasti Blanjong* or Belanjong Pillar) was discovered in the southern area of Sanur and is dated exactly to 914 CE. The low stone pillar is inscribed using both the old Balinese language and Indian Sanskrit, and it mentions King Sri Kesari of Bali, who commissioned the pillar. Three other inscriptions mentioning King

Kesari were discovered in central Bali, which indicates there was some regional struggle that required him to enforce his territory. King Kesari is the first known Balinese king to use the title Warmadewa (Varmadeva). Evidence of this title for the next century suggests kings that were linked in a monarchical sense, but there is insufficient evidence to confirm if Warmadewa refers to a biological dynasty or not. The most recent and final appearance of the title Warmadewa is on an inscription attributed to the well-known King Udayana Warmadewa, dated 1011 CE. King Udayana's most important historical claim is as the father of the renowned King Airlangga, who ruled Java from around 1020 to 1040 CE. The title Warmadewa was not seen again, and it is thought to have disappeared as Javanese expansion and rule expanded and overtook Bali.

The name "Bali" is believed to have originated in about the 7th century CE, although written evidence of its name dates from a little later. *Bali dwipa* ("Bali Island") was discovered in several inscriptions, including the Blanjong Pillar. The name "Bali" is thought to be derived from the word *bebali*, meaning "offerings," and spread by way of eastern Java through Hindu spiritualism and the concept of making donations to the spirit world, such as flowers, food, cloth, and decorations. Offerings are a core part of Balinese spirituality to this day, and the multitude of temples and sacred sites of the island are continually adorned with gifts to spirits and gods.

A concentration of archaeological finds in the Balinese regency of Gianyar suggests that this region may have been a political, religious, and cultural capital during the 10th and 11th centuries of the Common Era. At the same time, Shaivite (Shivaite) Hinduism was taking hold in Bali. Shaivism is one of the main Hindu traditions, in which Shiva is worshiped as the supreme being. It is one of the largest sects of Hinduism and is believed to be the oldest living religion in the world. The 11th-century stone-carved Elephant Cave (Goa Gajah) near Ubud and the adjoining bathing place are testimony to the Warmadewa kings' adherence to Buddhism as well as Shaivite Hinduism since the temple complex contains evidence of both religions in its stone carvings. A menacing figure has been carved at the entrance to the cave, which leads to a small chamber, assumed for meditation. Nearby, a bathing pool was carved out of stone and lined with seven stone women pouring water from pitchers into the pool.

King Udayana Warmadewa ruled Bali in the second half of the 10th century. At the same time, the Medang Kingdom of Java was flourishing. The Medang, also known as the Mataram, Kingdom was a sophisticated Hindu-Buddhist monarchy ruled by the Indianized Shailendra (Sailendra, Syailendra, or Selendra) dynasty. In Sanskrit, Shailendra means "King of the Mountain," and the emergence of the dynasty in the 700s CE in central Java began a cultural renaissance for Bali's closest and most influential island neighbor. During their approximate 300-year-long rule (from the mid-7th century to the early 11th century CE), the Shailendra dynasty's rulers filled Java with religious monuments, which were mostly Mahayana Buddhist. The Shailendras were a thalassocracy (a seaborne rulership), and most of their focus was on the intra- and inter-trade relationships of Southeast Asia. The Shailendras may have been more than the rulers of the Medang dynasty and could also possibly have been an important part of the Srivijaya Kingdom of Sumatra as well.

King Sri Kesari, who left the inscription on the Belanjong pillar, is thought to have been of Shailendra descent and could possibly have migrated to Bali from Java for the express purpose of establishing a Mahayana Buddhist government in Bali. The title Warmadewa could mean a connection to the Shailendra dynasty. The Medang Kingdom of Java flourished between approximately the 8th and 11th centuries, and it eventually spread to dominate eastern Java, thus moving ever closer as an influential power over Bali. This refined civilization focused heavily on rice farming and then later maritime trade. It was rich in spirituality, arts, and culture, and significant population growth and economic prosperity saw the Medang Kingdom spread to influence Sumatra, Bali, southern Thailand, and other areas of Indochina, as well as parts of the Philippines in time.

Eventually, the Medang Kingdom split into two warring factions, which alternately supported either Buddhism or Hindu Shaivism. The dynasties that headed up these factions were the Shivaist dynasty of Java and the Buddhist dynasty of the Srivijaya Kingdom of Sumatra. In 1006 CE, the Shailendra clan of the Srivijaya Kingdom triumphed when one of their vassals—King Wurawari of Lwaram—conquered the Shivaist capital of Watugaluh in eastern Java. Although the Srivijaya dynasty rose up to become the hegemonic empire of the region, lasting until the 14th century, the Shivaist dynasty continued and had reclaimed eastern Java by 1019.

King Udayana Warmadewa of Bali married an eastern Javanese woman, Queen Mahendradatta of the Isyana dynasty. The Isyana dynasty was the eastern Javanese arm of the Medang Kingdom and proceeded the Sanjaya dynasty of the same geographical region. The first ruler of the Isyanas (or the last ruler of the Sanjayas), Mpu Sindok, had initiated the establishment of rulership in the east of Java in 929 CE. Historical records are confusing, but the Hindu Sanjaya dynasty, which was established in central Bali, could have been an independent kingdom or could have been part of the Shailendras. Either way, they gave way to the Isyanas, and their seat of power was relocated to eastern Java for reasons that are not clear.

The Sanjaya dynasty was founded in approximately 732 CE by King Sanjaya, who was one of the rulers of Medang. Five more kings followed

Sanjaya until the eastward migration of the royal court and the establishment of Sindok's Isyana dynasty. Contrary historical records suggest that the Sanjayas and the Shailendras were interwoven and possibly related but were also at odds with one another, competing for dominance in religion and economics throughout Java and farther afield. Some historians deny the existence of the Sanjayas altogether and state that they were merely another branch of the Shailendras. Ironically, the legendary rivalry between the Buddhist Shailendra dynasty and the Hindu Sanjayas is supposed to have led to the establishment of two of the most famous and beautiful temples in Java: the Hindu Prambanan temple and the Buddhist Borobudur.

The marriage of King Udayana and Queen Mahendradatta is evidence of a historical link between the islands of Java and Bali. Queen Mahendradatta was the sister of the last king of the Medang Kingdom, Dharmawangsa (r. 990-1016 CE). These royal siblings claimed a direct lineage from Mpu Sindok as part of the Isyana dynasty. Since Dharmawangsa was supposed to have conquered Bali at some point in his reign, it is likely that the marriage of his sister to King Udayana was some kind of a strategic arrangement, albeit a loose one. The children produced from this union rose to rule eastern Java as well as Bali. Marakata Pangkaja and later Anak Wungcu (Wungsu) ascended the Balinese throne.

The eldest son of King Udayana and Queen Mahendradatta, Airlangga (or Erlangga), went on to establish the Kahuripan Kingdom of Java that arose after eastern Java's destruction by Wurawari. Airlangga was the only monarch to rule during the brief Kahuripan era of Java. He was born in Bali but crossed over to rule Java (his name meaning "jumping water"), and he was a descendent of both the Isyana and Warmadewa lineages. Certain apocryphal records suggest that Airlangga was born in Java to a different father than King Udayana. It is possible that both Airlangga and his mother, Mahendradatta, first crossed to Bali for her marriage to King Udayana. Airlangga may not have been the son of a Balinese king at all, and the fact that he was not first in line to the Balinese throne might corroborate his illegitimacy to the Balinese royal house. Airlangga was also sent back to his uncle, King Dharmawangsa, in his teenage years to be educated in the eastern Javanese royal court. He was betrothed to his cousin, a daughter of his uncle Dharmawangsa.

During this period, Bali may have been under the direct rule of the Medang Kingdom, which continued to be at war with the Srivijayas of central Java and Sumatra. The invasion of the eastern Javanese capital in 1006 by Wurawari includes a local legend that it occurred on Airlangga's wedding day and that he was the only one left alive, at sixteen years of age, after his entire family was slaughtered. After living as a hermit in the western jungle, by 1019, Airlangga had accumulated loyal allies, made peace with Srivijaya, and established his new kingdom of eastern Java, Kahuripan. Although Kahuripan thrived under the fair and equality-minded Airlangga, there were complications with the succession that saw the disintegration of his hard-fought-for kingdom.

Both of Airlangga's brothers (or half-brothers) who went on to rule Bali, Marakata Pangkaja and Anak Wungcu, were mentioned in historical Balinese inscriptions, and they were evidently fair and charitable leaders. Balinese inscriptions at that time were made on copper slit drums (*tongtong* or *kulkul*). By the 12th century CE, the descendants of Airlangga, Jayasakti (r. 1146-1151) and Jayapangus (r. 1178-1181), went on to rule Bali. Archaeological discoveries have been made of Jayasakti's *Prasasti Desa Depaa* copper plate inscriptions, as well as King Jayapangus's copper plate inscriptions regarding governance and taxes, which were written in the old Balinese script.

Bali's connection to China remained strong throughout the Javanese historical period. Chinese coins, or *Kepeng*, had been in use on the island since the 7th century CE. King Jayapangus (also known as Dalem Balingkang) married a Chinese princess, Tjin We, and the royal couple has been immortalized through the Barong Landung art form. The traditional Balinese Barong is closely linked with Chinese mythological creatures. The Barong is a lion-like creature, and as king of the spirit world, he is heralded as the ultimate victor in the never-ending battle of good versus evil in Balinese mythology. The Barong Landung is a cultural event and oral tradition that celebrates the long-held Balinese-Chinese association. It is a procession of people, music, and effigies that tells a legendary tale of the king and his Chinese queen. Furthermore, the names of several Balinese villages have Chinese words as their root.

Legends, specifically the Barong Landung, suggest that Jayapangus's marriage was without children, so at some point in history, the Warmadewa lineage died out. It is possible that a series of indigenous kings ruled the island in an interim period, which lasted more than a hundred years before the rise of Majapahit. Bali's formal connection to Java remained dormant, but its autonomy was shattered in 1284 by King Kertanegara of the Singhasari Empire. The Singhasari Empire was a 13th-century eastern Javanese stronghold and one of the Hindu-Buddhist Indianized kingdoms of ancient Southeast Asia. Historical Javanese sources tell that King Kertanegara invaded and overcame Bali, capturing the queen and forcing her to appear before the Javanese court. At this point, Bali became part of the Singhasari Empire. The preceding peace of several centuries gave way to Kertanegara's short eight-year-long rule. After he was assassinated during a rebellion, his empire fell. Bali enjoyed another interim period of independence. However, Bali's annexation by Java was renewed, this time with more vigor than in previous generations.

King Kertanegara's son, the renowned Vijaya (Raden Wijaya), took the throne and founded the Majapahit Empire in 1293, which was to have a long and lasting influence over Bali.

Chapter 4 – The Majapahit Empire

The Majapahit Empire (also known as the Wilwatikta Empire) was an Indianized kingdom based in central and eastern Java that lasted from approximately the end of the 13th century to the 1500s. Its decline coincided with the rise of Islam in Nusantara, specifically falling to the Islamic Sultanate of Demak of northern Java in 1527. The origins of Majapahit are unclear, although it was mentioned in ancient Javanese and Chinese historical records, particularly in Javanese religious records such as scriptural religious poems. Majapahit was considered a regional superpower of its time. The previous Singhasari Empire had given way to the Majapahit Empire, although the same ruling family—the Rajasa dynasty—continued to rule through the duration of both empires. The Majapahit Empire was a thalassocracy that subsequently developed a highly organized cultural and artistic society that was also economically productive, specifically in regard to rice cultivation. It was considered the last of the great Malay Archipelago Hindu kingdoms before colonial interference, and it is still heralded as one of Indonesia's greatest states, continuing to influence political rulership and identity in Indonesia in the modern day.

The golden age of Majapahit was marked by the rulership of Hayam Wuruk, who reigned from circa 1350 to 1389. During this era, the Majapahit Empire dominated large swathes of Indonesia, including Java, Bali, the southern Malay Peninsula, Borneo and Kalimantan, Sumatra, and the Philippines. The Majapahit coat of arms was the Surya Majapahit, or the Sun of the Majapahit, an emblem resembling a sun or a compass that has been found in many of the Majapahit ruins. A few generations into the Majapahit Empire, Hayam Wuruk, the grandson of the Majapahit founder, Vijaya, legitimately ascended the throne at the age of sixteen. Hayam Wuruk was also known as Rajasanagara. During Hayam Wuruk's rule, the Majapahit Empire dispatched with some of the last remaining maritime empires of the Malay Archipelago to emerge as the dominant thalassocracy in command of much of western and central maritime Southeast Asia.

At home on eastern Java, Majapahit society was refined, wealthy, and cultured. The Hindu court had developed a sophisticated system of religious rituals that became interwoven with everyday life and customs. The divisions between livelihood, religion, art, literature, spirituality, and community were significantly blurred to produce a unique blend of morals, beliefs, and behaviors, which created the foundation for Balinese life as it exists in modern times. The level of influence of the Majapahit Empire over its dominions is a matter of historical debate. Some historians propose more of a royal monopoly on trade and multiple vassal states rather than any form of interference or governance across the archipelagos. Since the empire also developed relationships with outlying countries, such as China and Indochina (Southeast Asian mainland), it is most likely that it held the most control over the islands closest to Java and its capital in eastern Java, Wilwatikta (modern-day Trowulan), and the least control the farther afield its empire stretched.

Around the same time the Majapahit Empire was founded, Muslim traders and proselytizers began entering the archipelagic regions of which Bali was a part, and eventually, sultanates were formed. After the death of Hayam Wuruk in 1389, the Majapahit Empire saw squabbles over succession for the next 130 years until 1519. The disintegration of the dynasty could not withstand the rising power of the Islamic Malacca Sultanate. After a series of battles with the Javanese Sultanate of Demak (part of Muslim Malacca centered on the Malay Peninsula), the Majapahit Empire was finally defeated by 1527. Demak had been one of the first Muslim sultanates to be formed with the newly Islamized Malay Archipelago in the 1400s. Many Majapahit nobles and courtiers moved south from the capital of Majapahit (modern-day Trowulan in Java) to Kediri, also in Java. Shortly after the fall of Majapahit, all of Java came under the control of the Islamic sultanate centered in northern Java, at Demak. Many religious and spiritual people (both Hindu and Buddhist), artisans, royalty and courtiers, and other literati, intelligentsia, and artists moved eastward to Bali rather than submit to a foreign religious and cultural power. In this way, although the formal rulership of the Majapahit era in Bali may have lasted for over two hundred years, the vanquished empire continued to significantly influence Bali until the mid-19th century (and beyond) with the advent of the island's modern historical period and pronounced Dutch intervention.

Abundant evidence of the culture brought across from Majapahit stills exists in Bali today. The split gateway entrances (*candi bentar*), so reminiscent of eastern Java, adorn most of the Balinese temples from this era. The Majapahit architects mastered the use of stone and, more uniquely, of brick for their temples (*puras*) and shrines (*candis*). (The

Majapahit red-brick candis may be visited in Bali today.) The Majapahits, like the Balinese in later times, venerated the death of loved ones and great people, and they celebrated the occasion with great pomp and ceremony, often continuing decades after the event. For funerals and religious ceremonies of all kinds, the people of the Majapahit Empire employed the work of artisans to create splendid floats, decorations, and music. Religious ceremonies adopted a carnival-like atmosphere, which included plays and narrations, and they went to extraordinary lengths to create beautiful offerings to the gods and the spiritual realms. Many Javanese and even Muslim states of western Southeast Asia later claimed to be related or at least linked to the mighty Majapahit Empire of the 14th and 15th centuries. However, it is Bali that can claim more than a historical recognition of the suzerainty of the Majapahits since their people are, in fact, the true heirs to the historical kingdom.

Along with the architectural and religious heritage brought from eastern Java, the Kawi script (the ancestral forerunner of the Javanese and Balinese written language common to Southeast Asia at the time), painting, sculpture, and the Wayang (Wayang Kulit or Wajang) puppet theater also lay claim to having their origins in Majapahit. The Wayang puppet shows are a particularly unique and fascinating piece of local culture and are recognized by the United Nations UNESCO as a vital part of Indonesia's ancient heritage. The Wayang puppets are either three-dimensional dolls or two-dimensional leather (or wood) shadow puppets with stylized features and clothing. The dramatic shows are watched behind lit screens and communicate indigenous knowledge, mythology, and folklore or important philosophies, such as those found in the two quintessential ancient Hindu epic poems—the *Ramayana* and the *Mahabharata*. These two pieces of ancient Hindu literature are dated between the 7th century BCE and the 4th century CE and are considered some of the main scriptural references of the religion. Over time, the tradition of Wayang has grown to include live action, singing, dancing, music, literature, painting, and other symbolic art forms. Although, interestingly, the Bali Aga were never brought into the cultural renaissance of the Majapahit era.

When the influx of Majapahit influences began in the 14th century with the overthrow of the Balinese royalty, eastern Javanese-style royal courts were established in Bali by royalty and priests alike. Intermarriages of prominent (or royal) Balinese families with Majapahit royalty began formulating the upper-class caste of future Balinese societies. Besides the family lineages, cultural and religious descendancies began to become entrenched as island ideologies, cultural norms, and art forms. The indigenous spoken language developed to incorporate elements of Javanese. Most importantly, a wealth of ancient Buddhist-Hindu literature, such as the *Nagarakretagama*, was maintained in the royal libraries of Bali and neighboring Lombok (also part of the Majapahit Empire). The palm-leaf eulogy poem *Nagarakretagama*, written in the 14th century by a Buddhist monk, tells the story of the ancient Hindu-Buddhist kingdoms and specifically speaks of the Majapahit Empire and its most influential leader, Hayam Wuruk. Hayam Wuruk ascended the throne in the same era that chief minister (*patih*) Gajah Mada, who'd led the attack on Bali, was at the pinnacle of his career. It is likely that Gajah Mada was a significantly influential person in guiding Hayam Wuruk's eventual domination throughout much of the Indonesian archipelago. After the end of Hayam Wuruk's reign, the Majapahit Empire began to decline as a power base, but its influence as a political and cultural phenomenon was transferred, mostly to Bali, and the island remains an icon of Hindu-Buddhist Javanese culture and fiefdom to this day.

The Majapahit period in history is marked by the extensive Indianization of Southeast Asia, and it was the most influential foreign power in the establishment of the socio-cultural historical landscape of Bali. The Majapahit influence reached as far afield as the Malay Peninsula and eastern Indonesia. The era bequeathed Bali with the most lasting influences of its present-day social structure and class system, as well as architecture, temples, and the royal hierarchy. The Majapahit migration had given rise to significant advancements in culture, arts, and the economy, eventually birthing a Balinese national identity consisting of several Hindu kingdoms. The geographical extent of these Hindu kingdoms is echoed in Bali's existing eight governing regencies (or *kabupaten*)—their extent has not changed much since their formation several hundred years ago.

The historical link between the Majapahit Empire and the resident rulers of Bali became intertwined from the time that Gajah Mada (the Javanese prime minister) led a successful attack on the Balinese king in Bedulu (near Ubud) in 1342, which culminated in 1343. Gajah Mada's general, Arya Damar, assisted in the overthrow of Bali, which was achieved after a series of battles that took place over the course of seven months. The Majapahit governance of Bali was handed over to Arya Damar's four younger brothers. The leading brother, Arya Kenceng, went on to become the ancestor of the Balinese kings of the Tabanan and Badung royal houses. According to the Balinese babad, the Majapahit capital was located at Samprangan (or Samplangan, Gianyar) and then later at Gelgel (southeastern coast beyond Gianyar). The babad, chronicles, or dynastic genealogies were a large and scattered set of mostly 19th-century Brahmin-authored texts of Balinese history, dating back to the start of the Majapahit era, although it is considered to be a mix of fact, legend, and indigenous myth. Specifically, a 20th-century babad known as the *Babad Buleleng* was scribed at a time (1920) when Bali's Dutch colonizers were seeking to reinstate the nation's traditional kingdoms and rulers. This babad was thought to have been contrived in support of the appointment of I Gusti Putu Jelantik as ruler of the Buleleng Regency. The *Babad Buleleng* could be an example of a summary of all of the babad that came in the centuries before, although nothing can be confirmed.

Three earlier texts, *Babad Dalem*, *Usana Bali*, and *Usana Jawi*, establish (at least in cultural terms) the lineage of certain Balinese royal families, tracing their origins back to the original Majapahit conquerors. These earlier texts (and sometimes poetic verses) appear to have been written at the start of the 18th century, following a time when Balinese political power was shifting from the dominant Gelgel to the emerging Klungkung dynasty (c. 1687). Since the babad were often written to ascertain genealogical descendancy for those gaining power, their accuracy is significantly questionable, but they do provide some idea of overarching historical truths or ideas as well as common historical linkages.

The *Babad Dalem* (the *Chronicle of Kings*) is the babad that deals specifically with the history of Gelgel and suggests that the kingdom remained the primary Balinese stronghold until the second half of the 17th century, well after the dissolution of Majapahit. The Gelgel domination gave way to the Klungkung dynasty as the rightful inheritors of the Balinese kingdom, at least according to the babad. Despite contest by other kingdoms of Bali, Klungkung continued to rule in one sense or another for more than two centuries until the final 20th-century conquest by the Dutch in 1908. The ability of Klungkung to retain power came largely from the *Babad Dalem*'s description of the dynasty as having descended directly from the Majapahit Empire! Although many Balinese kingdoms attempted to write and interlink babad that "proved" their ancestral lineage to the Majapahit and their "rightful" place to overrule the other Balinese kingdoms, these efforts were very obviously contrived. The creation of Balinese babad would surge at times when political change threatened to engulf the island, such as in the mid-18th century and during Dutch colonial rule.

According to the *Babad Dalem*, once Majapahit had conquered the king of Bali in the royal center of Bedulu, a vassal court was established in Samprangan, Gianyar, close to the previous royal center. Legendary sources such as the babad are confusing and contradictory, and their timelines are almost impossible to believe, especially when compared to early 16th-century accounts by the first European explorers. What is factually clear is that the Majapahit vassal royal courts of Bali consisted of eastern Javanese noblemen and priests, as well as warriors (Brahmin and Kshatriya), from whom many people on Bali in the modern day can claim descendancy (and not exclusively from the royal houses). Apocryphal evidence indicates that the Majapahit rulers moved to Bali in groups over periods of time after the conquest in 1343 and established vassal courts that provided the foreign support structures required to retain influence over Bali. The Javanese overlords may have set up more than one capital on the island and are likely to have met resistance, particularly from the independent Bali Aga of the mountainous regions. According to legend, one of the first rulers of Samprangan, Sri Aji Kresna Kepakisan, had three sons. The eldest (Dalem Samprangan) was incompetent, and when his younger brother, Dalem Ketut, succeeded to the throne, he moved the royal center to Gelgel (southern Klungkung coast). Samprangan lapsed into obscurity, and the royal center of Gelgel continued for at least a century.

Chapter 5 – Gelgel and the Muslim Era

Gelgel is on the southeastern coast of the Klungkung Regency of Bali. It is believed to have been an ancient seat of power from the early 1500s, coinciding with the fall of the Majapahit Empire as well as the arrival of Islam and early European explorers in Bali. The Gelgel kingdom continued as the dominant indigenous power until the mid- to late 1600s, being replaced by the Dewa Agung of Klungkung. It is likely that Gelgel achieved stability when the Sultanate of Demak fell in the mid-16th century and was replaced by the Javanese Muslim Sultanate of Pajang and later by the Mataram Sultanate—not to be confused with the Mataram (Medang) Kingdom of the 11th century CE. In its time, the *puri* (Balinese court) of Gelgel was a vital center of the island's polity and religion—two aspects of Balinese life that remain indivisible to this day.

Gelgel's link to the previous Majapahit dynasties is only recorded in babad and so cannot be verified. Some historians believe that there may be no direct ancestral link between the end of the Majapahit regencies and the more intrinsically "Balinese" court of Gelgel and later Klungkung. The babad, which were written several hundred years later, may have been an afterthought and a direct attempt by the authors to both promote their own bloodlines as those of the upper classes and also entrench Bali as a Hindu state, although the *Babad Dalem* can be backed up by European sources in certain instances. With the encroachment of Islamic forces beginning in the early 16th century, the Balinese became ever-insistent upon their true identity as ancestors of the mighty Hindu Majapahit. An account from the 19th century explains why it was difficult for the Balinese kingdoms to unite as one or even for a single foreign power to overcome the island throughout its history. Helen M. Creese's (an associate professor at the University of Queensland, Australia) *Bali in the Early 19^{h} Century the Ethnographic Accounts of Pierre du Bois* describes the poetic accounts of a Dutch governmental bureaucrat's experiences as a civil administrator in the 1830s in Badung. Pierre du Bois explained how the geography of Bali determined its governance structure since the regions were often divided by deep ravines or high mountains with no navigable rivers and few roads. He explained that the roads were dangerous because of tigers and malefactors—presumably bandits!

The Gelgel region was home to a series of powerful kings, the Raja Dalem of Gelgel, a powerful *patih* (prime minister), and a considerable royal harem. The dominions of Gelgel were known to extend at times beyond Bali itself to include the eastern islands of Lombok and Sumbawa and the far eastern Javanese area of Blambangan. Gelgel was in a continual state of unrest, as relatives of the ruling classes and other

Balinese kingdoms continued to disrupt the status quo and contest the right of Gelgel to rule. A VOC (Dutch East India Company) source in 1619 reported no fewer than thirty-three petty kingdoms operating under the Raja Dalem. The Dutch reported on a particularly painful uprising dating to approximately 1585 to 1587 in which the king overcame an attempted coup and ultimately banished the usurpers to a barren island just off Bali. Meanwhile, the Malay Archipelago was becoming increasingly Islamized, and this conversion was encroaching rapidly upon eastern Java, where the Hindu-Buddhist ancestors of the vanquished Majapahit Empire were considered to be heathens by the surrounding Muslims.

Although Muslim traders had been active in the Malay Archipelago since the 8th century CE, it would take another five hundred years before the spread of Islam began in earnest in Nusantara. Scholastic missionaries from South and Southeast Asia, as well as the Arabian Peninsula, brought the teachings of Islam to Bali's neighboring islands, including Sumatra and Java. The success of the spread of Islam was via its adoption at first by rulers and elites, as well as traders, from where it spread to the population at large. By the end of the 13th century, Islam had been established in northern Sumatra, which was noted by the European explorer Marco Polo (1254-1324 CE). Evidence of a Muslim sultanate and ruling dynasty dates from this time.

The spread of Islam was slow at first, but it gained momentum at certain times, such as during the 15th century with the Malacca Sultanate. The small but powerful regional historical capital of the Malay Peninsula, Malacca, was strategically positioned adjacent to a sea strait separating the mainland from Sumatra. The Malacca Strait was the main entry channel into Nusantara and the region of Malacca, and the Islamic sultanate that grew around it, the Malacca Sultanate, became central to the rise and fall of powerful influences across the Malay Archipelago. Of course, the spread and impact of Islam were heavily dependent upon the maritime trade routes. Sea traders spread the word of Islam and carried scholars and goods associated with the newly Islamized regions. The Malacca Sultanate's strategic position on the Malaysian trade routes gave it the military power to accelerate the spread of Islam. The decline of the Majapahit kingdom that had dominated trade until the early 1500s coincided with the rise of several powerful sultanates that had developed across Nusantara, including the Demak Sultanate of central Java. The Chinese joined the maritime trade race and created Chinese Islamic communities throughout the islands. An Islamized trade hegemony developed across maritime Southeast Asia, which was protected by mainland China and other Islamic states to the north.

By the end of the 16th century, Islam dominated Sumatra and Java. It should be noted that the conversion to Islam was not generally accompanied by bloodshed in the early centuries. Sufism (Muslim mysticism) was considered the vehicle whereby Muslims incorporated local elements of animism, Hinduism, and Buddhism into the Islamic faith, eventually converting believers by making established and local belief systems part of Islam. From the 17th century onward, more traditional Islamic influences began arriving from the Arabian Peninsula (rather than Asia), and they brought with them a more orthodox and forceful version of the religion. When the Dutch gained interest in the trade benefits of Nusantara in the early 17th century, they enabled the spread of Islam by displacing established Muslim traders, who then relocated to smaller ports throughout the archipelago.

A buffer empire between Bali and the fully converted western and central Javanese Muslim states still existed: the area of Blambangan. Blambangan, located in the far eastern corner of Java, was the last remaining stronghold of the vanquished Majapahit Empire. As the main inheritors of the Majapahit culture, Bali and Blambangan relied on each other for trade but also as the last remaining vestiges of a disappearing culture. At the same time, Balinese royal infighting forced the Raja Dalem to look outside the bounds of Bali for support. In 1639, the Sultanate of Mataram (the adjacent Islamic Javanese state to Blambangan) launched an invasion on Blambangan in order to spread the Islamic faith to all of Java. Gelgel supported its neighbor in rebuffing the Mataram troops, although Blambangan was ultimately forced to surrender. Luckily, however, once the Mataram troops had withdrawn, the death of the sultan of Mataram forced them to look inward, and they lost interest and momentum in pursuing an overthrow of Blambangan and Bali.

Both Blambangan and Bali had survived the full collapse of Majapahit in 1527, and Blambangan remained stubbornly "heathen" (Hindu-Buddhist) until the second half of the 18th century—250 years later. Bali's ability to remain outside of the Muslim fray until modern times is truly remarkable. The island's outlying location within the Indonesian arc of islands probably had the biggest role to play in Bali's ability to retain its identity, religion, and ethnicity. Aside from geography, Blambangan—as part of far eastern Java and Bali's closest connection to the rest of Nusantara—can be attributed as one of the factors that prevented Bali from being swept up in the tide of Islamic conversion in later centuries. Blambangan was the last remaining non-Islamic stronghold that extended from the Malay Peninsula, across Sumatra, and down through Java. This Hindu-Buddhist outpost protected Bali geo-politically from direct and overwhelming Islamic conversion. Blambangan spent so much time squabbling with its neighboring Muslim sultanates that Bali was perhaps both geographically and politically more removed from the Islamic states than would have been the case otherwise (such as if the whole of Java had become Muslim in the early 1500s.) As an example, the oldest mosque in Bali, the Masjid Nurul Huda Gelgel, in Gelgel was built in the late 16th century by Muslim missionaries from Java who refused to go home after failing to make converts! Evidence suggests that historically, the Islamic conversions that did occur in Bali happened gradually and peacefully.

Meanwhile, the indomitable rulers of Gelgel embarked on a series of unsuccessful wars with the eastern Javanese Islamic regional powers of Pasuruan and Mataram, which lay directly to the west of Blambangan. Both the Balinese babad and European sources (such as the Dutch register of the VOC, the Dagh-Register) reported both failed and successful skirmishes with Mataram, of which Gelgel was a part. (However, historical records mostly suggest that Bali's attempts to invade eastern Islamic Java were embarrassing and abortive.) Apocryphal evidence describes the leaders of Gelgel as despising Islam, although early European explorers noted that Bali traded peacefully with Muslims from across the archipelago. In about 1630, an envoy of the VOC (Dutch East India Company) was posted to Bali to create a treaty against the Javanese Muslim state of Mataram. However, the envoy (Van Oosterwijck) was met with refusal by the Gelgel king, who wished to remain on peaceful terms with both the Muslim sultanates and the Dutch. This contradiction in the Gelgel kingdom's handling of foreign Muslim powers may reflect the attitudes and behaviors of changing generations, which is supported in the babad.

By the mid-1500s, the successor of Dalem Ketut (the first Gelgel ruler), Dalem Baturenggong, was enthroned, and his reign marked the pinnacle of the Gelgel kingdom—the golden age of the Balinese Gelgel. Baturenggong's era extended until after the middle of the 16th century, after which his two sons, Bekung and Saganing (Seganing), reigned until the first quarter of the 17th century. Dalem Bekung was said to have ruled during a troubled time in which two rebellions, in 1558 and 1578, by his courtiers, as well as a severe military defeat against the Islamic Javanese kingdom of Pasuruan, threatened to destabilize his rule. His brother, Dalem Saganing, apparently enjoyed a long and peaceful rule. During Baturenggong's (Dalem Bekung's and Dalem Saganing's father) apogee, Bali, Lombok, and parts of easternmost Java were united under his suzerainty. However, the ownership of Lombok was contested, with the Makassar kingdom of south Sulawesi claiming it as well.

Justus Heurnius, a Dutch chaplain of Batavia—or Jakarta—assisted in translating the Bible into Indonesian languages. In his 1638 report, he describes a very close relationship between the kings of Gelgel and their priests or Brahmana. Dalem Baturenggong became the patron of a priest, or a Brahmin sage, named Nirartha, who had escaped the Islamic Javanese island and sought refuge in Bali. Ironically, along with advancing Islam, in around 1540, Bali experienced a Hindu renaissance led by Nirartha. As a Hindu-Buddhist high-priest, Nirartha was at the center of the spiritual and cultural revolution that occurred in Bali after the final collapse of Majapahit. Nirartha was intent upon spreading the concept of dharma ("righteousness") throughout Bali.

Dang Hyang Nirartha (Dang Hyang Nirarta Rauh or Pedanda Shakti Wawu Rauh), also known as "the Brahmin of Brahmins," was responsible for creating numerous literary works that formed the basis of Balinese Hinduism. These texts consisted mostly of high-quality hymns or kakawin. Kakawin are long narrative verses of ancient Javanese and Balinese origin. The verses are derived from Sanskrit literature in the style of ancient Hindu mythological and religious texts. The kakawin were most actively in circulation from the 9th to the 16th centuries and were brought to life in plays and recitals. The poems are rich sources of information on court life of the time, as well as spiritual ideologies threaded through intricate fables.

Nirartha was not only an advocate of religious texts and literature but was also an adherent of temple-building. Legends suggest that Nirartha was one of the first Hindu-Buddhists to arrive from Java after 1527 and that, while waiting for his family, he built the Perancak Temple. Perancak Temple in Jembrana—on the western side of Bali—stands to commemorate Nirartha's arrival on the island in circa 1537 from the Javanese royal court of Blambangan. Under his direction, Nirartha was responsible for erecting thirty-four temples throughout Bali, including several sea temples (Pura Segara). Nirartha oversaw the erection of a string of sea temples along the southwest coast of Bali, with each one being visible from the next. He was said to have done this to honor the sea gods and provide a chain of spiritual protection for the island.

In some instances, it is possible that Nirartha may not have been directly responsible for building all of the temples that were later attributed to him by the Balinese. He may have been more instrumental in bringing people's attention back to them and their prerequisite holiness. Essentially, Nirartha was a teacher and an advocate of spirituality within everyday life. He encouraged and prescribed the designs for the Balinese village temples, which are still an important element of life today. The Suranadi Temple in Lombok was apparently the work of Nirartha, and since Bali's closest island neighbor to the east was under the control of Gelgel during this time, it also became home to certain religious texts and babad. (Most of these were later removed by the Dutch and their Balinese consorts at the turn of the 20th century during a series of Dutch invasions.)

Amongst Nirartha's other accomplishments was his introduction of the padmasana (lotus throne) shrine in honor of the supreme god, Acintya. The padmasana formed the basis for Shiva worship later in Bali, which adopted a similar image. As a result, Nirartha is often ascribed as being a priest of Shaivite Hinduism. The padmasana temple architecture, as derived from the Javanese architecture of the same type, has become emblematic of Balinese religious structures. Nirartha's contribution to Bali's reputation as the "Island of the Gods" is noteworthy. He was also known as Wawu Rawuh ("coming together") in his close association with the king and by his appointment as a bhagawanta (royal priest). Nirartha enjoyed a prestigious religious lineage and was descended from renowned Javanese holy men. In particular, his grandfather, Mpu or Dang Hyang Tantular Angsokanatha, was the author of the critical Hindu-Buddhist work the *Kakawin Sutasoma*. The *Kakawin Sutasoma* is an ancient Javanese poem (c. 14th century CE) and the source of the Indonesian motto "Unity in Diversity." The poem teaches religious tolerance, particularly between Hindu and Buddhist religions.

Indigenous texts tell of Nirartha's psychic abilities and his prediction of the end of Javanese Hindu-Buddhist culture. The advent of a series of natural disasters around the end of the Majapahit Empire reinforced the priest's belief that their god did not intend the dharmic way to continue in Java, and this precipitated his move to Bali. Along with the reinvigoration that Nirartha brought to Balinese Hindu-Buddhism and the spread of dharma (right living) was the concept of *moksha*—a state of enlightenment that eliminated the need for rebirth. Nirartha is attributed with founding the Balinese Shaivite priesthood to which all Balinese priests (*pedandas*) of today can claim association. Legends say that he used his psychic abilities to select the correct locations for temples.

Although not attributed to Nirartha, Bali's "mother temple" is the Hindu Besakih Temple (Pura Besakih) on the slopes of the mystical volcano Gunung Agung (twenty-seven kilometers or seventeen miles north of Gelgel). Built almost one thousand meters above sea level, the temple complex has eighty-six separate but interlinked clan temples and shrines spread over six levels. It is considered Bali's largest and most important temple. The origins of Besakih date from the 8th century when a Hindu monk created a housing complex at the area called "Basuki," named after the dragon deity Naga Besukian believed to inhabit Mount Agung (from where the name evolved to Besakih). The complex was in use as a place of worship by the 13th century, and by the 15th century, it was the main temple used by the Gelgel kingdom. The temple has been added to over time and has fortunately escaped any damage by eruptions from Mount Agung. Locals claim this to be a sign from the gods. Like all Balinese temples, Besakih is an open-air compound of many separate walled areas joined by interleading gates. A series of stairways, terraces, pavilions (*bale*), courtyards, and shrines (*candi*) lead the worshiper up toward the sacred mountaintop and culminate in an inner temple and the padmasana, which was completed in the 17th century. Typical of Balinese temples, Besakih is punctuated with bamboo banners (long adorned poles), pagodas, sacred cloths, colorful plants, and offerings from worshipers.

Pura Besakih, Karangasem, Bali, showing the Javanese style split gateway entrance with Mount Agung behind

Photo by CEphoto, Uwe Aranas

https://commons.wikimedia.org/wiki/File:Besakih_Bali_Indonesia_Pura-Besakih-02.jpg

Pura Besakih, Karangasem, Bali, with Meru (multi-tiered tower) shrines.
Photo by CEphoto, Uwe Aranas
https://commons.wikimedia.org/wiki/File:Besakih_Bali_Indonesia_Pura-Besakih-01.jpg

As a royal consort during the golden age of Gelgel, Nirartha was most influential in contributing to the complexities of Balinese religion and the creation of a unique form of Hinduism and, subsequently, the idiomatic nature of Balinese culture. This uniqueness in culture and religion was one factor that enabled Bali to withstand the sweeping influences of Islam across Nusantara allow the population to resist mass conversion. More than 80 percent of modern-day Bali's population are practicing Hindus, and approximately 12 percent are adherents of Islam. Bali remains the only non-Muslim majority province of Indonesia. However, despite the Balinese *Babad Dalem* claiming that the Balinese Gelgel remained firmly in control of Bali, several historical sources suggest that Bali was more officially under Muslim rule, specifically in the second half of the 16th century. Bali's ability to resist complete Islamic domination is probably due to a combination of factors. The geopolitical buffer zone of Blambangan, Bali's unique geographical position, its historical resistance to excessive trade relations, and its individualized Hinduism and culture meant Bali was more impervious to total Islamic conversion than the rest of Nusantara.

In approximately the first half of the 17th century, Lombok was a part of Bali and possibly Sumbawa as well. Early European records suggest that Bali was a largely rural society, well populated and agriculturally successful, one over which the ruling classes enjoyed high (but perhaps remote) prestige. Gelgel may have flourished during this period in accordance with the Indonesian "age of commerce"—a time when Southeast Asian maritime trade was booming. Although Bali's formal role in trade during this period is questionable, there is no doubt that it was part of the Southeast Asian trade networks, specifically via Java. The Balinese exchanged cotton cloth manufactured on the island as well as spices. (The cotton industry came to Bali from India, via Java, in approximately 200 BCE.) In 1620, the Dutch made an abortive attempt to establish closer trade links with the Balinese. They reported that the king was headstrong, and the trade relationship was not established. The Dutch made detailed historical records at the end of the 16th century. Since they failed in their attempts to establish a formal commercial connection with the island, reports on Bali for the next few centuries were largely from diplomats and missionaries.

In the 1630s, the last documented king of Gelgel, Dalem Di Made, ruled tentatively until 1648, when his reign mysteriously ended. By this stage, the kings of Gelgel ruled in close association with two contesting families, the Agung and Ler lineages. Also, always closely intertwined with Balinese rulership was a hereditary line of Brahmana preceptors, as well as ministers introduced from various lineages. From 1651, the Gelgel kingdom began to break apart due to internal conflicts to the extent that multiple Dutch sources report a Balinese civil war occurring during this time. By 1686, a new royal center had been established in Klungkung, four kilometers (2.5 miles) north of Gelgel (modern-day Semarapura).

The interim period of more than three decades was punctuated by extreme dynastic infighting. Usurpers of the throne usually had some form of claim, such as ancestral lineage or as younger and overlooked sons of the king. When legitimate protests were ignored, stronger clans were not averse to simply grabbing the throne. One of these usurpers was the minister named Anglurah Agung (Gusti Agung Di Made or Gusti Agung Maruti), who is recorded as having ruled from 1665 to 1686. He is remembered as having briefly had interactions with the Dutch from around 1665 to 1667 and also helping to defend the island of Lombok before he took power in 1665. This was also the era when minor regencies, such as Buleleng, began to assert themselves, and Anglurah Agung struggled to retain power. In 1686, Anglurah Agung fell in battle against noblemen who were loyal to a more formal lineage of Gelgel, including aristocrats from the kingdoms of Buleleng and Badung. The babad tell of the rise of I Dewa (Agung) Jambe (r. c. 1686-1722) in Klungkung in 1683. He was a scion of the old Gelgel line, and Dutch sources corroborate his installment as the new king in 1686, three years after his emergence as a contender to the throne. The capital was moved four kilometers north, and a new Balinese royal rulership began that marked the end of the Gelgel period. (Technically, though, the new rulership retained the Gelgel bloodline.)

The new rulers of Bali, the Dewa Agung (Dewa Agung, or "Great God"), managed to retain some form of domination until the mid-19th century and the arrival of the Dutch colonists. However, the end of the Gelgel kingdom also marked the end of a single Balinese monarchy. The Dewa Agungs were really only responsible for a small area around the Klungkung Palace, as well as the lesser Balinese island of Nusa Penida. Under the Dewa Agungs (who were of the upper religious or Kshatriya caste), the island of Bali was split into nine minor kingdoms: Klungkung,

Buleleng, Karangasem, Mengwi (just north of Denpasar), Badung, Tabanan, Gianyar, Bangli, and Jembrana. Each of these nine kingdoms built their own palaces (*puri*), established their own local government, and eventually built their own dynasties. The principality of Mengwi claimed descent from Anglurah Agung.

The smaller local kingdoms of Bali developed their own rulerships and systems over the centuries, but they still pledged allegiance to the Dewa Agung of Klungkung as their primary overlord. Part of their power lay in their possession of ancient Balinese heirlooms (*pusaka*), which were believed to have magical powers that may have originated from Majapahit. (These *pusaka* were rumored to have been handed down from royal generation to generation and sometimes between lineages. Examples include kris or keris—ceremonial daggers—babad, and patterned cloths, like the Indonesian *Songket*.) The Klungkung dynasty remained, at least in nominal terms, as the kings of Bali. These original nine kingdoms of Bali developed into the eight modern-day regencies (*kabupaten*) of Bali (plus the urban node of Denpasar), though the country is run as a province of Indonesia. Before the arrival of the Dutch in the mid-19th century, the Balinese kingdoms fought amongst themselves. By the era of European intervention and colonization, the ruling arrangement on the island was complicated and fragmented. The Dutch used this incoherent Balinese regnal system to their advantage when they sought to take command of the island.

Chapter 6 – Early European Exploration

European influence in the Malay Archipelago was originally orientated around the region of Malacca on the Malay Peninsula. On the southwestern handle of the peninsula, Malacca was a small but strategic node adjacent to the Malacca Strait, which separates the mainland from Sumatra. The Muslim Sultanate of Malacca had been the dominant regional power for about a hundred years, and it was eventually subdued in 1511 by a combination of European forces, specifically the Portuguese and the Dutch. With the advent of modern shipbuilding and the era of oceanic exploration, the Europeans were intent upon controlling the trade routes of the Maritime Silk Road. The Portuguese remained in control of Malacca for a further 130 years until the Dutch overtook all other regional powers. For the first half of the 17th century, the Dutch and Portuguese fought against one another in what was known as the Spice War, as the ultimate aim for all parties was to control the spice trade of the Moluccas (the Maluku Spice Islands in eastern Indonesia). Essentially, the tension on mainland Europe, as well as the newly formed Dutch East India Company, pitted Dutch armadas against the Portuguese across their contested colonies worldwide. In the East Indies, the Dutch were ultimately victorious and remained the dominant power in the archipelagic waters until well into the 20th century.

However, before the advent of the Spice War, European explorers within Nusantara were rare, and their presence in Bali even more unusual. The era of the Italian merchant and explorer Marco Polo (1254-1324 CE) would have brought back indirect news of Bali to Europe since he explored the Indies in the late 13th century and wrote of his experiences whilst spending time on Sumatra and describing life there (there were no specific references to Bali). Historically, the consensus is that the first significant wave of European explorers to Indonesia involved the Portuguese, who were in search of spices and other goods for trade. The Portuguese explorer Vasco da Gama (c. 1460-1524 CE) led the first European ships around the Cape of Good Hope (southern tip of Africa) in 1498, and he was the first European to reach India by sea. Da Gama's expedition provided the maritime knowledge to open the sea routes from Europe to Asia for trade, and so began the Portuguese interventions into Southeast Asia. By 1511, the Portuguese had possession of the port and the greater strategic area of Malacca. The Portuguese colonialist-appointed governor of India at that time, Afonso de Albuquerque, had taken Malacca by force, overcoming the local sultanate in order to control the spice trade that operated primarily through the Malacca Strait.

In 1512, the first official European contact was made with Bali when the Portuguese sent a ship from Malacca to Bali. The expedition was led by António Abreu and Francisco Serrão, and they reached the northern coast of Bali. This was the first expedition of a series of biannual trips that the Portuguese took to the Spice Islands during the century, whereby they skirted the Sunda Islands on their way. In the initial trip of 1512, Francisco Rodrigues mapped Bali. Further interactions, or at least sightings of the island, occurred over the next decades. Bali was referred to as *Boly*, *Bale*, and *Bally* in early Spanish and Portuguese navigational maps. In 1580, Sir Francis Drake, sent by the government of Queen Elizabeth I of England, briefly visited the island in search of spices.

There was a failed attempt in 1585 by the Portuguese to establish a fort and a trading post on Bali. The ship that was sent was wrecked on a reef off the Bukit Peninsula. Five survivors made it to shore and apparently joined the Gelgel kingdom! They were provided with homes and wives. Twelve years later, in 1597, the Dutch explorer Cornelis de Houtman arrived in Bali with a greatly diminished crew (probably due to disease). They visited Jembrana, Kuta (Denpasar Peninsula), and finally assembled at Padang Bai (a southeast island, east of Gelgel), where they named Bali *Jonck Holland* (Young Holland). Upon meeting with the king, or Dalem, they became acquainted with one of the sailors from the 1585 wreck, Pedro de Noronha.

In 1601, the second official Dutch expedition of the 17th century was sent to Bali under Jacob van Heemskerck. The Balinese royalty took this opportunity to exchange friendly letters to trade with Prince Maurits, the leader of the Dutch Republic in Europe from 1585 to 1625. This open invitation by Bali for the Dutch to trade freely with their kingdom was misinterpreted and later used by the Dutch to claim overlordship of Bali. The openly friendly and welcoming style of the letter, as well as the obvious naivete of the Balinese Dalem in his statement of, "I grant permission for all who You send me to trade as freely as my own people may [trade] when they visit Holland and for Bali and Holland to be one," is a tragic example of colonial-era misrepresentation.

In 1597, a book was published in Europe in several languages entitled *Verhael vande Reyse by de Hollandsche Schepen gedaen naer Oost Indien* (*Description of a Voyage Made by Certain Ships of Holland into the East Indies*). The book was based on the private journals of an anonymous crew member on board the vessel *Hollandia* (of the VOC or Dutch East India Company) but was published under the name of Captain Cornelis de Houtman. The book included illustrations and descriptions of Balinese practices at the time, such as the Dalem being pulled on a chariot by two white oxen. The beasts were as ornately adorned as the chariot! In the image, the king is surrounded by his armed guards, and they are all naked to the waist, including the king. Another image describes the practice of *sati* (or *suttee*), the ritual sacrifice of a widow by fire after her husband's death. In the illustration, the corpse burns contentedly in a fire pit to which a happy-looking consort feeds fuel to the flames. The wife jumps unafraid into the pit while the local gamelan (indigenous Balinese orchestra) plays on.

In the meantime (until the mid-1600s), Bali experienced very little European interaction for trade or otherwise. Maritime traders of the time mostly sought goods that Bali did not provide, such as spices, silks, minerals, and metals. (Bali was mostly an agricultural rice economy.) The Spice trade, specifically, despite its ubiquity throughout recorded history, was focused primarily on the small island grouping of the Maluku Islands (Moluccas), east of Sulawesi in eastern Indonesia. The European traders were intent upon acquiring the nutmeg, mace, and cloves indigenous to the Maluku Islands, although the trading capital for these was eastern Java, 1,600 kilometers (995 miles) west of the Moluccas. The crops that were so coveted by the world came from just two types of trees on two small clusters of islands in the Moluccas. Cloves (the unopened flowers of the clove trees) were found on five islands, and nutmeg and mace came from the seed and kernel of a single species of tree found on ten islands (the Banda Islands).

In the 16th century, once the Portuguese had control of Malacca, they turned their attention to the Spice Islands. They dominated the regional trade of spices and other goods until the rise of the Dutch East India Company (Dutch: *Vereenigde Oostindische Compagnie* or VOC) in the early 17th century. The VOC was a public-private Dutch mega-consortium focused on maritime trade, and it was founded in the early 17th century. The VOC lasted for two hundred years from its foundation in 1602, and it posed considerable competition to other traders and colonizers around the world during its time. By 1603, the Dutch had established the first permanent trading post on west Java at Bantam (or Banten). The Dutch were intent upon dominating Malacca from the inception of the VOC. In the interim period of a century, starting with the conquest of Malacca in the early 1500s, the Islamic Sultanate of Aceh centered on northern Sumatra had grown into a regional power. The sultanate was not content with the Portuguese controlling the sea corridors of Malacca, and it joined an alliance with the Dutch to take control of Malacca. The alliance finally triumphed in 1641, and Malacca became a Dutch stronghold, with the Portuguese forced out as interlopers into the archipelago. The Dutch moved their headquarters to the Javanese capital of Jakarta, then called Batavia (or Batauia), which had been founded in 1619 by the Dutch. (Batavia was founded on the site of the ruins of Jayakarta, formerly of the Banten Sultanate of northern Java whose center was Banten, known as Bantam to colonialists.) Soon after the Dutch conquest of Malacca, the Portuguese ports of the Spice Islands also fell under the control of the VOC. Numerous European East Indies trading companies were started during this period, and East Indies colonies of European countries were also formed. Portugal was Holland's main rival until the mid-1600s when

England (and then Britain) competed with the Dutch for dominance. There were brief interludes by the French into the territory, and the Spanish held an East Indies colony across the Philippines (1565-1898) and other islands, including some of Sulawesi (known historically as Celebes) and the Moluccas (1580-1663).

From the mid-17th century, the Dutch dominated the Malay Archipelago. However, despite the material prosperity and prominent royal rule, the Balinese Gelgel kingdom's dealings with Dutch and Portuguese traders were incidental. Dutch records of the time indicate that the Balinese leadership was reluctant to enter into formal trade negotiations and could be "difficult." The all-powerful VOC were most interested in dominating the archipelagic regions of the Moluccas, Java, and Sumatra. They took less interest in Bali but tried to open a trading post in 1620 that was unsuccessful because of local hostilities. The mission for the trading post was given to First Merchant Hans van Meldert. He was instructed to purchase "beasts, rice, provisions, and women." He was reported to have returned with only fourteen female slaves and nothing else because trade negotiations had been unsuccessful. Other records of Dutch-Balinese relations in the mid-17th century are sketchy. In 1647 or 1648, a Gelgel king of Bali entered into diplomatic relations with the VOC, and in early 1648, a Dutch gift-giving mission left Batavia for Bali. The Dutch may have foundered on the reefs and never reached Bali, as the crew ended their journey on the neighboring island of Lombok.

During this earlier European era, Bali was mostly visited by private traders dealing in slaves and opium since the Dutch government had given the VOC the monopoly on the spice trade. These traders were primarily from China, Arabia, and other parts of maritime Southeast Asia (although some of these traders did include Dutch privateers). In its time, the VOC had free reign of any waters it traversed, as well as permission by its government to infiltrate and dominate any native culture it came across. The company ran its own financial system and minted its own coins; it conducted its own quasi-judicial system, including imprisonment and executions; it had permission to establish treaties or wage war; and it met with little opposition in colonizing new nations where it was strategically opportune to do so. Southeast Asia was no exception. The bounty of Nusantara's Spice Islands was apparently the cause of the formation of the VOC when a ship laden with profitable exotic spices arrived in Holland in 1596. The Dutch saw the opportunity to detach themselves from the dominant European superpowers of the time—specifically Spain—and form their own independent capitalist entity that could simultaneously carry out state objectives abroad. The VOC was both an international war machine for the Dutch as well as the main source for their treasury.

At the same time as the formation of the VOC, the establishment of the British East India Company was indicative of a worldwide periodical scramble for dominance of the maritime trade routes, which lasted well into the 1800s. (The French East India Company was established in 1664 and lasted for a century.) The British had also set their sights on Southeast Asia, as well as several other locations, and the spice trade. The Europeans had interrupted Arabic dominance of maritime trade in archipelagic Southeast Asia but were also instrumental in siding with the regional sultanates and playing one power off another in strategic attempts to gain control of the region. The European success in dominating the East Indies lay in the subsidence during this era of the sultanates into more fragmented oligarchies. The empire-like sultanates and thalassocracies of the Indian and Muslim kingdoms of Nusantara were disappearing at the same time that European explorers were arriving.

Foreign influences and powerplays within Southeast Asia were largely driven by commercial interests and public-private conglomerates that were actually thinly disguised national war machines. With the eventual collapse of the East India companies in the 1800s (the VOC at the beginning of the century and the British toward the end), foreign interests became "nationalized" interventions within the archipelago, and the introduction of a more formalized style of colonization was established via direct government control. The collapse of the VOC in 1800 marked the rise of the nationalist Dutch East Indies—the Dutch colonial arm of the European Dutch Republic in Southeast Asia, whose headquarters was at Batavia. The Dutch East Indies remained a dominant force in the archipelago until the 20th century except for a brief interim period from 1806 to 1815, known as the French and the British interregnum. The French ruled from 1806 to 1811 and the British from 1811 to 1815. Several factors led to the collapse of the VOC, but the final installment of its ruin was the Fourth Anglo-Dutch War in 1780, which involved worldwide contestation of political power and trading routes, in which the VOC lost half its fleet. Soon after the collapse of the VOC, its ports in Southeast Asia either became nationalized under the newly formed Dutch Republic or became British.

On the other side of the world, the Napoleonic Wars (1803-1815), led by the French military leader Napoleon Bonaparte following the late 18th-century French Revolution, were devastating Europe. Napoleon sought widespread domination, including of the East Indies. The time period from 1806 to 1811 was when the Dutch operated as a vassal of the French, who controlled their continental dominions back home on the European continent. However, constantly at odds with Britain, the French and Dutch powers lost their hold on the East Indies in 1811 when British forces invaded Java, set on dominating the spice trade and access to the

Maluku Islands. Java fell to the British in forty-five days, and it was a relatively easy task since it was defended mainly by paid French mercenaries who had little training or leadership.

In 1811, the British colonial official Sir Stamford Raffles (1781-1826) was employed by the British East India Company as secretary to the governor of Malacca. His governorship lasted until 1815, and it was at this point that Raffles decided to take over the government of Batavia. This was a strategic move by Raffles to prevent the French from usurping the British-dominant East Indies, whose power base was Java. Raffles was a key figure in rediscovering ancient Hindu and Buddhist temples and artifacts across Java, including elements of the Majapahit Empire. As an enthusiast of Javanese history, Raffles published a book titled *History of Java* in 1817. Within his East Indies administration, Raffles kept a small contingent of senior British staff but retained the overall Dutch government and civil service. Unfortunately, despite his love for the island and its history, he used high-handed tactics to overthrow local Javanese kingdoms, which resulted in the looting of their cultural and historical content, which were later seized by Raffles. Sir Raffles also attempted to limit the slave trade due to the changing British policies against slavery.

In 1816, after the end of the Napoleonic Wars and the collapse of French power in Europe, the Dutch reasserted their dominance in the region, taking Batavia back under the terms of the Anglo-Dutch Treaty of 1814. The Dutch were intent upon bringing in Europeans to settle the region as a colony to be governed by the Dutch. They were not successful in extending their influence across the archipelago and even caused antagonism on the islands of Sumatra and Java. However, the reestablishment of the Dutch East Indies lasted for another century and brought the wealth and political successes the Dutch had hungered for since the 1500s.

It is said that de Houtman of the late 16th century was fascinated by Bali and the easy charms of its landscape and people. It apparently took him a few months (some records say two years!) to round up his crew to leave. Most European explorers and navigators were motivated primarily by money and material gain, as well as the political control that ensured material gain. Historically, Bali's saving grace was that it didn't offer much in the way of economic gain, and its beauty was not enough to compete with the lure of the bounty of the Spice Islands (Moluccas). So, while the Dutch did not take control of Bali from the 16th to the 18th centuries, they instead established trading posts and used the island as a stopover. Unfortunately, by the mid-19th century, all that changed, and the peaceful island of Bali once again lost its independence.

Chapter 7 – Bali and Colonial Influences

The historical term East Indies broadly included the sum total of islands that stretch for more than 6,000 kilometers (3,728 miles) east of the Indian subcontinent, north of Australia, and south of the Asian mainland. Typically, this included the modern-day Republic of Indonesia (formerly the Dutch East Indies), the Malay Archipelago (including the Philippines), and all other islands of archipelagic Southeast Asia. In its broadest sense, the East Indies sometimes included mainland Southeast Asia as well as the Indian subcontinent, but generally, what colonial traders referred to as the Indies was maritime Southeast Asia.

During its two-hundred-year dominance of the East Indies, the VOC used its strong position in the archipelago to attain slaves to serve in its growing Cape Colony in South Africa, although they mostly took slaves from the Malay Peninsula and parts of East Africa. Within the Southeast

Asian archipelago itself, the Dutch used slaves from the region and, in many instances, people who had been enslaved themselves within their own homelands. Bali was in no way immune to the slave trade, and Balinese slaves were brought to Batavia under the VOC's dominion. The Dutch desire for slaves in the centuries of their domination was insatiable since they needed a workforce to settle their colonies across the world, particularly at the African Cape of Good Hope and in the East Indies. During the 18th century, over two-thirds of Batavia consisted of slaves working for the VOC, but by 1853, slavery in the region had technically been abolished due to international pressures. (The official date for the abolition of East Indies slavery may have been a little later—closer to 1860—but the practice continued illegally, particularly by privateers, for years to come, albeit at a vastly reduced rate.)

Balinese slaves were highly prized. The men were valued for their manual labor skills and the women for their beauty and gentle artistry. The kings of Bali were not hesitant to sell off orphans and widows, opponents to their government, criminals, and debtors to slave traders! Although the slaves were employed within Bali itself, on Java (specifically Batavia) and across the Dutch colonies, the biggest market for the slave trade was in French Mauritius (a small island in the Indian Ocean). Payment for the Balinese slaves would be made in opium, and the main port for the unhappy dealings in slaves and opium was through a northern exit in Buleleng known as Singaraja (or "Lion King"). Singaraja remained an important port throughout Bali's history, not only for the island but also for the entire Lesser Sunda Islands. The British were eager to get involved in this Balinese trade to the consternation of the Dutch. Dutch-Balinese relations had never been fortified, and during their 450-year-long association with Bali, their interactions swung from unclear to violent and back again. The two sovereignties realized that they needed each other in the changing and competitive times in which they lived, but neither seemed prepared to make the necessary sacrifices or commitment that was required for a long-term association.

The Sultanate of Mataram was the last Muslim stronghold that dominated Java before the final oppression by the Dutch in the mid-18th century under the auspices of the VOC. The independent sultanate had operated from central Java (not to be confused with the Mataram Kingdom of the 11th century) since the late 1500s. The sultanate reached the peak of its power in the first half of the 17th century during the reign of Sultan Agung Hanyokrokusumo but began to decline after his death in 1645. A century later, by 1749, the Sultanate of Mataram became a vassal state of the Dutch VOC. The Dutch had attempted to make alliances with Bali in their fight against Mataram and sent an envoy, Van Oosterwijck, in 1633 to obtain a treaty with the king of the Gelgel kingdom. The Dutch attempt was futile, but when Mataram invaded Bali six years later in 1639, the Balinese, in turn, sought Dutch help, which did not arrive. The Balinese Dewa Agung managed to repel Mataram alone. Shortly afterward, the Gelgel kingdom disintegrated to give rise to the Klungkung dynasty.

Bali experienced the brief French interlude into the East Indies at the beginning of the 19th century, but like many other interludes into Balinese life, the alliance passed by unmanifested. When the Javanese administration switched to Franco-Dutch in 1806, Napoleon Bonaparte assigned the "Iron Marshal" Willem Daendels as the new governor-general of Batavia. Bonaparte also sent ships and reinforcements to take control of the East Indies and embarked upon a flurry of fort-building along the Javanese coast. The French were most concerned about the British taking control of the East Indies, which they inevitably did from 1811 to 1815. Daendels signed a Franco-Dutch treaty of alliance with the

Balinese king of Badung (central-southern region) in 1806. Klungkung is not mentioned in this treaty. The main premise of the treaty was to provide workers and soldiers for the Franco-Dutch fortifications, mostly on Java. Five years later, Java fell to the British, and the Balinese treaty was not implemented in full.

Under the British governor of Java, Sir Stamford Raffles, several unsuccessful attempts were made with Bali to create positive Balinese-British relations. Raffles made himself extremely unpopular with various Balinese kingdoms when he began infringing on the slave trade in the region in alignment with the abolition policy that was beginning at home in Britain. (Slavery remained widespread during Raffles's tenure, and he was served by a large retinue of slaves at his official residence in Java!) He angered the rajas of Buleleng and Karangasem on Bali, who subsequently sent a military mission against the British-Javanese Blambangan in 1814, which fought British sepoys (Indian mercenaries trained and employed by the British East India Company). In the same year, Raffles sent an envoy to Bali to attain an acknowledgment of submission to his overlordship, and the following year, he himself visited the island. But whatever the outcome of these interactions, Bali once again slipped out of the colonial noose, as the Javanese government changed again to Dutch in 1816 at the end of the Napoleonic Wars.

The Dutch had been subservient to French and British colonial powers for a decade during the French and British interregnum, and they took the opportunity from 1816 onward to reassert their dominance in the Indies. A special commissioner, H. A. van der Broek, was sent to Bali to ratify "concept contracts" for overlordship, which the Balinese refused to accept. Despite Bali's disregard for colonialization, Dutch control expanded across the Indonesian archipelago in the early 1800s, including in Bali. Bali's independent kingdoms were already established, but interkingdom warfare was common and continuous between the Balinese rajas. They typically did not operate as a single homogenous unit with common ideals, and there was no clear hierarchy for rulership, governance, or even basic laws. The territory was ripe for foreign intervention, and it was really only the Dutch who made a delayed and unsteady grab for the island.

Denmark made a brief foray into Bali's history in the first half of the 1800s through the actions of a sailor named Mads Lange, who lived in Bali from 1839 to 1856. Lange entered Indonesia aboard a Danish commercial ship as a crew member. The ship harbored at Lombok as well as at Bali. Lange took the opportunity to side with the Balinese king during a Balinese-Lombok series of skirmishes that, luckily for him, saw Bali as the victor. Mads Lange was keen to use any rifts in local governance to establish himself as an independent tradesman. He traded anything that was available, from gold and precious stones to spices, fabric, and livestock, and based himself on the southern peninsula of the island in the Kuta region (southwest Denpasar).

Lange had created a revolutionary new style of independent trade (both importing and exporting to third parties) in an environment when nations had previously dominated the trade routes. Along with his increasing wealth came danger, and by the mid-19th century, the Dane—who became known as the "King of Bali"—had eventually built a compound complete with armaments and trained guards. He eventually had three children with Balinese women who integrated into Balinese royalty in time. His only child by a Chinese woman, Cecilia, married into the Indonesian Sultanate of Johor (south of Malacca on the Malay Peninsula), and Lange's grandson through this alliance, Ibrahim, eventually became the sultan of Johor. Lange's descendants rule the Sultanate of Johor to this day.

In 1843, a contract with the Dutch East Indies placed Klungkung (the main regency of Bali) under Dutch suzerainty. Contracts with other Balinese kingdoms were simultaneously constructed, but they were disputed by the Balinese, and controversies arose regarding their interpretation. This controversy led to Dutch intervention, and between 1846 and 1849, many wars were initiated by the Dutch in their attempt to capture and control Bali. As their influence over the East Indies grew, they became determined to be overlords of this unique but rebellious little island. The Dutch unsuccessfully invaded the north of Bali in 1846 and 1848, but by 1849, they had control of Buleleng and Jembrana. The considerable Royal Dutch East Indies Army fleet that arrived in 1849 to achieve this final overthrow of northern Bali consisted of one hundred ships, three thousand sailors, and five thousand trained soldiers, mostly Dutch.

The European overlords used various excuses to explain their desire for ruling Bali. These excuses mostly included a decision to eliminate the slave and opium trade, arms dealing, and the Balinese practice of plundering shipwrecks, or *tawan karang*. With the assistance of some Balinese kings, who used the colonizers to achieve their own ends, the Dutch eventually took control of the north of the island. The kingdoms of Buleleng and Bangli had always been at odds with each other, and Bangli eventually assisted the Dutch in overthrowing both Buleleng and Jembrana, giving the colonizers control of northern Bali. The chief advisor of Buleleng (I Gusti Ketut Jelantik) managed to escape to Karangasem (eastern Bali) with the raja of Buleleng, but they were killed soon after by Lombok soldiers, who were allies of the Dutch brought to Bali to fight. At this point, the raja of Karangasem committed ritual suicide. I Gusti Ketut Jelantik's open hostility and offensive efforts toward the Dutch invasions of the era have made him a national hero.

Unfortunately, the remainder of his household tragically participated in the *puputan*, or mass ritual suicide, which included at least four hundred of his followers. The Dutch had lost a handful of men, but the Balinese casualties were very high (possibly in the thousands).

The *puputan* would become a consistent part during the Dutch overthrow of Balinese royal houses from then on, much to the consternation of the Dutch, who preferred either surrender or open warfare. Reports indicate that the Dutch were horrified by the ritual suicides but that they were also unable to stop them. After the conquest of the north, the Dutch were reluctant to march their troops overland and chose to sail to the south (to Padang Bai) to invade Klungkung. However, the Dutch troops were beginning to slow due to tropical diseases, specifically dysentery. When the Balinese launched a nighttime attack on the Dutch, their commander general, A. V. Michiels, was killed by Klungkung warriors, and the Dutch retreated to their ships. The colonizers had been unable to strike a final blow on southern Bali, and they had suffered heavy causalities during the night raid in Kusamba, which was led by Dewa Agung Istri Kanya. The Dutch were repelled by a force of 33,000 Balinese from Badung, Gianyar, Tabanan, and Klungkung, and from the safety of their ships, the 1849 incursions had reached a stalemate. The standoff led to a peace treaty with the region, in which Klungkung enjoyed autonomous rule under the sovereignty of the Dutch. Holland still did not control the core of Bali despite this half-hearted attempt to gain Klungkung.

During these struggles, which lasted from 1846 to 1849, the Dutch took the opportunity to recruit troops from Lombok that they brought over in their ships to help overthrow Bali. The Dutch alliance with Lombok was not difficult to achieve since Bali had interfered in Lombok's rulership for centuries. Lombok had been part of the larger

Majapahit Empire from before the 14th century, although there had been little recorded of the island before the 17th century. Lombok had largely been made up of petty feuding tribes overseen by Sasak princes (the Sasak people compose the majority of Lombok's population today). The Balinese, specifically Karangasem or eastern Bali, had taken advantage of this fragmentation and took control of western Lombok (a populated area known as Mataram) in the early 1600s, which was already a Muslim state. The Dutch had completed their first treaty with Lombok in 1674 via the VOC and the Sasak princes. By 1750, Bali ruled most of Lombok. In the west of the island, the rulership was largely peaceful and homogenous, but in the east of Lombok, the Balinese were mostly considered as overlords and tax collectors, so they needed to defend their position. By 1838, the Mataram Balinese grouping controlled Lombok, and a rich Balinese court culture had developed through this neighboring island. But it was evident that the Lombok Mataram considered themselves to be not entirely under the spell of Bali since they signed a treaty with the Dutch in 1843 and then another in 1849 during the Dutch interventions in Bali. Ultimately, they were rewarded with the overlordship of Karangasem when northern Bali fell to the Dutch.

Mads Lange's strategic and powerful position had earned him a minor government position with the Dutch as harbormaster. The Dutch used his good relationships with the Balinese kings to include him in negotiating treaties with Bali. In 1849, the Dutch ratified themselves as having sovereignty over Bali, with the local royalty retaining a de facto rulership. Lombok gained suzerainty over Karangasem. Lange was part of these proceedings in a role as "peacemaker" representing all parties. It appears that he used his unique position mostly to gain commercially, as he continued to sell arms to the Balinese kings, both in their arguments with the Dutch as well as against one another. The Dutch ruled from

Singaraja in the north from 1855. From 1855 until 1908, the traditional Balinese royal houses were systematically dismantled by the Dutch and their members invalidated. Some members of the royalty were sent into exile, with their land being confiscated, but the dualistic approach of Dutch rulership saw ex-Balinese royalty employed as *punggawa* (local administrators—traditionally court officials), from where they ingratiated themselves with their Dutch overlords and sought to be of influence in the governance of their land. A well-known Balinese character who assisted the Dutch was I Gusti Putu Jelantik, the author of the infamous *Babad Buleleng*, a self-authored liturgy on his own ancestral claim to the Balinese throne. Jelantik worked as an advisor and an interpreter to the Dutch during their invasions of northern Bali, and this eventually gave him a position of prominence in the disabled royal households as the Dutch stronghold in Bali increased during the century.

In 1856, Lange prepared to depart Bali and return to Denmark, laden with wealth and local acquisitions. He mysteriously and unexpectedly died shortly before his departure. Most suspected the cause of death was assassination through poisoning—his past double-dealings and business affairs may have incited numerous enemies. This murder was never confirmed, and it is very possible he died of illness. Lange's grave and memorial can still be visited in Kuta to this day, as he never left Bali and was buried near his compound. His trading business, which had been in decline, was sold to Chinese merchants.

After the intervention of 1849, the Dutch proceeded to annex the northern territories of Bali. They nominated a Balinese royal but placed a Dutch prefect in control—Heer van Bloemen Waanders—who arrived in Singaraja in 1855. Waanders put his full force behind European-style reforms in the north and as far afield as the Dutch influence would stretch. The Dutch vaccinated against diseases, sought to ban the practice of *suttee* (ritual burning of widows), intervened in the slave and drug trades, sought to improve the agricultural irrigation systems, supported further agriculture, built roads and buildings, developed Singaraja (that is evident within Bali to this day), and built other infrastructure to improve commerce and interactions across the island. The Dutch raised taxes on commerce and agriculture, specifically on the opium trade. They developed the northern port into a major hub, which was visited by numerous local and European ships annually. They even attempted to Christianize the locals, but this proved to be a complete failure. In the half-century between the start of the Dutch hold on the north of Bali and the turn of the 20th century, the Balinese launched rebellions and minor skirmishes that were all quelled by their overlords. The Dutch may have remained as only partial overlords of the island for a long time, but they would not relinquish what they had attained.

By the late 1800s, differences between the southern kingdoms of Bali were being exploited by the Dutch in order to extend their control. A decade-long War of the Rajas, from 1884 to 1894, provided fuel for Dutch intervention. The Balinese raja of Gianyar was finally used by the rajas of Ubud in a devious stratagem to put their own self-interests above those of Balinese sovereignty, and they convinced the raja of Gianyar to relinquish his rule to the Dutch. In 1894, Lombok, Bali's closest neighbor to the east, rebelled against the last vestiges of Balinese rulership. Rebellions had been rife since 1891 when the Balinese overlord of Lombok had attempted to recruit Lombok troops to capture the whole of Bali. The western Lombok stronghold of Mataram (still under Balinese control) had two warships at their disposal—the *Sri Mataram* and the *Sri Cakra*—and they used these to surround rebellious Sasak villages and beat down the resistance to their rule. The Dutch took the opportunity to invade Lombok and unite with the native Sasak chiefs to fight against the Balinese overlords. The Sasak Lombok princes had sent an invitation to the Dutch to rule their island instead of the Balinese on February 20th, 1894. In June of 1894, the governor-general of the Dutch East Indies, Van der Wijck, ratified a treaty with the Sasak rebels and sent an army to Lombok. The Dutch also prevented the import of weapons and supplies from Singapore by the Balinese rulers.

By July 1894, the Dutch had sent warships from Batavia, including more than 100 officers, 1,300 European soldiers, 1,000 indigenous soldiers, and almost 400 horses. Battles between the Dutch and the Balinese rulers continued throughout 1894, in which the commander of the Dutch garrison, P. P. H. van Ham, was killed in a night raid in Mataram (western Lombok capital), along with five hundred of his contingent. By November, the Dutch had sent reinforcements under the new commander general, J. A. Vetter. Mataram was overcome in this final onslaught. Thousands died in the battles or committed ritual suicide, including Balinese royalty. The Balinese raja capitulated, and Lombok was annexed to the Dutch East Indies in 1895. The Dutch had gained Lombok and Karangasem (eastern Bali), and their hold on most of Bali became tighter (which included Bangli and Gianyar), but the southern kingdoms continued to refuse colonization. The older southern Balinese people preached peace, but overall, the citizens refused to yield to the Dutch, and a group of combative young princes defeated the colonizers in a surprise attack. This infringement made the Dutch even more determined to dominate Bali, specifically the kingdoms of Tabanan, Klungkung, and Badung. At the same time that the colonizers were seeking a cause for an all-out assault on Bali, they still struggled to justify their reason for wanting domination.

By 1906, the Dutch had launched offenses against the southern Balinese kingdoms of Badung and Tabanan, and they had weakened

Klungkung. Klungkung had remained the de facto head kingdom of Bali since the fall of Gelgel hundreds of years earlier. Finally, in 1908, the Dutch invaded Klungkung and cited containment of the opium trade as their reason for interfering (the details are explained in the following chapter). This final onslaught by the Dutch saw the end of the Balinese royal houses as they had existed since the days of Majapahit. The Dutch had secured their sovereignty as foreign rulers of the East Indies but at an extremely high moral cost. Bali was officially a Dutch protectorate—an ambition that had been initiated by the Dutch more than three hundred years before. The Dutch remained in control of Lombok until the Japanese occupation during the Second World War in 1942. They kept a light hold on Lombok by aligning with both Balinese and Sasak royalty to retain control with a tiny contingent of Dutch officers. Despite the fact that the Dutch seized a vast amount of royal treasure from Lombok (230 kilograms of gold and gold items, 7,000 kilograms of silver and silverware, and three chests of precious stones and jewelry) in the 1894 campaign, they were still considered by the Sasaks as heroic liberators of their island. Part of this treasure was returned to Indonesia in 1977.

Chapter 8 – Independence and Democracy

In 1904, a Chinese schooner wrecked on a coral reef near Sanur. Traditionally, the Balinese had rights to salvage in a common practice known as *tawan karang*, and they plundered the schooner, the *Sri Kumala*. However, the Dutch made unreasonable demands for compensation, which were refused by the raja of Badung and supported by the regions of Tabanan and Klungkung. The king of Tabanan also enraged the Dutch by reintroducing the practice of burning widows, known as *suttee*. These conflicts gave the Dutch a reason to launch a new attack on the southern ports of Bali in 1906 to assert their sovereignty. The arrival of the full force of the Dutch navy (the Dutch East Indies Army or the Sixth Military Expedition) at Sanur launched the Badung War. The Balinese were defiant in their continued desire not to be an occupied nation. The Dutch navy blockaded the southern ports, but their ultimatums were ignored. They subsequently launched naval and ground assaults and eventually marched on the palace of Badung. The Dutch assaults on various villages en route resulted in the Balinese burning their own palaces and refusing to fight or submit. Typically, the Balinese authorities at these villages committed ritual suicide.

The Badung War saw a massive defeat for the Balinese and was ironically not a war at all. The incidents of that time permanently compromised Holland's reputation as an even-handed and reasonable overlord. When the Dutch marched on the Badung palace (Denpasar), they were met within one hundred paces by the raja, who was carried on a palanquin, and thousands of his supporters. The only weapons carried by the Balinese were kris or keris (ceremonial daggers), and they moved silently and passively. The raja, dressed in white cremation clothing, was then ritually killed by a priest using a kris in a voluntary act of ceremonial suicide known as *puputan*. The remainder of the procession either killed themselves or were killed by priests in an act of mass suicide, a clear statement that they would rather be dead than ruled by the Dutch. The Dutch pleaded with the Balinese to surrender, but the Balinese would not, and the event ended in the deaths of approximately four thousand Balinese men, women, and children. Some accounts state that stray bullets resulted in the Dutch firing on the Balinese, but regardless, the result was that the Balinese were completely overcome. It was the end of the royal house of Badung.

Later that same day, a similar event took place at the palace of Pemecutan (Denpasar), claiming the lives of more Balinese people. The raja of Tabanan, Gusti Ngurah Agung, and his son surrendered but committed suicide two days later in a Dutch prison. Not surprisingly, the last remaining independent regency, Klungkung, brokered a peace deal with the colonists. The people of Klungkung were required to destroy their fortifications, give up all firearms, and renounce their import and export taxes. After the tragedy of the Badung War, the Dutch received overwhelmingly negative global attention for the events that had led to the unfortunate outcome of mass suicides and the extermination of a huge number of peaceful, indigenous peoples. Apparently, the Dutch troops plundered and looted the battle scenes and dead bodies and razed what was left of the palaces to the ground, but this is unconfirmed.

Unfortunately, the Dutch colonizers' transparency and economic motive in trying to gain control of the opium trade led to the breakdown in the peace deal negotiated with Klungkung. The Dutch sent troops to quell riots in 1908 that had erupted in retaliation to their attempts to get the monopoly on the drug trade. Riots erupted in Klungkung and in Gelgel. After quelling the riots (which resulted in about a hundred Balinese deaths) in Gelgel, the Dutch marched to Klungkung, to where the raja had fled. The raja of Klungkung, along with two hundred followers, purportedly bravely fought from his position of safety at the palace but was killed by a single Dutch bullet. The king had been armed only with a kris according to a prophecy that it would overthrow the enemy. His six wives and the remainder of the palace procession committed *puputan*, as had their predecessors in 1906. At least two hundred Balinese died that day (April 28th, 1908), and the palace was burned. With this final tragedy, the Dutch had full possession and control of Bali—albeit at a high and bloody cost.

This final occupation by the Dutch marked the end of the Balinese Majapahit Empire that had dominated Bali for four hundred years. Regrettably, the Dutch domination of Bali held little meaning for the Balinese, and it was more of a political and economic stratagem than a true moral victory. The Balinese continued with their daily and spiritual pursuits as they had done when being ruled by the Hindu kingdoms—it made an inconsequential difference to them whom they were governed by. However, politically, the Dutch hold on Bali was tentative, and by 1929, the colonizers sought to reinstate native chiefdoms, or what was referred to in Dutch as *volkshoofd*, in order to create a type of decentralized local government still under their suzerainty. The old kingdoms were to be reinstated as negara (Indonesian autonomous states), and the Balinese royalty was to be reestablished, which naturally led to an upsurge in the creation of babad, Balinese ancestral chronicles proving royal lineage. The Balinese impotency against the terror that the Dutch had instilled saw them using words rather than violence to achieve their ends of freedom or at least renewed tribal recognition and respect. Several babad created by the Balinese fiefdoms were sent to Dutch officials in a petition for the right to the throne of their particular regencies and also to motivate efforts for the creation of their regencies as independent negara. Some of these babad petitions ended up at the Dutch parliament in Holland and came to the attention of Queen Wilhelmina, the reigning Dutch queen of the time. Twenty years after the Badung War, in 1929, a nephew of the last Klungkung ruler, Dewa Agung Oka Geg, was appointed as a regent by the Dutch. About a decade later, in 1938, his status, as well as seven other Balinese regents, was elevated to raja (*zelfbestuurder*, or self-governor, in Dutch).

In 1912, a German visitor, Gregor Krause, took pictures and videos of topless Balinese women, which promoted a surge in European tourism after the First World War, particularly to the Singaraja area (modern-day Buleleng). This upsurge in international travel after the Great War not only brought increased attention to Bali but also an influx of international artists and intellectuals. Included in this number during the 1930s were anthropologists Margaret Mead (1901-1978) and Gregory Bateson (1904-1980), as well as renowned artists Miguel Covarrubias (1904-1957) and Walter Spies (1895-1942). Margaret Mead, an American cultural anthropologist, was a well-known media figure in the 1960s and 1970s. This controversial academic was a key influencer in the sexual revolution of the 1960s due to her work regarding the attitudes of sex and the South Pacific and Southeast Asia. Mead was a proponent of broadening sexual attitudes. Gregory Bateson was an English anthropologist and social scientist who was married to Margaret Mead. Miguel Covarrubias, a Mexican graphic artist and the discoverer of the Olmec civilization, along with his wife, Rosa (Rose), took several trips to Bali and created the book *Island of Bali*, which was filled with her photography of the island. This book was a significant contributor to the tourist rush to Bali that followed. Walter Spies was a Russian-born German primitivist painter, composer, musicologist, and curator. He lived in Bali from 1927 until his capture in 1942 during the Second World War. Spies was well acquainted with the other intellectuals and artists of the time. The musicologist Colin McPhee (1900-1964) communicated the image of Bali as "an enchanted land of aesthetes at peace with themselves and nature" in his book, *A House in Bali*. McPhee was a Canadian-born Indonesian composer and the first Westerner to make an ethnomusicological study of Bali. He composed music based on the ethnic sounds of Java and Bali that became world-renowned.

During the 1960s, the airport was renovated and began to facilitate international flights. Also, the first major tourist hotel was built in Sanur (the southeast coast of Denpasar), and it was called the Bali Beach Hotel. This era saw the start of mass tourism for Bali. Since ancient times, Bali had magnetized people with intellectual and spiritual inclinations, and the first prime minister of India, Jawaharlal Nehru (in office 1947-1964), described the island as "the dawn of the world." Western tourism brought international celebrities of the day, such as Noel Coward (English playwright), Charlie Chaplin (English comic actor), Barbara Hutton (a global socialite of her era from the 1930s onward), and Doris Duke (also a socialite and global heiress of the era). International celebrities helped to create an image of Bali as a modern-day Garden of Eden. By the 1970s, Australian filmmakers had started attracting multitudes of Australian visitors to Bali, specifically by producing surfing videos and building bars and nightclubs in tourist areas aimed at Australians and other international visitors.

But the lure and romance of Bali have never been without its tragedies. In 1963, Bali's only active volcano, Gunung Agung, erupted, causing at least 1,500 deaths and the evacuation of hundreds of thousands of people. Mount Agung, or the Bali Peak, rises above surrounding farmland to a height of more than 3,000 meters (9,842 feet). The volcano is known locally as "the navel of the world" and had been dormant for 120 years. Adding to the general social and political instability of the period surrounding the First World War had been a devastating earthquake in 1917, influenza that killed 22,000 people, and an atmosphere of unrest that necessitated the heightened decentralized administration of Bali. The Dutch also had altruistic reasons for empowering local negara, and they continued to support and establish the Balinese regencies toward self-rule until the start of the Second World War in 1938. These reasons included protecting Bali against harmful modernization and the threat of Islamic conversion and nationalism, which happened regardless after the close of World War II and Bali's incorporation into Indonesia. At the time, the Dutch thought that the best way to preserve and protect Balinese traditionalism was by reinvigorating the Hindu royal structures and their associated symbolism and ideologies.

When the regencies and ruling families of Bali were reinstated by the Dutch, the author of the *Babad Buleleng*, Jelantik, had his claim to the throne recognized, and he became the king of Buleleng. I Gusti Putu

Jelantik (1880-1944) was a character who had been particularly skillful in ingratiating himself with the Dutch, and as the author of the infamous babad, he eventually rose to power by simultaneously building temples to prove his worth to his fellow Balinese. (Not to be confused with I Gusti Ketut Jelantik of the mid-19th century.) Unfortunately, Jelantik's rapacious desire for rulership found him alongside the colonial oppressors as a translator when they marched against other royal houses, such as Badung, Tabanan, and Klungkung, in the Dutch conquest of southern Bali. Jelantik achieved his ends, but he was not trusted by the Balinese, and his precious *Babad Buleleng* was considered a putrid work of fiction by Balinese authorities of babad.

During these campaigns, Jelantik was complicit in acquiring the holdings of the royal Balinese libraries. Along with the contents of the libraries of the royal courts of Lombok, Jelantik acquired a considerable and impressive collection of private ancient Balinese works for himself. He went on to assist the Dutch in the establishment of the manuscript library Kirtya Liefrinck-Van der Tuuk (now the Gedong Kirtya library) in Singaraja in 1928 and served as its first curator. Despite Jelantik's perceived faults, he is attributed to making a considerable effort to preserve Bali's literary heritage. The Gedong Kirtya library is on the same grounds as the Museum Buleleng and can be visited today. The library houses a collection of Dutch and Balinese works dating back to the turn of the 20th century. This *lontar* (palm leaf manuscript) library also contains *prasati* or *prasasti* (copper metal plate inscriptions) and books regarding religion, architecture, philosophy, genealogy, homeopathy, *usada* (medical scripts), and even black magic! The contents of the library are written in the old Kawi Balinese script, as well as in Dutch, German, and English. The library was established by a Dutch resident, I. J. J. Calon, a government official in Bali and Lombok during the colonial period. The library enabled extensive research on Balinese culture, customs, and language by two Dutch scholars of the same period, F. A. Liefrienk and Dr. N. van der Tuuk. Gedong Kirtya means "to endeavor to build," and this repository remains a crucial source of inspiration and information for the study of Balinese culture to this day.

The Dutch occupation of Bali occurred far later than the colonization of most of the East Indies, such as Java and the Maluku Islands, which were more sought after for commercial gain and strategic positions. Also, the Dutch hold on Bali was never as well established as those of other colonized nations. and its 20th-century domination of the island only lasted until the Japanese occupation of Bali in 1942. Batavia (Jakarta) had remained a colonial city for 320 years until 1942 when the Japanese occupied the archipelago during World War II. After the end of the war in 1945 and once Indonesia had asserted its independence, Batavia was renamed Jakarta. (In 1527, the Demak Sultanate of central Java had renamed the capital, Sunda Kelapa, to Jayakarta—"precious victory"—when it had overthrown the Majapahit Empire, from which Jakarta was eventually derived. However, the Dutch occupiers of Java had seen the capital as "Batavia.")

Imperial Japan occupied Bali during World War II with the overarching objective of forming "a Greater East Asian Co-Prosperity Sphere," aiming to liberate Eastern countries from Western domination. Future rulers of Indonesia, such as Sukarno (the first ruler of Indonesia, who also had a Balinese mother), were promoted by the Japanese, but privately, Indonesia wanted independence from both the Dutch and the Japanese. Once the Japanese troops withdrew after their surrender at the end of the war in 1945, Bali assumed independence and issued a proclamation in this regard in 1945/46. However, the Dutch were not going to give up the hard-won island so easily, and they attempted to reinstate their pre-war colonial administration, reassuming governance in the following year. The Balinese now had Japanese weapons that had been left behind by the surrendered troops in their arsenal, as well as emboldened resistance leaders, such as Colonel I Gusti Ngurah Rai. Unfortunately, Colonel Rai died as a freedom fighter in the Battle of Margarana in east Bali in 1946. The brief Balinese military resistance had been entirely obliterated by a fresh Dutch onslaught. After a short and bitter battle to assert their independence, the Balinese were once again at the mercy of foreign powers.

The Dutch denial of Balinese sovereignty resulted in tentative rule for a further four years. Bali was one of thirteen administrative districts within the newly proclaimed Dutch state of Indonesia. In the meantime, the establishment and growth of the future Republic of Indonesia (ratified on December 27th, 1949) was becoming a reality. In the immediate aftermath of World War II, an evolving Indonesia, then consisting of a number of united states, was headed by Sukarno, or Kusno Sosrodihardjo (in office 1945-1967), a Javanese politician and the first president of Indonesia, and Mohammad Hatta (in office 1945-1956), the first vice president of Indonesia. For four years, from the end of the world war to 1949, the newly formed Dutch and Indonesian contenders for the former Dutch East Indies reached a climax. Also known as the Indonesian National Revolution or the Indonesian War of Independence, this was an era of armed conflict and diplomatic struggles, as the Indonesian government fought to assert post-colonial independence. The Dutch eventually conceded in 1949 after having reached a military stalemate on the ground, specifically in Java, as well as receiving overwhelming international pressure. Bali officially became part of Indonesia in 1950, along with the other twelve island states to which the Dutch had laid claim (including the Moluccas, Java, and the Lesser Sunda Islands).

Within the same interim time period that the United States of Indonesia and the Dutch state of Indonesia were developing, the State of East Indonesia (*Negara Indonesia Timur*) was in existence. It lasted from the end of the Second World War in 1946 to the declaration of Indonesian independence, at which time it became part of Indonesia in 1950. The only president elected to the office of the State of East Indonesia was Tjokorda Gde Raka Soekawati, who was born in Ubud, Bali, in 1899 (he died in 1967). Soekawati belonged to the highest Balinese caste of Kshatriya. After a political career in Bali and Indonesia, he studied in Europe and completed his education studying agriculture in the Netherlands. Tjokorda Gde Raka Soekawati negotiated the incorporation of the State of East Indonesia into the unitary Republic of Indonesia in 1949/50. States included within the State of East Indonesia were the islands under supposed Dutch suzerainty at the time: Celebes (Sulawesi), the Moluccas, Java, Bali, and the Lesser Sundas. The Dutch approved and oversaw the regulations for the formation of the interim state, although the independent constitution of the State of East Indonesia was never implemented since it became part of the Indonesian Republic before it could be initiated. The Dutch involvement with the creation of the State of East Indonesia, which would continue to be heavily influenced by the Dutch, may have been part of a compromise by the colonialists, and Indonesians supportive of a completely independent nation criticized the formation of the state.

Bali's independence with the formation of the Republic of Indonesia was perhaps not true independence. Rajasthan (local kingdom) rule was phased out in Bali and the rest of Indonesia by the new government. The tentative Indonesian federation, consisting of a profound seventeen thousand islands, was being led by Sukarno, a revolutionary whose role had merely evolved from democracy to autocracy and finally to authoritarianism. In 1958, Bali became an official province of Indonesia, and its first governor (regional head or *kepala daerah*) was appointed, Anak Agung Bagus Suteja—the son of the last raja of Jembrana—who was in power until 1966. By 1959, Sukarno had assumed full dictatorship of the archipelago. His anti-colonial sentiments and desire to right the wrongs of Indonesia's colonial past led him increasingly toward communist sympathies. In 1963, President Sukarno resisted the concept of an Indonesian federation since it was, according to him, too suggestive of continued European rule. He was unsuccessful in this, as well as his attempt to bring the disputed territories of northern Borneo (now a part of Malaysia) into the Indonesian fold. Since the removal of Dutch colonial influence, the power of local kingdoms had been reduced, including the former Rajasthans of Bali. Being part of Indonesia did not markedly improve economic fortunes or political leverage for Bali. The Dewa Agung title lapsed with the death of the Dutch *zelfbestuurder*, Dewa Agung Oka Geg, in 1964, although members of his family have since periodically played the role of regents (*bupati*) in Klungkung.

The economic cost of Indonesia's efforts during its War of Independence resistances and subsequent failures, coupled with Sukarno's openly hostile attitude to Western powers, created hyperinflation, which lasted through most of the first half of the 1960s. The resultant social unrest and his failing health weakened President Sukarno's power base. According to Sukarno, a group of communist renegades supposedly sought out and executed eight senior generals in September of 1965 to avoid a potential military coup, although this ruse was not widely accepted. In an attempt to stabilize the government, General Suharto convinced the remaining generals to conduct a countermove, and they regained control of the military. Although Sukarno remained in power, he was rivaled by the influential and politically authoritative Suharto.

Unfortunately, the incidents of 1965 created a communist backlash in which real and suspected communists across Indonesia were hunted down and summarily killed. In this mostly unwarranted attack on real and imagined threats to the government, Bali was the scene of some of the worst atrocities. In some instances, groups of suspected communists were rounded up by mobs and clubbed to death. Half a million potential communists and ethnic Chinese lost their lives in this unnecessary cleansing, and an estimated 100,000 of these were in Bali (5 percent of Bali's population at the time). In 1966, armed soldiers removed the former Balinese governor, Anak Agung Bagus Suteja, from his house in Senayan. He was never seen again, and his political rival, under the auspices of the Indonesian National Party (PNI), claimed he had committed voluntary execution (*nyupat*) near Jakarta. Suteja had been removed from his position the previous year due to his communist sympathies and his role as the "favored son" of Sukarno. Suteja had been heavily involved in the Indonesian Revolution to expel the Dutch, and he had been imprisoned by the Dutch from 1948 to 1949 for his efforts. In 1966, in the aftermath of the communist massacres, Sukarno fled the palace and went into exile. He remained a nominal president for a further year.

Sukarno's successor, Suharto, remained in power for over three decades, and he gradually created an authoritarian kleptocracy in which he, his family, and his associates benefited the most. Suharto's military-led regime controversially enabled a sustained period of economic prosperity that lasted until the global financial crisis of 1997. Civil unrest resulting from the financial crisis, as well as general discontent due to the corrupt Indonesian leadership, led to widespread riots and violence. Ultimately, by 1999, Indonesians had ousted the incumbent Suharto and participated in their first democratic election since 1955! In 1998, the resignation of Indonesian President Suharto after thirty-two years of rulership ignited Muslim-sponsored riots by Islamists across the archipelago, including in Bali. Islamists were angered about the new government's alignment with Western powers, such as the United States, Europe, and Australia. By the time of his death, Suharto's family owned and controlled most of the prestigious resorts in Bali. The Muslim riots on Bali caused the dislocation of many Chinese and Christians whose businesses were targeted, and they subsequently had to evacuate to Lombok for safety.

Five years of tentative peace ensued for Indonesia when Suharto's daughter, President Megawati, was voted in within a provisional democracy. Although she addressed the country's legacy of corruption and its shocking human rights record, she was also governing in the aftermath of an economic crisis and general political instability. Megawati was defeated by a former military general, Susilo Bambang Yudhoyono (or **SBY**). SBY was Indonesia's first completely democratically elected president and served more than one term (in office 2004-2014), as his anti-corruption and moral code of honesty policies resonated with the people of Indonesia. Following SBY's term of office was the installation of the seventh and current president of Indonesia, Joko Widodo.

In 2002, two terrorist bomb attacks in the southwest tourist area of Denpasar were attributed to an Islam extremist group called Jemaah Islamiyah. The attacks were claimed to have been in retaliation for the Indonesian government's support of the United States and Australia in accordance with a transitional democratic government opening up their foreign policies. The bombs killed over two hundred people, mostly Australian tourists, and injured many more. The biggest impact of this act of terrorism was a dramatic yet expected drop in tourist numbers to Bali. Three years later, in 2005, more Islamic extremist terrorist bombings were carried out in approximately the same area, Kuta. Similar to the

2002 attacks, the perpetrators were caught and jailed or executed.

By 2010, and with the advent of the Hollywood movie *Eat Pray Love*, starring Julia Roberts (based on the book by Elizabeth Gilbert), tourism in Bali increased and began to flourish, exceeding its 2002 levels with more than two million visitors per year. Between 2010 and 2015, Bali hosted many international events, such as the 2010 International Geothermal Congress and the 2012 East Asia Summit. Bali's first elevated highway was completed during this time, as well as an upgrade to the international airport (greater Denpasar), which allowed it to manage twelve million passengers a year. The mass influx of tourists has had positive economic results and assisted with a Balinese cultural revival. However, the natural environment is said to have suffered as a result, with overdevelopment, increased environmental degradation, and pollution being common.

Unfortunately, Bali's contemporary history has been consistently punctuated by setbacks as well as successes. Mount Agung erupted again in 2017 several times, remaining active for most of the year. Residents within the danger zone were once again evacuated by the government, displacing thousands of people. Although it was mostly local families and farmers that were evacuated for several months, the eruptions negatively affected tourism for the entire year and, therefore, the entire Balinese economy. In 2018, a new governor of Bali was elected, I Wayan Koster, from Singaraja. Koster is the ninth official governor of Bali since 1950. One of the greatest negative impacts on life and socio-economic circumstances in Bali was the unforeseen COVID-19 global pandemic. An estimated 5,000 people have lost their lives due to the disease so far, and the Balinese government closed all international travel. For a small developing island state that draws 80 percent of its economy from tourism and related sectors, the pandemic had a devastating effect on the island both economically and socially.

Chapter 9 – Existing Heritage

In 1901, the Dutch introduced the Ethical Policy, which sought to expand educational opportunities for indigenous peoples in the East Indies. They were eager to prove that their influence in the archipelago could not be equated with the extractive scramble of other European powers. Also, shortly after the 1906-1908 campaigns against the Balinese, the Dutch portrayal by the Western press was becoming increasingly negative, and they sought to correct these perceptions. Amongst other things, the Ethical Policy resulted in the establishment of universities in Jakarta during the first half of the 20th century, which still exist today, albeit under new names. The Ethical Policy claimed to be repaying a "debt of honor" for the wealth that they had drawn from the East Indies over the centuries. They sought to bring "peace, order, and modernity" to the indigenous peoples of the East Indies and to free them from the "tyrannous" rule of the monarchies. Along with the Ethical Policy, the Dutch began promoting tourism in about 1914 in an effort to display Bali as a "living museum" of preserved culture. These efforts by the Dutch were known as the "Balinization" of Bali.

True urban nodes (small cities) did not develop until the mid-19th century on Bali, with the influence of the Dutch, and the Balinese never experienced the mass urbanization that was common to people of medieval Europe. Overall, Balinese life is communal and centers largely on religion. Its modern-day religions include Balinese Hinduism, Buddhism, Malay ancestor cult, and animistic and magical beliefs and practices. The Balinese people also firmly believe in reincarnation. Muslims and Christians, as well as Chinese, also live in Bali, mostly in the west and north of the island. Known as "the Island of the Gods" or "Island of a Thousand Puras (Temples)," Bali is home to an abundance of places of worship. There are in excess of twenty thousand Balinese Hindu temples on the island, each dedicated to a particular aspect of life or Balinese spiritual geography. Balinese Hinduism developed from Shaivite Hinduism as well as Buddhism, which were brought to Bali throughout the island's history. Since Hindu practices are more focused on a spiritual way of life than a specific dogma, a unique type of Hinduism arose and flourished in Bali, outlasting the 16th-century Islamic conversion that was typical of the rest of Indonesia.

This Balinese Hinduism adopted the cultural style of the Balinese, who are enthusiastic about mixing ancient religious philosophies and ideas, as well as myths and legends, with modern-day festivities, arts, and traditions. Not long after Indonesia's independence in 1949, the Balinese needed to fight for the recognition of their unique island religion, and finally, in 1959, Balinese Hinduism was established as one of Indonesia's official faiths. Balinese Hinduism is a unique combination of Mahayana Buddhism and Shaivite Hinduism. The adherents of the religion only believe in one god—*Sang Hyang Widhi*, *Acintya*, or *Sang Hyang Tunggal*—although the followers still worship various forms of this god and continue with animistic rituals in daily life. Balinese Hinduism can also be referred to as Shiva-Buddhism, Hindu-Dharma, Tirtha religions, or the Holy Water Religion. The most important aspect of Balinese Hinduism is that its adherents find the spiritual meaning of their lives and the attainment of perfection through *moksha* (becoming one with the universe). The religion is not based on a prescribed doctrine but is more of a personal experience that draws from the ancient spiritual traditions and scriptures of Nusantara.

Although the Hindu caste system is observed in Bali, it is less socially entrenched than in places such as mainland India. The main reason for equality in Bali is that most of the population belongs to the lowest (Sudra / Shudra) caste. However, noble classes do exist in the form of priests (Brahman), the military and royal classes (Kshatriya), and merchants (Vaishya). Intermarriages across castes are not readily accepted (known as the practice of endogamy). The modern-day Balinese language is distinct from that of east Java, from which most of the Balinese culture developed, but upper-class Balinese contains many Javanese as well as Sanskrit words.

Balinese villages all contain temples, as well as assembly halls, which are usually located on a square that hosts markets and festivals. Families live in compounds surrounded by natural walls. Each village has its own orchestral club, and pantomimes (stage plays) and traditional dancing are a significant part of Balinese life. These plays serve as important sources of passing on indigenous knowledge through stories or preserving magico-religious beliefs. The Wayang puppet theater is thought to have lasted until modern times because the puppeteers have acted as teachers of history and have also played a crucial role in communicating key political and cultural ideas. Wayang is an intrinsic part of the indigenous culture of Bali, in addition to being an art form and a method of entertainment. The show is often accompanied by a local choir or orchestra. Wayang has grown over the centuries to include all Balinese art forms (visual and performance) and continues to evolve. It remains an important medium for information-sharing, teaching, preaching, philosophizing, and entertainment.

Balinese temples, aside from their religious, cultural, and community value, are timeless pieces that represent the lost empires of Bali. Dating from the early Indianized kingdoms through the Majapahit era and into the 20th century, the temples and shrines (and sometimes homes) of Bali provide a constant reminder of the island's exotic, spiritual past. Many of the temples exist in layers, as each new generation and culture added their additions and influences to these revered structures. Unfortunately, numerous palaces, such as the Klungkung Palace, were destroyed by the Dutch colonizers in the 1800s and 1900s, and these have been replaced since then, albeit in the traditional Balinese style. An example of ancient architecture on Bali are the towering paduraksa (or kori) gateways to temples—a multilayered roofed structure adorning the entrance archway, very typical of temples on Java and Bali.

The Balinese are extremely fond of music, poetry, dancing, and festivals. A Balinese orchestra (*gamelan, gamelang,* or *gamelin*) is the traditional music ensemble of Java, Bali, and the Sundas and an integral part of local Balinese culture. The gamelan usually consists of a multitude of percussion instruments (specifically metallophones, metal drums, and gongs, amongst others), two-string violins, and bamboo flutes. The gamelan can be accompanied by male and female vocalists as well. The Balinese people are supremely talented in arts and crafts and regularly indulge in betting games such as cockfighting. Bali's widespread artistic temperament is evident in their painting, sculpture, metalworking (gold, silver, and bronze smithing), spinning and weaving, musical instruments, and wood and bone carving. Even funerals are associated with beauty and festivities in Bali, and processions of flower-covered mourners accompany the dead, who lay in animal-shaped wooden coffins, to the cremation grounds. Bali painting and sculpture have been heavily influenced by the Hindu religion, as their purpose was mostly to inspire ethical values relating to the laws of adat (traditional law). In early Balinese painting, colorful two-dimensional drawings were done on cloth or bark paper. These paintings were of a distinctly religious inclination and were produced anonymously for temples and royal palaces. By the 20th century, the influx of visitors and Western artists allowed for more paintings that represented Balinese life rather than religious concepts, and they had a more commercial value as objects of art for tourists.

The foundation of Balinese performing arts is folk dancing and gamelan music, which are taught to young children by villagers. These highly stylized performances tell stories of ancient legends and are used to represent each individual's right of passage or other celebrations for the Balinese. The dance culture is a natural expression of Balinese religious beliefs brought to life through exaggerated, angular movements coordinated with intense eye, hand, and arm placements. Most of the dances involve the tyrannical character of the witch (demon queen), Rangda, who personifies the dark forces of the Balinese mythological kingdom. The Barong (Chinese-orientated lion beast) is also a common feature of a dance performance and represents the force for good. The constant contest between Rangda and the Barong represents the continual fight between good and evil for the Balinese. The dancers (usually girls) are dressed in colorful brocades of indigenous dress with tall, stylized gold-colored headpieces with heavy makeup and bold ornaments. Some Balinese dance is not religiously orientated and serves simply for celebrations and entertainment. The Balinese dances can also include a trance-like state by the dancers when benevolent spirits are believed to inhabit their bodies.

The Balinese living tradition of folk dance, showing girls in the Pendet (greeting) dance.
Christopher Michel from San Francisco, USA, CC BY 2.0 <https://creativecommons.org/licenses/by/2.0>, via Wikimedia Commons https://commons.wikimedia.org/wiki/File:Tari_Pendet.jpg

The Balinese artistic temperament was significantly influenced by the late 15th-century influx of Hindu intellectuals, literati, artists, and spiritualists after the collapse of the Majapahit Empire. This original series of influxes may have been the root cause for the Balinese ability to merge fact with fiction, history with literature, religion with folklore, and modern political maneuvering with ancestral power. For instance, the babad (Balinese chronicles) are considered more than legendary historical records. These textual heirlooms, or *pusaka*, embody monarchical and supernatural authority. The babad link ancestors from the past with the life and times of the present and ambitions for the future. Since nothing in Bali seems to be outside of the power of Saraswati, the Hindu goddess of arts and literature, the babad are part of the religious and artistic culture of the Balinese as well and are often interned, along with other items of court regalia, in shrines and temples.

One feature of Balinese entertainment and culture is the recital of babad and their exemplification in performing arts, such as the Wayang puppet theater.

Bali has unfortunately inherited a legacy of earthquakes and volcanic eruptions, with the latest seismic events occurring in 2018. The most detrimental effect of these natural disasters is the disruptive influence they have on everyday life, causing some of the population to be relocated. Tourism continues to draw millions of visitors each year to Bali, and they are intent upon enjoying the beaches and ocean, the nightlife, and the Balinese culture. The Balinese have developed their indigenous performing arts as well as crafts and handiwork to keep abreast of the demand by foreigners for their unique civilization. Klungkung, in the southeast and including Bali's three smaller satellite islands, is well-known for wood carving and its gold and silver industries, which are largely supplied by mines from Sumatra and Java. The ability to work with precious metals was brought by Majapahit smiths from Java and possibly from the Chinese Dong Son people during the Bronze Age. Today, most of Bali's silversmithing is centered around the village of Celuk, where metalworking skills stretch back for many generations. *Songket* (traditional Indonesian) textiles and pottery can be found in modern-day Gelgel. Exquisite baskets echoing the Austronesian craftsmanship are manufactured in the Bali Aga village of Tenganan. Gianyar's lively market, as well as the tourist destinations of Kuta, Sanur, and Nusa Dua (beachside locales in the south), draw many foreign visitors. Ubud, farther north in the foothills of Bali, is a center for international artists and includes the Agung Rai Museum of Art.

Although Indonesia does not recognize the Balinese royal kingdoms or their unofficial powers, some of these lineages exist in pockets across Bali and are adhered to within the communities, mostly through adherence to the caste class hierarchy. The ancestors of Balinese royal houses know who they are and from whom they are descended, and they sometimes enjoy special privileges, such as palatial homes. Bali's demographics are constituted of a mix of cultures originating from population influxes from different lands over millennia. Modern-day Bali consists of almost 90 percent ethnic Balinese, and the remaining groups—often distinguished by country of origin or religion—largely live separately from the traditional Balinese. As an example, the Aga Balinese, who originally crossed over from Java in the 8th century, now live in secluded isolation in the mountainous regions of Bali. The distinct tribes that developed as part of the Bali Aga are separated into a number of villages around the foot of Gunung Agung and have developed their own dialects of Balinese. The Bali Aga resist all forms of outside influence, and they prefer to maintain their removed societies according to *awig-awig* (customary rules). The Bali Agas' strict marital codes prevent marriage outside the community unless the person leaves the community and also prohibits divorce and polygamy. This isolation and the Agas' strict perpetuation of ancient customs have created communities preserved in time, which allow a glimpse into the past of what original Austronesian communities may have been like. From ancient cotton-dyeing techniques to uniquely Aga architecture, the Bali Aga continue to stand proudly and determinedly separate from the Balinese of the lowlands, who now freely mix with foreign tourists, although two Bali Aga villages now allow tourists to visit. Aga tourism is centered around artistry, festivities, and unique products, such as traditional geringsing fabric. The Bali Aga still celebrate the arrival of their ancestors of old in traditional Balinese fashion with music, dance, and artistry.

About a quarter of Bali's farmland is irrigated, and this is used mainly for rice. Other crops include coffee, yams, oil palms, cassava, corn, coconuts, and other fruits. Farmers raise cattle as well as smaller livestock. Surprisingly, fishing remains a minor occupation for the local communities. Unusually, the Balinese agricultural system is linked to their penchant for spiritual rituals and folk art. Bali's flourishing rice cultivation system and rich, fertile soils have ensured the population's supply of food for millennia and also provided excess for trade. This abundance of a staple food source has allowed the Balinese the time and energy to participate in and develop their numerous art forms and spiritual pursuits. In a world of rapidly changing ideals, the Balinese still employ the process of communal decision-making or *musyawarah*. The rice paddies are a communal affair (*gotong-royong*), which include in-built irrigation systems that channel water collected by the forests of higher altitudes. The terraced paddies are connected via a system of canals, weirs, and tunnels, and the workforce to maintain the paddies is drawn from local communities, who use hand tools to cultivate and harvest the rice.

Balinese rice terraces at Jatiluwih, one of the five rice terraces of the subak irrigation system and a UNESCO World Heritage Site.
Imacim, CC BY-SA 4.0 <https://creativecommons.org/licenses/by-sa/4.0>, via Wikimedia Commons https://commons.wikimedia.org/wiki/File:Jatiluwih_rice_terraces.jpg

Alfred Russel Wallace, a British explorer, had this to say about Bali when landing at Singaraja in 1860 after departing from Singapore:

> I was both astonished and delighted; for as my visit to Java was some years later, I had never beheld so beautiful and well-cultivated a district out of Europe. A slightly undulating plain extends from the seacoast about ten or twelve miles inland, where it is bounded by a fine range of wooded and cultivated hills. Houses and villages, marked out by dense clumps of coconut palms, tamarind and other fruit trees, are dotted about in every direction; while between them extend luxurious rice-grounds, watered by an elaborate system of irrigation that would be the pride of the best cultivated parts of Europe.

It seems that Bali's landscape has not changed significantly since Wallace's time. Strangely, the Balinese have never been keen seafarers or coastal navigators. The unusually treacherous approach to Bali via sea contributed to the island's ability to "turn its back on the world" as the mountainous north created a natural land barrier to passing maritime traders, not to mention its ports have always been small and few. Instead, Balinese attention is turned inward to their island home, and Balinese spirituality and cosmology are inseparably bound up with their beautiful land. The unique Balinese Hinduism is a combination of Hinduism, Buddhism, and Tantra (the esoteric aspects of both religions), as well as local indigenous beliefs and ancestor cult worship, nature worship, and animism. The three realms of the Balinese belief system might explain why they have never been avid seafarers. Higher powers are believed to occupy the higher realm of the mountains and skies (the *hyang* spirits), humans live in the interim world, and dark forces are ever-present below the depths of the sea. The sometimes frenetic worship and attendance at multiple temples reflect their beliefs that their island is constituted of gods, demons, and people and that it is their responsibility to manage these complex arrangements of entities.

The Balinese concept of Tri Hita Karana is one that brings together the realms of spirit, humanity, and nature in the pursuit of well-being and prosperity. Tri Hita Karana is similar to the Western idea of "sustainable development" and also includes unique alignments of entrances and structures (similar to the Eastern concept of feng shui) in all Balinese buildings, specifically the temples. But these spiritual ideologies are not confined to only buildings, and the complexities of Balinese Hinduism are included in each and every aspect of their lives, from the building of temples and homes to clothing, eating, dancing, and all forms of expression in an attempt to create a balance of life forces (*rwa bhineda*) on the island and amongst its people. There is no dedicated holy day in the weekly lives of the Balinese because every day is sacred and filled with numerous offerings to the gods, ceremonies, processions, and the burning of fragrant incenses. The local offerings, or *kriya bebali*, which are not only transient offerings and handmade objects but also permanent stone works and sculptures for the temples and shrines, are an expression of the Balinese collective life. Rituals and the social environment of Bali are inseparable, and the Balinese constantly put their aesthetic and communal efforts toward achieving balance.

The Balinese use art and beautifully created objects as a common visual language, and their talents have tied in well to the tourist industry through which the Balinese can sell their works and handicrafts. Art is such an important part of Balinese life that they don't define arts and crafts as separate acts because they are a part of their daily routine. The closest concept to sacred visual arts is *kriya bebali*, or "craft offerings." *Kriya* is crucial to the identity and culture of Bali (and Indonesia as a whole). Daily artistic creations and spiritual offerings are done regularly and do not necessarily last long. Natively, these offerings are called *kriya becik*, which translates as "complete, beautiful, and sacred." Village women carry piles of fruit on their heads to be blessed at the temple each day, palm leaves are woven into *lamak* (long hangings for rituals at shrines), and funeral towers for parades are all dispensable and can be burned or eaten soon afterward. Balinese arts, crafts, and sculptures are considered a method of honoring god or the gods on a daily basis. For the Balinese, beauty and the divine are a single concept that is the core of life and not separate abstract concepts that are apportioned certain hours in the week. In fact, the Hindu-based Balinese calendar is an expression of ten simultaneous cycles so that each day of the 210-day year can be defined by ten different names. Although the Balinese also use a solar/lunar calendar similar to the Western Gregorian calendar, it is not designed to numericize or stipulate a specific point in time as Westerners do. Both the Hindu (Pawukon) and the lunar (saka) Balinese calendars emphasize a more fluid sense of time, understood by the Balinese as the "motionless present."

The most unusual facet of Balinese religious worship, which is no different from their sense of "being" or "living," is that it has survived unchanged throughout the duration of Bali's history. Bali's parent country, Indonesia, is currently the world's largest Muslim majority country, but they still retain the symbol of their Hindu/Buddhist origins through the eagle-like Garuda bird as their national identity. Within three hundred years of the Dutch arrival in Nusantara (the early 1600s), Islam had become the method by which indigenous populations resisted colonialism. Islam continued to strengthen within Indonesia into the 20th century, and the Malay Archipelago's Islamic state exchanges with other Muslim countries grew stronger into the modern era. Bali's resistance to Islam and its perpetuation of the unique Balinese Hinduism has made the island vulnerable to Islamic terrorist attacks. The more Bali attracts foreign visitors from "the Western world," the more Islamic extremists estimate that Bali is aligning with foreign, non-Islamist societies. Terrorism remains an ongoing threat to the island, but Bali continues unchanged in culture and religion as it has done for at least the last millennium. The island has submitted to the waves of change that have inevitably engulfed this small, remote state within an immense archipelago. The constant influx of foreign powers or curious visitors still leaves Balinese resolute that they and the paradise they call home are unique and should remain so.

Conclusion

Bali is the most intriguing of the Indonesian archipelagic jewels of maritime Southeast Asia. It is a small, unique island, but it is big enough to draw the attention of migrants, invaders, and colonizers over thousands of years. Throughout Bali's history, the island has enjoyed an intriguing position within the Malay Archipelago trade routes. As Bali is closely neighboring Java and near to the Spice Islands, it has been submitted time and again to foreign rule as its people were forced to subjugate themselves to powers greater than themselves. Described as a nation of "aesthetes," the peaceful, spiritual, and culturally colorful societies that constitute Bali could not compete with the ambitions and interests of subcontinental India, Java, and Europe. In Bali's early history, the people took little action in repelling external forces and the endless waves of cultural and economic changes that engulfed their paradise. The Balinese adapted, integrated new cultures, and waited for each new independence that inevitably followed foreign rule.

During Bali's more modern history of the colonial period, the tragedy of the island's vulnerability caught up with it. Having been protected for hundreds of years from out-and-out exploitation, plunder, and colonization, it finally fell to the Dutch at the turn of the 20th century. Bali's lack of spices and other commodities for trade had kept the island safe from archipelagic interlopers that had harvested and plundered the East Indies for centuries. But the Dutch, who controlled so much of Indonesia and Java, would not rest until they completed their colonial arsenal of archipelagic control. The indigenous kingdoms of Bali, which traced their heritage back to the mesmerizing Majapahit Empire, were irrevocably dismantled. In a quick succession of uncontrollable circumstances, Dutch domination gave way to Japanese occupation during the Second World War, followed by Indonesia's overall claim of the former Dutch East Indies. Bali was swallowed up as a province of a far greater archipelagic republic, which remains its current status.

The island of Bali never entirely submitted to foreign powers, but it has also never been completely independent for any significant period of time. It has most often existed as a vassal state of a greater nation and dutifully incorporated different cultures, religions, and socio-political systems into its multifarious existence. In its current status as a province of the Republic of Indonesia, Bali is the only Hindu majority state of the Muslim-dominated island chain. Soon after its provincial independence, Bali had to fight for recognition of the unique Balinese Hinduism for which it is known—an eclectic blend of Buddhism, Hinduism, and other indigenous belief systems. The Balinese royal houses are still not recognized by its parent Indonesia in any official capacity, and the island's present echoes its past struggle for sovereignty or at least an individualized state identity.

Well-known historians herald Bali as an example of the extinguished Indo-Javanese societies of old. Bali is a living monument that celebrates the golden age of Hindu-Buddhist maritime empires that ruled the seas of Southeast Asia in pursuit of spices, exotic goods, and, most importantly, the sharing of philosophies and spiritual ideologies. Exemplifying a magnificent blend of ethnicities, cultures, and creeds, Bali continues as a timeless example of a magical and heroic past that evolved into the sublime, heterogenous tourist hotspot of today, one that is visited and loved by people from around the world for its singularity and faithful adherence to the past.

Part 5: History of the Philippines

A Captivating Guide to Philippine History

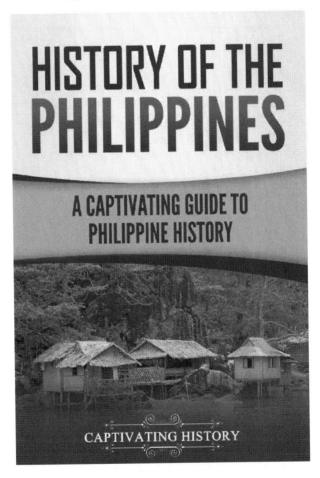

Introduction

The Philippines was known historically as the "Pearl of the Orient Seas," where beautiful goods were traded from around the world for centuries and abundant ocean treasures were bartered for crafted goods, exotic spices, and the extraordinary cultivars from Mesoamerica. Pearls, shells, seafood, indigenous woods, beautifully manufactured earthenware, Chinese porcelains, woven goods, Asian silks, South American chilis, vanilla, cocoa, coffee, precious metals, and exquisite gold and silver jewelry were just some of the high-value goods that changed hands, and cultures, in the vibrant, bustling ports of the ancient Philippines.

Over 150 cultures, which were spread across almost eight thousand islands, were eventually consolidated by the Spaniards in the late 1800s. It had taken them over three hundred years to unify parts of this magnificent archipelago, with the Moros—the Muslim principalities in the south—resisting until the very end. Since Spain's arrival in the 1500s, the waters of the Philippine isles were replete with traders, pirates, raiding parties, colonial galleons, and local tribal communities, all vying for their own independence and economic gain. The Philippines was ideally placed between the trading empires of Arabia, India, and western maritime Southeast Asia, as well as the trading giants of mainland and eastern Asia—Indochina, China, and Japan. The Spanish further enhanced the strategic position of the Philippines and its capital, Manila, by opening the first trans-Pacific trading route to Mexico. For over three centuries, the Spanish sent their galleons between Acapulco and Manila, exchanging the unique and demanded goods of Mexico and Peru with that of Asia and Arabia. The extensive Spanish empire became the "land upon which the sun never set," as it commanded territories in Europe, the East Indies, and in the New World of the Americas.

However, inter-cultural and powerful principalities had existed for millennia in the Philippines before the arrival of the colonists. The archipelago has always been and remains diverse in its cultural heritage, as well as the variety of its landscapes, from its clear blue coralline seas and magnificent beaches to its lush tropical forests and breathtaking mountains, with their ancient rice terraces and volcanoes. Some of the earliest known evidence of humanity has been found on the islands of the Philippines, and it claims hominid habitation from 700,000 BCE. It isn't possible to pay sufficient tribute to such an expansive paradise, with its considerable history and its peoples with their multitude of intriguing and ancient heritages, but the story of the Philippines is irresistible, and like its namesake, this pearl in the oyster needs to be opened to be discovered.

Chapter 1 – The Philippines within Southeast Asia

The Republic of the Philippines is an archipelagic country in maritime Southeast Asia consisting of between seven thousand and eight thousand islands (the final number is still under debate) and islets (very small islands). The land area of the Philippines is about 300,000 kilometers squared (115,000 square miles), with a total national population of 109 million people (it is the twelfth most populated country in the world). Most of the islands of the Philippines are small, and the eleven biggest islands account for 90 percent of the country's land area, with the two biggest islands—Luzon and Mindanao—consisting of half of the Philippine landmass. It is a slightly pyramidal-shaped archipelago bordered by the South China Sea to the west and north, the Celebes (Sulawesi) Sea to the south, and the Philippine Sea to the east. Most of the Philippine islands lie in a north-south direction, with Luzon at the far north and Mindanao at the far south. Two island arcs spread southwest from the lower half of the archipelago, and between them lies the Sulu Sea. The southernmost southwest arc is the Sulu Archipelago, which is still a part of the Philippines. The Sulu arc extends close to the Malaysian section of the large island of Borneo.

The Philippine archipelago stretches 1,850 kilometers (1,150 miles) from north to south and 1,130 kilometers (700 miles) at its widest along the southern portion of the islands. The Philippines' closest land neighbors are the string of Indonesian islands running west-east to the south of the archipelago (Sulawesi and the Maluku Islands) and, specifically, the large island of Borneo, which is an extension of the Philippines' southwesterly island arcs. Palawan Island is the main stretch of Philippine land that extends southwest toward Borneo (north of the Sulu Archipelago), specifically toward the northern Malaysian section of Borneo. Approximately 200 kilometers (125 miles) separates the eastern edge of Borneo from the western Palawan mainland. The majority of Borneo—most of the central and southern bulk of the island—is referred to as Kalimantan, and it is part of the Republic of Indonesia. The northern strip running west-east along the top of Borneo is Malaysian. The Malaysian strip of Borneo excludes the Sultanate of Brunei, which is an independent nation in the center of the very north of Borneo that occupies 1 percent of Borneo. The Philippines lies 800 kilometers (500 miles) east of the Vietnam coast (mainland Southeast Asia), and the island of Taiwan is about 400 kilometers (250 miles) north of the Batan Islands (the northernmost area of the Philippines). Hong Kong lies 1,116 kilometers (694 miles) northwest of Manila—the Philippine capital—as part of mainland China. Below, you can find a map of the Philippines.

The capital city of Manila is a coastal town on Manila Bay in the southwest of the Philippines' biggest island, Luzon, and it is in very close proximity to the adjacent urban node of Quezon City, which is just north of Manila. Both cities are part of the National Capital Region (NCR) or Metro Manila (including the principal Filipino port and its main international airport), which is the most densely populated urban area of the Philippines. The NCR technically includes sixteen cities and one municipal area over a land area of about six hundred square kilometers and is home to about thirteen million people. The most populous area, however, is Calabarzon—the expansive region southeast of Manila of lower Luzon—with over fourteen million people. Together, the areas of the NCR and Calabarzon contain about a third of the Filipino population. Other significant Philippine cities include Cebu (on Cebu Island), Jaro (on Panay Island), Vigan (northwest Luzon), and Naga (southeast Luzon), which were all previously given charters by the Spanish colonial government. Davao, on Mindanao, is also a considerable city. Fifty percent of the Philippines is urbanized. Of the archipelago's eighty-one provinces (and seventeen broader administrative regions), the Batanes (the Batan Islands) is a minimal cluster of islands that form the northernmost land area. Below the Batanes is another small cluster of islands called the Babuyan Islands that lie just above Luzon. Only about 40 percent of the Philippine islands have names, and only 5 percent have a land area of 2.6 square kilometers (1 square mile) or more.

The eleven largest islands fall into three groupings. The Luzon group to the north and west includes Luzon, Mindoro, and Palawan, as well as Masbate and eighteen other islands and island groupings. (The region of Kapampangan, which is often referred to in historical records, is Central Luzon or the areas stretching out from the NCR.) The Central Visayas grouping consists of Cebu, Panay, Negros, Bohol, Samar, Leyte, and ten other islands and island groupings. The island of Mindanao forms its own group in the south, along with seven other islands and island groupings, including the Sulu Archipelago.

Before the start of 16th-century colonialism, Filipinos lived in small, independent villages called barangays, each ruled by a datu (chief). In the modern day, the administrative divisions of the Philippines, besides the regions and provinces, include 146 cities, 1,488 provinces, and 42,036 barangays.

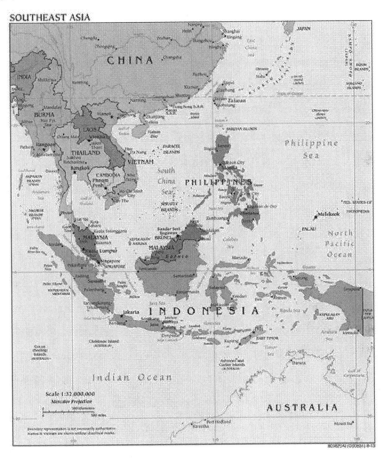

Map of Southeast Asia
https://commons.wikimedia.org/wiki/File:Political_Southeast_Asia.jpg

The Philippines is a part of the Pacific Rim of Fire (also known as the Ring of Fire), which is a ring of high seismic and volcanic activity that circumnavigates the Pacific Ocean. The horseshoe-shaped ring of more than 450 volcanoes stretches in an offshore arc from South America, running along North America, Asia, and Australia. The Rim of Fire was responsible for the creation of many Pacific island chains, specifically the easternmost archipelagos of maritime Southeast Asia. The violent geological conditions associated with the Rim of Fire are due to the movement of tectonic plates upon which Earth's landmasses rest. The tectonic plates generally define the subdivisions of the continents and are a part of Earth's crust and upper mantle. The tectonic plates create friction at their boundaries, as they have done for millions of years, as they move in the process known as continental drift. The friction along the plate boundaries is a result of tectonic plates pushing into each other, pulling apart from one another, or simply moving past one another.

The movement of the plates results in seismic activity (earthquakes), volcanic eruptions, the formation of oceanic trenches, and, most importantly, the creation of new land. In the case of the Philippines, magma (semi-molten rock lava) erupted from the Earth's crust below sea level and began building sub-oceanic mountains that eventually peaked above the surface of the sea. The magma was released during subduction, when one plate is pushed below another as they collide in their movement toward one another. This process of subduction generally results in the formation of island arcs, which are common in maritime Southeast Asia. The creation of the Philippine archipelago was specifically caused by the convergence of three tectonic plates: the Indo-Australian, Eurasian, and Philippine Sea Plates. The major Indo-Australian Plate to the south and far west of the Philippines contains the Indian subcontinent and Australia. The major Eurasian Plate to the immediate west of the archipelago contains the Asian and European continents. Finally, the minor Philippine Sea Plate lies directly below the island chain and includes the islands of Indonesia and Taiwan.

The Philippines remains a seismic and volcanic hotspot with prominent geological volcanic features making up its landscape, namely, the Philippines' highest active volcano, Mount Pinatubo, northwest of Manila on Luzon. One of the largest volcanic eruptions along the Pacific Rim of Fire was on June 9th, 1991, when Mount Pinatubo erupted, killing seven hundred people and destroying hundreds of thousands of homes. This eruption was the second largest of the 20th century. The last significant earthquake was the Luzon event in 1990, which killed an estimated 1,600 people, mostly in Central Luzon and the Cordillera region.

The Philippines is composed of volcanic rock and coral, and numerous mountain ranges run in a north-south direction like the archipelago itself. Similarly, the rivers of the Philippines mostly run northward. The archipelago is well-known for its unusual rock formations of various geological types, spectacular lakes, and narrow coastal plains. The central mountain chain of Luzon, the Cordillera Central, is the most prominent range in the Philippines and consists of two, at times three, parallel ranges running north-south along the northern half of Luzon. The average elevation of the Cordillera Central is about 1,800 meters above sea level (or 5,900 feet). The Sierra Madre is the longest Philippine mountain range. It is also on Luzon but runs along the eastern Pacific side of the island. The Cordillera and Sierra Madre meet in Central Luzon as the Caraballo Mountains.

Between the mountain ranges of the Philippines are fertile plains formed from eroded volcanic soils and ancient ash deposits. The extremely fertile plains of Cordillera on Luzon include rice terraces as part of a **UNESCO** World Heritage Site. The soils of the Philippines are ideal for rice and corn (maize) cultivation, as well as coffee, cassava, sugarcane, coconuts, fruit trees, bananas, pineapples, oil palms, abaca

(Manila hemp) and other fibrous plants, vegetables, and other crops. Eight major indigenous forest types are found within the Philippines (from beach forests to upper montane), and commercial forests are grown for timber harvesting. Mount Apo, at 2,954 meters (9,692 feet), is the highest peak in the Philippines on the southcentral coast of Mindanao. Of the Philippines' fifty volcanoes, about ten are active, and tremors and earthquakes are a common part of life on the archipelago. The most active of the Philippine volcanoes is Mount Mayon in southern Luzon. The Philippines is the world's second-biggest geothermal energy producer after the United States, supplying almost 20 percent of the country's energy needs.

Numerous important and large rivers drain between the mountain ranges toward the sea, with the largest, the Cagayan, in northern Luzon stretching for over five hundred kilometers (over three hundred miles). The capital of Manila on oceanic Manila Bay is connected via the Pasig River to the Philippines' largest lake, Laguna de Bay (or Laguna Lake), eighteen kilometers (eleven miles) away. The Pasig River, which flows through the city of Manila, was once a commercially important node for inter-island trade but is now no longer navigable except by small craft. The UNESCO World Heritage Site of the Puerto Princesa Subterranean River on the island of Palawan is a national park on the west-central coast of the island. Puerto Princesa is an 8.2-kilometer (5-mile) stretch of river that runs through a karst landscape (underground eroded caves with stalagmites and stalactites) before reaching the sea. This protected area at the mouth of the underground river allows visitors to explore parts of the waterways via boats that travel through the cave systems.

The Philippine undersea trench, Galathea Depth, Galathea Deep, or Emden Deep, is a 10,500-meter (34,500-foot) trench in the Philippine Sea and the third deepest in the world. The trench runs along the eastern side of the archipelago.

The Philippines constitutes a marine area of 2.2 million square kilometers (850,000 square miles) of the Coral Triangle, and some of its marine reefs contain the highest diversity of shore fish species in the world, along with numerous species of corals. The Coral Triangle is a triangular area of the western Pacific Ocean, which includes the waters of Indonesia, Malaysia, the Philippines, Papua New Guinea, Timor-Leste, and the Solomon Islands. The Coral Triangle is so named for its astounding number of corals (nearly 600 species of reef-building corals, or 75 percent of the total global coral species), 2,000 species of reef fish, and other special marine animals such as turtles, seahorses, and dugongs. The Tubbataha Reef in the Sulu Sea was declared one of the Philippines' impressive six UNESCO World Heritage Sites (with a further nineteen on the tentative list!) in 1993. Oysters naturally occur around the Philippine reefs, and pearls are the "national gem" of the islands. One species of oyster, the Pinctada maxima, produces a naturally golden pearl. The Sulu Archipelago is especially known for its pearl farms.

The national fish of the Philippines, the milkfish (similar to a herring), is an important food source and is found in abundance around the archipelago. The Coral Triangle is not only important for its beauty and as a tourist and scientific destination but also for its high commercial value as a fishing ground, specifically for tuna fish. In Donsol Bay (southwestern Luzon), tourists are drawn to the high number of whale sharks that accumulate to feed on nutrients released from the mouth of the Donsol River. Unfortunately, even though many internationally and locally driven environmental projects are underway to protect the magnificent marine waters around the Philippines (which is vital for local tourism and eco-tourism), overfishing, environmental destruction and pollution, and climate change continue to have negative effects on the Coral Triangle's ecosystem.

The Philippine coral reefs are critical as barriers to storms and rough seas (including tsunamis and typhoons), and they reduce flooding by almost half across the archipelago. Overall, the Philippines is home to a significant array of biodiversity (it is considered a country of megadiversity) and indigenous and endemic species of both fauna and flora, such as the Philippine (as well as the saltwater) crocodile, the Philippine eagle (the national bird), endemic bats, abundant ferns, hundreds of rare orchid species, and uniquely giant parasitic plants. There is even evidence that elephants once roamed the islands. Sadly, deforestation is a significant problem in the Philippines, and during the 20th century, forest cover declined from 70 percent of the land area to 18 percent, mostly due to logging, mining, and farming activities. When forests are removed, the groundcover is naturally replaced by low, coarse bushes (scrubland) or tall grasses. Along with environmental degradation and pollution, the Philippines continues to be extremely vulnerable to permanent biological destruction and the extinction of species due to human impact. Most of the Philippine vegetation is indigenous and is very similar to that of Malaysia, with some Himalayan elements at higher altitudes, as well as Australian species. The discovery of new species continues to this day.

The Philippines is tropical and has wet and dry monsoon seasons. The wet conditions are blown in from the southwest from May to October (summer), and the dry winds blow from the northeast from November to February (winter). The Philippines lies between four and twenty-one degrees north of the equator, and the temperatures remain fairly consistent all year round. In general, the temperature of the Philippines is moderate but is cooler at higher elevations, with the range of temperatures overall being between four degrees Celsius (forty degrees

Fahrenheit) and thirty-eight degrees Celsius (one hundred degrees Fahrenheit). However, the average conditions are warm and humid, with temperature ranges between twenty-one and thirty-two degrees Celsius (seventy and ninety degrees Fahrenheit). Cyclone season is from June to December and brings typhoons from the southeast, which can exceed twenty per season and be very destructive.

The Philippine people are referred to as Filipinos, and more recently, Filipino has become known colloquially for all things referring to the Philippines. (Originally, the Filipino people were specifically those living on the archipelago with a distinctively Spanish heritage.) Filipinos are now ethnically diverse, with over one hundred culturally and linguistically distinctive groups. Most Filipinos draw their ancestry from the Southeast Asian mainland, Indonesia, and Malay. The two most populous ethnic groups of the Philippines (constituting twenty percent each of the overall population) are the Tagalog of Luzon and the Visayans/Bisaya (including the Cebuano) of central Indonesia. Other larger groups are the Ilocano of northern Luzon and the Hiligaynon (Ilonggo) of the central Philippines (the islands of Panay and Negros), which constitute ten percent each of the nation's population. Another ten percent of the Filipinos consist of the Waray-Waray, who live on several islands in the Central Visayas, and the Bicol (Bikol) of the Bicol Peninsula, southeast of Luzon.

The "aboriginal" people of the Philippines were Negritos (small in stature and dark-skinned), which included various sub-groupings and who now only constitute a marginal percentage of the population. Influxes over the centuries from China, India, the United States, Europe, Latin America, and Spain contributed to ethnic variations within the last millennium and a current populace of mixed heritage. There are smaller communities of native Chinese, Japanese, Indians, and Arabs who live in the Philippines.

There are an estimated 150 to 186 native languages and dialects in the Philippines. Most of these languages are Austronesian in origin and are closely related, specifically Malayo-Polynesian. Also, many Spanish-based creole varieties are present on the island—referred to as Chavacano—as well as some original Negrito languages. The language proliferation reflects the ethnic areas, with Tagalog being the most spoken language in central and south Luzon (including Manila) and in Mindoro and Marinduque, the islands just to the south of Luzon. The national languages of the Philippines are Filipino (also called Pilipino), which is based on Tagalog, and English. Filipino sign language is also officially recognized. It should be noted that Spanish was the principal language of the Philippines from the colonial era until the beginning of the 1900s, when English came to dominate due to the United States' occupation.

The Philippines was named after its colonial-era Spanish sovereign, King Philip II, who ruled in the 16th century. Philippine history is the most strongly influenced by the West of all Southeast Asian countries. One-quarter of the population is fluent in English, with most being at least conversive in English, and it is the medium for several school subjects, including mathematics and science (with Filipino being the other major medium).

The Philippines is a secular state that protects the freedom of religion. Along with East Timor (Timor-Leste), the Philippines is one of only two predominantly Roman Catholic countries in Asia, and it is the world's third-largest Roman Catholic population after Brazil and Mexico, with at least 80 percent of Filipinos adhering to the faith. A further 10 percent of the population adheres to other Christian denominations. Islam was brought to the archipelago from Borneo, specifically Brunei, in the 15th century. Muslim adherents were established and grew around Manila, the Sulu Archipelago, and the southern zone of Mindanao by the time of the

Europeans' arrival in the mid-16th century. Since the European intervention in the last half-millennium, the existing Muslim communities constitute 6 percent (possibly up to 11 percent) of Filipinos, and they are limited to the southern islands and are known as Moros. A very small number of people practice Buddhism, and they are mostly of Chinese descent. Rural communities also practice local indigenous belief systems.

Although the Filipino people are distinctly Asian in culture and ideology, they are also strongly Euro-American in aspiration and outlook, mostly owing to their history and the educational policies instituted in the 20th century. By the late 20th century, the Philippines had emerged as a regional leader in education, with a well-established school and university system. By the early 21st century, the nation's investment in education led to one of the highest literacy rates in Asia.

The archipelago is run as a unitary state except for the Bangsamoro Autonomous Region in Muslim Mindanao (BARMM). Bangsamoro, in western-central Mindanao and the Sulu Archipelago, runs according to an autonomous legal system instituted in 2018, which will be in transition until 2022. It is the only Muslim-majority autonomous region in the Philippines, but along with the national government's considerations for governance decentralization, it acts as a testing phase for later conversations on constitutional reform and the potential federalism of the archipelago. The Philippines is run as a democratic and constitutional republic with an elected president (with a single six-year term). The current president, Rodrigo Duterte of the PDP-Laban political party, was elected in 2016. He is the first Philippine president from Mindanao. The PDP stands for the *Partido Demokratiko Pilipino-Lakas ng Bayan* (the Philippine Democratic Party-People's Power).

The Philippines continues to experience extreme income inequality. Wealthier people in the urban areas live in multi-story homes or apartment buildings, but much of the population lives in poverty, often in shacks made from bamboo, wood, sheet metal, and other scrap items. Those in poverty do not have regular access to basic services such as water, electricity, or even sewage.

As mentioned above, the Philippine archipelago has fertile volcanic soils and is rich in biological and mineral resources owing to its complex geological formations and high seismic activity. Metallic minerals (gold, iron ore, lead, zinc, nickel, chromite, palladium, and copper) are found mostly on the islands of Luzon and Mindanao. The archipelago is estimated to have the second-largest global deposits of gold after South Africa, as well as significant quantities of copper and the world's largest palladium deposits. Non-metallic minerals are primarily found in the Central Visayas (such as limestone, marble, asphalt, salt, gypsum, etc.). The Philippines' natural resources remain largely untapped due to social and environmental complications. Philippine oil and gas fields are found off the northwest coast of Palawan. Although the country has significant industrial potential, its economy remains largely agricultural, with manufacturing contributing to a quarter of the national GDP (gross domestic product). The national currency is the Philippine peso. Some of the Philippines' main exports are professional people and laborers who are educated and trained on the islands and then chose to move abroad, mainly to the United States and Canada as well as other Asian and Southeast Asian nations. Major tangible exports include electronic equipment, garments and accessories, coconuts and coconut products, and minerals—specifically copper, gold, and iron ore. The major destinations of these exports are to other Asian countries (Japan, China, Singapore, South Korea, Hong Kong, Taiwan, and Thailand), the Netherlands, Germany, and the United States. Tourism contributes approximately 10 percent to the economy and has been growing, with most visitors coming from South Korea, the United States, and Japan, as well as other Asian and Southeast Asian countries. Over eight million international visitors were recorded in 2019.

Filipinos exist as a unique blend of extraordinary heterogeneity in cultural and ethnic sub-groupings but operate homogeneously as a nation. The foundations of this homogeneity are due to hundreds of years of colonial rule and the establishment of broad and enduring faith-based institutions such as Catholicism and Islam. However, the more modern contribution to Filipino unity is the education system that was established by the United States in the first half of the 20th century and has been continued by the Filipino people and government. Elementary education in the archipelago is compulsory (lasting until the children are twelve years of age), but an alternative learning system exists for those who are not part of the traditional system. Vocational schools also offer technical education and skill development. Regardless, all Filipinos get a solid grounding in basic education and are highly encouraged and assisted in completing their full schooling and moving to tertiary pursuits. The Philippines provides many state-run universities and colleges for tertiary learning, particularly in the capital of Manila. (The oldest university in the archipelago, the University of Santo Tomas, was founded in 1611!) The Filipinos' emphasis on education has provided the basis for cultural unity and socioeconomic progress as the Philippines embarks on an Asian revival by reinstituting the barangay as the smallest unit of local governance, reviving dormant local traditions, and exploring Asian history and literature. It seems that the Filipinos have found a unique balance between the Western and Eastern influences of which they have always been a part.

Chapter 2 – Prehistoric Philippines (BCE)

The original indigenous peoples of the Philippines are believed to be the Negritos, which include the subgroupings of Agta, Aeta, Ati, Ata, and Batak, amongst others. These hunter-gatherers are thought to have occupied the archipelago sometime before 40,000 BCE. These small, dark-skinned peoples were nomadic and semi-nomadic hunter-gatherers who used their skills to hunt game throughout the centuries as a primary item for barter and trade; they even sold their hunting and fishing skills to colonialists into the 20th century. They are now a tiny sub-grouping of Filipino ethnicities, and in the 1980s, they numbered about fifteen thousand individuals, scattered mostly across the islands of Luzon, Palawan, Panay, Negros, Cebu, and Mindanao. Through the waves of colonialism over hundreds of years, this indigenous people's belief system has remained largely animistic (local indigenous folklore and nature worship). Unfortunately, however, since the colonial era, the number of

Negritos has declined dramatically. This decline is due mostly to the introduction of foreign diseases and the encroachment and degradation of lands, which has affected traditional hunting resources, enforced the alteration of lifestyles and livelihoods, and resulted in poverty for many.

The Negrito languages (as are all indigenous languages of the archipelago) are of Austronesian descent, although the Austronesian peoples were only thought to have occupied the islands a few thousand years before the Common Era and many tens of thousands of years after the Negritos were present on the Philippines. The Negritos are remarkably different in appearance from the dominant Asian progenitors of the Austronesian race of the Philippines, who currently outnumber the Negritos by four thousand to one. Despite being very dark-skinned, scholars accept that it is unlikely that the Negritos' ancestors came from continental Africa but rather believe they are the descendants of *Homo sapiens* that migrated into the Philippines during the Late Pleistocene period from mainland Southeast Asia. (However, scholarly debate around this subject continues since it is accepted that the first hominids of Southeast Asia, *Homo erectus*, journeyed from Africa over a million years ago. Theories continue over whether a subsequent wave of *Homo sapien* migration from Africa occurred thereafter. Evidence suggests a break in human evolution within Southeast Asia, and although it is unconfirmed, advocates believe that a later wave of the more evolved *Homo sapiens* must have come from Africa or Asia.)

The Late Pleistocene, or Tarantian Stage, was the last of the four stages of the Pleistocene era, lasting from approximately 126,000 to 11,700 years ago. During this era, global ice ages held oceanic waters captive in ice sheets and glaciers, creating lower sea levels. (In Southeast Asia, the sea levels may have been as low as 120 to 140 meters—or 394 to 460 feet—below current levels!) Land bridges between continents and islands existed that are not present today, which allowed people to migrate to more habitable locations. It is likely that most of the Philippine archipelago, except Palawan, existed as one or two more exposed islands separated from mainland Asia by narrow, navigable sea corridors.

The Sunda Shelf is the extension of the continental shelf of Southeast Asia upon which the landmasses of western maritime Southeast Asia rest, such as Malaysia, Sumatra, Borneo, Java, Madura, and Bali. A biogeographical boundary known as Huxley's Line divides the geographical distribution of fauna and flora between the areas included in Sundaland (of the Sunda Shelf) and the Philippines (except for Palawan). Thomas Huxley (1825-1895 CE) was an English biologist and anthropologist known as "Darwin's bulldog" in his support of the naturalist Charles Darwin's (1809-1882) theory of evolution. Between himself and Alfred Russell Wallace (1823-1913), a British naturalist and explorer, they demarcated a primordial theoretical line that runs through maritime Southeast Asia with distinct differences in fauna and flora on either side of the line. The line is known as the Wallace Line below the Philippine archipelago, but it has an extension that runs north—the Huxley Line—separating Sundaland from the Philippines (except for the island of Palawan). The Huxley Line also gives some indication of the likely distribution of early hominids who crossed from the mainland. Since evidence of prehistoric human remains on the Philippines, which is east of the Huxley Line, is more contemporary in evolutionary terms, it seems less likely that the archipelago was populated via distributions from the west of the biogeographical line. (Although, unfortunately, there is not enough evidence to either confirm or deny any of the evolutionary theories.)

Some of the earliest evidence of prehistoric man has been found on the island of Palawan, which is technically part of Sundaland and is west of the Huxley Line. The Tabon Caves have yielded the oldest human remains of modern *Homo sapiens*, the "Tabon Man," dating back to approximately between 58,000 to 16,500 years ago. (These dates can vary by 10,000 years. The discrepancies in dates are due to the human fragments being from more than one hominid individual.) The original excavations at Tabon were conducted by Dr. Robert B. Fox, a leading anthropologist and historian of the pre-Hispanic Philippines who lived from 1918 to 1985, along with members of the National Museum of the Philippines, in the 1960s. In addition to the human fossils (including a tibia fragment, a mandible, and a skull) were chert flakes (sharp rock flakes from human activity) and pebble tools (rocks used as tools). Paleolithic remains were also discovered beyond the Huxley Line in other parts of the Philippines, including on Luzon and in Cagayan Valley. Several caves within the northern Luzon area of Cagayan have produced evidence of early humans, as well as other paleolithic evidence, and additional prehistoric evidence (unconfirmed by date) has been found across the Philippine archipelago, including in Metro Manila, other parts of southern Luzon, and Davao, Mindanao.

In 2019, it was confirmed that the remains of an ancient man (pre-modern *Homo sapiens*) in the northern Luzon caves (specifically Callao Cave), which had originally been estimated to be more modern, were classified as being between fifty thousand and seventy thousand years old. These human remains indicate a previously unclassified species of human that is pygmy-like and was named *Homo luzonensis* after the island of its discovery. Overall, human presence on Luzon is now estimated as dating to at least 770,000 years ago! This approximate date is attributed to the remains of the extinct Philippine rhinoceros, *Rhinoceros philippinensis*, which had been clearly and purposefully butchered by humans at an archaeological site. Scholars could decipher this due to the remains of primitive stone tools and rock shards in the area, as well as the particular breaks in the animals' bones.

In the Rizal region of Calabarzon (lower Luzon, southeast of Manila), petroglyphs were discovered, known as the Angono Petroglyphs, of stick-like human and animal figures. The petroglyphs are believed to date back to before 2000 BCE due to the nearby discovery of fragmented earthenware, obsidian flakes, chert, flake stone tools, a stone core tool, and a polished stone adze. The Angono Petroglyphs were carved into a cave wall and are the oldest example of art in the Philippines. They have been declared a national treasure. The engravings are considered symbolic, and like most ancient indigenous art, they are associated with healing and sympathetic magic. The site is highly sacred to the Tagalog people (known as *dambana* or "holy ground") and is believed to be home to *anitos* (spirits or gods).

The Negrito ancestors are believed to have journeyed from Asia to the Philippines between 45,000 and 30,000 BCE. (Some scholars suggest that Negritos are of Australo-Melanesian descent—southwestern Pacific/Australian origins.) Regardless of the true origins of the Negrito ancestors, scientists agree that it is likely that these early people developed their physical characteristics from about 30,000 BCE in situ within their evolving island environment. (This localized evolution could have begun as early as 50,000 BCE.) This microevolution of the Negritos would have given rise to their unique phenotypic traits in terms of how their genetic evolution would have responded to the local environment. Other Pleistocene evidence of ancient mammals (such as *Stegodon*—elephant-like beasts—rhinoceros, the Philippine warty pig, giant turtles, and a type of bovid) suggests that early hominids in the Philippines may have lived in tandem with now-extinct fauna. The prehistoric evidence of slaughtered animals across the Philippine archipelago is a key indicator of early human presence since there is no evidence of ancient carnivorous predators in the Philippines (except for the tiger on Palawan, west of the Huxley Line).

The Philippines' human origins (and maritime Southeast Asia, in general) have always been contentious and widely debated amongst scholars, as is typical of the general movement of Austronesian peoples throughout Asian, African, and Pacific waters over the millennia. While the Negrito ancestors would have moved across land bridges during the ice ages (whether from Africa, Asia, or even Australasia) during paleolithic times (from the first evidence of hominids in the Philippines to the end of the Pleistocene age, c. 11,500 BCE), the Austronesian people were on the move from Neolithic times, which proceeded the Pleistocene age. The Austronesian people were avid seafarers, and their redistribution began after the close of the last ice age (approximately 11,500 BCE, which marked the end of the Pleistocene period and the beginning of our modern Holocene era), when ocean waters were higher. They used their highly developed maritime navigational skills to move between islands and landmasses. Typically, the Austronesians would have used multi-hulled or outrigger (including a lateral support float) canoes and sailboats, as are still seen across the maritime Austronesian domains today (from Madagascar in the Indian Ocean through maritime Southeast Asia, Micronesia, Melanesia, and Polynesia of the Pacific Ocean). The Negrito and Austronesian interactions on the Philippine archipelago are evidenced to have begun between three thousand and one thousand years ago. At first, it is likely that these two early peoples would have traded, but Austronesians later settled on the Philippines. Over time, there was a natural interracial mixing of these two groups, and modern Filipino genealogy is a varying genetic admixture of ancient Negrito and Austronesian peoples. However, by the first millennium before the

Common Era, societies had split into four groupings, of which the forest-dwelling Negritos have retained a form of separation and dominant Negrito genealogy to this day. The Austronesians (or Austronesian "mixes") eventually came to dominate the population of the archipelago to produce what is now referred to as the Filipino people.

Austronesian people are found throughout the Pacific islands, maritime Southeast Asia, and the Indian islands to this day. (They are mostly collectively identified by their genetics and languages but also through cultural similarities, rice cultivation, and other domestic livestock and cultivars.) Their ancestors journeyed via sea during Neolithic times, seeking new homes and fresh resources for their growing communities. There is still strong scholarly debate as to whether these seafarers originally came from southern mainland southeastern China (the coastal Yangtze Delta area) or from the island of Taiwan.

The Austronesians brought agriculture, polished stone tools, pottery-making skills, and, most significantly, their languages with them. This indirect population of the Philippines by Austronesians is one of the more widely accepted hypotheses of the influx of Neolithic peoples to the archipelago and is thought to have happened in waves from 4,000 BCE to 500 BCE. A genetic study in 2021 examined individuals of 115 indigenous communities in the Philippines and discovered that at least five separate waves of prehistoric immigration were likely, several Negrito and several Austronesian. Scholars estimate that these successive influxes of peoples to the Philippines were both heterogeneous (in terms of ethnicity and culture) as well as random and that much of the genetic lineage of the Philippine people was developed (evolved or mixed) once they were already residents of the archipelago.

The most likely sources of Austronesian influxes may have been from the Indonesian islands, as well as via the Malay Peninsula and then via

Borneo. Also, around 500 BCE, the possible influx of the rice-terrace building proto-Malays (ancient Malays) from central Asia took place, followed by a final wave of Deutero-Malays (direct ancestors of modern Malay people) from Indonesia during the 5th and 4th centuries BCE. In about 2200 BCE, some of the first Austronesian people settled the northern Batanes, as well as northern Luzon; they were presumably from Taiwan. They are believed to have spread south through the archipelago from there, but it is also possible that additional influxes of Austronesians came from other parts of mainland and maritime Southeast Asia. The presence of Taiwanese indigenous peoples in the northern Philippines is confirmed by the presence of jade artifacts dating to two millennia before the Common Era. The jade originated in Taiwan and was crafted on northern Luzon into lingling-o cultural items. Jade craftmanship spread first from China, where the oldest nephrite (jade) artifacts have been found, to Taiwan and then spread farther south to the Philippines. Lingling-o is double-headed pendant jewelry associated with Iron Age Austronesian cultures. Lingling-o was mostly crafted from jade that was sourced in Taiwan, but the crafting of the amulets became mostly associated with workshops in the Philippines (and partially in Vietnam).

In the 2000s CE, archaeologist Peter Bellwood (an English Emeritus Professor of Archaeology at the School of Archaeology and Anthropology at the Australian National University) proved the existence of lingling-o workshops in the northern Philippines (the Batanes) dating back as far as two and a half millennia ago. His discovery confirmed that lingling-o and other jade remains in the Philippines were not exclusively the result of trade. Lingling-o manufacturing in the archipelago continued until about 1000 CE. Although lingling-o was mostly made from nephrite jade (whitish-yellow but also green), they were also carved from shells, gold, copper, and wood. The jade artifacts discovered in the Philippines were not only restricted to jewelry. Jade beads, adzes, chisels, and other items were also discovered, tens of thousands of which were in a single site in the Batangas (southwestern Luzon).

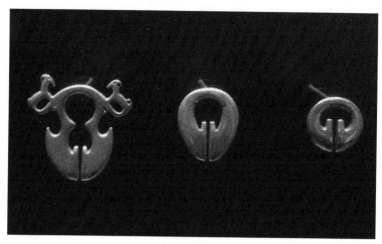

Examples of Filipino lingling-o jewelry currently housed in the Musée du quai Branly in Paris, France.
Chaoborus, CC BY-SA 4.0 <https://creativecommons.org/licenses/by-sa/4.0>, via Wikimedia Commons https://commons.wikimedia.org/wiki/File:Lingling-o-X3.jpg

The raw jade would also have come from mainland Southeast Asia, and cross-pollination of trade, as well as ancestry between the Asian continent and the islands, continued, often in stages, over the millennia. Another primary culture to influence the Philippines was the Sa Huỳnh of present-day Vietnam, who were also Austronesian. The Sa Huỳnh were prolific traders in items such as semi-precious gemstone beads, bronze mirrors, and other ornaments and items that they themselves imported and sometimes crafted themselves. Sa Huỳnh relics have been discovered in the Philippines as well as other Southeast Asian countries and islands. Ear ornaments were specifically found in the Tabon Caves of Palawan. More Sa Huỳnh evidence of pottery was discovered in the Kalanay Cave on the island of Masbate, dating to between 400 BCE and 1500 CE. These jars were presumably used for storage, cooking, and potentially for ritualistic purposes. Also, the Maitum anthropomorphic pottery, specifically Sa Huỳnh burial jars, in the Sarangani province of southern Mindanao are dated to approximately 200 CE. These burial jars are unique in that there are no other examples of their particular design in Southeast Asia. They were rediscovered in the 1990s in the Ayub Cave located in Maitum, and to date, a total of twenty-nine burial jars, thirty-three baskets, and four cubic meters (141 cubic feet) of archaeological material have been amassed. The average total height of the jars is seventy centimeters (eight inches), with its widest diameters at approximately thirty-six centimeters (fourteen inches).

An example of one of the anthropomorphic Maitum burial jars from Mindanao, c. 200 CE.
Gary Todd from Xinzheng, China, CC0, via Wikimedia Commons
https://commons.wikimedia.org/wiki/File:Mindanao_Burial_Jar_(24528966324).jpg

The Tabon Caves are dubbed the "Philippines' Cradle of Civilization," and the Philippine government has made great efforts to protect this site on the southwestern extent of the elongated Palawan Island. Towering above the ocean, the caves and their surrounding dense forests are part of a protected reservation and a living cultural museum. Of the 215 known caves, only 29 have been excavated, and 7 are open to the public. Tabon is a location of immense cultural and historical value and another one of the Philippines' seemingly endless national cultural treasures! It is one of the locations on the tentative list for a **UNESCO World Heritage Site**. Human habitation in the caves is estimated to have lasted from fifty millennia ago to approximately 1,300 CE. Other items in the caves include tools, jewelry, animal bones, and 1,500 burial jars! One of these jars, which is perfectly intact, is known as the Manunggul Jar. The exquisitely decorated ceramic jar dates from approximately eight hundred years before the Common Era and is topped with two figures rowing a boat. The jar was discovered near the Tabon Man in 1964 by Dr. Robert Fox and contains human bones painted red and multiple bracelets. Secondary burials were common throughout the Philippines during this historical period, with those who were not cremated being reburied at some point within the burial jars. The top third and lid of the Manunggul Jar are carved with curved wave-like designs that are painted with hematite (a black iron-oxide compound). The overall design of the jar reflects the nature-spirit (*anito*) belief systems of the early Filipinos, and the two figures are believed to be in convoy to the afterlife. The Sa Huỳnh people were known to have decorated their dead with agate, carnelian, and glass beads sourced in India and Iran. These, as well as similar jewelry of the Sa Huỳnh Vietnamese culture, were found in the caves.

The Tabon Caves are one example of the layers of human habitation in the Philippine archipelago over the millennia. Even though the exact timing of the influxes and origins of the early peoples cannot be pinpointed, nor their movements throughout the archipelago definitively mapped, the remains of eras past indicate an abundant and complex populating of the islands. The most likely patterns of Iron Age Austronesians would have been via maritime trade networks between the Philippines, Vietnam, Taiwan, Borneo, and southern Thailand. (The Sa Huỳnh route between 500 BCE and 1500 CE was known as the Sa Huỳnh-Kalanay Interaction Sphere after the Masbate findings.)

It was only in approximately the first millennium BCE that metallurgy was believed to have reached the archipelago as a result of trade with India. Evidence of metal tools from approximately 500 BCE exists, although stone tools used by proto-Philippine societies (the first societies) stretch from at least 50,000 BCE to past the start of the Filipino Iron Age. Anthropologist Felipe Landa Jocano (a Filipino anthropologist, author, and educator) refers to this Stone Age period as the *formative phase*, in which stone tools and ceramics were the most important elements that the early Filipinos used to interact with their environment. Jocano refers to the period of 500 BCE to the start of the Common Era as the *incipient phase*, when metallurgy and pottery were developing across the archipelago, making life more industrious and trade more propitious. Unlike most other ancient civilizations, it is very difficult to approximate when a "Bronze Age" or a "Copper Age" existed in the Philippine archipelago. The Iron Age finds from the 10th and 9th centuries BCE indicate the importation of iron tools and weapons, and there is only rudimentary evidence of ironmongery on the islands themselves. Whether most of the iron products were imported or mined and smelted on the archipelago itself, the use of metal brought an end to the Philippine Stone Age.

By 1000 BCE, Filipino societies were ordered into four approximate groupings: hunter-gatherer tribes confined mostly to the forests; warrior societies that practiced ritualized warfare and roamed the plains; highland plutocracies, mostly of the Cordillera highlands (controlling wealthy classes or families); and port principalities of the harbor estuaries who participated the most in trade. Two thousand years later, by the first millennium of the Common Era, some of these societies were so advanced that they could have been considered as states in their own right. The major conglomerations reflect some of the biggest cities of today, such as Maynila and Tondo (Manila); Caboloan (Luzon); Cebu; Madja-as and Panay (Panay); Bohol; Butuan, Cotabato, and Lanao (Mindanao); Sulu; and Ma-i (southern Luzon or Mindoro). Development of the archipelago had been mostly influenced by trade from approximately 300 to 700 CE, with the seafaring peoples of the Philippines using balangays (or barangays) to navigate the trade routes. The balangays were specialized Filipino boats, the oldest evidence of which dates to the 4th century CE and was the first wooden watercraft excavated in Southeast Asia. Access to Indianized kingdoms (such as Java), the Malay Archipelago, and East Asian principalities became more accessible and brought not only commercial opportunities but cultural and religious ones as well.

Chapter 3 – Pre-colonial Philippines (1–1565 CE)

The pre-colonial Philippines, from the start of the Common Era until Spanish occupation, which began in 1565, can be defined by principalities that started as the smallest unit of settlement known as the barangay. There is evidence of these settlement units dating back to at least the first half of the first millennium of the Common Era. During the Spanish colonial period (1565-1898), the communal regions were known as barrios, and during the first half of the 20th century (the American era), the barangays were referred to as municipalities.

The original barangays were family villages named after the groups of boats (balangays or barangays—they will be referred to as balangays in this book to avoid confusion), which carried small groups of people and their possessions to new parts of the Philippines. These settlers were most likely to have been Austronesian Malayo-Polynesians or perhaps Filipinos moving between the archipelagic islands. Naturally, most of the original barangays were coastal or riverine, and fishing was a critical aspect of their livelihoods. The balangays (the boats) carried family groups, slaves, cultivars for agriculture, and domestic animals to be farmed under the leadership of a datu, or chief. Once the balangays had landed at a new site, and a settlement was established and had grown, the word "balangay" took on a new form as "barangay," known as a village rather than a boat.

The village chief, or datu (also known as a rajah, *hajji*, sultan, or lakan depending on the area), of the barangay ruled through inheritance, physical prowess, and/or wealth. He was singularly the law, judiciary, and executive of village life. The datu was usually assisted in his rulership through a council of male elders, or *maginoo*, who were often chiefs who had retired. The barangay was the primary unit of protection in the first millennium and a half of the Common Era. Subsequently, it was natural for several neighboring barangays to coalesce into a conglomerate to strengthen their position and wealth. The strongest leader of these individual villages (usually by virtue of his being the largest and wealthiest barangay) became the overall de facto chief of the conglomeration. The datu of the barangay confederation would occasionally share his power with the lesser datus but never with the common people. This arrangement of hierarchical and localized governance in the Philippines was later used by the Spanish to their advantage, as the colonialists simply adopted and controlled the existing Filipino model at the start of their suzerainty.

However, this hierarchical model of combined rulership in the collective Philippine barangays may have been more theoretical and informal than how it seemed, at least perhaps in certain instances. Anthropologist Felipe Landa Jocano suggests that even when barangays were in alliances with one another, they were still ruled independently.

Grouping barangays was based more on a general and convenient consensus than on a permanent arrangement. "It was a living democracy," according to Jocano. When the Spaniards made attempts to forcefully consolidate Philippine principalities to govern the Filipinos more easily, they met resistance when they compelled certain datus and barangays to pledge subservience to localized barangays and their datus. As anthropologist Laura Lee Junker (Professor of Anthropology and Archaeology at the University of Illinois, Chicago) in a 1990 study on pre-Hispanic Filipino societies stated, "While political leadership followed an explicitly symbolized hierarchy of rank, this leadership hierarchy did not constitute an institutionalized chain of command from center to periphery. Political allegiance was given only to the leader immediately above an individual with whom a kin group had personal ties of economic reciprocity and loyalty." Allegiance to an overlord at that time seemed more of a personal choice than a political or geographical necessity.

The large conglomerations of barangays that accumulated at places like Maynila (ancient Manila), Tondo (much of Luzon), the Madja-as of Panay, Pangasinan (western Luzon around the Lingayen Gulf), Cebu (central-eastern coast of Cebu Island), the island of Bohol, Butuan (northern Mindanao), Cotabato (central Mindanao or current Davao), and Sulu became cosmopolitan polities or principalities. Maynila (centered on the existing district of Intramuros, which later became the epicenter of colonial rule) was the bayan (polity or country) of the Tagalog ethnic group. Exact historical references to the names of these ancient Philippine strongholds are confusing, but either Maynila or the entire Bay of Manila could once have been referred to as the Kingdom of Maynila or the Kingdom of Luzon, post-introduction of Indianized and Islamic influences. The adjoining bayans usually formed ritual alliances, such as the one created between Maynila and Tondo, which then collectively influenced the surrounding regions of Bulacan (northeastern region of Manila Bay above Manila and Quezon City) and Pampanga (northern region of Manila Bay and directly west of Bulacan).

The period from the 14th to 16th centuries became referred to as the Barangic Phase in Philippine history—the golden age of the Philippine barangays when they were at their most powerful. The first barangays had typically begun with approximately thirty to a hundred families, with populations of between one hundred and five hundred people. Upon the arrival of the Spanish in the 16th century, they discovered barangays consisting of as little as twenty people to large, wealthy principalities. The larger communities and principalities were naturally found on the coast since they could engage in trade and intercultural exchanges with Arabia, India, China, and Japan. Over time, the largest coastal communities developed into small, highly cultured kingdoms with their own social structures, sovereignty, and hierarchies of nobility and royalty. However, when the early Spaniards made their initial forays into the outer territories of these apex city-states, they discovered that any "king" of the Philippine principalities did not have any true territorial claim nor absolute command over the people. The hierarchical arrangements were loose, unenforceable, and more like the original agreement of chieftaincies prevalent at the beginning of Filipino settlement, when kinship and prowess were passed through the male line and allegiance to various datus was relatively subjective.

The title for the head of the barangays and principalities changed according to the geographical region of the Philippines and the culture that most influenced that particular area. Sultan was used in the most Islamized areas of Mindanao, the variation Sulotan in other Islamized areas, Lakan amongst the Tagalogs, Thimuay (or *Thimuay Labi*) amongst the Subanon (a tribe of the Zamboanga Peninsula of southwest Mindanao approaching the Sulu Archipelago), Rajah in the polities that traded most with Indonesia and Malaysia (the Indianized kingdoms or those most influenced by Indian cultures), and Datu, mostly in the Visayas and other regions of the Philippines. By the time of Spanish arrival, the upper echelons of certain societies were known as the datu classes, and in certain parts of unhispanized parts of the Philippines, such as Islamized Mindanao, some of the elites are still referred to as such (for reference, unhispanized refers to non-colonialized areas or areas that were able to keep their traditions intact).

In time, the *maginoo* (originally the council of elders) became a ruling class. Its members were referred to as *Ginoo* in Tagalog settlements, and both men and women could be a part of the class. This upper class adopted different names in various parts of the archipelago, though. *Maginoo* was mostly for Tagalog societies, *ginu* amongst the Kapampangan people, and *tumao* (or, for immediate royalty, the *kadatuan*) among the Visayans.

In most of the highly populated regions of the Philippines before Spanish arrival in the mid-16th century, three major social classes had developed, with different names in each tribal area. There were commoners, serfs, and slaves at the lowliest level of the social structure, the ruling classes at the highest and most influential level, and finally, a warrior class that was considered to be a higher class, more toward the nobility than the commoners. In certain more Indianized and Islamized populations of the Philippines, the ruling class structure, particularly the roles of principal influencers to the sultans and rajahs, including the line of inheritance, was considerably more complicated.

Another class of pre-colonial Filipino society was the shaman or *Babaylan* (*balian* or *katalonan*), who were usually directly descended from the prestigious classes and were held in high regard within society, potentially because they were feared for their assumed powers. The *Babaylans* were healers and spiritualists who could be men but were more likely women or even feminized men who dressed and behaved as women (known as *baklâ*). Before the advent of the monotheistic religions of Hinduism, Buddhism, Islam, and Christianity in the Philippine archipelago, indigenous and animistic (nature-orientated and mythological) belief systems dominated the islands. The overall term for local Filipino beliefs is Anitism and includes gods (*anitos*), minor deities and demigods (*diwatas*), nature spirits, mythological creatures (such as nymphs), and connection to ancestors. Beginning in the 7th century, Buddhism and Hinduism were brought to the Philippines from the Indianized Kingdom of Nusantara—mostly from Sumatra and Java. There is evidence that many Filipino people adopted elements of both religions and incorporated them into their indigenous belief systems.

The disintegration of the Indianized kingdoms (1300s to 1500s) coincided with the rise of Islam and the subsequent conquest of Hindu kingdoms by Muslim sultanates in maritime Southeast Asia, and Muslim belief systems were added to the general milieu of beliefs in the Philippines. Islam potentially reached the Philippines as early as the 1200s, mostly from Muslim traders, missionaries, and proselytizers from Arabia and western Nusantara. However, Islam only became entrenched within the Philippines in the 1400s and 1500s, most specifically across the southern island states (Mindanao and Sulu). The Spaniards brought Christianity—specifically Catholicism—in the 16th century, and over the three centuries of their domination of the Philippines, they had mixed success converting the Filipino people, despite their considerable efforts to do so. (Ironically, the Philippines is now a predominantly Roman Catholic nation.)

Although Filipino maritime trade was evident from the original settlements of the archipelago, from the 900s (the Song period in Chinese history) and for the next six hundred years until Spanish colonization, the Philippines engaged in the trade and barter of "prestigious goods" with China and other mainland Asian states. Chinese porcelain, as well as other high-value goods such as silks, magnetite mirrors, glass beads, and metal jewelry, were seen as articles of prestige with Filipino elites. Both Chinese and Spanish sources state that the trade of prestigious goods reached its peak in the 15th and 16th centuries. Naturally, this boom in trade and inter-maritime policy coincided with the growth and development of the various significant Philippine principalities that were positioned and organized along the trade routes, allowing them to reap the maximum benefits from trade activities. For these principalities to remain competitive in the trade boom during this era, they were required to significantly increase the complexity of their societies, tax collection systems, and warfare strategies. Evidence suggests that certain principalities grew tenfold in the thousand years from the 6th century to Spanish occupation in 1565.

Within the Philippines, whether these goods were acquired via trade or produced locally by attached specialists or by those who had learned specific trades, the accrual of high-value items became the pre-colonial local currency. Prestigious goods were necessary for political control and power in the millennium before the Spanish arrived, and they were often used as items of patronage to gain allegiances. This prestigious goods economy became one of the most significant catalysts in Filipino political, cultural, and social development. Not only was there an intra-archipelagic race to dominate long-distance trade routes, but the local Filipinos were also significantly persuaded to craft and garner their own resources and handiwork for international trade, such as forest items like hardwoods or metal tools and weaponry. Included within the complexities of increasingly stratified Filipino societies was the control of agricultural livelihoods through restricted land tenure, as well as extracting surplus agricultural product through tributes (taxes). The Philippine chieftaincies also controlled the metal-producing sectors, such as gold artisans, by sponsoring their work.

Evidence of this thousand-year-long rise in materialism was found in images of the elites adorned in ornaments, with the common usage of these valuable items being for high-profile burials, and records of objects of wealth being used in the households of the hereditary elite through archaeological findings. Foreign luxury goods became the currency for political authority, and these powerful status symbols could buy loyalties, labor, and protection to further increase the power of the chieftaincies and nobility. Within principalities, nodes of wealth and poverty developed, along with divisions in income and living standards. Historians have uncovered significant evidence of ancient income inequality amongst the Filipinos within the densely populated principalities. The locations of the most expansive and oligarchical communities were those at Jolo (Sulu), Maynila, Cebu, and Cotabato (adjacent to Davao, Mindanao).

Some excavated sites of the Philippine archipelago date back to at least four thousand years before Spanish occupation (or 2500 BCE), during the peak of Austronesian settlement within maritime Southeast Asia. The Philippines' primary agricultural product that was introduced, along with the Austronesian peoples, was rice. However, important crops have also been abacá (banana hemp), along with other natural, indigenous produce that was mostly traded from highland, plain, or forested regions, such as rattan, beeswax, honey, tree resins, and spices. Products that came from coastal regions were largely manufactured and included pottery, textiles, and metal tools, as well as natural products such as fish, seafood, and salt.

These items were part of the internal island trade as well as offshore barter.

Archaeological evidence confirms that early Philippine societies, particularly at sites of high coastal and estuarine trade activity, showed evidence of high cultural diversity and social stratification. One confirmation that this complexity increased in the 15th and 16th centuries are the discoveries of porcelains from trade with the Chinese Ming dynasty (as opposed to less evidence of porcelains from the earlier Chinese Song, Yuan, and early Ming dynasties of the 10th to 14th centuries). It seems that the Filipino appetite for luxury items at this time was insatiable, as one historian (Dr. Robert Fox) suggests that Chinese vessels arrived at Filipino ports "laden with large quantities of cheaply manufactured, homogenous, and aesthetically inferior wares from specific kilns." It appears that the Chinese were engaging in the mass manufacture of porcelains to keep abreast of Filipino demand! However, the Filipinos were not only sourcing their porcelains from China (which constituted an estimated 20 to 40 percent of the total trade wares at many ports and 15 percent of archaeological ceramic remains) but also from Thailand and northern Vietnam.

The Philippine trade with China was reciprocal, and most likely, the trade missions sent out from the Philippines were aimed mostly at procuring favoritism with tradespeople associated with the royal courts of China. The well-known and highly coveted Spice Islands of maritime Southeast Asia (the Moluccas or the Maluku Islands, including the Banda Islands) lie approximately 1,300 to 1,500 kilometers (807 to 932 miles) south of the Philippines' southern Sulu Archipelago. A direct route from China to the Spice Islands naturally passed along the western perimeter of the Philippine archipelago—western Luzon, northern Mindoro, western Mindanao, and the Sulu Archipelago. During the period that China was most active as a global maritime power, during the late 14th to the early 15th centuries, China received a flurry of trade envoys from the Philippines bearing gifts, according to ancient Chinese court records. These trade missions were primarily from the principalities located along the western coasts of the archipelago that had direct and regular contact with the Chinese on their way to the Spice Islands. The court visits (and gift-giving) from all Southeast Asian nations to China were assumed by historians to be competitive strategies to gain favor with the Chinese and thereby entice them into further and more frequent trade. The Philippine polities would set out on separate missions, taking retinues of hundreds of people, including noblemen and slaves, and bearing gifts such as pearls, spices, and metal ores.

One example of this practice of foreign economic policy took place in 1373. The Chinese Ming dynasty (1368-1644) court records identify a mission from Luzon and the polity of "Ma-li-lu." This initial record was followed three years later by a joint mission from Luzon (presumably Manila), Pangasinan (western Luzon), and a mysterious polity known as "Soli" (most likely from southern Luzon). The Luzon polity was considered important enough to warrant a reciprocal visit by an ambassador to the Yongle Emperor (r. 1402-1424) in 1405. This ambassadorial visit prompted an incursion of Philippine principality trade visits to China in the early 15th century, and the Filipinos were determined to win the favor, attention, and goods from the powerful Chinese dynasties of the time! Before the 14th- and 15th-century visits, the Philippine principalities that were known to have visited China were a series of early envoys from "P'u-tuan" (most likely Butuan along the northern Mindanao coast) during the Song dynasty (960-1278) and "Ma-i" (probably northern coast of Mindoro) in the Yuan period (1279-1368 CE).

Imported trade goods were accessible to all echelons of Philippine society if they could afford them, and the goods were moved inland up riverways, as well as to higher settlements. By the 15th and 16th centuries, the Filipinos were producing their own thin, fine-textured, red-slipped (fired and polished) earthenware, as well as coarse redware with stamped, impressed appliqué, and incised decorations. The trade boom in the century or so before the arrival and settlement of the Europeans was not only limited to international trade, as intra-island trade within the archipelago also increased substantially. Also, trade within the islands themselves needed to increase in response to growing demand in the coastal principalities. The Chinese required many Filipino forest products, such as tropical hardwoods (for example, mahogany, molave, kamagong, birch, and others), spices (like cinnamon and abacá, a banana harvested for its fiber known as Manila hemp), and metal ores (such as copper, gold, and iron). Coastal Filipino chiefs required these products to trade with foreigners, and they needed to grow internal trading systems to secure inland commodities. Historical records suggest that internal island trade had continued informally for a long time and that a symbiotic relationship existed between the larger chiefdoms of the coastal principalities and the more scattered tribes of the forests and highlands. It is possible that coastal chieftaincies put military pressure on upland tribes to provide items for trade, but there is also evidence that coastal principalities also used other less violent methods of gaining inland commodities, such as creating major trading nodes closer to the sources of inland trade routes and increasing the production of their own products with which to barter.

The degree of internal trade-related transgressions between the islands of the Philippines and, indeed, within the islands themselves cannot be quantified except that, as early as the 13th century, Chinese records warn of

Filipino raids, reminiscent of pirating, through the central archipelago. These intercoastal raids were mostly an attempt by the Philippine people to destabilize neighboring islands of the archipelago and capture booty from trading ports, but naturally, foreign trading missions would also have been vulnerable to the skirmishes. (There are ancient Chinese records by the historian Zhao Rukuo, 1170-1231, of the Song dynasty that might suggest the Filipino raids reached as far as Chinese coastal shores.) By the 1500s, the Spanish reported the presence of sophisticated weaponry such as Chinese-styled (but locally manufactured) iron cannons at principal Philippine ports, as well as fortifications. Interlopers of the Philippines over the centuries were also aware of the highly specialized warrior class of Filipino society. China's interest in the Spice Islands south of the Philippines is mentioned in classical herbal anecdotal Chinese literature and refers to the use of spices, such as cloves, from as early as the 3rd century BCE. (Courtiers would chew clove pods to keep their breath sweet when conversing with the Chinese emperors.) Thus, the Chinese interest in Southeast Asian goods kept them returning for millennia to the archipelagos, despite the potential challenges and threats.

Chapter 4 – Pre-colonial Independent Principalities and Sultanates (900–1565 CE)

The Indianized kingdom with which the Philippines traded, specifically within the Barangic Phase, was the Majapahit of Java. Legends also tell that the archipelago traded with the Srivijaya Empire. Although no factual evidence can support this, most indigenous legends tell of the significant migration of Srivijayans who relocated to the Philippines for various reasons—particularly to the middle Philippines or the Visayas. The Srivijaya Empire became the first dominant thalassocracy (seafaring empire) that coincided with the decline of Austronesian movements throughout maritime Southeast Asia, from approximately the 7th to the 12th century. Srivijaya was primarily responsible for the spread of Buddhism throughout its area of dominance. It was based in Sumatra, and it spread out to include parts of Java to the south, the Malay Peninsula to the north, and mainland Southeast Asia.

The Indianized Hindu Majapahit Empire of Java was an Indianized thalassocracy that existed from around 1293 to 1527. "Indianized" refers to the empire's development through considerable and ongoing direct exchanges and cultural blending with India. Architecture, religion, literature, art, ideologies, foods, and goods from the Indian subcontinent had a significant and lasting impact on certain regions of Southeast Asia before the advent of colonialism. The golden age of Majapahit was from 1350 to 1389, while it was under the rulership of Hayam Wuruk (r. 1350-1389), when Majapahit dominated trade in maritime Southeast Asia, including the Philippines. The Majapahit Empire was considered one of the most expansive and greatest thalassocracies of the era and the last major Hindu empire of the Malay Archipelago.

There are suggestions in legends that parts of the Philippines were under Majapahit rulership during the 14th century (specifically during Hayam Wuruk's time), but this cannot be confirmed. These legends are drawn mostly from the poem *Nagarakretagama*, also known as *Desawarnana*, an ancient Javanese eulogy to Hayam Wuruk written in 1365 by a Buddhist monk. This legend tells that Majapahit held the territories of Luzon (at Manila or Saludong) and Sulu (or Solot). The legends state that Majapahit was unable to dominate the Visayas because it was a stronghold of Srivijaya. A battle in Manila in 1365 was said to have liberated the northern Philippines from the Majapahit Empire, so it was possible that at certain times, the Philippines may have been under both Srivijaya and Majapahit control. Mostly, there is considerable evidence of trade between Majapahit and the Philippines, as well as between the coastal regions of Vietnam and China. For example, a gold pendant found in the Tabon Caves of Palawan includes an image of a

Garuda bird—the Hindu eagle that represents Vishnu. Many more examples of Hindu imagery and ornaments were found in the Tabon Caves, as well as artifacts linking Palawan with both India and China during the Song and Yuan dynasties.

The Indianization of parts of maritime Southeast Asia occurred due to successions of powerful dynasties that ruled subcontinental India during the first millennium of the Common Era, such as the Pallava dynasty (3rd century to 9th century CE of southern India) and the Gupta Empire (3rd century to 6th century CE that ruled most of India). A multitude of influential Indian kingdoms spread Hinduism and then Buddhism throughout Southeast Asia, but there is little evidence to suggest that the Philippines had much direct contact with subcontinental India; rather, this influence came indirectly through the Indianized Kingdom of Nusantara. The earliest material evidence of Indianized influences in the Philippines is a copperplate inscription (known as the Laguna Copperplate Inscription) that dates from 900 CE. This inscription is also the oldest surviving written historical record discovered in the archipelago. The plate is written in the Kawi script, which was a common written language in archipelagic Southeast Asia from the 8th to 16th centuries CE. Kawi is a derivation of an Indian script and was the method that best communicated ancient Sanskrit as well as Old Javanese. The Kawi script is the ancestral root of modern Javanese, Balinese, and Filipino writing. The copperplate was discovered in Laguna (southeast of Laguna Lake below Manila) and mentions surrounding principalities and kingdoms such as Tondo (Luzon) and Medang (the Hindu-Buddhist Mataram Kingdom of Java, c. 752-1006). The plate clears the name of a man, as well as his descendants, who owed a debt to the ruler of Tondo. The Laguna Copperplate provides evidence of early Filipino knowledge of weighing and measuring, mathematics, and astronomy.

Another old script of the Philippines is Baybayin, which was evident in several historic findings before the advent of the Latin-based Hispanic script of the colonial era. An ivory seal from Butuan dating from the first half of the second millennium of the Common Era is written in both Kawi and Baybayin. Also, a pot from Calatagan (southwestern peninsula of Luzon) dated to the early 1500s is inscribed with Baybayin.

The most important regional power within Nusantara for the ancient Filipinos was Brunei, a small sovereign sultanate in northern Borneo. It was one of the first regions in the area to become Muslim (probably in the late 1300s to early 1400s) and was known to the Filipinos as *Burnay*, *Brunyu*, or *Po-ni*. The Sultanate of Brunei was critical for maritime trade in the Philippine archipelago since it linked the Hindu-Buddhist kingdoms of western Southeast Asia with the eastern states of China, Japan, and Taiwan. The sultanate had particularly strong relationships with the southern Islamic islands of the Philippines, specifically the Moro people of Mindanao and Sulu. Sulu, in particular, as well as parts of Palawan, may have been under Brunei's suzerainty for centuries, and at one point, Brunei ceded a large portion of northeastern Borneo—a region known as Sabah—to Sulu.

Under the rulership of Sultan Bolkiah (r. 1485-1528), Sulu is believed to have been annexed to Brunei, and it is possible Manila was as well. Whether Brunei ever held political and military sway over the Philippines is debatable, but the various prominent principalities of the Philippines (particularly the Islamized ones) maintained close trade relationships with Brunei, often through intermarriages that ensured royal successions and definitive lineages. Brunei was small, powerful in traded wealth, strategically positioned, and well administered. Its people were generally peaceful, and the social structure was organized. However, Brunei's establishment as a capable, independent state, as well as its alliances with

Philippine principalities, arose only after 1400 and with the advent of Islam. Before this time, Brunei had been noted as a poor and vulnerable principality under the suzerainty of the Hindu-Buddhist Majapahit Empire. Thereafter, the sultanate reached the peak of its power from the 15th to the 17th centuries, mostly through maritime trade.

In the centuries of the Common Era leading up to the colonial period, there was no unifying force amongst the various powerful principalities or the scattered rural tribes of the Philippines. In the millennium and a half of the Common Era before Spanish arrival, there were too many settlements, clans, ethnicities, and principalities to name, although they were numerous, ever-changing, and represented the multicultural landscape of the archipelago. There were highland societies, such as the Ifugao and Mangyan. The Ifugao highland tribe resided in the landlocked Cordillera Administrative Region of Luzon—the central area of the northern main island. The area is famous for its rice terraces, including the Cordillera and Banaue Rice Terraces. The Banaue Rice Terraces are referred to as "the eighth wonder of the world," as they represent millennia-old traditions whereby indigenous peoples have mastered the delicate balance between natural beauty and human bounty. The rice terraces are one of the main living cultural monuments of ancient Filipino people and were declared as a UNESCO World Heritage Site in 1995.

The historic terraces cover a vast expanse of land but are technically only five groupings that lie across four modern municipalities. The rice fields are the work of the Ifugao tribe and date back to before the Common Era. They are maintained and utilized to this day through a dedicated and sustainable communal effort. In 2008 and 2015, the Ifugao Hudhud chanting and the ritual tugging game (like tug-of-war) of *punnuk* were included in the UNESCO Intangible Cultural Heritage Lists. The Hudhud include narrative tales for important occasions, and the chanting can continue for three to four days, particularly during the rice-harvesting season. The Ifugao, meaning "people from the hill," is a matrilineal society led primarily by women and was a plutocracy of principal families in ancient times. The Ifugao was one of the most sophisticated and peaceful polities of its time, possibly due to a communal method of rulership, including the democratic method of a council of elders. Ifugao's prosperity and position, safely tucked in the highlands of Luzon, has ensured the survival of its culture and society into the modern day.

Rice Terraces of the Philippine Cordilleras showing human settlements between the cultivated hills and natural mountains.
Seventide, CC BY-SA 4.0 <https://creativecommons.org/licenses/by-sa/4.0>, via Wikimedia Commons
https://commons.wikimedia.org/wiki/File:Batad_Rice_Terraces,_Ifugao_Province,_Philippines.jpg

The Mangyan people were (and still are) residents of the island of Mindoro, southwest of Luzon, and they have a number of sub-tribes according to geographical settlement. They originally dwelled in the coastal regions, but many moved inland to avoid influxes of other Filipinos, such as Tagalogs and Moros, and later to avoid the Spanish. The Mangyans' ways have not changed much through the centuries, and they lived in the remote areas of Mindoro, relying on hunting and agriculture but occasionally coming to the coast to trade their forest products for consumer goods. There is an abundance of evidence that shows they had extensive trade with the Chinese, and the Mangyan who remained on the coast were eventually Christianized by the Spanish. Historians have concluded that the Mangyan people arrived at different times from different places to populate Mindoro, and their ethnicities (including physical features) and languages differ to a noticeable extent.

Like the Ifugao, the Mangyan societies were peaceful and avoided trouble. Their tribes were highly skilled in basket-weaving and handicrafts. The Mangyan have a form of poetry called ambahan. This poetry predates Spanish intervention and was written on bamboo cylinders in an ancient local script of Indian Brahminic origins from before the Common Era. Ambahan is traditionally sung as a chant and concerns emotional aspects of life as a form of communication. An example of ambahan can be found below:

You girl, I would like to love, if you wish to close the door while I am staying outside, let it be closed from the floor, reaching to the heavens wide!

The Kingdom of Maynila (essentially metropolitan Luzon around the Bay of Manila and the Pasig River) was the largest and most influential territory of the Philippines. However, there was a multitude of Philippine territories mentioned in historical records that competed for the same maritime trading waters and beneficial alliances with foreigners. The Taytay of northeastern Palawan were well known abroad (the southern sections of Palawan were under Sulu control). The Taytay became most famous when their king and queen were taken for ransom by the first Spanish conquistadors in 1521 after their leader, Ferdinand Magellan, was slaughtered on the island of Mactan, which is a part of Cebu. The crew demanded resupplies for their escape to the Portuguese-occupied Moluccas and safety. The Taytay provided more than was demanded by the Spanish, and it seems they parted on good terms!

The beautiful island of Coron at the northern extremities of the Palawan island chain was known to the locals as Calis and is now protected by law for its unique geological features and supreme snorkeling and scuba diving areas. In 1998, the Tagbanwa tribe of Coron Island was awarded a Certificate of Ancestral Domain Title (CADT). This area covers more than 220 kilometers squared (85 square miles) of land and sea under their jurisdiction and protection.

The Tagbanwa, who were also present in central Palawan, were historically considered fearsome and wild. A Spanish chronicler named Antonio Pigafetta, who was part of the Magellan expedition, recorded that this tribe practiced blood compacts in which they slit their wrists and poured the blood into a vessel, which, when mixed with other liquid, was then drunk by both parties. They are also believed to be descended from some of the oldest inhabitants of the Philippines and possibly directly descended from the Tabon Man. The Tagbanwa had an early and strong relationship with the Sultanate of Brunei.

A view of some of Coron Island, Palawan, showing the shallow coralline waters ideal for snorkeling and scuba diving. The ancestral tribe of the island, the Tagbanwa, made blood pacts and hunted with blowpipes, and they were considered dangerous and wild by the first European explorers.
Ray in Manila, CC BY 2.0 <https://creativecommons.org/licenses/by/2.0>, via Wikimedia Commons https://commons.wikimedia.org/wiki/File:Coron_Island,_Palawan,_Philippines_1.jpg

Tondo was a fortified banyan (principality) centered around Manila Bay, and it was heavily involved with Chinese, Japanese, Malaysian, and other Asian trade. The Tagalog Kingdom of Tondo operated under a paramount ruler known as a Lakan, and at the height of Philippine power (the 15th- and 16th-century trade booms), it shared a monopoly on trade with the Rajahnate of Maynila during the period of the Chinese Ming dynasty. This trade relationship with China was significant enough that a governor named Ko Ch'a-lao (under the resident Chinese Yongle Emperor) was appointed to oversee it. The trade connection was so important to China that even during their national ban on maritime trade during the Ming dynasty, trade with the Philippines continued, mostly under the guise of a tribute (gift-giving) system or through lesser-known ports. (The complicated and multi-tiered Chinese Ming dynasty experienced rises and falls in its oceanic forays, but the emperors limited maritime trade when they wanted to increase control of the governance of the mainland empire. These limitations were known as the *Haijin* or sea ban laws. The *Haijin* was highly ineffective and not enforced.)

The Tondo, as the ruling ethnicity of this principality, belonged to the caste known as Maharlika, the feudal warrior class. They ruled most of Luzon from at least the 900s CE to the advent of colonialism, and the Spaniards referred to them as Hidalgos. Although the primary religion amongst the Tondo was Hindu-Buddhism and adherence to Rajadharma (which included Indianized beliefs, codes of conduct, and court practices based on Hindu-Buddhism), they were essentially an indigenous Philippine society and similar to the Kapampangan people of Central Luzon. Although the predominant religions of Tondo were Hinduism and Buddhism, which had been introduced over the centuries by the Indianized kingdoms, ancient animism (natural and indigenous belief systems) of the archipelago was still practiced, particularly in remote areas. The people of Tondo were good agriculturalists, which included aquaculture.

Tondo and the Kingdom of Maynila were the most significant bayans when the Spanish arrived in the 16th century. The Kingdom of Tondo traded significantly with China and Japan, and Japanese tea merchants established offices on Luzon in the 16th century. One particularly enthusiastic Japanese merchant even changed his surname from Naya to Luzon, becoming Luzon Sukezaemon. The Chinese were known to keep extremely tight controls on their trade routes, and the Filipinos involved in Chinese trade almost came under their suzerainty whilst engaged in these exchanges. Although the Philippine principalities traded freely with Japan, Chinese-Japanese trade was limited by the Chinese themselves as part of their controlling measures. (The Japanese often retaliated with frequent acts of piracy to acquire Chinese goods!)

While Tondo was considered the area north of the Pasig River Delta, which empties into both oceanic Manila Bay and the inland Laguna de Bay, joining the two, as well as most of the greater surrounding regions of Luzon, both north and south, the Kingdom of Maynila was the urban node south of the Pasig. Maynila, being more concentrated and centered entirely on the coastal bay area, was mostly influenced over the centuries by external forces, specifically in terms of trade and religious and cultural impacts. Islam was the predominant religion introduced to the Kingdom of Maynila via the Sultanate of Brunei in the 13th century. It is possible that Islam was introduced by force when a certain Rajah Ahmad attacked Maynila, but it is also possible that the transfer of Islam to Maynila was a natural result of its close trade and kinship affiliations with Brunei.

It was perhaps Maynila's adoption of the Muslim faith that maintained its position as a very strong trading partner with Brunei and, along with its proximity to Tondo and its strategic position on the coast, ensured its establishment as part of the Philippine trade oligarch. Maynila retained a strategic relationship with Brunei through intermarriages of the ruling classes. Although there is no hard evidence that the Sultanate of Brunei was ever politically an overruling power of Maynila, Bruneian legends tell of an important marriage in 1500 during the reign of Sultan Bolkiah of Brunei that united the two kingdoms more permanently. Other sources claim Brunei "attacked" Maynila and established a satellite state named Seludong, which later was renamed Maynila. Majapahit legends also refer to an area called Saludong or Selurong and Solot (or Sulu) that were under the rulership of Majapahit in the 14th century, and Chinese sources state that later in the century, Brunei was attacked by Sulu pirates. Malay apocryphal sources also refer to the area known as Seludong, and it is apparent that the name "Maynila" only became significant after the colonial occupation of the Philippines. (Bruneian traditions state that Seludong was under the direct rulership of the rajahs of Maynila—or the House of Sulayman—from 1500 onward, although the local leaders of Tondo, the Lakandula, were permitted to keep their titles and lands.)

In truth, until the advent of the colonial era, complete dominance of the archipelagic islands and principalities was unrealistic due to distance and the logistical problems of oceanic approaches. Even the large Indianized thalassocracies were unable to put real and lasting governance structures into place but were influential because of their accumulated wealth through trade and the extent of their maritime fleets.

The combined areas (or even the individual bayans) of Tondo and Maynila were often referred to abroad, particularly in China and Japan, as simply Luzon. Over time, they included the influx of ethnicities with whom they traded, and intermarriages and immigrant settlements arose to alter the genetic and cultural landscape of the Philippines.

The principality of Pangasinan was located along the Lingayen Gulf, north of Manila, and halfway up the western coast of Luzon. This independent region was referred to as Caboloan or Kaboloan and was centered around the fertile Agno River Delta that empties into the Lingayen Gulf. The capital of Caboloan was Binalatongan, which is now modern-day San Carlos. Like the other principalities of the Philippines, this bayan flourished in the 15th and 16th centuries and sent emissaries to China in the early 15th century, as well as traded with Japan and other Asian states. The Pangasinan kingdom was referred to as a "Wangdom" after the Chinese word for king (*wang*). The Chinese also referred to the kingdom as "Feng-chia-hsi-lan," and it expanded significantly into the surrounding territories as an independent principality in the same period that the powerful Indianized thalassocracies of Srivijaya and Majapahit were active in the archipelago. From the time of Spanish conquest in the late 16th century, the colonizers referred to the area as the "Port of Japan," as the population wore an abundance of Chinese and Japanese clothing, both cotton and silk. The Caboloan people adopted many cultural traits of the Chinese and Japanese, and they used their traded goods, such as porcelains, extensively in their daily lives. The polity, in turn, traded Chinese and Japanese goods with other Southeast Asian states, as well as gold, slaves, animal skins, and other local products.

Ma-i was a principality first mentioned in the 10th-century Chinese Song dynasty documents (*Zhu Fan Zhi*, written by the Song Dynasty historian Zhao Rukuo). Ma-i was also mentioned in the 10th-century records of the Sultanate of Brunei. The Chinese regularly traded with Ma-i and noted that its citizens were "honest and trustworthy." Some gold artifacts known as Piloncitos or Bulawan may have been punch-marked with the symbol of Ma-i. These small, rounded gold nuggets were considered the first official currency of the Philippines, as all trade conducted prior to the appearance of Piloncitos was through barter. Overall, gold rings and gold, in general, were historically the currency of the archipelago prior to colonial intervention. The Spanish named the golden beads Piloncitos, meaning "little weights," and it was unlikely that they would have been manufactured before the 1300s.

The Sultanate of Sulu dominated the Sulu Archipelago, as well as parts of Palawan, Mindanao, and northeastern Borneo (Sabah) during the height of its power. This Muslim sultanate was founded sometime between the late 14th and mid-15th centuries, although it was settled as a principality before being ratified as an Islamic state. Local people, known as the Tausūg (Suluk, Jolo Moros, Sulu Moros, Sulus, or *Taw Sug*), were evident on the Sulu archipelagic islands from at least the 11th century. The Tausūg were mostly centered around Sulu's second-biggest island of Jolo in the central archipelago, with the largest island being Basilan, closest to Zamboanga. Tausūg means "people of the sea current," and besides the Sulu Archipelago, this ethnic group can also be found on the Zamboanga Peninsula of southwestern Mindanao, as well as farther inward of Mindanao, Sabah, Palawan Island, and even Malaysia. The Tausūg are believed to have migrated to Sulu from Mindanao during times of intensive Chinese maritime trade, specifically in the Song dynasty and the Yuan dynasty. Sulu was mentioned in Yuan court records, including accounts of tributary trade missions from that area.

By the end of the 1200s, the Tausūg was considered an elite commercial society and had gained power through trade. The exact timing of Islamic intervention is uncertain but is most likely to be the 13th century when Arab merchants began using Sulu (via the Sultanate of Brunei) as a direct trade link to China. Proselytizing began from various sources, including Muslim Chinese and Sufi (Islam mystic) missionaries from Arabia and Iraq. The Sufis arrived via the Malay Peninsula and

Sumatra. Specific individuals are mentioned in more recent annals that describe the exact process of Islamization of Sulu, but it is far more likely that it was a centuries-long process that developed through the influx and influence of Muslims to the archipelago and through marriages with the Sultanate of Brunei. Malaysian Muslim religious scholar Sharif ul-Hashim was said to have arrived in the 1450s when the establishment of the Sultanate of Sulu began in earnest. He was apparently a Malaysian from Johore on the southern end of the Malay Peninsula. In 1457, he married a local Sulu princess, the daughter of Rajah Baginda, the latter of whom had arrived from Sumatra as a proselytizing Muslim, and Sharif ul-Hashim officially founded the Sultanate of Sulu. He renamed himself "master" or "paduka," with his full title being Paduka Mahasari Maulana al Sultan Sharif ul-Hashem. (As a side note, the dates for the founding of Sulu as an Islamic kingdom range from the late 14th century to the mid-1400s—there is no consistency in the historical records.)

The Sultanate of Sulu reached the height of its power in the 18th and early 19th centuries when its influence through the southern Philippines, Mindanao, and Sabah was at its greatest. There was high demand for the Sulu sea slugs that were a popular ingredient in Chinese medicines and cuisine. Pearls, shark fins, rattan, birds' nests, camphor (from cinnamon trees), and mother-of-pearl were also highly demanded commodities. Sulu was an epicenter of trade and piracy, particularly in regards to the sale of slaves from the island of Jolo, most of whom were taken in the Christianized areas of the Philippines—those most under the influence of the Catholic Spanish. The Spanish conquest of the Philippines in the mid-16th century left Sulu in a continual state of warfare with the colonizers and the Moros, who refused to submit. The city of Jolo was first attacked by the Spanish in 1578, but it was only by 1876 that the Spanish managed to establish a permanent garrison on the island! Spain instead proceeded with a series of agreements concerning trade and territorial negotiations with Sulu. Unfortunately, good diplomatic relations between Sulu and the French and British in the first half of the 1800s encouraged Spain to exert sovereignty over Sulu to protect its waters. After an initial pact of friendship in 1851, by 1878, Spain had asserted its dominance and practically had Sulu as its protectorate.

Sometime between the mid-17th century and the early 18th century, Sulu gained northern Borneo from the Sultanate of Brunei through a peaceful alliance that had seen Sulu quell an uprising against the sultan of Brunei. At the same time, Sulu ceded the island of Palawan to the sultan of Maguindanao (a sultanate in Mindanao), who had married a Sulu princess. However, Palawan came under Spanish suzerainty shortly afterward. The Muslim thalassocracy of Sulu finally gave up its independence in 1915. From interactions with the Portuguese to the Spanish, Dutch, French, German, and English, the Sultanate of Sulu was officially dissolved in 1915 through the United States' Carpenter Agreement, which aimed to abolish slavery, confiscate firearms, and curtail piracy and feuding. The reigning sultan, Jamalul Kiram II, relinquished secular power but retained religious dominance. However, in 1962 (under Philippine President Diosdado Macapagal) and then again in 1974 (under Philippine President Ferdinand Marcos), along with Philippine independence, the sovereignty of the Sultanate of Sulu was once again recognized. Sultan Mohammed Mahakuttah Kiram (r. 1974-1986) was the last official sultan of Sulu.

Another principal kingdom of the pre-colonial Philippines was Madja-as. A considerable mystique surrounds the legendary kingdom of Madja-as, which was centered in the Visayas (central Philippines) around the island of Panay. Believed to have been established by high-ranking members of the disintegrating Indianized Srivijaya Empire, legends tell that they purchased and renamed the island of Panay after the destroyed Srivijayan state of Pannai on Sumatra. Although Sumatra had been the epicenter of the primarily Buddhist Srivijaya for almost eight hundred years, its strategic location, which dominated the Strait of Malacca—the critical channel of entry into maritime Southeast Asia—had always been challenged by other powerful kingdoms and states. Srivijaya's demise in the 13th century was mostly due to the expansion of the Hindu thalassocrat empires of Java (such as Majapahit and Singhasari, the latter being a 13th-century eastern Java empire. Although Srivijaya was located in Sumatra, this extensive thalassocracy extended and influenced much of maritime Southeast Asia during its time. The datus that escaped the collapsing empire came from Borneo and were apparently escaping the Muslim rajah of Brunei, Makatunao. Legends tell that nine high officials and their families and households were escorted out of Brunei by the rajah's chief minister, Datu Puti. These predecessors of Madja-as sailed their balangays to the Visayas, and after landing on the island now called Panay, they purchased the land from Negrito Chief Marikudo. (Some sources dispute that the people of Panay were Negrito, believing they were possibly of the Austronesian Agta tribe.)

Legends suggest that initial negotiations for the island included a large tract of land (most likely on the southeastern coast) that was bartered for peacefully between the two tribes, who remained on good terms and integrated over time to become one kingdom. The first datu of the Madja-as was Sumakwel, and eventually, the growing community split into separate groups that now form the most populated settlements of Panay—Iloilo (southern coast), Capiz (northeast), and Antique (western coast). The people of Madja-as made their capital in the north near present-day Kalibo, and the kingdom began to grow to include many other islands of the Visayas. Madja-as reached its zenith in the 15th century during the leadership of Datu Padojinog, becoming a considerable, although warlike and pirating, power. It threatened the centers of Tondo and Maynila, other rajahnates and sultanates of the Philippines, and even China. Like much of the Philippines before the colonial era, the religious beliefs of this kingdom were a mixture of Buddhism, Hinduism, and animism that included indigenous cultural folklore.

Other minor kingdoms in the Visayas included Dapitan (or the Bool Kingdom) on Bohol Island and the Rajahnate of Cebu. The Kedatuan ("the realm of Datu") of Dapitan developed around the Tagbilaran Strait—southwest Bohol across from the small island of Panglao. The original inhabitants of Bohol are believed to have arrived on the Anda Peninsula in southeastern Bohol. Ancient Anda petroglyphs and petrographs were included in the **UNESCO World Heritage Site** tentative list in 2006, along with the Singnapan Caves' charcoal petrographs of southern Palawan, the Angono Petroglyphs of southern Luzon, the Alab Petroglyphs of Mountain Province (north-central Luzon), and the charcoal-drawn Penablanca Petrographs of Cagayan (northeastern Luzon). The new migrants to the Anda Peninsula created the red hematite petrographs that have remained a sacred site for ethnic communities.

However, Dapitan was settled by migrants from Mindanao, who developed separately from those on the other side of Bohol. All the peoples of Bohol Island were constantly under threat from the Sultanate of Ternate (of the Moluccas or Spice Islands to the south), and by 1563, it was aligned with the Portuguese. After a significant battle, the people of Kedatuan fled to the northern coast of the Zamboanga Peninsula of Mindanao, where they usurped the resident Sultanate of Lanao and integrated with the people.

The Spanish Jesuit missionary and historian Francisco Ignacio de Alcina (1610-1674) spent thirty-seven years in the Philippines, mostly in the Visayas, where he referred to the locals as "my beloved Bisayans." There was a principality in the Visayas that he called the "Venice of the Visayas," and this is thought to be Dapitan. Alcina documented Visayan literature and poetry and eventually died in Manila.

The ancient Cebu (or Sugbu) kingdom was an Indianized polity on the island of Cebu. The kingdom was officially established by Sri Rajamuda Lumaya, better known as Sri Lumay, who was a minor prince of the Chola dynasty. The Cholas were an Indian thalassocracy that occupied Malaysia and Sumatra and existed from at least the 3rd century BCE until the 13th century CE. They were the most dominant and longest lasting subcontinental Indian maritime empire of the era. Sri Lumay was dispatched by the Indian Hindu maharajah of Chola to establish bases for expeditionary forces, but he disobeyed his instructions and established his own independent node on Cebu instead!

Sri Lumay is believed to have founded his empire in the 1400s, and he focused his attention on defending his dominion against slave traders from Mindanao and Moro Muslim raiders (*Magalos* or "destroyers of peace"). His application of scorched-earth tactics (burning things to the ground and destroying everything) granted him the name of Kang Sri Lumayng Sugbu ("Sri Lumay's great fire"), which was shortened to Sugbu. Sri Lumay had several sons who continued his legacy, and their island domain became known as *Pulua Kang Dayang* or *Kangdaya* ("the islands which belong to Daya").

As with all other coastal principalities of the pre-colonial Philippines, Cebu became an important trading zone. Cebu was known for its harbors that colloquially became known as "the place for trading" or *sinibuayng hingpit*, which was then shortened to *sibu* or *sibo*, "to trade" (which obviously became the later Castilian *Cebú*). Cebu traded with mainland Asia, Japan, and India, amongst others. The ports of the island were alive with barter in agricultural products, ivory, perfumes, glass products, leather, and precious and semi-precious stones.

Sri Lumay's grandson, Sri Humabon (or Sri Hamabar), was rajah when he granted or perhaps was forced to cede parts of the Cebu dominion to a mysterious character from Borneo known as Lapu-Lapu. Lapu-Lapu was specifically given the small island of Mactan just off the coast of Cebu (it is so close that in contemporary times, these islands are joined by aerial highways). Mactan is sixty-five thousand square kilometers (or twenty-five square miles) in size. In Rajah Humabon's time, Mactan was known as Opong, and Lapu-Lapu was also granted a section of the coastal Cebu port known as Mandawili (now Mandaue). Whoever Lapu-Lapu really was (or if he even existed, for some historians suggest he did not), he must have been of considerable importance to gain prime trading areas directly from the rajah of Cebu. Opong (Mactan) was the site of a pivotal battle with the first Spaniards to reach the Philippines in 1521, and Lapu-Lapu has been immortalized through statues in tribute to his honor as a key figure in repelling the Europeans.

The Rajahnate of Cebu was said to be on good terms with the rajahs of Butuan (on Mindanao), and apparently, they were linked by blood relations. Certain evidence suggests that the bayan of Maynila held those from Cebu (the Cebuanos) in low regard and ridiculed Visayans in general because they were easily conquerable (and perhaps posed some kind of competitive hereditary threat since the ruling classes all seemed to originate from Brunei). In general, all recorded history (mostly via Chinese chronicles and colonial reports) indicates that regardless of the religion or culture of the various archipelagic principalities and settlements, they continually experienced intra-regional peace as well as rivalry, including violence and destruction. Piracy and raiding were common during the pre-colonial era of extensive Asian maritime trade, and the various principalities maneuvered against one another for economic and political dominance. It was perhaps this archipelagic incoherency in mutual agendas and lack of permanent alliances that made the Philippines easier for the Spanish to conquer half a century after the Battle of Mactan in 1521.

The Sultanate of Butuan was located in the north of the island of Mindanao at the current location of the city of the same name. Like all the other rajahnates of the Philippines, it traded prolifically across Nusantara and even as far as Persia (Iran) to the west. Butuan was best known for its gold and gold products. Prolific evidence of balangays along the Agusan River that runs through Butuan proves that it was a significant trading port. Antonio Pigafetta (c. 1491-1531) was an Italian explorer and scholar who assisted the first Spanish conquistador, Ferdinand Magellan, to the Philippines on his journeys. Pigafetta kept a journal and made the first inroads into translating the Cebuano language. His comments on Rajah Siagu of Butuan and Butuan, in general, from the early 16th century were as follows:

> Pieces of gold, the size of walnuts and eggs are found by sifting the earth in the island of that king who came to our ships. All the dishes of that king are of gold and also some portion of his house as we were told by that king himself...He had a covering of silk on his head, and wore two large golden earrings fastened in his ears...At his side hung a dagger, the haft of which was somewhat long and all of gold, and its scabbard of carved wood. He had three spots of gold on every tooth, and his teeth appeared as if bound with gold.

Apparently, gold was so abundant that people decorated the outside of their homes with it, and the small Butuan kingdom is thought by historians to have been even richer than the mighty Sumatran Srivijayan Empire in gold bullion! Chinese records state that their first tribute visit from the Philippines was in 1001 CE and that it came from Butuan. The people of Butuan, as well as the Visayas in general, practiced the ritual deformation of human skulls known as head binding, as is evidenced in human remains of the region. This practice did not seem to occur in the northern Philippines. Skull molding was believed to enhance beauty, and cranial deformation was enforced by binding the heads of children to distort the normal growth of their heads. The bindings were used to fasten rods to babies' foreheads to broaden the faces, recede the foreheads, and flatten the noses of the growing children. With the advent of colonialism, the standards of beauty began changing more toward a European look, and the practice of skull deformation ceased.

Two further Muslim sultanates of the ancient Philippines that were associated with the Sulus and the other "Moros" of the southern Philippines were Maguindanao and Lanao. Maguindanao was a sultanate on the island of Mindanao, and it ruled in the province of modern-day Maguindanao (in the center of the island) and the city of Davao (southeastern coast). Even before the advent of the first established Islam sultan, Muslim influences had been arriving over the centuries, such as with other regions of the southern Philippines. The island was formerly known as the Great Moluccas (*Gran Moluccas*), and later, the sultanate adopted its name from the "people of the flood-plains," or *maginged*, and "people of the marsh," or *danaw*. This was one of the few inland dwelling principalities of the pre-colonial Philippines, and it relied mainly on the cultivation of rice, fishing, and weaving fine baskets and mats. At its greatest extent, Maguindanao ruled the entire island of Mindanao as well as its smaller satellite islands. The sultans were said to be on good terms with the various trading empires, such as China, as well as with the colonial powers of Britain and Holland (the Dutch). The sultanate's sovereignty ended in the late 19th century when the Spanish governor, General Emilio Terrero y Perinat (in off. 1885-1888), captured the island, which was under the leadership of Datu Uto at the time. In 1888, Uto signed a peace treaty with the Spaniards, as a famine in 1872 and Spanish insurgencies (and repeated failed attempts at Christianization) had weakened his empire.

Maguindanao was most likely officially Islamized in the mid-1500s, and like Sulu, it was purportedly done by a Malay from Johore. He was called Shariff Muhammad Kabungsuwan. Just like the founder of the Sultanate of Sulu, he married a local princess to further legitimize his position. The center of the sultanate remained mostly near modern-day Dulawan and the valley of Cotabato in the protected highlands (southwest-central island). Maguindanao mostly managed to fend off Spanish invasions until Terrero's incursion, and in 1705, Maguindanao gave away the island of Palawan (given to them by Sulu) to the Spanish to keep them in abeyance. The most famous sultan of Maguindanao was Muhammad Dipatuan Kudarat, who ruled from 1619 to 1671. Kudarat fiercely fought off Spanish invaders and prevented the spread of Catholicism. He claimed direct descendancy from Shariff Muhammad Kabungsuwan and attacked his fellow Filipinos in Luzon and the Visayas, punishing them for giving in to the Spanish. However, overall, Kudarat's relationships with the various colonial powers were peaceful enough, and he eventually allowed the Spanish access into select pockets of his kingdom to perform conversions.

The Sultanate of Lanao was also a part of Mindanao, but it was unique in the decentralization of its four constituent kingdoms, the *Pat a*

Pangampong a Ranao, which were further constituted of sixteen royal houses. Lanao was said to have developed at the same time as Maguindanao and under the same Islamic influences. Lanao's territories were approximately north of Maguindanao and included Unayan, Masiu, Bayabao, and Baloi. Lanao managed to sufficiently repel the Spaniards and Christianization until the advent of the Americans in the early 20th century.

The southern Muslim kingdoms of the Philippines were not considered a hegemony, but they were linked through ideologies, behaviors, and sometimes marriage. The Muslim populace, or Moros, of the archipelago had most of the monopoly on the Philippine slave trade and were notorious raiders and pirates of the surrounding islands and waters.

However, like most of the monarchical structures across the Philippines, the sultan was not an all-powerful dominant force but was rather often assisted by other royalty, advisors, and councils in the rulership of his Muslim lands or "Dar-al-Islam." Subjects were able to switch allegiances, and sometimes there were various datus in a sultanate operating with separate agendas and with varying support of the people. Tradition enabled any free man (non-slave) to transfer his support between datus (in the Muslim areas, the governors were also referred to as panglimas). (In terms of sultanate lineage, the Sulu were a slight exception in that they retained the Sulu *Tarsila*, a documented genealogy of sultans. However, the beginnings of this genealogy are unclear.)

In terms of enslaved persons, there were three types: those born into slavery, those owing a debt of slavery, and those captured specifically to become slaves. Slaves were able to own land, choose their occupations, and attain their freedom through services rendered. Payment to the ruling classes could consist of goods or slaves, and the accumulation of slaves increased a person's (usually a datu's) loyalty structure, almost as if the slaves were unpaid subjects or mercenaries acquired to perform a datu's bidding, including following him into war. Eventually, if a datu (or a collection of datus) acquired a significant following of people—both free men and slaves—they would find a way to claim an ancestral right to form a monarchy and elect a sultan. Whether Muslim, Hindu-Buddhist, animistic, or Christian, the Filipino structure of monarchical governance remained flexible throughout history. Their fluid attitude to loyalties applied to relationships with foreign trading powers and colonialists alike, as relentless cycles of diplomacy and war followed one another over the centuries between the same polities, both regional and international.

Chapter 5 – The Spanish Colonial Era (1521–1898 CE)

Plant-derived spices, such as pepper, cinnamon, cloves, nutmeg, and mace, became extremely valuable commodities to Europeans during the Renaissance—the 15th- and 16th-century period that brought the continent from the Middle Ages to the modern era. Spices became one of the primary commodities for trade during this period. The applications for the spices were numerous and included culinary, medicines and general health, scientific discovery and enhancements, textile dyeing, and aphrodisiacs and sexual aids, amongst others. The European maritime trade boom of the Renaissance period owed its acceleration to advances in ocean-going vessels, as well as significant interest by monarchies to dominate the global maritime trade routes. It was the time of oceanic exploration and pioneering voyages to far-flung and previously "undiscovered" domains. European rulers of the time put the full force of their wealth and political power behind launching fleets and eventually companies to benefit economically and politically from the rush in the trade of slaves and other exotic goods from Southeast Asia, as well as other places. This era of maritime political and economic maneuvering lasted into the mid-20th century, whereafter most foreign colonial powers dissipated after the close of World War II.

Many of the spices were sourced from Nusantara, specifically a small group of islands south of the Philippines known as the Moluccas (Maluku Islands), including the Banda Islands. Clove, nutmeg, and mace were the three commodities that grew naturally on this tiny island grouping that became known as the Spice Islands, whose produce, at certain points in history, became more valuable than gold. As cultivars (such as chilis, cocoa, and corn) from the New World of the Americas became more readily available with exploration, demand for Asian spices diminished, and prices stabilized. Initially, beginning in the early 1500s, the Portuguese dominated the trade in Southeast Asian spices, but later (by the mid-17th century), the Dutch and then the British were the dominant forces within maritime Southeast Asia, although the French and the Spanish also played their parts. The Dutch and British began their activities in Southeast Asia through the Dutch and British East India Trading Companies, respectively, both founded in the early 1600s, and then later directly through the monarchies and governments of their respective countries as ruling colonial powers. The Spanish, however, did not create an East India trading company and operated entirely on directives from the king of Spain and the Holy Roman Catholic Church.

Holy Roman Emperor Charles V, who was also the king of Spain (r. 1519-1556), was the monarch of much of western and central European Roman Catholic domains of the first half of the 16th century. Not to be outdone by his European neighbors, Charles V's reign encompassed the long-lasting colonization of parts of the Americas. Spanish motivation to conquer the New World was centered mostly around resource extraction (gold, cultivars, and high-value tradeable goods) but also by a desire to convert indigenous peoples to Roman Catholicism. Spain's ability to claim territories from the Americas to Southeast Asia afforded them the title of having realms known as "the empire on which the sun never sets." As well as spending considerable time and resources on the European continent to defend his territories, Charles V was responsible for sanctioning the Mesoamerican Aztec and South American Inca conquests by the Spanish conquistadors. The conquistadors were the conquering knights, soldiers, explorers, and overlords dispatched by their government to overrun parts of the unchristianized civilizations. The conquistadors were accompanied by Catholic missionaries and sometimes entire ecclesiastical retinues, who were intent upon converting the people of the conquered dominions. These conquered regions, including the Philippines, were incorporated into the Spanish Empire in various forms from 1521 to 1572. The new Spanish empires in the Americas were renamed as New Spain—now western Mexico and Peru—which both gained independence from Spain about three hundred years later in 1821. In 1556, Charles V divided his immense territories through a series of abdications that saw his son, Philip II, inherit Spain.

Early in Charles V's reign, in 1519, he commissioned the Magellan expedition that dispatched explorer and seaman Ferdinand Magellan (c. 1480-1521) to make the first full circumnavigation of the globe in recorded history. Included in the specifications for his voyage was the discovery of the renowned Spice Islands of the East Indies (maritime Southeast Asia). Magellan was of Portuguese nobility, but he was prevented from fulfilling his plans of finding a westward route to the East Indies by his own king. King Charles I of Spain instead employed Magellan and provided the explorer with a fleet of five vessels. Magellan headed west from Europe and passed the bottom of South America via a sea strait now known as the Magellan Strait and entered the "peaceful sea," or the Pacific Ocean. Magellan had visited India and Southeast Asia on previous trips but by sailing around the eastern approach via the Cape of Good Hope at the southern point of Africa. He arrived with a reduced fleet and crew in Southeast Asia in 1521—two years after setting out from Europe.

Magellan's second stop after Guam (east of the Philippines) was the Philippines itself, where they remained for six weeks. At first, they were stationed at Homonhon in the east of the archipelago, then at Limasawa, a small island southeast of Cebu and directly below Leyte Island. Magellan named the islands he saw as the Archipelago of Saint Lazarus and claimed them for the king of Spain. He erected a cross and began converting the local people to Christianity. Magellan allegedly converted over two thousand people, including Rajah Humabon of Cebu and the leaders of surrounding islands.

However, on the island of Mactan, the locals, led by the legendary Lapu-Lapu, resisted violently, and in the ensuing battle, Magellan was killed. According to the scribe Antonio Pigafetta, forty-nine Spaniards were attacked in shallow waters off Cebu by 1,500 Mactan warriors. There were reports that Christian-converted Visayan warriors assisted the Spaniards.

With further imminent hostilities from the Rajahnate of Cebu likely, the Spanish fled to the Moluccas, where they knew that the resident Portuguese would assist them. (This was after making the infamous stop on Palawan for resupply and where they took the royal family of the Taytay hostage.) Of the 270 men and five vessels (containing two years of supplies) that had left Spain in 1519, one ship, the *Victoria*, limped back to Spain under the command of Spanish Juan Sebastián Elcano, reaching its destination in 1522. Mutinies, storms, disease (mostly scurvy), and wars with indigenous locals had left only nineteen survivors, but the Spanish had completed the "impossible" and circumnavigated the globe. (The next successful circumnavigation was by Queen Elizabeth I of England's naval explorer Sir Francis Drake fifty-eight years later.)

Three or four further expeditions left Spain for the Philippines over the next forty-four years, and they retained their interest in the area from a distance. By 1559, King Philip II of Spain renewed the Crown's interest in the Philippines and sent an expedition of five hundred men to the archipelago, who would establish a permanent presence on the islands. In February 1565, an expedition led by Miguel López de Legazpi (1502-1572) arrived in Cebu, and they went on to establish the first Spanish settlement in the region. However, it was only by 1570 that the colonists had conquered the primary principality of Maynila under the soldier Martín de Goiti (c. 1534-1575), who was taken from Mexico for the purpose. With the assistance of local Visayans, the Spanish first intimidated Tondo into surrendering and then gained Maynila. The rajah of the time, Rajah Sulayman (r. 1571-1575), who was technically a vassal of the Sultanate of Brunei and Tondo, made alliances with the Spanish rather than defending Maynila. De Legazpi founded the city of Manila and pronounced it the capital of the Spanish East Indies. He also became the first governor general of the Philippines. Philip II's intention, as well as the missionaries who accompanied the colonists, was to take the islands peacefully, but the reality on the ground was that infractions and skirmishes forced the Spaniards to be fairly aggressive in their approach. (On several occasions, the Spanish needed to repel the Portuguese from taking hold of the archipelago.) Within a short time, the Spanish were enforcing the practice of *encomienda*—a form of enforced indigenous labor—but by 1574, slavery was officially abolished by royal decree (almost 240 years before slavery was abolished in Spain, around 260 years before the United Kingdom, and nearly three centuries before the United States declared abolition).

The Philippines eventually came under the viceroyalty of New Spain and was governed directly from Mexico City via the *Real Audiencia* (Royal Audience) of Manila. Manila was officially established on February 6th, 1579, through the papal bull *Illius Fulti Praesidio* by Pope Gregory XIII, which encompassed all Asian Pacific territories under the Archdiocese of Mexico. (After the Mexican Revolution of 1821 that brought independence to New Spain, the Philippines were governed directly from Spain until 1898.) Within twenty years after the passing of the bull, the Spanish had established a cathedral in Manila, including an episcopal palace and Augustinian, Dominican, and Franciscan monasteries, including a Jesuit house. Just before the death of King Philip II of Spain in 1598, he issued a decree to return all ill-gotten taxes to local Filipinos, therefore, in a sense, returning a large degree of their autonomy. However, there was a year's delay before his death or the decree was known in the Philippines, and during 1599, a referendum was held whereby local Filipinos acknowledged Spain as their overlords. Spain was officially in control of the Philippines.

The early settlers in the colonial Philippines were explorers, soldiers, government officials, and religious men who were born in Spain, Mexico, or Peru. The incoming peoples from New Spain were of Spanish ancestry as well as indigenous Mesoamerican, and the mixed-race descendants became known as mestizos, mulattos, or indios. Immigrating Spanish nationals sometimes married into the noble indigenous classes (the Ginoo and Maharlika castes) to entrench their position within the archipelago. Chinese immigration to the archipelago also flourished during the Spanish colonial occupation, as the Europeans imported thousands of

Chinese migrant laborers to construct necessary colonial infrastructure on the islands, such as houses, government buildings, hospitals, and churches. In order to defend the parts of the Philippines they had gained, the Spanish built fortresses called presidios at key locations to protect their territories from foreign powers, such as the British, Dutch, Portuguese, and Muslim and Asian pirates. Japanese traders also settled on the islands during the colonial era. In the late 16th century, Japanese pirates known as *wakōs* built a trade, specifically for piracy of Chinese shores and seas, on northern Luzon. In 1582, the Spanish repelled these pirates and their infamous warlord Tay Fusa in the Cagayan battles. Tay Fusa had attempted to establish a Japanese city-state on Luzon (called Luçon by the Spanish) to support his piratical trade.

Fending off pirates—whether Muslim, Japanese, or Chinese—was a regular occupation of the Spanish. In 1574, shortly after the Spanish had gained Manila, the Chinese warlord Limahong (Lim Hong or Lin Feng) invaded the northern Philippines via a series of raids in search of silver and gold. He failed to invade Manila despite several calculated and planned attacks, mostly due to the foresight and counterattacks of conquistador Juan de Salcedo (1549-1576), master of the Spanish camp at Manila and close relative of de Legazpi (either his grandson or his nephew). De Salcedo had played an active role in the conquest of the Philippines, and once he had repelled the pirate Limahong from Manila in 1574, he besieged the *wokou* (Chinese pirates) in Pangasinan for four months before they fled, never to return to the Philippines. Renowned historian William Henry Scott (1921-1993) refers to Salcedo as the "last of the Conquistadores," and he died at twenty-seven years of age, most likely from dysentery. To further enhance Salcedo's romantic image of Spanish gallantry, he is known as the erstwhile lover of Princess Kandarapa of Tondo. Their forbidden romance became the fodder of a legendary local tale reminiscent of English playwright William Shakespeare's play *Romeo and Juliet*, with both lovers dying young with an unresolved misunderstanding between them.

The Plaza de Roma in Manila—the capital of the Spanish-era colonial Philippines. This administrative area was called Intramuros, meaning "within the walls" since it was a protected, walled-off area for the ruling colonists and settlers.
Judgefloro, CC0, via Wikimedia Commons
https://commons.wikimedia.org/wiki/File:01063jfIntramuros_Manila_Landmarks_Buildingsfvf_19.jpg

Although the Spanish laid claim to the entire area of what we now know as the Philippines, they never truly got the southern Muslim islands under control, and this created the foundations for Filipino infractions centuries later in modern times. The Spanish-Moro wars were a series of battles between the Spanish and the Muslim sultanates of the southern islands that lasted from the late 1500s to the late 1800s. The Castilian War in 1578 was a Spanish-Christian war against the Muslim Bruneians, who had considered themselves as the de facto rulers of the Muslim Philippine sultanates at various times over the centuries. The two powers fought for control of the Philippines, with Spain invading Brunei and burning a multi-tiered mosque to the ground. However, the Spanish did not remain in Brunei due to heavy losses from cholera and dysentery and returned to Manila. In some instances, the Spanish were permitted small military and religious retinues in certain areas of the Muslim principalities, but they never got a firm hold on governing these regions.

Overall, besides infringements from the Moros and foreign powers, over the centuries that Spain ruled the Philippines, they also needed to contend with regular uprisings and skirmishes by local Filipinos, although these were always subdued. Many local Filipinos often fought voluntarily alongside their Spanish overlords to defend the islands against foreign invaders and protect Spain's suzerainty. However, it was also the case that many soldiers brought in from New Spain, India, and other foreign locations escaped their commissions and integrated into the local populations of the Philippines as civilians.

One of the biggest disappointments of the Spanish was that the Philippines did not produce the most coveted of global spices—pepper, nutmeg, cloves, and mace—but could only produce cinnamon, which is in the bark of an evergreen tree indigenous to the archipelago. This tree, *Cinnamomum mindanaense*, was discovered by the Spanish growing on the island of Mindanao (as well as some islands of the Visayas), and it can be used as a flavoring and additive for food. In addition, camphor oil can be extracted from its bark, wax from its fruit, and its wood can be used for furniture-making. The natives referred to the tree as "sweet wood" (*caiu mana*).

Although there are no historical records regarding earlier European exploration in the Philippines, it is possible that the Portuguese explorers had already visited the archipelago, and owing to its lack of marketable spices, they had not attempted to colonize the islands. The next real European intervention to Nusantara was the Dutch East India Company in the early 1600s, by which time Spain had claimed the Philippines. In 1646, the Battles of La Naval de Manila saw three Spanish galleons fend off eighteen Dutch ships that were preparing to invade and capture the Philippines. This offensive was also part of the Eighty Years' War (1568-1648) that saw European territories under Spain's control and that of the Holy Roman Empire—including Holland—struggle for independence, which they eventually achieved. The Battles of La Naval de Manila, which included five separate battles, were later investigated by the Catholic ecclesiastics and declared as a miraculous event that is still celebrated in the Philippines.

Spain was one of many nations to take control of previously unchartered areas, and in the case of the Philippines, they united an area in which many different cultures and landscapes existed. (Without Spanish intervention in the 1500s, the Philippines may have been split up in a multitude of different ways.) In fact, they eventually encompassed an area that included over 150 ethnolinguistic groups. The spread of the islands, as well as the difficult terrain across many of the landmasses, not to mention the disparate communities outside of the main principalities, would always make the Philippines difficult to govern.

The Philippines was named by the Spanish explorer and Dominican priest Ruy López de Villalobos (1500-1544) in a 1542 expedition from Mexico as *Las Islas Filipinas* ("the Philippine Islands") in honor of King Philip II of Spain. Even before Spain had laid its first settlement in the archipelago, de Villalobos was charting potential borders for a future nation. When the Hispanic era of the Philippines began, the first Spaniards to arrive on the archipelago were at pains to understand the various origins of the people they encountered on its shores. They referred to the Negritos as *Negrillos*, the non-Negrito pagans as *Indios* (Indians) or *Indigentas* (indigents), and the Muslims as *Moros*. Later, in the 19th century, it became more evident that the Indios were really of Malay (Austronesian) ancestry. The early Spanish colonialists referred to the locals as Filipinos, but later in the 19th century, this term was associated with Filipino-born Spanish natives, who resented being referred to as "Filipinos" and preferred the term *hijos del país* ("sons of the country"). Meanwhile, certain indigenous Filipinos began referring to themselves by the colloquial name of *Pinoy*.

Mosques had been established in the Philippines hundreds of years before, with the first one on the Sulu island of Simunul by the scholar, trader, and Sufi missionary Karim ul-Makhdum in 1380. The Spaniards established themselves through the building of churches and garrisons first, which later developed into complete colonial settlements. Each Spanish town had a central plaza for the hosting of festivities, around which government buildings, churches, and a market area were established. Besides religion, the Spanish brought the peso, new foods from America such as cocoa, chilis, pineapples, and maize (corn), as well as new cultivars such as coffee, tobacco, sugarcane, and indigo plants (used to extract dye for textiles). The colonists brought European architecture, music, and clothing fashions to the Philippines. Most influentially, the Spanish introduced education systems and colleges, and although many of these were originally religiously orientated, in time, they formed the foundation of a strong and effective education system that is present in the Philippines today. The Jesuits founded a college in Manila in 1590, and in 1611, the oldest university of the Philippines (and of all Asia), Santo Tomas, was founded, also in Manila.

One of the first books published in the Philippines was the *Doctrina Christiana* (Christian Doctrine). This book on Catholic catechism was written by Fray Juan de Plasencia (1520-1590), a Spanish friar of the Franciscans who lived in the Philippines from 1578 to 1590. The book was written in Spanish and Tagalog. The Franciscans were a Christian order that operated primarily under the Catholic Church, and Fray de Plasencia was part of the first group of missionaries to arrive on the archipelago after the Spanish conquest. In 1590, what is now referred to as *The Boxer Codex* (or the *Manila Manuscript*) was commissioned by the Spanish to illustrate ethnic groups of the Philippines and other Asian states. The codex contains hand-drawn illustrations and descriptions of the Philippines and other Asian places, including their people, belief systems, and even mythological creatures!

The first efforts made by the Spanish to translate Filipino were by the missionaries who wished to convert the local populace to Roman Catholicism. One of the most significant of these dictionaries was the *Vocabulario de la lengua tagala* (*Vocabulary of the Tagalog Language*) by Augustinian missionary Fray Pedro de San Buenaventura in 1613. It is believed that Fray de San Buenaventura drew on the *Doctrina Christiana* to create his dictionary, which became a crucial reference source for later missionaries to the Philippines.

Illustration of a Manila Spanish galleon being received by the local peoples off the coast of the Philippines from the Boxer Codex, also known as the Manila Manuscript, 1590.
https://commons.wikimedia.org/wiki/File:Reception_of_the_Manila_Galleon_by_the_Chamorro_in_the_Ladrones_Islands,_ca._1590.jpg

After 1570 and the conquest of Manila, the Spaniards began proselytizing Christianity and making concerted efforts to convert the locals to the Catholic faith and away from their indigenous animistic belief systems. This process was easiest for them along the populated coastal regions of the larger northern islands. It was difficult for the friars to access the remote, central highland regions of the archipelago, and the southern islands were predominantly Muslim and had been so in some cases for more than five hundred years. Unfortunately, by the 18th century, the Spaniards took Christian indoctrination far more seriously and punished locals who were found practicing indigenous belief systems. This process of installing Christian domination included burning bamboo scripts of the Filipinos and destroying cultural artifacts. The Catholic Church and their imported religious proselytizers and ordained hierarchies shared power with the Spanish Crown, which included the governing officials and conquistadors.

At first, the Spanish retained the barangay and its resident datu, but the chief's powers were restricted, and the administration of Philippine villages came mostly under the jurisdiction of both lay and ecclesiastical Hispanic authorities. The datu was mostly a figurehead who formed the primary negotiation unit with the Spanish, specifically for tax collection and the execution of Spanish policy. The Spanish used the existing regional social institutions and rulership hierarchies for the implementation of a highly centralized, autocratic colonial regime. During the three and a half centuries of Spanish rule, the European overlords didn't make drastic changes to the arrangement of existing Philippine local governments but rather used existing structures toward their own ends, making alterations or advancements where and when necessary to streamline their suzerainty of the islands. The Spaniards instituted four levels of governance: provinces, cities, towns, and neighborhoods (wards or municipalities).

Spanish intentions to reconfigure the existing independent villages of the Philippines, or the barangays, included establishing small towns, or *poblaciónes*, and capitals that then assumed much of the barangays' original political functions. This was known as the process of *Redducción* (reduction or perhaps simplification and centralizing). These towns were created where it was most geographically and administratively convenient for the Spanish. Filipinos were moved from disparate barangays into central locations in which a church was established, and the process of population control, taxation, and religious conversion (Christianization) began. Roads extended radially from the *poblaciónes* along which villages, or barrios, arose, which were further divided into small neighborhood units or *sitios*. By the late 19th century, the Spanish had reconfigured the towns, or pueblos, into barangays of fifty to a hundred families, although this new configuration of amalgamated barangays was artificial in comparison to the principalities that the Spanish had found upon their arrival in the archipelago. (Elements of both indigenous and Spanish settlement patterns still exist in the Philippines today.) A new type of chief called a cabeza de barangay was appointed as the overseer under the Spanish command of the principalía—the elite Spanish ruling classes and statesmen. The cabeza de barangay could appoint a few sub-administrators and was exempt from paying taxes.

The Spanish rearrangements of the Filipino population ensured that taxes were collected for the Spanish Crown so it could continue to fund Spanish sovereignty in the archipelago. Although, ironically, for much of Spanish domination in the Philippines, the colonization of the archipelago cost them more than it produced in saleable goods and commodities, and resources from other parts of the Spanish Empire were used to fund the governance of the Philippines. This was true particularly in the first period of Spanish occupation of the islands, when the Spanish Manila government ran at a constant loss that could only be offset by subsidies from New Spain in the Americas. Questions over how to fund the occupation of the islands continued into the 18th century, but the archipelago remained a "white elephant" (not particularly useful) possession of Spain's. Basic community services were provided mostly by the religious fraternities or *cofradías*—specifically education and medical assistance. Otherwise, the Filipino neighborhoods needed to rely on themselves for assistance with daily life, and the community members took turns assisting each other with activities such as building houses, farming, and other labor-intensive projects. This method of informal labor exchange continued until Philippine independence in the 20th century.

The Spaniards' intense interest in Central and South America led to their holding a monopoly on the commodities from those places, such as gold, chilis, vanilla, cocoa, and other high-value items of trade. By 1571, the Spaniards had established the first trans-Pacific maritime trade route that linked its territories of the Philippines with Mexico, known as *tornaviaje* or "journey home." (The first direct voyage of Philippine-Spanish trade occurred in 1767 by the frigate *Buen Consejo*—it was not considered a legitimate trade link for the first two hundred years of Spanish suzerainty.) This Manila-Acapulco (Philippine-Mexican, respectively) trade reached its peak in the 18th century, with cinnamon as the main export from the Philippines. Even though the Mexican, as well as Dutch, demand for this Filipino "gold dust" was insatiable and remained profitable (it was used prolifically to flavor chocolate at the time), it still didn't necessarily warrant Spain's efforts at occupying and governing the Philippines. So, even after two hundred years of occupation, they still weren't sure if their suzerainty was worth the effort! Spain's Mexican domains were still supplementing the Spanish Philippine government with an annual subsidy known as the *situado*.

However, the potential of the Philippines was (and remains to this day) immense if only a coordinated effort at agriculture, mining, and industry could have been mobilized and maintained by the Spaniards. Some historical European records referred to the Filipino Spanish as "indolent, negligent, and proud." Apathy and corruption were ever-present and increasing in the Hispanic home government on the continent. Efforts by foreign (non-Spanish) Europeans to salvage the Philippines as an economic vassal were constantly overlooked or thwarted. The resident Philippine Spanish were suspicious of other foreign interlopers and unsure of their intentions. For the indigenous Filipinos, the Spanish had fundamentally changed their concept of land usage. The ancient communities employed communal land ownership—and, in some parts of the Philippines, still do—whereas the Spanish introduced the concept of private land ownership and commercial cultivation. It would not have been possible for the local populations under the suppression of the colonists to understand, let alone conduct, commercial farming practices.

One Englishman (although naturalized in Spain), Nicholas Norton Nicols, eventually persuaded the Spanish Philippine government to begin cultivating cinnamon on a grander scale, using alternative cultivars and methods to enhance the indigenous cinnamon. Unfortunately, after beginning his work in 1762, he met with a tragic and untimely death just one year into the start of his project. A few years later, a former assistant of Nicols, Francisco Xavier Salgado (1713-c. 1792), took over the cinnamon agricultural project that aimed to cultivate (and hopefully, in time, produce a globally competitive emporium) a refined form of Zamboanga cinnamon. Salgado had been authorized to continue with Nicols's work by the dynamic and economically-minded governor general of the time, Simón de Anda y Salazar (in off. 1770-1776). However, even though Salgado had success within the first few years of his cultivation, starting in 1774, he could not sustain his efforts without the financial and political support of the Spanish government, especially after de Anda's death in 1776. Although he received support from the European sovereign, the Spanish Philippine bureaucracy, slow communications, and despotic attitudes of the local government brought his efforts to a closing failure.

The Spanish continental Bourbon Reforms (*Reformas Borbónicas*) were a set of economic and political legislation updates by the Spanish Crown during the 1700s that brought considerable changes to the Spanish colonial territories, such as in the Americas and the Philippines. Instituted by a new lineage of kings (the French-originated Bourbons), as opposed to the Habsburg dynasty under which Charles V and Philip II had ruled, the Bourbon government code was less complicated and more decentralized than previous lines of monarchical control originating from Spain. It aimed to improve the hierarchy and define the independence between Spain and its colonies. (Some theorists suggest that the reforms were the root cause for Spanish colonies demanding and gaining independence within the next century or so.) For the Philippines, the Bourbon reforms were a positive influence on Spanish rule, as the Spanish gained increased economic independence toward the end of the 18th century. The reforms provided space for increased local entrepreneurship and privatization to an extent. It must be considered that many of the Spaniards who were born or naturalized in the Philippines were part of the upper classes, who considered industry, commerce, and agriculture beneath them. Individuals such as Salgado had been the exception, and in the atmosphere of the strangling effect of the Hispanic officialdom of the day, it was difficult, if not impossible, to make commercial progress as an individual (even for wealthy individuals like Salgado had once been).

In the 18th century, the Royal Audience of Manila wrote a letter to King Charles III of Spain (r. 1759- 1788) urging the Crown to abandon the colony that always seemed to be leaking funds, but the Catholic Church opposed the abandonment of the islands because it believed it could make ecclesiastical inroads into the rest of Asia from the Philippines. Despite this fiscal request, as well as experiences such as Salgado's, historians mark the 18th century as a watershed time in the archipelago's economic, cultural, religious, administrative, and military development. This period advanced the archipelago, forming the foundation for contemporary Filipino life. Salgado had begun his Philippine career as a government official and, by 1762, held the lofty position of secretary of the central government. He was one of the few, along with his superior Simón de Anda, who managed to escape during the British occupation of Manila—a twenty-month-long incursion from 1762 to 1764, which was part of the Seven Years' War (1756-1763). (The Seven Years' War was a global war that included five continents and many contested maritime regions, such as Nusantara, and has been equated with the first real World War. Although the conflict began in Europe between England, France, Prussia, Austria, and Sweden, it extended to the colonies of the various nations, such as North America and Asia.) Together, Salgado and de Anda managed to salvage enough Spanish pesos from the royal treasury before their escape to Laguna de Bay that helped finance the retaliatory war with Britain.

The British were intent upon using Manila as an entry point to trade with the East, specifically China. The Spanish paid a ransom to the British to prevent them from destroying Manila, and the exiled Spanish governor of the capital, de Anda, along with Filipino troops, prevented the British from spreading their occupation beyond Manila during the two years of occupation. Salgado used his personal wealth along with the salvaged pesos to finance a resistance movement against the British, as well as General Antonio Bustos, the chief Spanish military commander. Combined with Salgado's efforts to intercept bullion (probably silver pesos) from Mexico arriving on northern Samar Island on the ship the *Filipino*, the Spanish eventually gained enough currency, and therefore weaponry, to win the local war against Britain and reclaim Manila.

At the same time, the 1763 Treaty of Paris ended the Seven Years' War and required Britain to return foreign territories, such as the Philippines, although this news reached Manila late, and the Spanish had already recaptured Manila. The treaty also included a promise by Britain to protect Roman Catholic territories in the New World. (Unfortunately, Salgado's only son, José Eslava, was captured during the incursions and died in a British prison cell from disease.) Some British and Indian sepoy troops remained in Manila after the close of the Seven Years' War and integrated into Filipino society. (Another ethnicity to settle in the Philippines during the colonial era were the Cambodians, who were fleeing persecution.)

Through the centuries of Spanish rule of the Philippines (333 years from 1565 to 1898), it gained and lost territory consistently to other forces, and although the existing conglomeration of islands that is known as the Philippines is impressive and extensive, Spain could have, at certain points, been the overlords of the large island of Borneo and even Cambodia on the Asian mainland. The unusual geographical and social arrangement of governing an archipelago meant that over the centuries of colonial rule, some Filipinos were entirely under Spain's suzerainty and oftentimes almost enslaved to the Spanish, whilst other remote and rebellious communities ignored their presence and continued their customs and way of life—in certain instances, they continue to do so this day. The Spanish Philippine government considered their ongoing struggles with the southern Muslim principalities of the Philippines as an extension of the continental Reconquista, or the reclamation of European Mediterranean territories from the Muslims that had lasted from 718 to 1492. During the entire colonial era, the Spanish-Moro conflict continued, with the Spanish only managing to subjugate parts of Mindanao and Jolo toward the end of the 19th century.

The opening of the manmade Suez Canal in 1867 brought a flood of Westerners to the Philippines, who were keen to engage in regional trade. The canal also enabled Spanish-Filipino intelligentsia (the Ilustrados) to enroll in European education systems and universities. In 1863, Queen Isabella II of Spain (r. 1833-1868) issued a decree that established a free public school system in the Philippines but in the medium of Spanish. The Spanish also invested heavily in infrastructure during this century, advancing the Philippines far beyond its Asian neighbors and, in some cases, beyond many European countries (specifically when it came to building and transportation). The first regional bank, *El Banco Español Filipino de Isabel II*, was created in 1851 to deal with a 19th-century economic boom that was mostly bolstered by the export of agricultural products. Along with the establishment of the bank was the introduction of the first exclusively Filipino currency—the Philippine peso. Although the peso had been used previously on the islands, it was mostly in the form of silver bullion from Acapulco (specifically the Spanish dollar or the "piece of eight"), and it had been used in tandem with other currencies.

The Spanish were internationally applauded by this stage as having been successful and fair colonizers who had improved the livelihoods of the local peoples, who were generally content and prosperous. But not all Filipinos appreciated being colonized. Certain Filipinos that had settled in New Spain or other parts of the world, or even those employed in the navies and armies of foreign countries, were clearly discontent with colonialism and intent upon achieving anti-imperial societies—whether for their homelands or for others (specifically in the Americas and Asia-Pacific). During the colonial era, native Filipino communities abroad became known as Manilamen or Manila men, Tagalas (from Tagalog), and Lucoes (from Luzon). These men were slaves, indentured servants, sailors, mercenaries, and tradesmen. Communities of Manilamen sprung up from slaves who had escaped the Spanish Navy or were recruited from other parts of the world as sailors and pearl divers—such as from Louisiana, northern Australia, and the Torres Strait Islands (north of Australia). In Mexico (specifically the states of Guerrero and Colima), Filipino immigrants arrived in the 16th and 17th centuries on Spanish Manila galleons (built in the Philippines) and were referred to as *chino*. This naming created confusion with the later Chinese immigrants who arrived in the 19th and 20th centuries. A 2018 study revealed that one-third of the population of Guerrero has 10 percent Filipino ancestry.

Mexico achieved its independence in 1821 after over a decade of continued struggles that had been ignited by the reign of the French insurgent Napoleon Bonaparte (r. 1804-1815) and his supplantation of the king of Spain, Charles IV, with his own brother Joseph! (Joseph Bonaparte was the king of Spain from 1808 until Napoleon Bonaparte's fall from power in 1813.) Naturally, this instability in Europe incited Mexico to fight for independence from an artificially installed head of state. Once Mexico gained its independence (which was again ratified by Queen Isabella II in 1836), its leaders expressed a desire to assist the Philippines to similarly gain liberation from the Spanish since many Filipinos had been present to liberate Mexico. A secret memorandum was sent from the new Mexican government to this effect. The irony of the memo was that it included the statement, "we must resume the intimate Mexico-Philippine relations, as they were during the halcyon days of the Acapulco-Manila galleon trade."

This statement intimates that the centuries of the Spanish colonial trans-Pacific era were apparently blissful for both Filipino and Mexican communities! This begs the question of why the "freedom" referred to earlier in the memorandum of the "less fortunate countries" such as the Philippines was entirely necessary.

Uprisings against the Spanish in the Philippines only began in 1872, half a century later, but the colonizers were aware that changes needed to be made in their governance of the isles. By 1893, the Spanish aimed to create more local autonomy in the Philippine governance structure and drafted the Maura Law. This law was a belated attempt, and it was never implemented. The Maura Law took greater and detailed strides to integrate and elevate the role of the cabeza de barangay into a town board of executors (like a mayor), making him more connected to the provincial government. One of the parameters for the position of cabeza de barangay was that the individual needed to be of Filipino or mixed Filipino descent. Along with the cabeza de barangay, a series of lieutenants was appointed, including a chief lieutenant. Although this final 1893 Spanish law was never implemented, it laid the foundation for the American municipal system that came shortly after.

Chapter 6 – The Philippine Revolution and the American Period (1872–1935 CE)

Revolutionary movements against Spanish colonization had begun in the 1700s in the Philippines, and it was done mostly through narratives of intellectuals rather than by violence. The growing dissatisfaction with colonial rule arose ironically from the opening of the Suez Canal in the 19th century and a growing and educated middle class of Filipinos who questioned foreign suzerainty. In the late 18th century, revolutionary outbreaks had been quelled by the Spanish (including the Catholic Church) using underhanded tactics such as assassinations. Within the next hundred years, many more revolutionaries emerged, but it was not until 1896 that the extended rule of Spain (for all its benefits and injustices) could be considered to have been brought to an end.

In 1872, the Spanish executed three Filipino Catholic priests under suspicion of being involved in revolutionary activities, although the evidence was weak. These executions by garotte (an archaic mechanism form of strangulation) ignited propaganda movements in Spain by Filipinos abroad. Of the agitators, future national hero (*pambansang bayani*) José Rizal boldly infuriated the colonial government with the publication of *Noli Me Tángere* (*Touch Me Not*, 1887) and *El Filibusterismo* (*The Subversive*, 1891). Rizal (1861-1896) was executed in 1896 by the Spanish government at the end of the Philippine Revolution for the role his writings had played in igniting a rebellion, even though he had not been actively involved in any part of the rebel actions and was en route to Cuba at the time.

The revolutionary Emilio Aguinaldo y Famy (1869-1964) is considered the founder of the Filipino nationalist military rebellion, and under his leadership, his combatants assisted the Americans to remove the Spanish from the capital of Manila in 1898 at the end of the Spanish-American War. From 1898 to 1902, Aguinaldo was considered the first (and youngest) president of an Asian constitutional republic—even though it was technically under the shadow of a change in colonial overlords—that had drawn up its own constitution and assigned high-level positions (technically a political cabinet). Aguinaldo began his military career by joining the Philippine Revolution from 1896 to 1898, which was led by the secret revolutionary organization the Katipunan. The Katipunan was known by many other names and was established by Andrés Bonifacio y de Castro (1863-1897) in the same year that nationalist intellectual, José Rizal, was banished to Mindanao for his political views and proselytizing (in 1892, the same year he returned to his homeland from Spain). The Katipunan employed armed forces rather than reason with the Spanish, as Rizal had attempted. The Philippine Revolution officially began in

1896 when the Spanish government discovered the Katipunan and its revolutionary intentions. The revolution continued for three years and included the replacement of Spanish colonial power by American power. This happened due to the Spanish-American War, which was followed immediately by the Philippine-American War that lasted a further three years, ending in 1902.

Bonifacio is recorded as being a leading member who started the Philippine rebellion against the wishes of other members of the organization, as well as individuals such as Aguinaldo and Rizal. Emilio Jacinto (1875-1899), a close comrade of Bonifacio, was a high-ranking member of the Katipunan and a leading general in the revolution. Once the revolution against Spain occurred, Bonifacio (who fought with his brothers in the rebellion) was eventually executed by his own people under Aguinaldo's orders for blatantly disobeying the pre-agreed terms of warfare, specifically laying waste to parts of the Philippines and mistreating his own Filipino people and their possessions. Historians are split on whether any of these accusations are true since there is abundant evidence that Aguinaldo was threatened by Bonifacio and was looking for an excuse to punish sedition. (He was not the only general that died unpardonably at the hand of Aguinaldo. Military leader Antonio Luna (1866-1899), who took part in the Spanish-American War, the Philippine-American War, and the Philippine Revolution, was strangely assassinated by his Filipino comrades, allegedly by the orders of Aguinaldo.) Aguinaldo's decision to execute Bonifacio divided militant loyalties, with certain guerilla soldiers and generals remaining behind Bonifacio's close comrade, Jacinto, and refusing to pledge allegiance to Aguinaldo. Jacinto died from malaria in Luzon in 1899.

In 1897, the Pact of Biak-na-Bato was signed. This was a truce between the revolutionaries and Spain, and Aguinaldo went into voluntary exile to Hong Kong, only to return one year later with the Americans (who had requested his return and offered him transport) to redeclare revolution under the guise of the Spanish-American War. The Spanish-American War of 1898 was fought over ten weeks in the Caribbean Sea and the Pacific Ocean. The battles had been instigated by the Americans' desire to assist Cuba to gain independence from Spain, and when a US battleship, the USS *Maine*, mysteriously sank in February 1898 in Havana Harbor, Cuba, from an internal explosion, the Americans felt forced to go to war with Spain. They believed the battleship was blown up by the Spanish without any hard evidence. The major newspapers of the day were quick to jump on this moneymaking opportunity, fanning the flames of war. It is believed the ship actually sank due to a problem with its coal bunker.

The Battle of Manila Bay (or the Battle of Cavite) in May of that same year was the first major engagement of the war and one of the most decisive naval battles in history since it brought an end to European colonial rule in the Philippines. American Commodore George Dewey (1837-1917) is accredited with having lost only one crewman during the battle (apparently from illness, not injuries) and went on to attain the highest rank of Admiral of the Navy—the only person to ever have achieved this rank. His squadron fought against Spanish Rear Admiral Patricio Montojo y Pasarón (1839-1917), whose career was ruined by his failure in the battle, even though the Spanish were heavily outmanned and outgunned and were using antiquated, ill-equipped ships.

The Spanish were significantly less prepared and equipped for the battle, and unlike the "miracle" of the Battles of La Naval de Manila against the Dutch in 1646, the Spanish gave in to defeat, even sinking some of their own fleet (a tactic known as scuttling). In the interim, a German fleet arrived at Manila Bay, hoping for the opportunity to ambush Manila after an American defeat and a presumably weakened Spanish Navy. Dewey summarily dispatched the Germans (they left without a fight) as he had done with the Spanish!

Four months later, in August of 1898, the Americans and Spanish secretly met to create the illusion of a battle over Manila, now known as the Mock Battle of Manila. The Westerners' intentions (knowing that Spain had lost the Spanish-American War) was to get the Americans ensconced in the walled and defended Manila capital, or Intramuros ("within the walls"), without allowing any influx of Filipino revolutionaries or guerilla fighters into the administrative capital. This divisive tactic by the colonizers to exclude Filipino nationalists from an opportunity to take control of their own state laid the foundations for the Philippine-American War, which began the following year in 1899. The period from 1898 to 1901 was one in which the rebels had declared the First Philippine Republic. The date upon which Aguinaldo declared independence, June 12th, 1898, is now the day celebrated by Filipinos as their Independence Day. However, Aguinaldo was considered a Philippine president with a constitution and cabinet, and his government was never formally recognized internationally.

America won the overall Spanish-American War mostly due to their advanced firepower, and Spain surrendered, leading to the Treaty of Paris in 1898, in which America gained territories from Spain, including Guam, Puerto Rico, and the Philippines (and temporary control of Cuba). The US paid twenty million dollars to Spain to compensate for their infrastructural investments in the Philippine archipelago. It isn't clear why the United States was interested in the Philippines except that it was a strategically positioned global location for military and naval warfare. This interest was proved when America assisted the Philippines with a transitional government leading to full independence by 1946 but maintained their military bases on the islands until the early 1990s, only relinquishing them under duress. America's success in the Spanish-American War established them as the dominant power in the Caribbean and the Pacific, which would prove a decisive positioning for World War II. The United States' newfound position was not only tactically and politically improved but also economically, as their proximity to Eastern markets increased.

However, before America could take full possession of the Philippines, Emilio Aguinaldo led a war between Filipino nationalists and American forces. Aguinaldo, who had assisted the Americans in taking Manila from the Spanish, had done so under the impression that the US would grant the Filipinos a substantial role in the governance of their islands, if not ultimately outright independence. When the Filipino activists were excluded from occupying the capital in 1898, this insult was the fuel for further Filipino revolutionary action.

The Philippine-American War lasted for three years and resulted in the death of over 4,000 American troops (of the 126,000 American soldiers dispatched) and 20,000 Filipino combatants (of the 80,000 to 100,000 Filipino soldiers). An estimated two hundred thousand to one million Filipino civilians lost their lives to disease (mostly cholera and malaria), famine, and collateral violence during the war. At first, Aguinaldo and his supporters seized control of the main island of Luzon and declared the independent Philippine Republic. When it became clear to the Filipinos that a direct onslaught against the Americans would ultimately end in failure due to the Americans' superior military training and resources (and refusal to negotiate), Aguinaldo's troops changed to guerilla warfare, in which they were far more successful. However, the Filipinos' guerilla tactics could never have created a homogenized and ultimate win because of the practical difficulties of the Philippine terrain and the coordination of disparate troops throughout the archipelago, as well as the lack of foreign support and inaccessibility to resources and weaponry. Aguinaldo was captured in 1901, after which the resistance dissipated. By 1902, the United States had retaken control of Luzon, and US President Theodore Roosevelt (in off. 1901-1909) declared a general amnesty. The new overlords occasionally needed to deal with insurgencies thereafter, but nothing sufficient to destabilize their suzerainty over the Philippines.

In a similar fashion that the Spanish used to regulate the Philippines, by leveraging existing administrative governance infrastructure, the Americans retained the Spanish pueblos (or towns) and other units and renamed them municipalities. The barrios remained as sub-divisions, with a barrio lieutenant in charge of each as the chief administrative officer. The president of the United States at the time, President William McKinley (in off. 1897-1901), specified the United States' commitment to archipelagic governance: "The establishment of municipal governments in which the natives of the islands, both in the cities and in the rural communities, shall be afforded the opportunity to manage their own local affairs to the fullest extent they are capable."

However, the commission responsible for the implementation of American governance eventually relapsed into restricting Filipino autonomy. The American interference in local politicking virtually reverted Philippine governance structures to the Maura Law, which was drawn up at the end of Spanish intervention. The Americans' reasoning for their supervision was purportedly corruption and inefficiency in the ruling Philippine elite classes. The colonial government had the power to intervene in local affairs and overrule any decision taken by Filipino administrators. This American intervention made McKinley's original statement pointless, as the Americans ruled the Philippines as tightly and intentionally as the Spaniards had done.

The central government remained in Manila. As at the end of the Spanish-led government, the barrios were led by a barrio lieutenant, who was the main representative of municipal government in village life. The lieutenant was appointed by municipal officers but was not paid a salary and had no legal authority. The lieutenant was really a de facto peacekeeper for the Americans, and he was required to relay communications between the villages and their overlords and vice versa. It seems that the villages kept their own internal system of chieftaincy in addition to the colonial municipal system, and a leader in the form of the ancient datu continued to guide village life.

The Americans attempted to institute rural structures of decentralized local governance (local councils) that equated to colonial micro-management of jurisdictions. It could be considered immoral since the local Filipino positions were not paid ones. Unsurprisingly, the rural governance arrangements remained largely unimplemented and were a "paper organization." During the early turn of the 20th century, when the Americans began exploring and "taming" the Philippines, resident scientists and expatriates often referred to the outlying indigenous tribes as wild and unpredictable. In 1914, US Captain Wilfred Turnbull of the Filipino-American military force was ordered to "reform" the Negrito Agta way of life. The Americans moved 150 Agta families onto a reservation, and these previously semi-nomadic hunter-gatherers were forced into farming. Those men who resisted were chain-ganged together and forced to clear forest land (previously their indigenous hunting grounds) for planting.

However, the Americans were sincere in their desire to eventually deliver an independent Philippines. During the Philippine Revolution that preceded the Spanish-American War, as well as over the next few years until the end of the Philippine-American War, the Americans launched a pacification campaign known as the policy of attraction. It aimed to make alliances with Filipino elites who were not necessarily supporters of Aguinaldo and his bloody, revolutionary tactics. The policy sought a long-term solution to empowering the Filipinos, enabling self-government, and building economic development and social reforms. Over time, this program gained support and ultimately undermined Aguinaldo's efforts to take the Philippines by force. When the Filipinos lost their rebellion against the United States in 1902, the Westerners set up an insular government to replace the military government that had been in place. The insular government was part of a larger organic mechanism through which the United States governed the civil aspects of their overseas territories. The structure was a form of an interim government that aimed to tutor local administrators to eventually control their own independent government. (The governing laws, the Philippine Organic Act, established Filipinos as sovereign citizens of their own state for the first time in history.)

The US remained true to its promises, and in 1907, the Philippines convened its first elected assembly, with the Jones Act of 1916 assuring future national independence. The Jones Act replaced previous US laws for the Philippines and included a constitution as well as a provision for the first Philippine elected legislature. Like Spanish rule, the American era had successes and failures and times of peace as well as minor uprisings. Socio-economic conditions were strong, and trade was booming. English became the lingua franca of the islands. In 1907, the first political party of the Philippines was formed, the Nacionalista Party (which was for immediate nationalization), but its members retained a good relationship with the Americans. The archipelago officially became a member of the American Commonwealth in 1935 and held its first democratic election. The new government included the new Constitution of the Republic of the Philippines, and the date of July 4th was established as Independence Day.

Emilio Aguinaldo lost the presidency to Nacionalista member Manuel Luis Quezon y Molina (1878-1944), who remained in office until his death. Quezon died in exile in the United States from tuberculosis. He had been forced to leave the Philippines during the Japanese occupation in the Second World War. Aguinaldo is, nevertheless, heralded as a national hero of the Philippines, and his crest of a yellow sun on a white background remains part of the Philippine flag. The date for total and final independence of the isles happened in 1946.

Philippine President Manuel L. Quezon was considered an exemplary president, as he was focused on social justice and inequality and built a national culture. He is attributed with saving more than a thousand Jewish people from Nazi Germany and resettling them into the Philippines in the Marikina Valley of the Manila Metropolitan Area. After the outbreak of World War II in 1938, the Philippines became directly involved when Japan invaded the islands in 1941. The Second Philippine Republic was created as a puppet state under Japanese suzerainty in 1943, which lasted for two years until the Japanese surrender in 1945 at the end of World War II.

Chapter 7 – The Second World War to the Modern Era (1935–21st century CE)

The Philippines officially became involved in World War II when Japan attacked the Clark Air Base in Pampanga on December 8th, 1941, just hours after its infamous attack on the American Pearl Harbor naval base in Hawaii. Shortly after the aerial attack, Japan began landing troops on Luzon, and being overwhelmed and unprepared, the Americans and Filipinos could not resist and immediately fled or submitted. The American general at the time, General Douglas MacArthur (1880-1964), withdrew with his forces to Bataan Peninsula (western edge of Manila Bay, north of Manila) and Corregidor Island at the entrance of Manila Bay. General MacArthur declared Manila an open city to protect and preserve its heritage and prevent the destruction of Intramuros by

Japanese forces.

The United States officially surrendered the region to Japan in April of 1942 after three months of fighting on the peninsula, thus beginning the official occupation of the Philippines by Japan. Eighty thousand prisoners of war were forced to take the Bataan Death March to a prison camp more than a hundred kilometers (sixty-two miles) north to be loaded onto trains for prisoner of war camps. More than eleven thousand prisoners (both Filipino and American) died during this walk due to exhaustion, starvation, disease, and gross mistreatment and unlawful killings by the Japanese troops. (The Japanese responsible for the death march were later charged with war crimes.) President Manuel Luis Quezon and his vice president were part of the march but then left to go into exile in the United States. MacArthur was sent to Australia to regroup and prepare for a counterattack on the Japanese.

The Japanese reasons for invading Southeast Asian countries during the Second World War were motivated by their desire to create a Greater East Asian Co-Prosperity Sphere and to overthrow colonial oppression. This was a thinly veiled attempt to use the world war as a ruse for gaining Asian-Pacific territories and their resources. Once ensconced in the Philippines, the Japanese proceeded to create an independent government council, eventually pronouncing the archipelago as an independent state in 1943. José P. Laurel (1891–1959), a Nacionalista Party member and judge, was installed as the president. However, Japan's decisions were unpopular with Filipinos, and the "independent" government was, in reality, considered an inauthentic move by Japan to give the illusion of independence while Japan remained as overlords. President Laurel remained in office for two years until Japan surrendered in 1945.

The Filipinos remained loyal to the Americans, and the Japanese occupation of the Philippines was drastically diminished (from forty-eight states to twelve) through the actions of underground guerilla warfare. The guerillas were constituted of the Philippine Army, US Army combatants of Southeast Asia (that provided supplies and weapons via submarine and parachute drops), and indigenous Filipino rebel armies. Half a million Japanese troops were killed in the ongoing guerilla warfare that continued until their formal surrender from World War II in August 1945 and which was ratified on September 2nd. One of the most important Filipino guerilla armies was the Huks (the *Hukbong Bayan Laban sa Hapon*, or the *Hukbalahap*, which translates in English to the People's Army Against the Japanese). This communist organization was formed by a group of farmers in Central Luzon, whose numbers reached at least thirty thousand during the war. Their considerable efforts to undermine the Japanese occupation were heralded in the Philippines, but unfortunately, they furthered their fight into 1946 after the close of the war. The Huks rebelled against the independent Philippine government of the time, but they were defeated and outlawed. (They returned in 1950 under the new name of the People's Liberation Army, wreaking havoc throughout the villages and undermining the government. By 1955, the organization had weakened and disbanded.)

Leyte Gulf—the gulf east of Leyte Island in the Visayas—became the site of the most conclusive and largest naval battle of World War II. The Battle of Leyte Gulf, which lasted from October of 1944 to July of 1945, involved over 200,000 naval personnel from Japan and America (led by MacArthur), as well as Australia, who were allied with the Americans. It was, in reality, a series of four separate battles and is considered the last true naval battle ever fought. The conflict also included Japanese kamikaze attacks, in which the aviators commit suicide by flying their planes at high speed into battleships. The Japanese navy, headed by General Yamashita Tomoyuki (1885-1946), suffered great losses of its vessels and crew, and they inevitably lost their hold on the Philippines and subsequently the remainder of their strongholds in Southeast Asia. The most important result of the Japanese loss of territory in the region was that their sources of fuel and oil were removed, which considerably contributed to their eventual loss of World War II. The Japanese had not only lost their hold on the Philippines but had also lost command of the seas.

However, General Yamashita held onto parts of Luzon until the end of the Second World War and only relinquished the capital after the battles of Manila Bay, which took place several months after the start of the Battle of Leyte Gulf. The Battle of Manila in February/March of 1945 was the final battle of Manila Bay in the history of its seemingly endless "Manila Bay Battles." The battle led to the death of hundreds of thousands of innocent Filipino civilians at the hands of Japanese troops or by being caught in the crossfire, as well as the complete destruction of historic colonial Manila. (Manila, along with Warsaw and Berlin, were considered the three most devastated cities at the close of World War II.) Intramuros was liberated by the Allied forces on March 4th, 1945, but the beautiful city had been devastated, and the Filipinos in its proximity had been brutalized, murdered, and traumatized by the Japanese. In 1946, Yamashita was executed by the Allied forces after being tried for war crimes that had been committed by the troops under his command, even though there was no evidence that he had knowledge of or had condoned these offenses. His execution led to a legal precedent known as the Yamashita standard, which enforced that military authorities should be aware of and responsible for their subordinates' actions in times of war.

Unlike other Southeast Asian countries, the Philippines welcomed America's presence, heralding the troops as heroes who had liberated their country from the Japanese. The US helped to reestablish a government since Quezon had died in exile and spent two billion dollars over five years to fix the destruction caused by the world war. The original date of independence of 1946 was achieved peacefully, and for the next two decades, the Philippines retained good relations with the US under a democratic, elected, and national constitutional government. (One of the consequences of the war and the departure of the Americans was the proliferation of Amerasian children who remained behind.)

The Third Philippine Republic began in 1946 with the installation of President Manuel Roxas (in off. 1946-1948) of the newly formed Liberal Party. This era lasted for twenty years until 1965 and the start of the Marcos era, which was marked by dictatorship, civilian intimidation, and atrocities that brought an end to good Philippine international relations.

After Philippine independence in 1946, local governance structures were clearly disordered and undemocratic. After the Second World War, there were no legal mechanisms in place to generate funds for the running of the barrios, which were still contained within the municipalities. Residents were not empowered to collect taxes to use toward local economic development and infrastructure. The services provided by the municipal government were limited, and the rule of law and chain of governance were disordered and confusing. This situation necessitated the newly independent Philippine government to organize legal governance structures at the local government level, specifically in the rural areas, and centralize community development programs. To avoid the influence of communism, which was beginning to infiltrate the thinking of certain groups that were now required to be self-dependent in their daily governance, the government created the elective Barrio

Council Law in 1956. The creation of this local government policy was the Philippine government's effort to centralize government control while promoting localized development communities.

The Barrio Council Law charter was found to be seriously flawed since all legal frameworks still reverted to the municipalities and the barrios continued to find themselves disempowered. This law was replaced by a new Barrio charter a few years later. The new Barrio Charter Act, although not perfect, gave official recognition to barrio self-rule and autonomous community development, creating the underpinnings of democracy in the rural Philippines. The election of the barrio lieutenant defaulted to elected members of the village, which, like their predecessors in the 1500s and before, was heavily influenced by wealth, position, and prowess, with perhaps a new dimension of modern politicking included. The barrios could now conduct their own tax collection and administrate their own treasuries while exercising their own legislative powers. By 1963, a revised barrio charter included more specific alterations to the law, but it was minor in terms of the overall governance framework of the document.

During the Third Philippine Republic, the United States continued to assist the Philippines economically, particularly via efforts to bolster trade deals. In 1947, the Philippines signed a ninety-nine-year lease that allowed the US to maintain their military bases on the islands—a factor that had always been strategically critical to the Americans. When Roxas died suddenly of a heart attack in 1948, he was replaced by Elpidio Quirino of the Liberal Party, who served one term, leaving office in 1953. Three further presidents served during this era: Ramon Magsaysay (in off. 1953-1957), an extremely popular president at home and abroad who regrettably died in a plane crash; Carlos P. Garcia (in off. 1957-1961), who convinced the United States to return large military reservations to the Philippines; and Diosdado Macapagal (in off. 1961-1965), who introduced massive land reforms and changed the national Independence Day back from the American-selected July 4th to Aguinaldo's June 12th.

The Fourth Philippine Republic started with the democratic election of the Nacionalista Party's Ferdinand Emmanuel Edralin Marcos Sr. in 1965, who remained unlawfully in office until 1986 (the Philippine constitution at that time allowed a president to serve for a maximum of two terms of four years each). When Marcos's legitimate second term of leadership expired, he ruled as a dictator from 1972 using martial law and election rigging to retain his position, as well as changing the constitution in 1973 to suit his own ends! Marcos used the excuse of the double threat of the Communist Party and the Moro Islamic Liberation Front as an excuse to maintain military command and the presidency, citing them as violent extremists. He controlled the press and abolished other media, ordered the arrest or assassination of members of opposition parties, shut down congress, and forced swathes of democratic protestors into exile for fear of their lives. Marcos is remembered as a brutal kleptocrat under whom corruption was rife. Tens of thousands of Filipinos who opposed his rulership were tortured, found murdered and mutilated in the streets, or simply disappeared. Marcos imprisoned an estimated seventy thousand of his opponents. There were no limits to the atrocities performed in order for him to stay in power.

Since World War II, the Islamic strongholds of the southern Philippines had remained a center for religious separatism and the birthplace of many of the original leaders of the Moro Islamic Liberation Front (MILF). It has been the site of some of the most destructive political and ideological fighting. Unfortunately, during the fighting between MILF and the Philippine forces in the 1970s, irreparable damage was done to the ancient anthropomorphic pottery artifacts of

Ayub Cave, southern Mindanao.

Under Marcos, the original Philippine barangays were reinstated in 1974, and this law was ratified in 1991 after the end of the Marcos era. The barangay is currently the smallest unit of local governance in the archipelago, of which there are over forty-two thousand. The primary difference between the barangays of the modern day and those of the pre-colonial era is that contemporary barangays are established according to geographical arrangement and that historical barangays were formulated in allegiance to a chief (as well as being roughly geographically). During Marcos's period of martial law, the barangays were used as instruments to enforce his dictatorship. Although his regime pretended to extend democracy through the institution of citizen assemblies, they were really used to increase his control down to the neighborhood, or *sitio*, level by sending out spies and control squads. Marcos's allies were routinely reelected to positions of power at the community level. Once again, like in the colonial era, the Philippines was in a position where the illusion of a decentralized, participative, democratic governance system was being used to disguise a tightly controlled central government.

By 1986, local and international pressure in retaliation to Marcos's government resulted in a snap election in which he finally lost power. A peaceful resistance movement in Manila in 1986, the People Power Revolution, included over two million Filipinos who used the assassination of opposition Senator Benigno Simeon "Ninoy" Aquino Jr. (1932-1983) as the basis of their protest. The resultant election heralded in the Fifth Philippine Republic, which is the current phase of the Philippine government. Marcos lost the election to the first female Philippine president, Maria Corazon Cojuangco Aquino, known as Cory Aquino (in off. 1986-1992), who was the widow of the late Benigno Aquino and a member of the Liberal Party. (In this first election of the

Fifth Republic, Marcos once again attempted to snatch back power by electing himself the winner by popular vote. However, independent electoral observers, including members of the international community—specifically the US—declared vastly different results and declared Aquino the winner. American involvement was partly due to the previous colonizers still retaining two military bases on the islands.) The People Power Revolution, which had formed a quasi-military presence, forced Marcos into exile. In 2016, the government gave permission for the late President Marcos to be buried in the country's cemetery for heroes against significant public protest.

Cory Aquino was in office for one term of six years, and she was the most prominent figure during the People Power Revolution. Since her husband's assassination had begun her political career, she rallied for change. Once in office, Aquino instituted a new permanent constitution. Her constitution disabled the ability of presidents to unilaterally declare martial law, restored congress, and proposed the creation of autonomous regions in the Cordilleras and Muslim Mindanao. Although democracy was restored under her leadership, Cory Aquino was inexperienced in politics, and her government was considered slightly weak and fractured. This instability led to six unsuccessful coup attempts by the Philippine military (the most serious of which was in Manila in 1989). A series of natural disasters also negatively affected Aquino's term, including the eruption of Mount Pinatubo in 1991, which left 700 dead and 200,000 homeless.

The most important historical event of Aquino's presidency was the denial of her senate to allow the continuation of the US military bases, with the Americans returning the spaces to the Philippines in 1992. The final total withdrawal of American presence in the Philippines ended after almost a century of their intimate involvement with the archipelago. A further four presidents followed from 1992, with the sixth and current president of the Fifth Republic, Rodrigo Duterte, having been elected in 2016. Defense Secretary Fidel V. Ramos (in off. 1992-1998) of the Lakas-CMD (Lakas-Christian Muslim Democrats) followed Cory Aquino. From 1998 to 2001, Joseph Estrada, Ramos's vice president and a former movie actor, sat as president. Estrada was forced to resign halfway through his first term due to an impeachment crisis (including accusations of being a recipient of massive bribery), with which he would not comply.

Estrada's vice president, Gloria Macapagal-Arroyo, who was also the daughter of former President Diosdado Macapagal of the 1960s, took office as president in 2001 and completed a one-and-a-half term (nine years), leaving in 2010. Her presidency was relatively stable, although marked with controversy and military uprisings. In 2010, the son of Benigno and Cory Aquino, Benigno Simeon Cojuangco III, also known as "PNoy" or "Noynoy," served one six-year term under the Liberal Party until 2016. Aquino III's leadership was marked with successes and difficulties, including natural disasters and the continued tensions with the various Islamic separatist groups. The most noteworthy milestone of his term was the 2014 ratification of the Comprehensive Agreement on the Bangsamoro (CAB) with the Moro Islamic Liberation Front. This agreement, which had been seventeen years in the making, had the intention of eventually bringing peace to the Sulu and Mindanao regions.

The agreement stressed the cessation of armed conflict in lieu of independent, autonomous Islamic regions that would retain a form of power-sharing with the overall Philippine government. This was an agreement aimed to transition certain regions into full autonomy, but by 2019, it was clear that the Autonomous Region in Muslim Mindanao (ARMM), which was subsequently established after the agreement to implement this change, was failing. In 2018, President Duterte stepped in with a reconfigured plan for an interim government for the Islamic Philippines, replacing the defunct ARMM with the Bangsamoro Autonomous Region in Muslim Mindanao (BARMM). (Bangsamoro being a composition of the words "bangsa" or "nation" and "Moro" or "Muslim.") The new plan, ratified in 2019, includes the Bangsamoro Organic Law (BOL) and a constitution of the Bangsamoro Transition Authority. The autonomous regions, which include several Philippine provinces of Mindanao and Sulu, will eventually be transitioned into power-sharing arrangements with the overall Philippine government, with the BARMM having its own constitution, regional government, and ability to practice Sharia law while still being a subsidiary of the full Philippine government and presidency, its military, and foreign policy. The transition period is set to end in 2022.

Another agreement that began during Aquino III's presidency that continues into Duterte's era is the 2014 Enhanced Defense Cooperation Agreement (EDCA) with the United States of America. This military agreement does not aim to allow America any permanent military bases in the Philippines but does allow for the creation of significant facilities for both American and Filipino military forces and resources. Under the agreement, America is also permitted to rotate troops on impermanent bases. The original agreement was signed between US President Barack Obama (in off. 2009-2017) and Benigno Aquino III of the Philippines. In 2016, the agreement was deemed constitutional by the Philippine Supreme Court.

Plans, such as the BARMM, help to recognize ancient cultural claims to heritage, such as the sultanates of the Islamic Philippines. Legally, royalty is not recognized in the modern Philippine constitution, but many Filipinos claim descendancy from the royal houses or chief principalities (principalía families) of old, sometimes even adhering to the ancient caste system of social hierarchy. In some instances, principalía councils still make decisions on behalf of communities.

After the Marcos era, the Philippine government knew it needed to reinstate truly decentralized and democratic governance systems, and the 1987 Philippine Constitution restored autonomy to local government units. The 1992 Local Government Code defined the new powers of the barangays, guaranteeing their independence. Included in the various new local codes and acts were a significant proportion of powers to the private sector, non-governmental organizations, and civil society. This new arrangement for the local government was to be as broad-based as possible. Since the early 1990s, the various administrations of the Philippines have sought to continue to increase transparency and democratization in Philippine politics, particularly at the local level. Technically, the barangays have full authority over their own governance and, most importantly, participate in efforts in their own disaster management systems and drive the collection of local data for policy-making through the Community-Based Monitoring System (**CBMS**). Unfortunately, despite the government's efforts, predatory politics has ensued, including clientelism (political bribery). Philippine politics is currently dominated by well-known figures, often celebrities or members of political dynasties. A form of "cacique democracy" has developed at a local level that echoes the ancient barangay-style homage to a powerful "boss." Even though, technically, the barangays are the smallest unit of hierarchical government in the Philippines, a type of street law exists at a local level, where leaders with warlord-like authority have significant influence.

The existing Negritos of the Philippines consist of an estimated twenty-five different linguistic groups, but in the 1980s, their numbers were a meager fifteen thousand. Widely scattered throughout the archipelago, they battle for their land rights since their previously hunter-gatherer societies have turned to agriculture. Their societies are considered to be in various stages of deculturation. Despite the influx of acculturative forces over the centuries, the Negritos were still living a semi-nomadic existence in the mid-20th century. The Filipino population explosion since the end of the Second World War saw the movement of other ethnicities into the sparsely populated lands previously occupied by Negritos. The Negritos have inevitably found themselves as landless squatters on their own ancestral lands and have been forced into more modern occupations of subsistence agriculture, communal barter, or trading labor. The intrusive and damaging influences of logging and mining have also had a highly detrimental effect on the Negritos, as their lands continue to shrink and be destroyed by private and public corporations. Over the centuries, as roadways and other transport links were placed through previously Negrito land, not only were their hunting, fishing, and gathering grounds disrupted or destroyed, but it also provided more outsiders with access to their previously remote lands.

Like other Southeast Asian islands, the Filipino people adhere strongly to community and family life. Historical arts and culture include Spanish, Muslim, and indigenous influences, and folk dancing and music often include remnants of several cultures. Art and literature continue to be a part of the ever-curious and questioning Filipino lifestyles, and the archipelago's long list of existing and potential **UNESCO World Heritage** Sites and intangible cultural aspects are proof of the Philippines' critical role in human and natural history.

Conclusion

It might be difficult to understand why the Filipino indigenous people gave in so readily to Spanish occupation. In many instances, there were minor battles and great displays of resistance by the locals to colonial suzerainty, but essentially, they were passive people who were never too concerned with who held sway over their lives. Whether it was the local ruling classes of the hierarchical caste system, foreign powers such as Brunei and Majapahit, or the colonizers intent upon ultimate domination, Filipinos didn't put up too much of a fight at being ruled. However, their capitulations came with an attitude of dismissiveness in many cases, and if they could flee to the uncolonized highlands, remain within the Muslim-dominated south, or even abscond aboard a vessel destined for more freedom, they did.

Another critical factor in their eventual colonization was due to the geopolitical arrangement of their island polities upon Spanish arrival. The disparate and disunited nature of the Philippine archipelago was a natural development from ancient times owing to the spread of more than 150 ethnicities with their own unique cultures and languages over thousands of islands through the millennia. The purposeful placement of the powerful principalities was an obvious result of maritime trade and the economic and cultural opportunities it afforded. However, it also made the Filipinos more vulnerable to conquest since they did not operate as a single unit, and they even sometimes sided with foreign powers against communities within their own archipelago. The Spanish quietly employed a tactic of "divide and conquer," taking full advantage of the unhomogenized power centers.

The people of the Philippines could very easily have become a Muslim majority if Spanish intervention had not been successful in the 1500s. Like the Battles of La Naval de Manila fought with the Dutch in the mid-17th century, it is perhaps a miracle that the Philippines are now a majority Roman Catholic group of islands. The monotheistic religion seems worlds away from the original indigenous animistic Anitism of ancient times that was mostly about nature, mythology, and ancestors. Ironically, it was the pomp and pageantry of Catholicism that most attracted the indigenous Filipinos to the new religion brought by their colonizers. Today, a unique form of Folk Catholicism, which incorporates aspects of animism, is practiced in the Philippines, but 85 percent of Catholic Filipinos remain part of the formal global Catholic Church under the guidance of the pope.

It was through Catholicism that education was introduced to the Philippines, with the first universities being established at the end of the 16th and the beginning of the 17th centuries. The Philippines has continued with this concept of a substantial focus on education and has one of the highest literacy rates in Asia. The influence of its colonial past has left an indelible mark on the country, with many Filipinos bearing Spanish names despite not necessarily having a Spanish lineage. The influence of the United States has also had a significant impact on the islands, and American popular culture, such as the widespread use of English, basketball, fast food, and media, are ingrained in Filipino life. However, what has not changed over the millennia of external influences is their inherent value system and basis of loyalty based on personal alliances of kinship, friendship, and commerce. A common thread amongst the diverse and disparate Filipinos is to maintain social harmony through ongoing communal relationships and shared objectives. A sense of belonging has held the heterogeneous island grouping of the Philippines unified despite all odds. Any slight deviation from the history that unfolded for this archipelago could have created a very different Philippines, but by some magic—whether through the Catholic saints of the orthodox religion or the mystical beliefs of indigenous folklore—the Philippines has remained true to the Southeast Asian concept of unity in diversity.

Here's another book by Captivating History that you might like

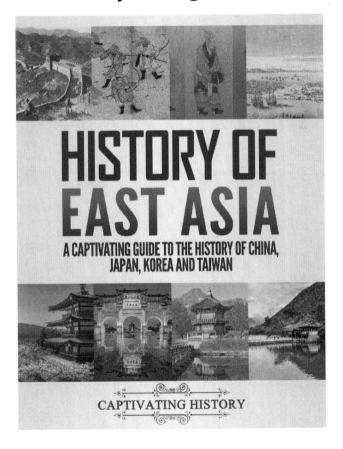

Free Bonus from Captivating History (Available for a Limited time)

Hi History Lovers!

Now you have a chance to join our exclusive history list so you can get your first history ebook for free as well as discounts and a potential to get more history books for free! Simply visit the link below to join.

Captivatinghistory.com/ebook

Also, make sure to follow us on Facebook, Twitter and Youtube by searching for Captivating History.

Reference

Hall, D. G. E. *Burma.* 1950.

Hannigan, Tim. *A Brief History of Indonesia.* 2015.

Lockhard, Craig. *Southeast Asian World History.* 2009.

Myint-U, Thant. *The Making of Modern Burma.* 2001.

Reid, Anthony. *Charting the Shape of Early Modern Southeast Asia.* 1999.

Stuart-Fox, Martin. *A Short History of China and Southeast Asia: Tribute, Trade, and Influence.* 2014.

Tully, John. *A Short History of Cambodia: From Empire to Survival.* 2005.

Yellen, Jeremy A. *The Greater East Asia Co-Prosperity Sphere.* 2019.

Ancient Origins. "Kingdom of Sukhothai and the Birth of Thailand." Ancient Origins. April 17, 2020. Accessed December 2020. https://www.ancient-origins.net/ancient-places-asia/sukhothai-kingdom-0013580 .

Anto, Meiri. "Thai Students Overthrow Military Thanom Regime, 1973." Global Nonviolent

Action Database. May 13, 2013. Accessed January 2021.

https://nvdatabase.swarthmore.edu/content/thai-students-overthrow-military-thanom-regime-1973.

Asia Highlights. "Sukhothai Kingdom." Asia Highlights. May 28, 2020. Accessed December 2020. https://www.asiahighlights.com/thailand/sukhothai-kingdom.

Asiaweek. "Newsmakers." *Asiaweek*, July 30, 2000. https://web.archive.org/web/20060322141459/http://www.pathfinder.com/asiaweek/magazine/2000/0630/newsmakers.html.

BBC. "Kneeling before a King: The Moment That Shook a Nation." *BBC*, October 13, 2016. Accessed January 2021. https://www.bbc.com/news/world-asia-37650466.

BBC. "Thailand Profile - Timeline." BBC News. March 7, 2019. Accessed December 2020. https://www.bbc.com/news/world-asia-15641745.

Bentley, R. Alexander, Michael Pietrusewsky, Michele T. Douglas, and Tim C. Atkinson. "Matrilocality during the Prehistoric Transition to Agriculture in Thailand?: Antiquity." Cambridge Core. March 10, 2015. Accessed December 2020. https://www.cambridge.org/core/journals/antiquity/article/matrilocality-during-the-prehistoric-transition-to-agriculture-in-thailand/641E2C761F097C80C13C153698AE9599.

Britannica, T. Editors of Encyclopedia. "Khmer." Encyclopedia Britannica. April 18, 2020. Accessed December 2020. https://www.britannica.com/topic/Khmer.

Britannica, The Editors of Encyclopedia. "Sukhothai Kingdom." Encyclopedia Britannica. April 10, 2009. Accessed December 2020. https://www.britannica.com/place/Sukhothai-kingdom.

Britannica, The Editors of Encyclopedia. "Lan Na." Encyclopedia Britannica. April 02, 2009. Accessed December 2020. https://www.britannica.com/place/Lan-Na.

Britannica, The Editors of Encyclopedia. "Tai." Encyclopedia Britannica. July 7, 2011. Accessed December 2020. https://www.britannica.com/topic/Tai-people.

Britannica, The Editors of Encyclopedia. "Ayutthaya." Encyclopedia Britannica. August 18, 2015. Accessed December 2020. https://www.britannica.com/place/Ayutthaya-Thailand.

Britannica, The Editors of Encyclopedia. "Toungoo Dynasty." Encyclopedia Britannica. August 8, 2017. Accessed December 2020. https://www.britannica.com/topic/Toungoo-dynasty.

Britannica, The Editors of Encyclopedia. "Chakkri Dynasty." Encyclopedia Britannica. April 26, 2017. Accessed December 2020. https://www.britannica.com/topic/Chakkri-dynasty.

Britannica, The Editors of Encyclopedia. "Dvaravati." Encyclopedia Britannica. May 29, 2018. Accessed December 2020. https://www.britannica.com/place/Dvaravati.

Britannica, The Editors of Encyclopedia. "Baht." Encyclopedia Britannica. September 23, 2019. Accessed January 2021. https://www.britannica.com/topic/baht.

Britannica, The Editors of Encyclopedia. "Mon." Encyclopedia Britannica. April 18, 2020. Accessed December 2020. https://www.britannica.com/topic/Mon-people.

Britannica, The Editors of Encyclopedia. "Ramkhamhaeng." Encyclopedia Britannica. December 2020. Accessed December 2020. https://www.britannica.com/biography/Ramkhamhaeng.

Britannica, The Editors of Encyclopedia. "Naresuan." Encyclopedia Britannica. December 2020. Accessed December 2020. https://www.britannica.com/biography/Naresuan.

Britannica, The Editors of Encyclopedia. "Trailok." Encyclopedia Britannica. December 1, 2020. Accessed December 2020. https://www.britannica.com/biography/Trailok.

Britannica, The Editors of Encyclopedia. "Hsinbyushin." Encyclopedia Britannica. 2020. Accessed December 2020. https://www.britannica.com/biography/Hsinbyushin.

Britannica, The Editors of Encyclopedia. "Taksin." Encyclopedia Britannica. April 13, 2020. Accessed December 2020. https://www.britannica.com/biography/Taksin.

Britannica, The Editors of Encyclopedia. "Rama I." Encyclopedia Britannica. September 3, 2020. Accessed December 2020. https://www.britannica.com/biography/Rama-I.

Britannica, The Editors of Encyclopedia. "Rama II." Encyclopedia Britannica. July 17, 2020. Accessed December 2020. https://www.britannica.com/biography/Rama-II.

Britannica, The Editors of Encyclopedia. "Rama III." Encyclopedia Britannica. March 29, 2020. Accessed December 2020. https://www.britannica.com/biography/Rama-III.

Britannica, The Editors of Encyclopedia. "Mongkut." Encyclopedia Britannica. October 14, 2020. Accessed December 2020. https://www.britannica.com/biography/Mongkut.

Britannica, The Editors of Encyclopedia. "Chulalongkorn." Encyclopedia Britannica. October 19, 2020. Accessed December 2020. https://www.britannica.com/biography/Chulalongkorn.

Britannica, The Editors of Encyclopedia. "Somdet Chao Phraya Si Suriyawong." Encyclopedia Britannica. December 2020. Accessed December 2020. https://www.britannica.com/biography/Somdet-Chao-Phraya-Si-Suriyawong.

Britannica, The Editors of Encyclopedia. "Vajiravudh." Encyclopedia Britannica. 2020. Accessed December 2020. https://www.britannica.com/biography/Vajiravudh.

Britannica, The Editors of Encyclopedia. "Prajadhipok." Encyclopedia Britannica. November 4, 2020. Accessed December 2020. https://www.britannica.com/biography/Prajadhipok.

Britannica, The Editors of Encyclopedia. "Pridi Phanomyong." Encyclopedia Britannica. May 7, 2020. Accessed December 2020. https://www.britannica.com/biography/Pridi-Phanomyong.

Britannica, The Editors of Encyclopedia. "Luang Phibunsongkhram." Encyclopedia Britannica. July 10, 2020. Accessed December 2020. https://www.britannica.com/biography/Luang-Phibunsongkhram.

Britannica, The Editors of Encyclopedia. "Ananda Mahidol." Encyclopedia Britannica. September 16, 2020. Accessed January 2021. https://www.britannica.com/biography/Ananda-Mahidol.

Britannica, The Editors of Encyclopedia. "Sarit Thanarat." Encyclopedia Britannica. December 4, 2020. Accessed January 2021. https://www.britannica.com/biography/Sarit-Thanarat.

Britannica, The Editors of Encyclopedia. "Thanom Kittikachorn." Encyclopedia Britannica. August 7, 2020. Accessed January 2021. https://www.britannica.com/biography/Thanom-Kittikachorn.

Britannica, The Editors of Encyclopedia. "Chuan Leekpai." Encyclopedia Britannica. July 24, 2020. Accessed January 2021. https://www.britannica.com/biography/Chuan-Leekpai.

Britannica, The Editors of Encyclopedia. "Thaksin Shinawatra." Encyclopedia Britannica. July 22, 2020. Accessed January 2021. https://www.britannica.com/biography/Thaksin-Shinawatra.

Court of Justice Thailand. "History of the Court of Justice." Court of Justice Thailand. 2020. Accessed December 2020. https://www.coj.go.th/th/content/page/index/id/91989.

Devex. "Ministry of Interior (Thailand)." Devex. 2021. Accessed January 2021. https://www.devex.com/organizations/ministry-of-interior-thailand-135202.

Erlanger, Steven. "Thailand Seeks to Shape a 'Golden Peninsula'." *The New York Times*, April 30, 1989. Accessed January 2021.

https://www.nytimes.com/1989/04/30/world/thailand-seeks-to-shape-a-golden-peninsula.html.

Government of Singapore. "Bowring Treaty Signed with Bangkok." History SG. August 1, 2019. Accessed January 2021. https://eresources.nlb.gov.sg/history/events/ae996879-bb92-4dab-a62b-594824b803e6.

Hafner, J. A., Keyes, Charles F. Keyes, and Jane E. "Thailand." Encyclopedia Britannica. January 24, 2021. Accessed December 2020. https://www.britannica.com/place/Thailand.

Hamilton, Elizabeth. "Bronze from Ban Chiang, Thailand: A View from the Laboratory."

Expedition Magazine Bronze from Ban Chiang Thailand A View from the Laboratory

Comments. July 15, 2001. Accessed December 2020.

https://www.penn.museum/sites/expedition/bronze-from-ban-chiang-thailand/.

Hays, Jeffrey. "Ancient History of Thailand, Origin of the Thais and the Thai Name and World's First Bronze Age Culture." Facts and Details. May 2014. Accessed December 2020. http://factsanddetails.com/southeast-asia/Thailand/sub5_8a/entry-3184.html.

Hays, Jeffrey. "Military Rule in Thailand after World War II." Facts and Details. May 2014. Accessed January 2021. http://factsanddetails.com/southeast-asia/Thailand/sub5_8a/entry-3189.html.

Hays, Jeffrey. "Thailand in the 1990s: The 1992 Demonstrations, Short-Lived Leaders and the 1997 Asian Financial Crisis." Facts and Details. May 2014. Accessed January 2021. http://factsanddetails.com/southeast-asia/Thailand/sub5_8a/entry-3193.html.

Hays, Jeffrey. "Sukhothai and Early Thai Kings." Facts and Details. August 2020. Accessed December 2020. http://factsanddetails.com/southeast-asia/Thailand/sub5_8a/entry-3185.html.

Hollar, Sherman. "Samak Sundaravej." Encyclopedia Britannica. November 20, 2020. Accessed January 2021. https://www.britannica.com/biography/Samak-Sundaravej.

Hulme, Kyle. "This Is How Thailand Really Got Its Name." Culture Trip. March 10, 2018. Accessed December 2020. https://theculturetrip.com/asia/thailand/articles/land-of-the-free-how-thailand-got-its-name/.

Insight Guides. Insightguides.com. 2020. Accessed December 2020. https://www.insightguides.com/destinations/asia-pacific/thailand/historical-highlights.

Institute for Southeast Asian Archaeology. "The Ban Chiang Project." Institute for Southeast Asian Archaeology ISEAA. 2018. Accessed December 2020. https://iseaarchaeology.org/ban-chiang-project/background/.

Institute for Southeast Asian Archaeology. "The Ban Chiang Project – METALS MONOGRAPH." Institute for Southeast Asian Archaeology ISEAA. 2018.

Lim, Eric. "Phibun Songkhram - the Master of the Coup D'état." Tour Bangkok Legacies. 2018. Accessed January 2021. https://www.tour-bangkok-legacies.com/phibun-songkhram.html.

Lim, Eric. "Pridi Banomyong the Father of Thai Democracy." Tour Bangkok Legacies. 2020. Accessed January 2021. https://www.tour-bangkok-legacies.com/pridi-banomyong.html.

Lithai, Frank Reynolds, and Mari B. Reynolds. *Three Worlds According to King Ruang, a Thai Buddhist Cosmology*. Berkeley, CA: Center for South and Southeast Asian Studies, University of California., 1982.

Mishra, Patit Paban. *The History of Thailand*. Santa Barbara, CA: Greenwood, 2010.

Mudar, Karen M. *Evidence for Prehistoric Dryland Farming in Mainland Southeast Asia: Results of Regional Survey in Lopburi Province, Thailand*. Report. University of Hawai'i Press (Honolulu). 1995.

Muntarbhorn, Vitit. "Lessons of 'Black May' 1992 and the 2006 Coup." *Bangkok Post*, May 23, 2014. Accessed January 2021. https://www.bangkokpost.com/opinion/opinion/411309/lessons-of-black-may-1992-and-the-2006-coup.

Nationsonline.org, Klaus Kästle. "History of Thailand." History of Thailand. 2020. Accessed December 2020. https://www.nationsonline.org/oneworld/History/Thailand-history.htm.

Phattanarat, Siwanit. "Cradle of the Thai Nation: Sukhothai, the Dawn of Happiness." Thailand Guide. January 2003. Accessed December 2020. http://www.thailand-guide.com/benjarong/beyondphuket/sukhothai.htm.

Pike, John. "Thailand - Thonburi Period (1767-1782)." Global Security. August 4, 2012.

Accessed December 2020. https://www.globalsecurity.org/military/world/thailand/history-thonburi.htm.

Renown Travel. "Sukhothai Kingdom History." History of the Sukhothai Kingdom. 2020. Accessed December 2020. https://www.renown-travel.com/historicalsites/sukhothai/history.html.

Royal Thai Consulate. "Thailand History." Royal Thai Consulate General, Hong Kong. 2020. Accessed December 2020. http://www.thai-consulate.org.hk/webroot/ENG/Thailand/History1.htm.

Smith, Brian K., J.A.B. Van Buitenen, Wendy Doniger, Vasudha Narayanan, Edward C. Dimock, Arthur Llewellyn Basham, and Ann G. Gold. "Hinduism." Encyclopedia Britannica. November 30, 2020. Accessed December 2020. https://www.britannica.com/topic/Hinduism.

Stowe, Judy. "Obituary: Seni Pramoj." *Independent*, July 29, 1997. Accessed January 2021. https://www.independent.co.uk/news/people/obituary-seni-pramoj-1253268.html.

The New York Times. "New Thai Premier Named as Students Battle Troops." *The New York Times*, October 15, 1973.

https://www.nytimes.com/1973/10/15/archives/new-thai-premier-named-as-students-battle-troops-student-rioting.html.

The New York Times. "Another Coup in Thailand." *The New York Times*, October 21, 1977. Accessed January 2021. https://www.nytimes.com/1977/10/21/archives/another-coup-in-thailand.html.

The Phra Racha Wang Derm Restoration Foundation. "King Taksin The Great." King Taksin. 2013. Accessed December 2020. http://www.wangdermpalace.org/King Taksin.html.

The Times. "General Kriangsak Chomanan." *The Times*, January 22, 2004. Accessed January 2021. https://www.thetimes.co.uk/article/general-kriangsak-chomanan-jnxhzflxncv.

Tim's Thailand. "About the Ramkhamhaeng Inscription." Tim's Thailand. May 8, 2018. Accessed December 2020. https://www.timsthailand.com/about-ramkhamhaeng-inscription/.

Tourism Authority of Thailand. "The King Taksin Shrine." The Official Website of Tourism Authority of Thailand. 2020. Accessed December 2020. https://www.tourismthailand.org/Attraction/the-king-taksin-shrine.

TravelOnline. "Thailand Culture & History." TravelOnline. 2020. Accessed December 2020. https://www.travelonline.com/thailand/history.

U.S. Embassy & Consulate in Thailand. "Policy & History." U.S. Embassy & Consulate in

Thailand. November 19, 2019. Accessed January 2021. https://th.usembassy.gov/our-relationship/policy-history/.

UNESCO World Heritage Centre. "Ban Chiang Archaeological Site." UNESCO World Heritage Centre. 2020. Accessed December 2020. https://whc.unesco.org/en/list/55/.

Vandenberg, Tricky. "History of Ayutthaya - Historical Events - Timeline 1300-1399."

Ayutthaya History. 2020. Accessed December 2020. https://www.ayutthaya-history.com/Historical_Events13.html.

Wiener, James Blake. "Sukhothai." Ancient History Encyclopedia. October 12, 2018. Accessed December 2020. https://www.ancient.eu/Sukhothai/.

Wyatt, David K. *Thailand: A Short History.* New Haven, CT: Yale University Press, 2004.

สารนิเทศสัมพันธ์ มหาวิทยาลัยรามคำแหง. "The Inscription of King Ramkamhaeng the Great." ๐๕๋๚ ๑. 2020. Accessed December 2020. http://www.info.ru.ac.th/province/Sukhotai/srjsd11-4en.htm.

Asia for Educators, Columbia University. "Living in the Chinese Cosmos." Asia for Educators | Columbia University. https://afe.easia.columbia.edu/cosmos/irc/classics.htm.

Duiker, William J. *Ho Chi Minh: A Life,* 2012 ed. New York: Hachette Books, 1989.

"Feng Shui of Saigon." Oriental Culture, Philosophy and Management. https://www.guiculture.com/fs16saigon.htm.

Grant, R. G. *1001 Battles That Changed the Course of History.* Chartwell Books, 2017.

Hays, Jeffrey. "CAO DAI AND HOA HAO RELIGIONS: THE BELIEFS, HISTORY AND MILITARY WINGS." Facts and Details. Accessed September 30, 2020. https://factsanddetails.com/southeast-asia/Vietnam/sub5_9d/entry-3379.html.

Kiernan, Ben. *Viet Nam: A History from Earliest Times to the Present.* New York: Oxford University Press, USA, 2019.

Morgan, Ted. *Valley of Death: The Tragedy at Dien Bien Phu That Led America into the Vietnam War.* Random House, 2010.

Nguyen, Viet T. *The Sympathizer: A Novel (Pulitzer Prize for Fiction).* New York: Grove/Atlantic, 2015.

"Professor Stephen Young History of Vietnam Part 1 of 6." YouTube. 2014. https://www.youtube.com/watch?v=T9yg9uv0SXU&ab_channel=TrungHo.

The Vietnam War. Directed by Ken Burns, and Lynn Novick. 2017. PBS, 2017. Film.

Hinduism in Bali, https://bali.com/bali-travel-guide/culture-religion-traditions/balinese-hinduism-religion/, accessed February, March 2021.

Baliaround.com: *Barong Landung: Balinese Legend*, https://www.baliaround.com/barong-landung/, accessed February, March 2021.

Bellwood, Peter, et al., editors. *Austronesian Prehistory in Southeast Asia: Homeland, Expansion and Transformation*. The Austronesians: Historical and Comparative Perspectives, ANU Press, 2006, pp. 103-118, accessed via *JSTOR*, www.jstor.org/stable/j.ctt2jbjx1.8, February, March 2021.

Britannica: *Austronesian Languages*, https://www.britannica.com/topic/Austronesian-languages, accessed February, March 2021,

Bali, https://www.britannica.com/place/Bali-island-and-province-Indonesia, accessed February, March 2021,

Dong Son Culture, https://www.britannica.com/topic/Dong-Son-culture, accessed February, March 2021,

East Indies, https://www.britannica.com/place/East-Indies, accessed February, March 2021,:*Indonesia*, https://www.britannica.com/place/Indonesia, accessed February, March 2021.

DiscoverBaliIndonesia.com: *Balinese Arts and Crafts*, http://www.discover-bali-indonesia.com/encyclopedia-balinese-art-craft.html, accessed February, March 2021,

Balinese Calendar, http://www.discover-bali-indonesia.com/encyclopedia-balinese-calendar.html, accessed February, March 2021,

Balinese Cosmology, http://www.discover-bali-indonesia.com/encyclopedia-balinese-cosmology.html, accessed February, March 2021.

Farram, Steve, 1998. *The Dutch Conquest of Bali: The Conspiracy Theory Revisited, Indonesia and the Malay World*, 26:76, 207-223, DOI:10.1080/13639819908729924 accessed via www.tandfonline.com,

February, March 2021.

Frommer's.com. *History in Bali,* https://www.frommers.com/destinations/bali/in-depth/history, accessed February, March 2021.

Guampedia.com, 2019. *Canoe Building,* https://www.guampedia.com/canoe-building-2/, accessed February, March 2021.

Gunadi, Ari. *Besakih Temple in Bali,* accessed via Hotels.com, https://au.hotels.com/go/indonesia/besakih-temple, February, March 2021.

Gunther, Michael D., http://www.art-and-archaeology.com/indonesia/indonesia.html, accessed February, March 2021.

Hagerdal, Hans, 1995. *Bali in the Sixteenth and Seventeenth Centuries: Suggestions for a Chronology of the Gelgel Period.* Bijdragen Tot De Taal-, Land- En Volkenkunde, vol. 151, no. 1, 1995, pp. 101-124, accessed via *JSTOR,* www.jstor.org/stable/27864631, February, March 2021.

Kalpavriksha, 2019. *Dang Hyang Nirartha, Reformer of the Indonesian Dharma,* accessed via https://medium.com/@Kalpavriksha/dang-hyang-nirartha-reformer-of-the-indonesian-dharma-26ac19dbea8c, February, March 2021.

Kapil, Iris. Iris Sans Frontieres Blog:

Rice and Slavery in Colonial America, 2018, https://irissansfrontieres.wordpress.com/category/bali/, accessed February, March 2021,

The Artful Crafts of Bali, Part 1, 2016, https://irissansfrontieres.wordpress.com/2016/12/03/the-artful-crafts-of-bali-part-i/, accessed February, March 2021,

The Artful Crafts of Bali, Part 2, 2017, https://irissansfrontieres.wordpress.com/2017/01/01/the-artful-crafts-of-bali-part-ii/, accessed February, March 2021,

The Artful Crafts of Bali, Part 3, 2017, https://irissansfrontieres.wordpress.com/2017/01/31/the-artful-crafts-of-bali-part-iii/, accessed February, March 2021.

Lalor, Ailish, 2020. *What was the VOC? The Dutch East India Company Explained*, accessed via DutchReview.com, https://dutchreview.com/culture/history/voc-dutch-east-india-company-explained/, February, March 2021.

Lansing, J. Stephen et. al., 2001. *Volcanic fertilization of Balinese rice paddies*, accessed via Elsevier, Ecological Economics 38 (2001) 383 – 390.

Lonelyplanet.com: : *Gelgel*, https://www.lonelyplanet.com/indonesia/klungkung-semarapura/attractions/gelgel/a/poi-sig/1554081/1002205, accessed February, March 2021.

Mahavidya, *The Sanjaya Dynasty*, http://www.mahavidya.ca/2012/06/18/the-sanjaya-dynasty/, accessed February, March 2021.

National Geographic:

Rutledge et. al., 2011. *Monsoon*, https://www.nationalgeographic.org/encyclopedia/monsoon/, accessed February, March 2021.

Newworldencyclopedia.org: :*Majapahit*, https://www.newworldencyclopedia.org/entry/Majapahit, accessed February, March 2021.

NowBali.co.id: :*Mads Lange: Why a Danish Man has a Kuta street named after him*, https://nowbali.co.id/mads-lange-bali-history/, accessed February, March 2021.

NusaStudio, *Balinese Silver-making*, https://www.nusa.studio/balinese-silver/, accessed February, March 2021.

Rivers, P.J., 2004. *Monsoon Rhythms and Trade Patterns: Ancient Times East of Suez*. Journal of the Malaysian Branch of the Royal Asiatic Society Vol.77, No.2 (287) (2004), pp.59-93, *JSTOR*, https://www.jstor.org/stable/41493525?read-now=1&seq=1#page_scan_tab_contents, accessed February, March 2021.

Speake, Jennifer, 2003. *Literature of Travel and Exploration: G to P*, accessed via Google Books, February, March 2021.

Sunarya, I Ketut, 2021. *Kriya Bebali in Bali: its essence, symbolic, aesthetic*, accessed via tandfonline.com, https://doi.org/10.1080/23311886.2021.1882740, February, March 2021.

Thomas, Prof. David R., 2011, *Origins of the Austronesian Peoples*, University of Auckland, New Zealand, accessed via ResearchGate, https://www.researchgate.net/publication/236169876_Origins_of_the_Austronesian_Peoples, February, March 2021.

Tatu, Robin, 1999. *I Gusti Putu Jelantik's Babad Buleleng Placed within Historical Context*, Explorations in Southeast Asian Studies, A Journal of the Southeast Asian Studies Student Association, Vol 3, accessed via the University of Hawaii, https://scholarspace.manoa.hawaii.edu/bitstream/10125/2540/1/I%20Gusti%20Putu%20Jelantik%27s%20Babad%20Buleleng%20Placed%20within%20Histori.pdf, February, March 2021.

Tripati, S., 2017. *HISTORICAL NOTES, Early users of monsoon winds for navigation*, accessed via ResearchGate, https://www.researchgate.net/publication/321418755_HISTORICAL_NOTES_Early_users_of_monsoon_winds_for_navigation, February, March 2021.

Villa-Bali.com: *What's Behind the Name Bali*, https://www.villa-bali.com/guide/whats-bali/, accessed February, March 2021.

VisitBali.id. *Bali Aga Tribe: Indigenous People of Bali*, https://visitbali.id/property/the-bali-aga-of-trunyan-traditional-village, accessed February, March 2021.

Wikipedia: *Airlangga*, https://en.wikipedia.org/wiki/Airlangga, accessed February, March 2021,

Anak Agung Bagus Suteja, https://en.wikipedia.org/wiki/Anak_Agung_Bagus_Suteja, accessed February, March 2021,

Anglurah Agung, https://en.wikipedia.org/wiki/Anglurah_Agung, accessed February, March 2021,

Austronesian Peoples, https://en.wikipedia.org/wiki/Austronesian_peoples, accessed February, March 2021,

Bali, https://en.wikipedia.org/wiki/Bali, accessed February, March 2021,

Bali Kingdom, https://en.wikipedia.org/wiki/Bali_Kingdom, accessed February, March 2021, :*Bali Temple*, https://en.wikipedia.org/wiki/Balinese_temple, accessed February, March 2021,

Balinese Dance, https://en.wikipedia.org/wiki/Balinese_dance, accessed February, March 2021,

Batavia, Dutch East Indies, https://en.wikipedia.org/wiki/Batavia,_Dutch_East_Indies, accessed February, March 2021,

Colin McPhee, https://en.wikipedia.org/wiki/Colin_McPhee, accessed February, March 2021,

Coral Triangle, https://en.wikipedia.org/wiki/Coral_Triangle, accessed February, March 2021, *Dang Hyang Nirartha*, https://en.wikipedia.org/wiki/Dang_Hyang_Nirartha, accessed February, March 2021,

Dewa Agung, https://en.wikipedia.org/wiki/Dewa_Agung, accessed February, March 2021, *Dutch East India Company*, https://en.wikipedia.org/wiki/Dutch_East_India_Company, accessed February, March 2021,

Dutch Intervention in Bali (1906), https://en.wikipedia.org/wiki/Dutch_intervention_in_Bali_(1906), accessed February, March 2021,

Dutch Intervention in Bali (1849), https://en.wikipedia.org/wiki/Dutch_intervention_in_Bali_(1849), accessed February, March 2021,

Dutch Intervention in Lombok, https://en.wikipedia.org/wiki/Dutch_intervention_in_Lombok_and_Karangasem , accessed February, March 2021,

East India Company, https://en.wikipedia.org/wiki/East_India_Company, accessed February, March 2021,

Geringsing, https://en.wikipedia.org/wiki/Geringsing, accessed February, March 2021,

History of Bali, https://en.wikipedia.org/wiki/History_of_Bali, accessed February, March 2021,

Flora of Indonesia, https://en.wikipedia.org/wiki/Flora_of_Indonesia#Sundaland, accessed February, March 2021,

French and British interregnum in the Dutch East Indies, https://en.wikipedia.org/wiki/French_and_British_interregnum_in_the_Dutch_East_Indies, accessed February, March 2021,

Gelgel, Indonesia, https://en.wikipedia.org/wiki/Gelgel,_Indonesia, accessed February, March 2021,

Gregory Bateseon, https://en.wikipedia.org/wiki/Gregory_Bateson, accessed February, March 2021,

Indonesian National Revolution, https://en.wikipedia.org/wiki/Indonesian_National_Revolution, accessed February, March 2021,

Islam in Indonesia, https://en.wikipedia.org/wiki/Islam_in_Indonesia#History, accessed February, March 2021,

Jakarta, https://en.wikipedia.org/wiki/Jakarta, accessed February, March 2021,

Kakawin, https://en.wikipedia.org/wiki/Kakawin, February, March 2021,

Kakawin Sutasoma, https://en.wikipedia.org/wiki/Kakawin_Sutasoma, accessed February, March 2021,

Lesser Sunda Islands, https://en.wikipedia.org/wiki/Lesser_Sunda_Islands, accessed February, March 2021,

Lombok, https://en.wikipedia.org/wiki/Lombok#History, accessed February, March 2021,

Mads Johansen Lange, https://en.wikipedia.org/wiki/Mads_Johansen_Lange, accessed February, march 2021,

Maluku Islands, https://en.wikipedia.org/wiki/Maluku_Islands, accessed February, March 2021,

Margaret Mead, https://en.wikipedia.org/wiki/Margaret_Mead, accessed February, March 2021,

Mataram Sultanate, https://en.wikipedia.org/wiki/Mataram_Sultanate, accessed February, March 2021,

Medang Kingdom, https://en.wikipedia.org/wiki/Medang_Kingdom, accessed February, March 2021,

Miguel Covarrubias, https://en.wikipedia.org/wiki/Miguel_Covarrubias, accessed February, March 2021,

Moon of Pejeng, https://en.wikipedia.org/wiki/Moon_of_Pejeng, accessed February, March 2021,

Nagarakretagama, https://en.wikipedia.org/wiki/Nagarakretagama, accessed February, march 2021,

Nusantara, https://en.wikipedia.org/wiki/Nusantara, accessed February, March 2021,

Pejeng Drum, https://en.wikipedia.org/wiki/Pejeng_drum, accessed February, March 2021, *Portuguese Malacca*, https://en.wikipedia.org/wiki/Portuguese_Malacca, accessed February, March 2021,

Provinces of Indonesia, https://en.wikipedia.org/wiki/Provinces_of_Indonesia, accessed February, March 2021,

Ring of Fire, https://en.wikipedia.org/wiki/Ring_of_Fire, accessed February, March 2021,:*Shailendra Dynasty*, https://en.wikipedia.org/wiki/Shailendra_dynasty, accessed February, March 2021,

Singaraja, https://en.wikipedia.org/wiki/Singaraja, accessed February, March 2021,

Singhasari, https://en.wikipedia.org/wiki/Singhasari, accessed February, March 2021,

Sir Stamford Raffles, https://en.wikipedia.org/wiki/Stamford_Raffles, accessed February, March 2021,

Spanish East Indies, https://en.wikipedia.org/wiki/Spanish_East_Indies, accessed February, March 2021,

Spice Trade, https://en.wikipedia.org/wiki/Spice_trade, accessed February, March 2021,

Sunda Shelf, https://en.wikipedia.org/wiki/Sunda_Shelf, accessed February, March 2021,

Tjokorda Gde Raka Soekawati, https://en.wikipedia.org/wiki/Tjokorda_Gde_Raka_Soekawati, accessed February, March 2021, *Trade Route*, https://en.wikipedia.org/wiki/Trade_route, accessed February, March 2021, *Wayang*, https://en.wikipedia.org/wiki/Wayang, accessed February, March 2021, *Wallace Line*, https://en.wikipedia.org/wiki/Wallace_Line, accessed February, March 2021, *Walter Spies*, https://en.wikipedia.org/wiki/Walter_Spies, accessed February, March 2021.

WonderfulBali.com: :*Lontar Library Gedong Kirtya Singaraja*, https://www.wonderfulbali.com/lontar-library-gedong-kirtya-singaraja/, accessed February, March 2021.

Britannica.com: Borlaza, Gregorio C., Hernandez, Carolina G. and Cullinane, Michael et. al., 2021. Philippines. Encyclopedia Britannica, https://www.britannica.com/place/Philippines, accessed March, April 2021, Rafferty, John P. Tarantian Stage, https://www.britannica.com/science/Tarantian-Stage, accessed March, April 2021.

Dulay, Prof. Sofronio (Toti), University of the Philippines. *Lakan Dula of Tondo: His True Story and His Descendancy*, https://sites.google.com/site/truelakandula/, accessed March, April 2021.

Earth.org: :*What is the Coral Triangle?*, https://earth.org/coral-triangle/, accessed March, April 2021.

Encyclopedia.com: :*Spices and the Spice Trade*, https://www.encyclopedia.com/history/news-wires-white-papers-and-books/spices-and-spice-trade, accessed March, April 2021,

Tausug, https://www.encyclopedia.com/humanities/encyclopedias-almanacs-transcripts-and-maps/tausug, accessed March, April 2021.

Escoto, Salvador P., 1998. *Francisco Xavier Salgado, Civil Servant and Pioneer Industrialist in Eighteenth Century Philippines*. Southeast Asian Studies, Vol. 36, No.3, accessed via *Kyoto-seas*, https://kyoto-seas.org/pdf/36/3/360301.pdf, March, April 2021.

EveryCulture.com: :*Philippine Negritos*, https://www.everyculture.com/East-Southeast-Asia/Philippine-Negritos.html, accessed March, April 2021.

Headland, Thomas N., 1984. *Agta Negritos of the Philippines* https://www.culturalsurvival.org/publications/cultural-survival-quarterly/agta-negritos-philippines, accessed March, April 2021.

Herrera, Dana R., 2015. *The Philippines, An Overview of the Colonial Era*, Volume 20:1: Southeast Asia in the Humanities and Social Science Curricula, accessed via the Association for Asian Studies, https://www.asianstudies.org/publications/eaa/archives/the-philippines-an-overview-of-the-colonial-era/, March, April 2021.

History.com: :*Seven Years War*, https://www.history.com/topics/european-history/seven-years-war , accessed March, April 2021.

Jean-Christophe Gaillard, Joel P. Mallari. The peopling of the Philippines: A cartographic synthesis. *Hukay: Journal of the University of the Philippines Archaeological Studies Program*, 2004, 6, pp.1-27. ⟨halshs-00119458⟩

Junker, Laura Lee, 1994. *Trade Competition, Conflict, and Political*

Transformations in Sixth to Sixteenth Century Philippine Chiefdoms. *Perspectives* Vol.33, No.2, Special Issue: Regional Perspectives on States in Asia (Fall 1994), pp. 229-260 (32 pages), published by the University of Hawaii Press, *JSTOR*, https://www.jstor.org/stable/42928321, accessed March, April 2021.

Knowledgia, 2020. YouTube Video: *The History of the Philippines,* https://www.youtube.com/watch?v=P-I4Bay5SXo, accessed March, April 2021.

Majul, Cesar Adib, 1965. *Political and Historical Notes on the old Sulu Sultanate,* Journal of the Malaysian Branch of the Royal Asiatic Society Vol. 38, No, 1 (207) (July, 1965), pp.23-42 (20 pages), accessed through *JSTOR*, https://www.jstor.org/stable/41491838, March, April 2021.

Mallari, Francisco, 1974. *The Mindanao Cinnamon.* Philippine Quarterly of Culture and Society, vol. 2, no. 4, 1974, pp. 190-194. *JSTOR*, www.jstor.org/stable/29791158,

accessed March, April 2021.

McCormickScienceInstitute: :*History of Spices,* https://www.mccormickscienceinstitute.com/resources/history-of-spices, accessed March, April 2021.

NationalGeographic.com: :*Know before you go: the Philippines,* https://www.nationalgeographic.com/travel/article/partner-content-know-before-you-go-the-philippines, accessed March, April 2021.

Nationsonline.org: :*History of the Philippines,* https://www.nationsonline.org/oneworld/History/Philippines-history.htm, accessed March, April 2021.

NewworldEncyclopedia.org: :*Majapahit,* https://www.newworldencyclopedia.org/entry/Majapahit, accessed March, April 2021, :*Sulu Sultanate,* https://www.newworldencyclopedia.org/entry/Sulu_Sultanate, accessed March, April 2021.

Phillife.co: :*Skull Moulding,* https://www.phillife.co/skull-moulding/, accessed March, April 2021.

Porio, E., and Roque-Sarmiento, E., 2019. *Barangay*, Orum, A. (ed), The Wiley Blackwell Encyclopedia of Urban and Regional Studies. John Wiley & Sons Ltd., New Jersey. DOI:10.1002/9781118568446.eurs0016, accessed via ResearchGate, https://www.researchgate.net/publication/332425401_Barangay, March, April 2021.

Porter, Catherine, 1945. Office of War Information, formerly with Institute for Pacific Relations. *Pamphlet EM 24: What Lies Ahead for the Philippines? (1945)*, Aquino, Belinda A. (ed), accessed through the American Historical Association, https://www.historians.org/about-aha-and-membership/aha-history-and-archives/gi-roundtable-series/pamphlets/em-24-what-lies-ahead-for-the-philippines-(1945), March, April 2021.

Quirino, Karl, 2010. *Sultanate of Maguindanao*, accessed via Bulwagan Foundation, https://thebulwaganfoundation.wordpress.com/2010/09/01/sultanate-of-maguindanao/, March, April 2021.

Shackford, Julie, 1990. *The Philippines: Historical Overview*, partially funded by the Henry Luce Foundation, Inc. Center for Philippines Studies, School of Hawaiian, Asian, and Pacific Studies, University of Hawaii, https://scholarspace.manoa.hawaii.edu/handle/10125/15373, accessed March, April 2021.

UNESCO.org: :*Rice Terraces of the Philippine Cordilleras*, https://whc.unesco.org/en/list/722/, accessed March, April 2021.

Wikipedia: :*Angono Petroglyphs*, https://en.wikipedia.org/wiki/Angono_Petroglyphs, accessed March, April 2021, :*Bangsamoro*, https://en.wikipedia.org/wiki/Bangsamoro, accessed March, April 2021, :*Barangay State*, https://en.wikipedia.org/wiki/Barangay_state, accessed March, April 2021, :*Boxer Codex*, https://en.wikipedia.org/wiki/Boxer_Codex, accessed March, April 2021, :*Brunei*, https://en.wikipedia.org/wiki/Brunei, accessed March, April 2021, :*Cebu, Historical Polity*, https://en.wikipedia.org/wiki/Cebu_(historical_polity), accessed March, April 2021, :*Charles V, Holy Roman Emperor*, https://en.wikipedia.org/wiki/Charles_V,_Holy_Roman_Emperor, accessed March, April 2021, :*Doctrina Filipino*, https://en.wikipedia.org/wiki/Doctrina_Christiana, accessed March, April 2021, :*Emilio Aguinaldo*, https://en.wikipedia.org/wiki/Emilio_Aguinaldo, accessed March, April, 2021,

:*Enhanced Defense Cooperation Agreement*, https://en.wikipedia.org/wiki/Enhanced_Defense_Cooperation_Agreement, accessed March, April 2021, :*Ferdinand Magellan*, https://en.wikipedia.org/wiki/Ferdinand_Magellan, accessed March, April 2021, :*Filipinos*, https://en.wikipedia.org/wiki/Filipinos, accessed March, April 2021, :*History of the Philippines*, https://en.wikipedia.org/wiki/History_of_the_Philippines, accessed March, April 2021, :*Homo Luzonensis*, https://en.wikipedia.org/wiki/Homo_luzonensis, accessed March, April 2021, :*Ifugao*, https://en.wikipedia.org/wiki/Ifugao, accessed March, April 2021, :*Island Groups of the Philippines*, https://en.wikipedia.org/wiki/Island_groups_of_the_Philippines, accessed March, April, 2021, ;*Juan de Salcedo*, https://en.wikipedia.org/wiki/Juan_de_Salcedo, accessed March, April 2021, :*Kawi script*, https://en.wikipedia.org/wiki/Kawi_script, accessed March, April 2021, :*Limahong*, https://en.wikipedia.org/wiki/Limahong, accessed March, April 2021, :*Lingling-o*, https://en.wikipedia.org/wiki/Lingling-o, accessed March, April 2021,

:*List of World Heritage Sites in the Philippines*, https://en.wikipedia.org/wiki/List_of_World_Heritage_Sites_in_the_Philippines, accessed March, April 2021, :*Mangyan*, https://en.wikipedia.org/wiki/Mangyan, accessed March, April 2021, :*Manunggul Jar*, https://en.wikipedia.org/wiki/Manunggul_Jar, accessed March, April 2021, :*Metro Manila*, https://en.wikipedia.org/wiki/Metro_Manila, accessed March, April 2021, :*Mexican War of Independence*, https://en.wikipedia.org/wiki/Mexican_War_of_Independence, accessed March, April 2021, :*Muhammad Kudarat*, https://en.wikipedia.org/wiki/Muhammad_Kudarat, accessed March, April 2021, :*Philippines*, https://en.wikipedia.org/wiki/Philippines, accessed March, April 2021, :*Piloncitos*, https://en.wikipedia.org/wiki/Piloncitos, accessed March, April 2021, :*Pre-History of the Philippines*, https://en.wikipedia.org/wiki/Prehistory_of_the_Philippines, accessed March, April 2021, :*Religion in pre-colonial Philippines*, https://en.wikipedia.org/wiki/Religion_in_pre-colonial_Philippines, accessed March, April 2021, :*Subduction Tectonics of the Philippines*, https://en.wikipedia.org/wiki/Subduction_tectonics_of_the_Philippines, accessed March, April 2021, :*Tabon Caves*, https://en.wikipedia.org/wiki/Tabon_Caves, accessed March, April 2021, :*Tagbanwa*, https://en.wikipedia.org/wiki/Tagbanwa, accessed March, April 2021. :*Wallace Line*, https://en.wikipedia.org/wiki/Wallace_Line, accessed March, April 2021.

United States, Department of State, Office of the Historian:

:*The Philippine-American War, 1899-1902*, https://history.state.gov/milestones/1899-1913/war, accessed March, April 2021, :*The Spanish-American War, 1898*, https://history.state.gov/milestones/1866-1898/spanish-american-war, accessed March, April 2021.

WorldAtlas.com: :Sawe, Benjamin Elisha, 2018. *How Were the Islands in The Philippines Formed?*, https://www.worldatlas.com/articles/how-were-the-islands-in-the-philippines-formed.html, accessed March, April 2021, :Wee, Rolando Y., 2017. *What Is the Ring of Fire?*, https://www.worldatlas.com/articles/what-and-where-is-the-pacific-ring-of-fire.html, accessed March, April 2021.

WorldWildlife.org: :*Coral Triangle*, https://www.worldwildlife.org/places/coral-triangle, accessed March, April 2021.

World Heritage Encyclopedia: :*Sultanate of Maguindanao*, accessed via *Project Gutenberg Self-Publishing Press*, http://self.gutenberg.org/articles/eng/Sultanate_of_Maguindanao, March, April 2021.

Zamora, Mario D., 1967. *Political History, Autonomy, and Change: The Case of the Barrio Charter*, accessed via Asian Studies: Journal of Critical perspectives on Asia, https://asj.upd.edu.ph/mediabox/archive/ASJ-05-01-1967/zamora-political-history-autonomy-change-barrio-charter.pdf, March, April, 2021.

Made in the USA
Columbia, SC
17 December 2023